MW01286331

The Baptism
and
Gifts of the Spirit

The Baptism and Gifts of the Spirit

D. Martyn Lloyd-Jones

Edited by Christopher Catherwood

© Bethan Lloyd-Jones 1984, 1985, 1994

Published by Baker Books
a division of Baker Book House Company
P.O. Box 6287, Grand Rapids, MI 49516-6287

Cloth edition published 1996

This edition issued by special arrangement with Kingsway Publications, Lottbridge Drove, Eastbourne, East Sussex, England BN23 6NT

Previously published in England under the title *Joy Unspeakable*

Printed in the United States of America

All rights reserved. No part of this publication may be reproduced, stored in a retrieval system, or transmitted in any form or by any means—for example, electronic, photocopy, recording—without the prior written permission of the publisher. The only exception is brief quotations in printed reviews.

ISBN 0-8010-1117-5

Unless otherwise indicated, biblical quotations are from the Authorised Version, Crown copyright.

Contents

Foreword

The past thirty years have seen the widespread growth of two radical and potentially mighty movements in Great Britain. These are the reformed movement with its stress on doctrine, expository preaching and total loyalty to Scripture; and the charismatic movement with its stress on the Holy Spirit's baptism and gifts, its strong sense of personal guidance and its bold freedom in worship.

The weaknesses of the reformed churches have often been their traditionalism, their lack of evangelism and their contentment with sound doctrine sincerely approved. The weaknesses of the charismatics have tended to be their self-indulgent and sometimes uncritical enjoyment of 'experience', their lack of interest in doctrine and their naïvety in church policy.

Both of these groupings have known considerable blessing in recent years, but both may well expect an element of divine rebuke to enter their life if they do not now begin to learn from one another. Already the charismatic movement is finding the Spirit withdrawing his blessings and the devil sowing his confusion wherever doctrine is despised and neglected. Correspondingly, in many places the reformed movement is beginning to go stale; its congregations replete with sound doctrine but cramped in regard to experience and self-expression are looking wistfully at less instructed but often more effective congregations 'down the road'. In both camps *a sense of something more* is beginning to rise up from the people.

Happily a reaching out to each other and a sharing with each other of 'things new and old' is also beginning to occur. We are beginning to see an appreciation of expository and doctrinal preaching and teaching among 'charismatics' and a real attempt to introduce greater congregational participation and more contemporary expression of praise into certain 'reformed' churches and meetings. At a deeper level, the profounder reaches of spiritual experience are already sought and shared by both alike. For many reasons – biblical, historical and experiential – it is becoming increasingly untenable and even absurd to see these two movements as fundamentally alien to one another. Nothing in my opinion is calculated to show that more satisfactorily than this book, both because of its subject and because of its author.

Dr Lloyd-Jones was undoubtedly *the* leader in the burgeoning reformed movement in Britain. His London ministry was outstanding, not only for the great congregations which flocked to his rich biblical and doctrinal ministry, but also for its evangelistic emphasis with its penetrating analysis of modern society and its remarkable unction as he passionately proclaimed the present power of Jesus Christ.

At a time (in the forties and early fifties) when doctrine was so often and so widely ignored by evangelicals and even feared as 'divisive', he showed how apostolic truth in all its breadth and depth ('the whole counsel of God' as our fathers called it) was no optional extra in the church's life but a vital source of her power and a constant demonstration of the holiness, wisdom, justice and love of God in Christ. Under his advice and inspiration books began to flow from the press in which Reformers and English Puritans once more exercised their incomparable ministry to a new generation of believers; great revival leaders and preachers like Whitefield and Edwards, Ryle and Spurgeon, became widely known in the fullness of their ministries to present-day evangelicals.

For Dr Lloyd-Jones, the history of the church was alive with the activity of God, and it was from such an historical as well as biblical perspective that he was able to evaluate movements and trends in our own day. For him, everything was to be rooted in Scripture, but nothing was to be left in Scripture. He maintained that apostolic history was, in its essence, the typical story of the church in revival and that even at the level of individual experience God has never left Pentecost as an isolated moment in the past but has given it as the promise 'to you and to your children' of a new and mighty dimension of spiritual experience available to us all.

Dr Lloyd-Jones' loyalty to Scripture, his sense of history, his breadth of reading and his profound humility before the things of God led him to welcome (though not uncritically) many aspects of the rising charismatic movement and to see its fundamental compatibility with historic evangelicalism, including the reformed tradition in which he stood.

His understanding of revival, however, led him to call the church *on* from both reformation and renewal. Anyone who reads the history of revivals will soon learn how much they are beyond anything that the church in Britain has known in our generation. Revival is a spiritual phenomenon utterly incomparable in the sweep and depth of its effect in the churches and staggeringly effective in its awakening of vast numbers of people in the world at large.

If the combination of the best elements of the reformed and charismatic movements is potentially explosive, revival is the match which will ignite it! Committees cannot organize it; festivals and celebrations cannot duplicate it; we cannot work it up: only God can send it down. Acts chapter 2 and the ensuing history of the apostolic church is more than charismatic experience and doctrinal insight – it is revival in archetypal form.

May it please Almighty God, by the Spirit of his exalted Son, to use not only this volume, but the many books and tapes of Dr Martyn Lloyd-Jones' historic ministry to lead many thousands of Christians in this land into a profounder understanding and deeper experience of God's grace; and may it please him further to lead the church of our day into a time of world revival in which nations shall be born in a day and all peoples shall call his Son our Lord Jesus Christ 'blessed'.

PETER LEWIS
The Cornerstone Evangelical Church
Nottingham

Introduction

In a churchyard in the middle of Wales, outside the town of Newcastle Emlyn, in the Teifi Valley, lies a simple grave. On it are inscribed the words 'Martyn Lloyd-Jones 1899-1981: 'For I determined not to know anything among you save Jesus Christ and him crucified.' The church nearby had once been that of Evan Phillips, his wife Bethan's grandfather. It had seen revival – the great outpouring of the Holy Spirit with power – in the famous Welsh Revival of 1904-5. It seemed appropriate that my grandfather should have chosen to be buried there, because it had such a close link with the passion that he held throughout his ministry – that of revival, a visitation of the Holy Spirit upon the people of God, the church. From his study of Scripture he felt that it was only if people were baptized with the Holy Spirit, as in the book of Acts, that the power of the message of Jesus Christ crucified would be seen in the land.

My grandfather – or 'the Doctor' as he was called by evangelical Christians across the world – was one of the men primarily responsible for the resurrection in interest in reformed doctrine in Britain after the war, with its emphases on solid expository preaching and confidence in the sovereign power of God. Much of this renewed interest sprang from a reading of the great British Puritans of the seventeenth century and of eighteenth-century preachers such as Jonathan Edwards. (It should be said that my grandfather always insisted that he was a 'Bible Calvinist' and never a system one.) At a time when English evangelicalism had become rather flabby, afraid of both doctrine and intellect, this change came like a gust of fresh air. But after some years, the Doctor realized that many reformed people had become dry and arid in their Christian lives – that although their doctrine was sound, their day-to-day faith lacked the fire and sense of the presence and power of the Holy Spirit that should be present in the Christian's life.

In his booklet 'Christ our Sanctification', designed to confute the false perfectionist tendencies still present in many evangelical circles, he put forward the view that the sealing of the Spirit which Paul refers to in Ephesians took place simultaneously with conversion – a stand taken today by men such as John Stott. By the time in the mid-1950s that he himself came to preach on Ephesians, he had changed his mind. He still rejected perfectionism – indeed continued to do so till his death – but now felt that it was evident from Scripture that the sealing of the Spirit was indisputably separate from conversion. He read many of the Puritans, and discovered that they too testified both from Scripture and from their own experience that the two events were not necessarily simultaneous in the Christian's life. The Christian should not just believe the truth, and know it, the Puritans felt, but have a day-to-day living experience of it – what they called 'experimental' truth.

So the conviction as to what Scripture taught, and the concern that he had about the increasing aridity in the lives of many Christians around him, caused him to change both his views and his emphasis. He became increasingly burdened to pray for revival – indeed the desire for a revival was to dominate the rest of his ministry. He saw that this was a theme upon which it was vital to preach, and the result is the sermons on John that are in this book (delivered in Westminster Chapel 1964-65), which form part of a longer series of expositions on John's Gospel.

The sermons demonstrate my Grandfather's ability to achieve a biblical balance. He believed passionately in the baptism with the Holy Spirit as a distinct, post-conversion experience. But he equally realized that it was a filling with power that made those who had received it into better witnesses for Christ. His indeed was a Christ-centred message, emphasizing that a deeper knowledge of and relationship with Jesus Christ was at the heart of the baptism with the Spirit. Similarly, while he believed that all the gifts existed today, he refused to hold, on the basis of Scripture, that any one gift was necessary as proof of baptism with the Spirit. He was quite consistent with his views of the sovereignty of God when he maintained that we cannot induce baptism with the Spirit – it is something that can be given by God alone. He was thus both reformed and charismatic, in the biblical senses of the terms.

Furthermore, he firmly believed from Scripture that 'the baptism of the Spirit may itself be present in great power and yet none of these gifts may be manifest as such'. As he makes clear, the whole purpose of baptism with the Holy Spirit is to make us witnesses of Jesus Christ, in a time and place that has forgotten the message of the cross. The Holy Spirit is sovereign, and is sent not to draw attention to himself, but to make Jesus Christ central in all our lives. This is clear not only from Scripture itself, but again and again from the history of the Christian church.

'Jesus Christ and him crucified' was the great theme of my grandfather's life. It was why he regarded this issue of baptism with the Holy Spirit as so important – so that all may know of the glorious message of salvation. This is also why he was so anxious to safeguard the doctrine as he saw it, and why he was concerned that Christians test or 'prove' all things from Scripture. Tragically, today Christians are often more concerned with fighting each other, including over issues such as the gifts of the Holy Spirit, than seeking to win and save the lost with the gospel of Jesus Christ.

Whatever we may think the Bible's phrase 'baptism with the Holy Spirit' actually means – whether we agree with the interpretation given by my grandfather or not – we should never forget that at the very heart of our message are the words on that tombstone in Wales: 'Jesus Christ and him crucified'.

CHRISTOPHER CATHERWOOD

Chapter 1

Baptism with the Spirit and Regeneration

The words to which I should like to call your attention are to be found in John 1:26, 33 – 'John answered them, saying, I baptize with water: but there standeth one among you, whom ye know not.... And I knew him not: but he that sent me to baptize with water, the same said unto me, Upon whom thou shalt see the Spirit descending, and remaining on him, the same is he which baptizeth with the Holy Ghost.'

I take these two verses and put them together because of this great truth which they bring out, namely, that John the Baptist was constantly telling the people that he was not the Christ, and that the essential difference between them was that he baptized with water whereas the Christ would baptize with the Holy Spirit.

Now why are we looking at this? Well, we are doing so because the statement in John 1:16 shows us that the truth about the Christian should be this statement of John 1:16 – 'And of his fulness have all we received, and grace for [or upon] grace.' That is what the Christian is meant to be like. He is a man who has received something of the fullness of Christ and he goes on receiving it increasingly. That is the Christian life. And I am suggesting that John, the Evangelist, shows us that the way in which this can become true of us, and increasingly true of us, is that we receive of his fullness in large and great measure when we are truly baptized with the Holy Spirit by the Lord Jesus Christ.

John the Baptist himself drew this contrast clearly in his ministry. When we read Luke 3:1-17 we see some of the striking contrasts between John's baptism and our Lord's baptism; putting it very roughly, we see the difference between religion and Christianity; or indeed, we can go further, the difference between being content with only the beginnings or 'first principles' (see Hebrews 6:1) of the doctrine of Christ, and this same doctrine in greater fullness.

Now we are doing this, and I must go on repeating it, because this is no academic exercise. Indeed, it seems to me that this is the thing we need above all else at the present time. We need it as individual Christians, but we need it still more because of the state of the world that is round and about us. If we have no sense of responsibility for the condition of humanity at this moment, then there is only one thing to say – if we are Christians at all we are very poor ones. If we are only concerned about ourselves and our own happiness, and if the moral condition of society and the tragedy of the whole world does not grieve us, if we are not disturbed at the way in which men blaspheme the name of God and all the arrogance of sin – well, what can be said about us?

But I am assuming that we *are* concerned, and that we are concerned for ourselves, that we may receive what God has intended us to receive in his Son. 'God so loved the world, that he gave his only begotten Son' – and if we are not receiving what he has made possible, it is an insult to God. So these two aspects must be borne in mind – our own individual states and needs, but, still more, the condition of the world around us. That, then, is what we are doing, and I am trying to show that the great and constant danger is that we should be content with something which is altogether less than that intended for us.

Let me put it like this. Perhaps the greatest danger of all for

Christian people is the danger of understanding the Scriptures in the light of their own experiences. We should not interpret Scripture in the light of our experiences, but we should examine our experiences in the light of the teaching of the Scripture. This is a fundamental and basic point, which is particularly important just at this moment in view of the things that are happening in the Christian church.

There are two main ways in which, it seems to me, we can go wrong in this question of the relationship of our experiences to the teaching of the Scripture. The first danger is that of claiming things which either go beyond the Scripture or which, indeed, may even be contrary to it. Now there are many who have done that throughout the centuries, and there are people who are still doing it. There have been people – they were to be found in the early church – who have claimed that they were uniquely inspired. The apostle calls them 'false apostles'. And there were people who claimed that they were receiving 'revelation' who did not care what the teaching was; they said they were directly inspired by God.

I remember once hearing a man saying he did not care what the apostle Paul or anybody else said, he knew! He had had an experience. Now the moment a man says that, he is putting his own experience above the Scriptures. That opens the door to fanaticism; not enthusiasm but fanaticism and other possible dangers. So there is one danger – that we put what we experience subjectively over the Scripture.

Another way in which this is done is to put tradition or the teaching of the church above Scripture. This has been the Roman Catholic heresy; it says that tradition is co-ordinate with the Scripture. And that means in the end that tradition is superior to the Scripture. There is nothing in the Scripture about the so-called Assumption of the Virgin Mary, a doctrine which says that she never died and was buried, but literally rose in the body into heaven. But they teach it, and it is their authority alone that sanctions such a teaching. That is the kind of thing I mean.

But forgetting something as obvious as the Roman Catholic heresy, there are many (and they are generally the most spirtually minded) who are always prone to become so interested in the experimental side that they become indifferent to the Scripture. The early Quakers were particularly subject to this, with their emphasis on the 'inner light'. They, too, said that, whatever the Scripture may say, they knew a doctrine had been revealed to them directly. One of them (poor man) claimed that he was the incarnate Christ again, and rode into the city of Bristol on a horse with many misguided people following him who believed his teaching, because he spoke to them with authority.

Now that is fanaticism, and it is a terrible danger which we must always bear in mind. It arises from a divorce between Scripture and experience, where we put experience above Scripture claiming things that are not sanctioned by Scripture, or are perhaps even prohibited by it.

But there is a second danger and it is equally important that we should bear it in mind. The second is the exact opposite of the first, as these things generally go from one violent extreme to the other. How difficult it always is to maintain a balance! The second danger, then, is that of being satisfied with something very much less than what is offered in the Scripture, and the danger of interpreting Scripture by our experiences and reducing its teaching to the level of what we know and experience; and I would say that this second is the greater danger of the two at the present time.

In other words, certain people by nature are afraid of the supernatural, of the unusual, of disorder. You can be so afraid of disorder, so concerned about discipline and decorum and control, that you become guilty of what the Scripture calls 'quenching the Spirit'; and there is no question in my mind that there has been a great deal of this.

People come to the New Testament and, instead of taking its teaching as it is, they interpret it in the light of their experience, and so they reduce it. Everything is interpreted in terms of what they have and what they experience. And I believe that this is very largely responsible for the condition of the Christian church at this present time. People are so afraid of what they call enthusiasm, and some are so afraid of fanaticism, that in order to avoid those they go right over to the other side without facing what is offered in the New Testament. They take what they have and what they are as the norm.

Let me just put it in a nutshell in this way. Compare, for instance, what you read about the life of the church at Corinth with typical church life today. 'Ah, but,' you say, 'they were guilty of excesses in Corinth.' I quite agree. But how many churches do you know at the present time to which it is necessary to write such a letter as the First Epistle of Paul to the Corinthians? Do not put your emphasis entirely on the excesses. Paul corrects the excesses but see what he allows, what he expects.

Take your New Testament as it is. Look at the New Testament Christian, look at the New Testament church, and you see it vibrant with a spiritual life, and, of course, it is always life that tends to lead to excesses. There is no problem of discipline in a graveyard; there is no problem very much in a formal church. The problems arise when there is life. A poor sickly child is not difficult to handle, but when that child is well and full of life and of vigour, well, then you have your problems. Problems are created by life and by vigour, and the problems of the early church were spiritual problems, problems arising because of the danger of going to excess in the spiritual realm.

Would anybody like to claim that speaking generally that is the danger in the church today? Well it is not, of course, and the reason is that we have been tending to interpret the New

Testament teaching in the light of our own experiences.

These, then, are the two great dangers, which are both wrong, and both equally wrong. The excesses, of course, and the fanaticism are most spectacular and they always attract attention, but the other is equally bad, if not more so. There is all the difference in the world between a man in a state of delirium when he is ill, and a man suffering from some terrible growth which is just eating out the vitals of his life and of his body and reducing him more or less to a state of paralysis and of helplessness. But the two things are equally bad, and therefore we have to remember them both.

And so as we handle this whole matter I would lay down this fundamental proposition – that everything must be tested by the teaching of Scripture. We must not start with what we think, what we like. Some of us would like the spectacular, others are so dignified that dignity is the one thing that matters; everything must be ordered and dignified and orderly, working like a clock with all the mechanism and mechanistic characteristics of a clock or of a machine. So if we start with ourselves and what we like and our experience we will already go wrong. No, we have got to start, all of us, with the New Testament and its teaching.

Now fortunately for us there is plenty of it. If we look at two incidents in Acts, the end of chapter 18 and the beginning of chapter 19 – the case of Apollos and the case of the disciples whom Paul found at Ephesus – we discover the following things: there are obviously steps, or stages, in the Christian life. The New Testament is full of that. 'Babes in Christ', 'young men', 'old men', 'growing in grace, and in the knowledge of the Lord', and so on. But not only that, this is more than supported and fulfilled and substantiated in the subsequent history of men in the long story of the Christian church, and we see, especially in those two instances to which I have referred, that what really makes the difference is this baptism of the Holy Spirit, or with the Holy Spirit, or this 'receiving' of the Spirit.

Let me try to put this teaching of the New Testament as I understand it in the form of a number of principles. We must do this because John tells us at the beginning of his Gospel that the thing that is going to differentiate the new era from the old, even including John the Baptist, is this baptism with the Spirit. Here is the first principle. It is possible for us to be believers in the Lord Jesus Christ without having received the baptism of the Holy Spirit.

But let me clarify this, because it is often misunderstood – and this to me is the crux of the whole interpretation of the New Testament at this point, it is the key point. Do not start thinking about phenomena; I will come to that later. That is the fatal mistake that people make. They start with phenomena, they have their prejudices and they take up their lines and their points and the New Testament teaching is entirely forgotten. No, we must start with the teaching of the Scripture.

How? Well, in this way. It is obvious that no man can be a Christian at all apart from the work of the Holy Spirit. The natural man, the natural mind, we are told, 'is enmity against God: for it is not subject to the law of God, neither indeed can it be.' The apostle Paul in that whole passage in Romans 8:7 which I have just quoted, draws his great distinction between the 'natural' man and the 'spiritual' man, and that is the great difference. The spiritual man is a man, he says, who is 'led by the Spirit' and who 'walks after the Spirit, not after the flesh'. Basically, therefore, you have to start by saying that no man can be a Christian at all without the Holy Spirit. The natural mind is – 'enmity against God, is not subject to the law of God, neither indeed can be'.

Again, in 1 Corinthians 2:14 Paul puts it in this way: 'The natural man receiveth not the things of the Spirit of God: for they are foolishness unto him: neither can he know them, because they are spiritually discerned.' In that chapter, too, the apostle is drawing a distinction between the Christian and the non-Christian. He says, 'Even the princes of this world' – though they are great men in great positions and men of great ability, are not Christians. Why? Well, they have not believed on the Lord Jesus Christ – 'Had they known him, they would not have crucified the Lord of glory.'

How then do we believe, how does anybody believe in him? Well, he says, 'God hath revealed them unto us by his Spirit: for the Spirit searcheth all things, yea, the deep things of God.' And again he says, 'We have received, not the spirit of the world, but the spirit which is of God; that we might know the things that are freely given to us of God.'

He says we are Christians because the Holy Spirit has worked in us and has given us this enlightenment and knowledge and understanding, this ability to believe. A man cannot believe without the work of the Holy Spirit. In every believer the Holy Spirit is of necessity a resident. That is a fundamental statement of the whole of Scripture. It is the Spirit who convicts us and who gives us the enlightenment and the ability to believe. No man by nature can believe the gospel. This is fundamental right through the whole Bible.

But then we can go further. It is the Holy Spirit who regenerates us, it is he who gives us new life. The Christian is a man who is born again. Yes, he is a man who is 'born of the Spirit'. Now in the Gospel of John, as we shall find, there is great teaching about this. You get it at once in our Lord's teaching to Nicodemus of all men. 'Except a man be born of water and of the Spirit, he cannot enter into the kingdom of God' (John 3:5). That is it. This is something that happens as the result of the operation of the Holy Spirit. Regeneration is the work of the Holy Spirit; it is a secret work of the Spirit. It is not something experimental but is a secret work, and a man only knows that it has happened to him.

But we have got a very specific statement in Romans 8:9,

which puts this matter quite tersely, once and for ever. Paul says, 'But ye are not in the flesh, but in the Spirit, if so be that the Spirit of God dwell in you. Now if any man have not the Spirit of Christ, he is none of his.' So that, clearly, any man who is a Christian is a man in whom the Holy Spirit of God dwells.

I take it that that is therefore abundantly clear – you cannot be a Christian without having the Holy Spirit in you. But – and here is the point – I am asserting at the same time that you can be a believer, that you can have the Holy Spirit dwelling in you, and still not be baptized with the Holy Spirit. Now this is the crucial issue. Why do I say this? Let me give you my reasons.

All I have been describing is the work of the Holy Spirit in us, the work of convicting, the work of enlightening, the work of regenerating and so on. That is what the Holy Spirit does in us. But as you notice in the teaching in the first chapter of John's Gospel and which we see so clearly in the preaching of John the Baptist, the baptism of the Holy Spirit is something that is done by the Lord Jesus Christ not by the Holy Spirit. 'I indeed baptize you with water ... he shall baptize you with the Holy Ghost.' This is not primarily some work of the Holy Spirit. It is the Lord Jesus Christ's act. It is his action – something he does to us through the Spirit or his giving to us, in this particular way, of the Spirit.

Now here it seems to me is something that is there, plain and clear, on the very surface of this whole subject and yet people get confused over it, and quote 1 Corinthians 12:13 – 'For by one Spirit are we all baptized'. Of course we are. Our being baptized into the body of Christ is the work of the Spirit, as regeneration is his work, but this is something entirely different; this is Christ baptizing us with the Holy Spirit. And I am suggesting that this is something which is therefore obviously distinct from and separate from becoming a Christian, being regenerate, having the Holy

Spirit dwelling within you. I am putting it like this – you can be a child of God and yet not be baptized with the Holy Spirit.

Let me give you some proof. I start with the Old Testament saints. They were as much the children of God as you and I are. Abraham is 'the father of the faithful', a child of God. Now I could give you endless Scriptures to prove that. Our Lord himself says, 'You shall sit in the Kingdom of God with Abraham, Isaac, and Jacob.' And yet some of these Jews are going to be outside, though they kept on boasting that Abraham was their father. But that is what it means to be in the kingdom of God, to be with Abraham, Isaac, and Jacob.

Paul, in Galatians 3, shows at great length that all the children of faith are children of Abraham; he is the father of the faithful. Indeed, the apostle Paul, as the apostle to the Gentiles, goes out of his way to emphasize this great thing: that when the Gentiles became Christians, what happened to them was that they became 'fellow-citizens with the saints' – that is to say, the saints of the Old Testament – 'and joint heirs with the saints of the Old Testament.'

You remember, also, that great contrast in Ephesians 2:11 and following: 'Wherefore remember, that ye being in time past Gentiles in the flesh, which are called Uncircumcision by that which is called the Circumcision in the flesh made by hands; That at that time ye were without Christ, being aliens from the commonwealth of Israel, and strangers from the covenants of promise.' That is where they were. 'But now in Christ Jesus ye who sometimes were afar off are made nigh by the blood of Christ.... Therefore ye are no more strangers and foreigners, but fellow-citizens with the saints, and of the household of God.' Abraham, Isaac, Jacob, Moses, David – all these men of the Old Testament – they all belong to the household of God. And when we become Christians, as Gentiles, we become 'fellow-citizens' with them and 'members of the household of God'.

And then, to make this thing abundantly clear, the apostle repeats it in Ephesians 3. He says that the revelation had been made known to him of the mystery. What is it? Well, here it is: 'Which in other ages was not made known unto the sons of men, as it is now revealed unto his holy apostles and prophets by the Spirit; that the Gentiles should be fellow heirs, and of the same body, and partakers of his promise in Christ.' If you think that the Old Testament saints were not children of God you are denying the whole of the Scripture. They were. But they had not been baptized with the Holy Spirit.

Abraham believed in Christ. Our Lord says, 'Abraham saw my day' – he saw it afar off – 'and he rejoiced.' These men did not understand it fully, but what made them children of God and men of faith was this – that they believed God's testimony about this 'Coming One'. No man can be saved except in Christ. There is only one way of salvation, Old Testament and New. It is always in Christ, and by him crucified.

But what about John the Baptist himself? Our Lord makes this quite clear. He says, 'Among them that are born of women there hath not risen a greater than John the Baptist.' John the Baptist is a son of God, he is a child of God, and yet John was not baptized with the Holy Spirit.

'Notwithstanding,' says our Lord, 'he that is least in the kingdom of heaven is greater than he' (Matthew 11:11). That is a reference to the kingdom of heaven taking the form of the church, that though John the Baptist is the last of the prophets, though he is a child of God and a unique servant of God, though the man is as saved as any Christian, he is not enjoying the benefits which those who have received the baptism of the Holy Spirit, which Christ is to give, are able to enjoy.

And then you remember that most important statement in John 7:37-39: 'In the last day, that great day of the feast, Jesus stood up and cried, saying, If any man thirst, let him come unto me, and drink. He that believeth on me, as the scripture hath said, out of his belly shall flow rivers of living water. (But this spake he of the Spirit, which they that believe on him should receive: for the Holy Ghost was not yet' – the Authorized Version adds 'given', quite rightly – 'was not yet given', 'was not yet', 'had not come in that way yet'.

The Holy Spirit always was, of course; you read about him in the Old Testament. But he was not given in this way 'yet'. He was given like that on the day of Pentecost – 'for the Holy Ghost was not yet given; because that Jesus was not yet glorified.' Now there again is one of the crucial statements.

But let us go on and add to that. All this it seems to me becomes much clearer when you come right on to Acts and look at the case of the apostles themselves. Now surely it is quite obvious that the apostles were regenerate and were children of God before the day of Pentecost. Our Lord has already said, 'Now ye are clean through the word which I have spoken unto you' (John 15:3). In the great High Priestly prayer in John 17 he keeps on drawing a distinction between them and the world. 'I have manifested thy name unto the men which thou gavest me out of the world: thine they were, and thou gavest them me; and they have kept thy word. I pray for them: I pray not for the world, but for them which thou hast given me; for they are thine'. Throughout the whole of that seventeenth chapter the emphasis is that these people are already regenerate, our Lord keeps on saying that. He says, 'I have given unto them the words which thou gavest me; and they have received them, and have known surely that I came out from thee, and they have believed that thou didst send me.' Nothing could be clearer.

And then we are told that after the resurrection our Lord met with them in an upper room and he 'breathed on them'. He breathed on them the Holy Spirit. You remember that incident: it is recorded in John 20. 'Then said Jesus to them again, Peace be unto you: as my Father hath sent me, even so send I you. And when he had said this, he breathed on them, and saith unto them, Receive ye the Holy Ghost.' These men are not only believers, they are regenerate men, the Holy Spirit has been breathed upon them, yet they have not been baptized with the Holy Spirit.

Acts 1:4-8 makes this very clear: 'And being assembled together with them, [he] commanded them that they should not depart from Jerusalem, but wait for the promise of the Father, which, saith he, ye have heard of me. For John truly baptized with water' – here it is again – 'but ye shall be baptized with the Holy Ghost not many days hence. When they therefore were come together, they asked of him saying, Lord, wilt thou at this time restore again the kingdom of Israel? And he said unto them, It is not for you to know the times or the seasons, which the Father hath put in his own power. But ye shall receive power, after that the Holy Ghost is come upon you: and ye shall be witnesses unto me both in Jerusalem, and in all Judea, and in Samaria, and unto the uttermost part of the earth.'

And these self-same men, already believers and regenerate, already having received the Holy Spirit in one sense, were 'baptized' with the Holy Spirit. This is my way of substantiating that a man can be a true believer on the Lord Jesus Christ and a child of God, and still not baptized with the Holy Spirit.

But come, let us go on to the evidence which we have already seen in Acts 8, where it is perhaps still more clearly put before us. Philip went down from Jerusalem to Samaria to preach the gospel to those Samaritans and we are told this: 'The people with one accord gave heed unto those things which Philip spake, hearing and seeing the miracles which he did.... And there was great joy in that city.' This is followed by the incident about Simon.

But let us concentrate on these others. 'But when they believed Philip preaching the things concerning the kingdom of God, and the name of Jesus Christ....' Now this is not the teaching of John the Baptist, this is the teaching of Philip, filled with the Holy Spirit, baptized with the Holy Spirit after the day of Pentecost, the plain Christian teaching. '... when they believed Philip preaching the things concerning the kingdom of God, and the name of Jesus Christ, they were baptized, both men and women.'

Here they are then, believers, and they are rejoicing in their belief. They have been baptized not with John's baptism but they have been baptized 'in the name of Jesus Christ'. But then comes verse 14: 'Now when the apostles which were at Jerusalem heard that Samaria had received the word of God, they sent unto them Peter and John: Who, when they were come down, prayed for them, that they might receive the Holy Ghost: (For as yet he was fallen upon none of them: only they were baptized in the name of the Lord Jesus.) Then laid they their hands on them, and they received the Holy Ghost.' These people were already true believers on the Lord Jesus Christ and him crucified as their Saviour. They had been baptized into his name because they had become believers, but still they were not baptized with the Holy Spirit.

The next case we must consider is none other than that of the apostle Paul himself. We are, at this point, let me remind you, just going through the Scriptures. Later we shall be drawing lessons and working this out in detail. It is so vital that we should start with the Scriptures, not with our prejudices, not with what we think, not what we are afraid of.

'Ah,' you may say, 'now you have said that tongues are all right.' I am sure many are already thinking that. You wait a minute; I shall deal with the question of gifts when it comes at the right place. You do not start with that. That comes towards the end of this treatment. But that is how the devil gets us to bypass the Scriptures in the interests of our particular point of view, whichever of the two extremes it may chance to be.

Look, then, at the case of Paul himself. You get that in Acts 9. There, on the road to Damascus, he sees the risen Lord and says, 'Lord, What wilt thou have me to do?' He becomes as helpless as a little child; undoubtedly the apostle at that point believed on the Lord Jesus Christ. He saw it. He was given the vision that enabled him to see it.

But this is what I read in verses 10 and 11: a man named Ananias was called by the Lord. 'And the Lord said unto him, Arise, and go into the street which is called Straight, and inquire in the house of Judas for one called Saul, of Tarsus: for, behold, he prayeth, And hath seen in a vision a man named Ananias coming in, and putting his hand on him, that he might receive his sight.' Paul was rendered blind, you remember.

Then you go on in verse 15 – 'The Lord said unto him,' – Ananias did not seem to want to go – 'Go thy way: for he is a chosen vessel unto me, to bear my name before the Gentiles, and kings, and the children of Israel: For I will shew him how great things he must suffer for my name's sake. And Ananias went his way, and entered into the house; and putting his hands on him said, Brother Saul, the Lord Jesus, that appeared unto thee in the way as thou camest, hath sent me that thou mightest receive thy sight, and be filled with the Holy Ghost.'

He does not instruct him on the way of salvation. He is sent to heal him and to fill him with the Holy Spirit, to give him the baptism with the Holy Spirit. 'And immediately there fell from his eyes as it had been scales: and he received sight forthwith, and arose, and was baptized.' You can, you see, receive the Holy Spirit before you are baptized, or the other way round, it does not matter at all. 'And when he had received meat, he was strengthened. Then was Saul certain days with the disciples which were at Damascus. And straightway he preached Christ in the synagogues, that he is the Son of God.' There, then, is another striking example of the same thing.

I come now to my last example from Acts. I am not going to use the case of Apollos, though I believe it could be used quite easily. It seems to me this is the only adequate explanation of the story about him. This was the thing that Priscilla and Aquila recognized as lacking in Apollos and about which they told him, and it made all the difference to him.

But leaving that out of account, come to the beginning of chapter 19, where you read, 'It came to pass, that, while Apollos was at Corinth, Paul having passed through the upper coasts came to Ephesus: and finding certain disciples,' – and you remember that we have seen the full connotation of that, for in Acts, without a single exception it always means 'believers in the Lord Jesus Christ' – 'and finding certain disciples, He said unto them, Have ye received the Holy Ghost since ye believed?'

All right – I know what you want to say and you are quite right. You say, 'You are reading from the Authorized Version.' I am. You say, 'That is not the right translation.' I agree. So let me give it you in the Revised and the other translations. 'Did you receive the Holy Ghost when you believed?' Right; that is the correct translation and, of course, it shows that the old Authorized translation is after all not wrong: 'Have ye received the Holy Ghost *since* ye believed?' (my italics). The implication there, obviously, is, of course, that you can believe without receiving the Holy Spirit, that it happens to you afterwards.

'All right,' you say, 'but the other is the correct translation: "Did you receive the Holy Ghost *when* you believed?"' But what does that tell us? Well that, too, tells us that it is obvious that you can believe without receiving the Holy Spirit.

Let me use an illustration which I think I have used before. You may say to me, 'I had a cold last week.' I then put to you this one question – 'Did you run a temperature when you had your cold last week?' What does that question mean? Well it obviously means that you may have a cold without running a temperature. On the other hand, you may run a temperature when you have a cold. I want to know, Did you or did you not have one? And that is the very question that is put here by the Apostle.

It is possible for a man to be baptized with the Holy Spirit virtually simultaneously with his belief. Take the case of Cornelius and his household. You remember that there we are told in Acts 10 that as Peter was still speaking, the Holy Spirit fell upon them. There it seems that the baptism with the Holy Spirit happened 'as they were believing', 'almost simultaneously'. But it is clear from the question put by the Apostle that that is not always the case, that it is possible for a man to believe without receiving the Holy Spirit. 'Did you receive the Holy Ghost when you believed?'

Paul, obviously, saw that there was something wrong with these people and he was quite clearly of the opinion himself that they had not been baptized with the Holy Ghost, so he puts his question: 'When you believed, were you baptized with the Holy Spirit?' So you see, even the Revised translation and the others come to exactly the same thing in the end as the old Authorized Version, except that these others are more accurate.

From the purely linguistic standpoint the Authorized translation is wrong, but, as so often, these Authorized translators get the right point, the right meaning but they over-emphasize it a little, so that it looks as if it is always something subsequent. But what is established beyond any doubt is that one can be a believer without being baptized by the Holy Spirit.

But if that does not satisfy you – and it should – pay attention to this. In Acts 19:4 Paul addresses these men and gives them further instruction and then we read: 'When they heard this, they were baptized in the name of the Lord Jesus.' The apostle is perfectly happy that these men are true believers. But they have had John's baptism only, so he says,

'But you must be baptized in the name of the Lord Jesus Christ.' So he baptized them 'in the name of the Lord Jesus Christ'.

They are true believers, children of God, but still they have not been baptized with the Holy Spirit, because we read in verse 6: 'When Paul had laid his hands upon them, the Holy Ghost came on them; and they spake with tongues, and prophesied.'

Now there is an absolute proof that you can be a true believer in the Lord Jesus Christ and still not be baptized with the Holy Spirit; that incident proves it twice over. Twice over! The question at the beginning and what actually happened subsequently. The important point is that there is a difference, that there is a distinction between believing and being baptized with the Holy Spirit.

So I give you my last bit of evidence, which is in Ephesians 1:13. Paul is here reminding these Gentile Christians of how they became Christians. 'In whom ye also trusted, after that ye heard the word of truth, the gospel of your salvation: in whom also after that ye believed, ye were sealed with that Holy Spirit of promise, Which is the earnest of our inheritance until the redemption of the purchased possession, unto the praise of his glory.'

'All right,' you say again, 'Authorized Version once more, and again they have made exactly the same mistake: "In whom also *after* that ye believed". It should not be that.'

'What should it be?'

Well, as the Revised has it – 'In whom, having also believed, ye were sealed with the Holy Spirit.' But you see once more that it does not make any difference to the meaning and to the truth. It is only the believer who is baptized with the Holy Spirit or receives the seal of the Spirit. 'In whom, having believed, were sealed.'

It is the same order again. The believing is the first thing, but being baptized is something that does not of necessity happen at the same time. It may – it may not. But it is distinct and separate, so the Apostle does separate them. 'In whom, having also believed, ye were sealed with the Holy Spirit of promise, Which is the earnest of our inheritance until the redemption of the purchased possession.'

That, then, is our first great principle. All I am trying to establish is this – that you can be regenerate without being baptized with the Holy Spirit. The Scriptures that I have adduced to you show quite clearly that to say, as so many have said, and are still saying, that every man at regeneration is of necessity baptized with the Holy Spirit, is simply to fly in the face of this plain, explicit teaching of the Holy Scriptures.

Chapter 2

Blessed Assurance

In the prologue to John's Gospel we are told that a Christian is one who has received of God's fullness, and grace upon grace. The New Testament gives us a picture and portrayal of what a Christian should be, and obviously in that connection nothing is more vital or important than that we should understand the doctrine of the baptism with the Holy Spirit.

This is not only that we may enjoy the full blessing of the Christian salvation, but also, more urgently, because of the times in which we live. We see the Christian church in a more or less parlous condition, ineffective in a world of sin and shame, a world which is increasingly manifesting, in a horrifying manner, godlessness and hatred and antagonism to God. There is only one hope for such a world and that is a revived church. So the most urgent need of the hour is revival in the Christian church, and that means revival in individual Christians. There is no such thing as the church apart from people, so we start with the personal, and through that we see how the general can be effected.

In order to try to bring out this doctrine, I have suggested that perhaps the most convenient thing to do is to consider a number of general principles or propositions. We have started with the first, which is that it is clear from the teaching of both the Old Testament and the New that it is possible to be a believer and a Christian without having received the baptism of the Holy Spirit. You cannot be a Christian at all without having the Holy Spirit in you. A Christian is a man who is born of the Spirit; the Spirit does the work of regeneration in him. 'If any man have not the Spirit of Christ, he is none of his' (Romans 8:9). So while a Christian, by definition, is a man who has the Holy Spirit dwelling in him, that does not mean that he is baptized with the Holy Spirit.

This, then, is the basic proposition and it is the aspect of the teaching that is most frequently controverted, not to say attacked. So I propose to go into this still further. If it is true to say that you cannot be a Christian without being baptized with the Spirit, that it is something that is virtually synonymous with regeneration, then the whole position is changed. That is why I am holding you with this particular general princple, because to me it is very vital that we should see that there is an essential distinction, that you can be regenerate, a child of God, a true believer, and still not have received the baptism with the Holy Spirit.

We must substantiate this yet further. So what I propose to do now is give you certain additional reasons or arguments why it is so vital and essential for us to hold this distinction.

An argument that is very often brought against the teaching which separates regeneration and the baptism of the Holy Spirit is as follows: 'Yes, but all of you who hold that view always seem to base it all upon the book of Acts. You must not found your doctrine on the history in Acts – that is a very dangerous thing to do. You must found your doctrine only upon the teaching of our Lord himself and upon the teaching of the epistles.'

Now this is frequently said, and the answer, of course, is quite simple. You should never pit one section of Scripture against another. You should never say that it must either be this or that. The true position is to take both Acts and the epistles. It is characteristic of the higher critical attitude to put Scripture against Scripture, to depreciate one at the expense of the other. So there is that fundamental answer to this criticism.

But, furthermore, we must go beyond that and say this: surely one of the main purposes of Acts is to show us the fulfilment of this promise concerning the baptism with the Holy Spirit – 'the promise of the Father'. In the very first chapter of Acts our Lord himself, after the resurrection and just before the ascension, turns to his disciples, who with their materialistic outlook were still concerned about 'the restoration of the kingdom to Israel' and says, 'It is not for you to know the times or the seasons.... But ye shall receive power, after that the Holy Ghost is come upon you: and ye shall be witnesses unto me both in Jerusalem, and in all Judaea, and in Samaria, and unto the uttermost part of the earth' (Acts 1:7).

In that context Jesus quoted the statement about John the Baptist baptizing with water but added that he would baptize with the Holy Spirit, and the remainder of Acts is just to tell us how this happened. Chapter 2 tells us how the Holy Spirit actually came, as our Lord had prophesied, upon the early church, upon the hundred and twenty on the day of Pentecost and later upon the three thousand who had believed; and it goes on to give us further examples and illustrations as we have already seen.

Now surely this is quite basic to any doctrine of the baptism with the Holy Spirit. We are told in Acts how it happened, what its results were, how it was recognized, and its essential, vital part of the teaching. And when people come along and say, 'Ah yes, but that was only at the beginning you know,' that is a very serious charge – namely that the Scripture does not apply to us. One agrees, of course, that there are exceptional times in the history of the church, but it is always wrong to say that any teaching in Scripture has nothing to do with us, that it was exceptional. What we read in the whole of the Scripture must be applied to ourselves. It is a kind of pattern or standard or norm of what we should expect individually and in the case of the Christian church.

Let me illustrate what I mean. What is a revival of religion? It is generally agreed that the best way of defining a revival is to say that it is the church returning to the book of Acts, that it is a kind of repetition of Pentecost. It is the Spirit being poured out again upon the church. And this, of course, is a very vital and essential bit of doctrine.

But to go still further – and this to me is perhaps the most important point of all – there is nothing which is more fatal than to fail to see that the teaching of the epistles always presupposes the history which we have in Acts. You see, what some people are trying to do – they have done it in the past and they are still trying to do so – is to say, 'Ah well, what you have got in Acts is very exceptional, it is just the beginning of the church; the norm is what you get in the teaching of the epistles.'

My reply to them is quite simple. Take, for instance that great first epistle to the Corinthians. Its teaching is obviously based upon the fact that the members of the church at Corinth had been baptized with the Spirit in the way that we read of in Acts. We are sometimes told, 'You never find the epistles exhorting people to be baptized with the Spirit.' That is perfectly right, but the answer is obvious. They are not exhorted to be baptized with the Spirit because they were already baptized with the Spirit!

What is the meaning of those three chapters, 12, 13 and 14 of 1 Corinthians? The answer is that they are dealing with certain excesses which had arisen and certain misunderstandings in people who had been baptized with the Spirit. As I have often put it – how many churches do you know at the present time to whom you need to write 1 Corinthians? How many churches are there today that need to have the teaching of 1 Corinthians 12, 13 and 14? And the answer is, 'Precious few.' Why? Well, you see, there was a church whose members were baptized with the Spirit, and because of that, because the kind of thing that is described in Acts had happened to them, problems and difficulties had arisen.

This is surely therefore a very important matter. It shows that this attempt to differentiate between the teaching of Acts and the epistles is completely false. The epistles were generally written to correct errors and faults in situations that had arisen. That is not only true of 1 Corinthians, but is equally true of the teaching of an epistle like that to the Galatians.

Let me illustrate what I mean by a passage from a fairly recent writer on these matters. In dealing with Galatians he says, 'further, it is a fundamental principle of biblical interpretation to begin with the general, not with the special.'

He is illustrating the point that the history of Acts is 'special' but the general, the ordinary, is to be found in the epistles. So he goes on to say, 'If it be asked what the general teaching as distinct from the special teaching of the New Testament is regarding the reception of the Holy Spirit, we can give a plain and definite answer. We receive the Holy Spirit "by hearing the gospel with faith" Galatians 3:2. Or, more simply still, through faith, Galatians 3:14.' Thereby the writer thinks he has established his case. Here he says what we should expect for ourselves. We are not in the days of Acts, which are special, but in the ordinary.

Let us look, then, at the verses which he quotes from in Galatians 3. 'O foolish Galatians,' says Paul, 'who hath bewitched you, that ye should not obey the truth, before whose eyes Jesus Christ hath been evidently set forth, crucified among you? This only would I learn of you, Received ye the Spirit by the works of the law, or by the hearing of faith?' And then verse 14 reads like this: 'That the blessing of Abraham might come on the Gentiles through Jesus Christ;

that we might receive the promise of the Spirit through faith.'

Now that writer identifies receiving the Spirit or being baptized with the Spirit with believing the gospel, with regeneration, with becoming a Christian, and he says this is the normal way; you believe and receive the Spirit by faith. So you must not say that the baptism with the Spirit is something which is different and distinct from belief and regeneration. But in a most interesting way he evidently fails to remember what we are told in verse 5. Now this is the kind of confusion people get into when they do not draw this distinction between baptism with the Spirit and regeneration. Look at what we find in Galatians 3:5 – 'He therefore that ministereth to you the Spirit, and worketh miracles among you, doeth he it by the works of the law, or by the hearing of faith?'

Is that the general and the normal? 'Worketh miracles among you', 'ministereth to you the Spirit'? This is not just a description of how people came to believe. That is not what the apostle is asking. He has, incidentally, already dealt in the first two chapters with how you believe and are justified by faith. He is now producing an additional argument. Not only, he says, do you believe, not only are you saved by faith rather than by circumcision, and so on, but....

Let me put it to you like this: 'When you received the Spirit, when the Spirit came upon you, when you received the baptism of the Spirit, tell me, was that the result of keeping the works of the law or was it this whole matter of your faith relationship to God in Christ?' And, of course, the proof that that is what he is talking about is that fifth verse: 'He that ministereth to you the Spirit, and worketh miracles among you.' Are we to say that this is the general and the ordinary and the usual? No, this church of the Galatians was baptized with and filled with the Spirit, it was a church in which miracles were being demonstrated. Of course, this was true of every single New Testament church. Not only the Corinthian church but also that at Galatia.

In other words I am establishing my point, that you really cannot truly interpret nor understand the teaching of the epistles unless you do so in the light of the history of Acts.

When we come later to consider the effects of the baptism with the Spirit, we shall find that one of the main effects and results of the baptism with the Holy Spirit is to give us an unusual assurance of our salvation, and that is why, of course, I am dealing with this whole subject. The greatest need at the present time is for Christian people who are assured of their salvation. If we confront the world saying, 'Well, I hope I am saved, I am not sure, but I hope', we will be depressed and we will depress others and we shall not attract. The thing that was so obvious about the New Testament Christians, as seen in Acts 2 or anywhere else, was their spirit of joy and of happiness and assurance, their confidence; they were so certain, that they were ready to be thrown to the lions in the arena or put to death. And this has always characterized every great period of reformation and revival in the history of the church.

So we are entitled to say this: if you identify the baptism with the Spirit with belief in the Lord Jesus Christ unto salvation, you are automatically saying that there is no difference between saving faith and an assurance of faith, and this is a very serious matter.

Of course, people who do not draw this distinction actually say that. Let me give you a quotation again from the same writer. 'As a result,' he says, 'all God's sons possess the Spirit, are led by the Spirit, and are assured by the Spirit of their sonship and of God's love; while those who do not possess the Spirit do not belong to Christ at all.'

Think about what he says: 'All God's sons possess the Spirit' – that is all right – 'are led by the Spirit' – is that true of necessity? – 'and are assured by the Spirit of their sonship, and of God's love' – Romans 8:15-16, and 5:5. And the contrast is that those who do not possess the Spirit do not belong to Christ at all.

Here, then, is the question that I would put to you. Is it true to say of all believers that they possess this great and full assurance of salvation? Look at Romans 8:15-16, 'Ye have not received the spirit of bondage again to fear; but ye have received the Spirit of adoption, whereby we cry, Abba, Father.' Paul uses a word there which expresses this, that out of the depth of our being comes an elemental cry 'Abba, Father'. And then he goes on and says, 'The Spirit itself beareth witness with our spirit, that we are the children of God.' It is the highest form of assurance, an absolute certainty, a glorying and a crying out of 'Abba, Father'. We are told that this is true of every Christian.

Now you see the consequence of that. Do you all possess that assurance? Have you got this elemental cry in you, crying out 'Abba, Father'? Do you know beyond any doubt or dispute or peradventure or hesitation that you are the children of God, and joint heirs with Christ? Are you rejoicing in a full assurance? You see the consequence of this confusion. It is to say that large numbers of people who are regarded as Christian are not Christian at all.

Now there is nothing new about this. This was something that was fought out at the end of the sixteenth and the beginning of the seventeenth centuries. Some of the early Reformers in order to counteract the false teaching of Rome had said that you could not be a Christian unless you had assurance. There is no difference, they said, between saving faith and assurance of salvation. But on reflection Protestant leaders came to see that this was quite wrong and therefore in a document like the Westminster Confession of Faith, and indeed all the other great Confessions, you will find that they are very careful to draw a sharp distinction between saving faith and assurance of faith, and it is very important.

The Bible never says that we are saved by assurance, we are

saved by faith. In other words, there are many Christian people who have come to see and to know that they are sinners, that they are under the wrath of God, that they are helpless and hopeless, and who are afraid of the judgement; who realize, furthermore, that should they spend the rest of their lives in a monastery trying to live a good life and to please and to satisfy God and to work up righteousness, but they will be no further on at the end than they were at the beginning. Then just as they are, in simple faith, they say, 'I trust myself only to the Lord Jesus Christ.' They believe the truth concerning him, they believe on him, and they rest on that. They are constantly having to go back and do it again; the devil attacks them and they are terrified. They fall into sin and they feel they are not Christians at all but they say, 'I have nothing but Jesus Christ and the fact that he died for me.'

Now the Bible says that such people are Christians, but they are Christians who are not enjoying full assurance of salvation and of faith. They are like the people to whom the Apostle John was writing in his first epistle: 'These things write I unto you that believe on the name of the Son of God; that ye may *know* that ye have eternal life' (1 John 5:3, italics mine).

There is no question about this. There have been saints who have testified to this throughout the centuries, that for years – even all their lives – they believed but did not enjoy assurance. They were uncertain, unhappy, and always came back and said, 'I have nothing but Christ.' You must not disenfranchize these people, nor say they are not Christians. But if you say that every son of God, every Christian, has full assurance by the Spirit of sonship and of God's love, you are saying that these people are not Christian at all. And that is not only wrong but it is a very cruel thing to say. O yes, you can be a Christian without assurance. Of course, Christians should not be in that fearful state. Sometimes it is due to psychological conditions, or sometimes to wrong teaching.

And it is a terrible thing, not only a wrong thing, to confuse saving faith with full assurance of faith.

And you see, the moment you begin to do things like this you get into difficulties and you begin to contradict yourself. For the writer I quoted earlier goes on to say this, 'Sometimes the Holy Spirit may do His distinctively new covenant work of glorifying the Lord Jesus, that is revealing and manifesting Him in such a way as to make us '– then he quotes 1 Peter 1:8 – "rejoice with unutterable and exalted joy".' My point here is that he uses the word 'sometimes'. '...Sometimes we may have visions and revelations or have some such experience as Paul had in 2 Corinthians 12: 1-4.' Then he adds this: 'I do not for a moment deny any of these things, nevertheless these are not the usual, general, or common purpose of God for all His people, but the unusual, particular and exceptional ministries of the Holy Spirit to some; nor should such people who have these, urge the same experiences upon others as if they were the spiritual norm.'

Why, then, do I emphasize this? Well, this is very interesting. I do so because what he is saying is that the position in which one rejoices with a joy unspeakable, and full of glory, is 'exceptional, unusual, particular, it is something that happens sometimes. But what does the Scripture say? To whom is the apostle Peter writing? He starts off like this – 1 Peter 1:1 – 'Peter, an apostle of Jesus Christ, to the strangers scattered abroad throughout Pontus, Galatia, Cappadocia, Asia, and Bithynia, Elect according to the foreknowledge of God the Father, through sanctification of the Spirit, unto obedience and sprinkling of the blood of Jesus Christ.'

Is he writing there to exceptional Christians; to a body of apostles or church leaders only? Is he writing to people and saying, 'Now you are a most unusual people'? No, he is writing to ordinary church members, whose names he does not even know, to 'strangers scattered abroad'. He says, 'I am writing to you and I know that this is true of you, "Whom having not seen, ye love; in whom though now ye see him not, yet believing, ye rejoice with joy unspeakable and full of glory".' Peter himself makes it clear that he is not writing about something exceptional, something that *sometimes* happens. He is assuming it to be the norm and the normal experience of ordinary unknown members of the Christian church. And yet, you see, because of a wrong doctrine our writer says this is 'sometimes', this is 'exceptional'. No, this is the ordinary and the usual.

'Very well, then,' says someone, 'are you yourself now saying that we all of us should be able to say that we rejoice in Christ with a joy unspeakable, and full of glory?'

My answer is quite simple: we all ought to be able to say that, but I do not say for a second that if you cannot say that then you are not a Christian. What is the explanation? Well, let me repeat it again. It is that all the teaching of the epistles is based upon and presupposes the history of what happens in Acts. In other words, there is only one way you can understand the New Testament epistles and it is this: God started the Christian church by pouring down his Spirit upon them. So the New Testament church is a church that is baptized with the Spirit. And all the teaching of the New Testament assumes that. Often the church today is not like that; she often has not been anything like that in her long history; she is not like that today. But that is what she should be like.

Now in the New Testament epistles you obviously do not get exhortations to people to seek the baptism of the Spirit. Why? Because they had already had it. In exactly the same way, when there is a time of revival and the Spirit is outpoured you do not urge this. Indeed, your problem then will be to deal with the tendencies to excesses and a certain element of riot that comes in, and you have to preach order. In other words, you will be back in the position of the New Testament church. But the apostle Peter knew that these people, having been baptized with the Spirit, were filled with a joy unspeakable, and full of glory. He, far from saying that it was exceptional, takes it as the standard and as the norm. Therefore I would urge once more that there is nothing more dangerous than to start by saying you must ignore Acts and look for your teaching only in the teaching of our Lord or in the teaching of the New Testament epistles.

Let me now give you a third answer to this difficulty that people seem to be in. If regeneration and the baptism of the Spirit are one and not to be differentiated, then I think we can say, from what we have already seen, that obviously the apostles had it in their power to regenerate people. You remember the story in Acts 19 of the people at Ephesus? The apostle expounded the truth to them, they believed it, and he baptized them in the name of the Lord Jesus Christ. Then he laid his hands upon them and they were baptized with the Spirit. If therefore you identify baptism of the Spirit with regeneration you must say that it was the apostle who, by laying hands upon those people, regenerated them, and the same with all the other examples – Peter and John when they went down to Samaria must have done the same thing. But the answer, as we have already seen, is that these people were already regenerate – they had believed the gospel. In all these instances it was afterwards, after they had been regenerated, that hands were laid upon them, after which they received the baptism of the Holy Spirit (Acts 8 and 19).

But let me come to a fourth argument, which is rather interesting. There are certain sections of the Christian church who believe in what they call confirmation and they hold what they call 'confirmation services'.

The Anglican Church in this country does it, as do the Roman Catholic and Lutheran Churches. Now where does this come from? Well, they say that it is derived from what we read in Hebrews 6:2 about laying on of hands: 'the doctrine of baptisms, and of laying on of hands'. And it is also based, they say, upon what the apostles Peter and John did in Samaria and what Paul did with those people in Ephesus.

Now there are some who write like this: 'Confirmation is the way that the Anglican Church has chosen to receive into full membership those who have been baptized, usually in infancy, and have themselves repented and believed.' They say further that 'it is something that God may use as a sign to certify the candidate of his (God's) favour'.

Now the answer to that is this: confirmation is not something that the Anglican Church has 'chosen' as a manner of receiving people into full membership. The actual history is that the Anglican Church has just continued what the Roman Catholic church had been doing throughout the centuries. It is simply a part of the incompleteness of the Reformation of the sixteenth century. They continued with a number of customs, and the Puritans of course objected to these things. Confirmation is one of them.

But what is interesting to us is this. I do not believe in confirmation, but nevertheless it is an argument which is of great value at this point. Where did confirmation ever come from? Well I have just told you something about its origin. You see, from the beginning there was a distinction between believing and being baptized in water, and receiving the baptism of the Holy Spirit. I have shown you, and you see in the Scriptures, that there was always this distinction between the two things. Paul baptized these men at Ephesus, then, having finished that, he laid his hands upon them and they received the baptism of the Holy Spirit, and began to speak in tongues. The two things are separate and distinct.

Now the early church perpetuated that, and the historians are agreed in saying (I have taken considerable trouble to make quite sure of all the facts) that in the early days the overseer, the bishop, was the man who did the baptism with water and the laying on of hands. But as the numbers greatly increased he found that he could not do this, so then there was a division. The act of baptism in water was given to the parish priest but the one of laying on of hands was reserved for the visit of the overseer or, as he became known increasingly, as the bishop. Now there is clear evidence about this in the writings of one of those great Church Fathers – Tertullian – who wrote at the end of the second century, and by the fourth century this was the common practice. And of course it has continued until today. The local parson preaches and does the baptizing, but the bishop is the man who comes to do the confirming.

Now I am only putting this evidence before you in order to substantiate this point – that this distinction which is so plain in the New Testament has been recognized throughout the centuries. The place where we disagree, of course, is this: we say that the bishop is not necessary in this respect and that this is something that can happen apart from him, and so on. But that is not the material point.

The point that I am establishing is that in accordance with the teaching of the New Testament, you find that church history from the earliest times continues to show that there is this distinction between regeneration and the baptism of the Spirit.

It seems to me, therefore, that those who are in the Anglican position are in real difficulties about their whole service of confirmation, because in connection with the baptism of an infant this is what the priest has to say: 'Seeing now, dearly beloved brethren, that this child is by baptism regenerate and grafted into the body of Christ's Church, let us give thanks unto Almighty God for these benefits' – and so on. The same thing is repeated in the service of confirmation: 'Almighty and ever living God, Who hast vouchsafed to regenerate these Thy servants by water and by the Holy Ghost, and hast given unto them forgiveness of all their sins, strengthen them etc.' It seems to me that if you identify belief or regeneration with the baptism of the

Holy Spirit there really is no point in a confirmation service.

Let me come finally to what is the most important thing of all, and this is no longer quoting anybody or refuting error. This is positive assertion: the teaching of the New Testament itself. To me the ultimate proof of this vital distinction between regeneration and the baptism of the Spirit, the teaching which says that you can be regenerate and still not baptized with the Spirit is none other than the case of our Lord and Saviour Jesus Christ himself. It is interesting to notice that people who do not recognize this distinction never refer to him at all in this manner. And yet here it is – it is so vital. It is time for us to look at the accounts of his baptism.

Here he is, the eternal Son of God, more than regenerate, the Word which always was the Son of God, the incarnate Son of God. Here he is now as a man in the flesh, and yet you remember what happened to him? In order to fulfil all righteousness, as he puts it to John the Baptist, he submitted to baptism, and this is what we read: 'Now when all the people were baptized, it came to pass, that Jesus also being baptized and praying, the heaven was opened, And the Holy Ghost descended in a bodily shape like a dove upon him, and a voice came from heaven, which said, Thou art my beloved Son; in thee I am well pleased' (Luke 3:22).

And you notice what happens after that? Luke 4:1 says, 'And Jesus being full of the Holy Ghost' – it happened when the Holy Spirit came down upon him as he was there in the Jordan – 'full of the Holy Ghost returned from Jordan, and was led by the Spirit into the wilderness.' And again look at verse 14: 'And Jesus returned in the power of the Spirit into Galilee.' But look again at the later verses. He went into the synagogue, the book of Isaiah was handed to him, 'And when he had opened the book, he found the place where it was written, The Spirit of the Lord is upon me, because he hath anointed me to preach the gospel to the poor.... And he began to say unto them, This day is this Scripture fulfilled in your ears' (verses 17-18, 21).

Then you have statements saying the same thing in John's Gospel. Look at John 3:34: 'For he whom God hath sent speaketh the words of God: for God giveth not the Spirit by measure unto him.'

Then the last statement is in John 6:27: 'Labour not for the meat which perisheth, but for that meat which endureth unto everlasting life, which the Son of man shall give unto you: for him hath God the Father sealed.' We have already met that word 'sealed' in Ephesians 1:13: 'In whom having believed ye were sealed with that Holy Spirit of promise.' God the Father has sealed the Son – and he sealed him at the Jordan when he sent the Holy Spirit upon him. He there received the Spirit in fullness.

What for? Here is the crucial point. Our Lord was there beginning to enter on his public ministry. He had lived as a man, he had worked as a carpenter, but now at the age of thirty he was setting out on his ministry, and – here is the teaching – because he had become a man and was living life in this world as a man, though he was still the eternal Son of God, he needed to receive the Spirit in his fullness, and God gave him the Spirit. The Spirit descended upon him. So then we read of him, that 'filled with the Spirit' he went, in the 'power of the Spirit' (Luke 4:14) and began to preach. He said, 'I have been anointed with the Spirit in order to proclaim.' In other words, our Lord himself could not act as witness and as preacher and as testifier to the gospel of salvation without receiving this enduement of the Spirit. And that, I hope to be able to show you, is the purpose of the baptism with the Holy Spirit.

Now you see the argument. Our Lord is eternally the Son of God, but though he was the Son of God, in order to do his work as the Messiah in the likeness of man, in the form of a servant, he needed this 'baptism' with the Spirit, and so the

Spirit came upon him even as it came upon the disciples and the hundred and twenty in the upper room, and upon Cornelius and his household, even as it comes upon people in every time of revival. And in the power of the Spirit he was enabled. We are told that he spoke and lived in the power of the Spirit, he died through the power of the eternal Spirit, and rose from the dead through the power of the Spirit.

Here you see, then, is established, beyond any dispute or doubt whatsoever, this essential distinction between regeneration, being born again, being a partaker of the divine nature, and the baptism with the Holy Spirit. Not only do you get into difficulties if you do not recognize these distinctions, but you find yourself above all in a position in which you simply cannot explain what we read of as having taken place in the case of our blessed Lord and Saviour himself.

Chapter 3

Something that Happens to Us

We have been considering the fact that people can be true Christian believers without having received the baptism of the Holy Spirit – that was my first proposition. Now my second proposition – and I regard this too as a very important statement – is that baptism with the Holy Spirit is something that happens to us. That is clear surely, in all these cases that are recorded in Acts which is, as I have tried to show, our ultimate authority in this matter. It is this history that is taken for granted as background to the teaching of the epistles. And there as you read of these different cases that have obviously been recorded for our instruction and enlightenment, you find that it is something that happens to men and women, to Christian believers.

Now I am not so concerned at this point to consider exactly the way in which it does happen. That will be one of the things that will come nearer the end of our consideration. All I am concerned to do here is to emphasize this big fact, that it is something that happens to us. Now it is not something that happens automatically to all who believe, we have seen that there is a distinction. There may be an interval between the two, sometimes short, at other times longer. Sometimes there scarcely seems to be an interval at all. But it does not happen automatically the moment a man repents and believes on the Lord Jesus Christ.

I am equally anxious to emphasize that it does not happen as the result of something that we do. Now there are many who teach something like that. They say, 'You can have this whenever you like; as long as you do this or that.' I do not find a single instance of that in the New Testament. It seems to me to be entirely wrong teaching. So we must not say that we can receive the Spirit in this sense of baptism whenever we like. I want to try to show you that the teaching is almost the exact opposite of that. Neither does it happen automatically on condition that we do this or that.

Now here is a great principle of course. Any teaching which would say that any blessing in the spiritual realm can be received in a kind of mechanical automatic manner – 'Do this, and there it is' – seems to me to violate a very vital principle in the whole realm of this teaching.

In other words it is the Lord's action. That is what comes out in this our basic text: 'He shall baptize with the Holy Ghost and with fire.'

'I,' says John, 'I baptize with water, but he will baptize' – it is his action, his prerogative. So that in all these cases which are described, what is emphasized above everything else is what I would call this 'given' element. Take the terms that are used – he is 'poured out', 'they were filled', or he 'fell upon them'. Here are these people, they are the recipients; but the action is outside, it is objective if you like, it is given, it is the Lord who does it.

Now the very variations which you will find in the different instances described in Acts help to bring out this element very prominently. We remember how in the case of the apostles themselves they had been praying for some ten days in Jerusalem in that upper room, and then on that morning of Pentecost he suddenly came.

We remember, too, how, as we read in the fourth chapter that they were again praying, and again the Holy Spirit descended upon them and the building shook. But as far as the Samaritans were concerned, you remember there was an interval. Many had been converted through the preaching of Philip, and the news went up to Jerusalem, so Peter and John were sent down to speak to them and pray for them and lay their hands upon them. But in the case of Cornelius, even while Peter was speaking, the Holy Spirit fell upon them. Then we have already considered the account in Acts 19 of what happened in Ephesus.

The point I am establishing, then, is that these very variations in the way in which this happens all point to the same fact, that the given element is the important one. You cannot stereotype or systematize this, or say, 'Very well then, this is what you have to do.' No, it is always this given element, the pouring out, the falling upon, the being filled. In other words, all these variations establish the lordship of our Lord Jesus Christ in this entire matter. It is he who is the giver, it is he who is the baptizer. He does so in his own way and in his own time, and we must never lose sight of this all-important principle.

Perhaps it will help us to grasp this if we put it like this. The same thing is true, of course, of all the great revivals in the history of the church. They are most important in this matter. The difference between the baptism of the Holy Spirit and a revival is simply one of the number of people affected. I would define a revival as a large number, a group of people, being baptized by the Holy Spirit at the same time; or the Holy Spirit falling upon, coming upon a number of people assembled together. It can happen in a chapel, in a church, it can happen in a district, it can happen in a country.

There is nothing more fascinating than the history of the great revivals in the history of the church and, as you read about them, you see that they are but illustrations of this. It is a truism to say that every revival of religion is in a sense but a repetition of Pentecost. Pentecost was the beginning, the first, but then there are these repetitions in Acts, upon the household of Cornelius, the people in Ephesus and so on.

In the light of all this, therefore, there is nothing that is so clear about the history of revivals as the sovereignty and the Lordship of our Lord and Saviour Jesus Christ. You cannot get a revival whenever you like, or work one up. It is wrong to say that if you fulfil certain conditions, or do certain things a revival will come. So many have said that. I have known many who have taught and practised that, who have done everything that they have been instructed to do, but the revival has not come. The answer is that it is entirely his gift, and entirely in his hands. He is the Lord, he is sovereign, and as the Holy Spirit gives gifts to people according to his sovereign will, so the Son gives this gift, this baptism, according to his own sovereign will.

So that any mechanical notions that are introduced into this matter are, it seems to me, a contradiction of what is plain obvious teaching. It is something that happens to us, it is something that takes place with respect to us, it is given, it is his action and not the result of something that you and I do.

I emphasize that in order that it may lead us into the next proposition which is, perhaps, a still more important one. It is that the baptism with the Holy Spirit is always something clear and unmistakable, something which can be recognized by the person to whom it happens and by others who look on at this person. This is obviously a most vital and important principle. Those, of course, who tend to identify the baptism of the Holy Spirit with regeneration, and say that all who become Christians receive the baptism of the Holy Spirit on conversion naturally minimize this, as they must do, of necessity. Regeneration is something unconscious, not experimental; and the great point is that it is a mysterious, miraculous act worked in the depths and the vitals of the soul, and no man can tell you the moment when he was regenerated. Everybody is agreed about that – that regeneration is non-experimental. You later begin to discover the fact that you have been made regenerate and give evidence of it.

But now here we are dealing with something which is very different. The very essence of this is that it is conscious, that it is experimental, obvious, plain, and clear; not only to the recipient but also to those who are familiar with him.

I regard this as in many ways the nerve of the difference of opinion between good Christian people who are all equally generally concerned to preach and to arrive at a knowledge of the truth. I could quote many to you. In one volume on systematic theology there is a great heading which says, 'Baptism with the Holy Ghost non-experimental.' Other writers put it in the form of a question by saying, 'What biblical warrant is there for supposing that people cannot receive the gift or baptism of the Holy Spirit in a quiet and unsensational way?' Or: 'The fullness of the Spirit leads to restrained and rational moral behaviour.'

You see the emphasis, the restraint, the quietness; you see sentences like: 'The Spirit's fullness involves not a private, mystical experience so much as a relationship to God'. This is all a minimizing of the experimental aspect of the matter. You read: 'Neither the baptism nor the fullness of the Spirit need be accompanied by spectacular signs. The initial baptism of the Spirit may be quiet and unsensational.' Now we are all agreed that there is no need or necessity for spectacular signs, but this other statement that it may be 'quiet' is quite logical for people who identify regeneration with the baptism of the Spirit, or who say that it happens to everyone at the time of regeneration. They must of necessity say this and minimize the experimental side, the emotional or mystical aspect if you like, and stress the fact that it is mainly a matter of moral life and living and behaviour.

But now therefore we come to the vital question. We are asked what biblical warrant there is for supposing that it is not like that. Well, I want to put the biblical evidence before you because I think the Bible makes it perfectly clear, it makes it quite beyond any doubt, that this is something essentially experimental, which involves a mystical experience, to use such a term. The whole emphasis, in the instances that we are given in the Scriptures, and from what we can deduce from the teaching about the need for restraint and control in the church at Corinth, all this indicates that far from being something quiet and unsensational, it tends to be obvious and patent, essentially experimental.

Now do not misunderstand me; I am not concerned to emphasize anything spectacular, although we have got to say this: in the New Testament it was highly spectacular, and in the great revivals of religion there has always been a very prominent spectacular element. Also, in the lives and experiences of individuals who talk about this experience and who testify to receiving it, there is invariably something which, again, you are almost compelled to call a spectacular element; to them, anyway, it was the most spectacular thing that had ever happened to them. So that any impression that is given that this is something quiet and restrained and almost unobserved seems to me to be coming very near to what the apostle calls, 'quenching the Spirit'. Let me, then, give you the evidence, because it is abundant and it is most interesting.

It seems to me that, in a very remarkable manner, even in the foreshadowings or the prophecies of the coming of this great fullness of the baptism of the Spirit there is clear evidence of the fact that this is something that is obvious, clear and patent. Now you find that in the Old Testament; the Holy Spirit comes upon certain people occasionally, Bezaleel and others, and upon the prophets, to do a certain work. Do not misunderstand me – that is not the baptism with the Spirit but it is of the same order. The big difference between the Old and the New is that it happens there occasionally to exceptional men for particular purposes, whereas the prophecy of Joel tells us it is going to be more extensive and include more types and kinds of people, indiscriminately almost, in the New. But these fore-shadowings are extremely interesting, and perhaps the most interesting ones of all are those which are found in the New Testament itself.

In Luke 1:41-42, for example, we are told about Elisabeth, the mother of John the Baptist. In verses 39-40 we read that Mary paid Elisabeth a visit: 'Mary arose in those days, and went into the hill country with haste, into the city of Judah; And entered into the house of Zacharias, and saluted Elisabeth.' Then notice how it goes on: 'And it came to pass that when Elisabeth heard the salutation of Mary, the babe leaped in her womb.' Some of the Puritans writing on this subject made great use of that, saying that this is the kind of thing that happens to man when the Spirit comes upon him in this way – a kind of babe leaps in his womb. In other words, the babe was already there, already regenerate, but all has been very quiet until there is a 'leaping' of the babe in the womb. I do not want to make too much of that, but what I am emphasizing is, 'And Elisabeth was filled with the Holy Ghost.' Here is the evidence, 'And she spake out with a loud voice, and said....'

It was obvious to her that something had happened: she was filled with the Holy Spirit and spoke out. She was aware of it, and those who were listening to her were equally aware of it. It was not something quiet – we are told that 'she spake out with a loud voice'. This is the authority of the Spirit, the same kind of thing that you read about in Acts 2. When Peter becomes the spokesman he is no longer the craven, fearful individual that he has been, but speaks with a boldness and with an authority. And so they all do, and so they have continued to do throughout the centuries.

But look at Luke 1:67 – where you are told something about Zacharias himself. Verse 66 introduces the account: 'And all they that heard them laid up in their hearts, saying,

What manner of child shall this be! And the hand of the Lord was with him.' Verse 67 continues: 'And his father Zacharias was filled with the Holy Ghost, and prophesied, saying....' Then we have this great prophetic utterance of Zacharias, who was clearly inspired, filled with the Spirit. It is exactly the same thing that had happened with Elisabeth but is, if anything, even more remarkable.

Now the point I am making is that when this happens it is manifest, there is a power given, an insight, an understanding, an authority, a speaking loudly and boldly. This does not suggest something quiet and controlled, almost unobtrusive and unobserved. It is the exact opposite. However, those are but the preliminary anticipations. We have seen with our Lord himself that once the Spirit had come upon him, he began his ministry, he began to speak and to act and to do his great works, even as Peter summarized them in preaching to Cornelius and his household.

But then you come right on to Acts and here, surely, it is almost impossible to see how anyone reading the facts can dispute this proposition that when the Spirit comes down, it is something that is clear and evident. Take Acts 2:4: 'They were all filled with the Holy Ghost, and began to speak with other tongues.' Now that is highly sensational! 'They began to speak with other tongues, as the Spirit gave them utterance.' And they were aware of it, of course. The men were in a state of ecstasy, they were filled with the Spirit and they were doing something most unusual, something that had never been done before. It is the Scriptures that say this, but look, too, at verses 6 and 7: if the apostles themselves were aware that something had happened, you would see the effect upon others. 'Now when this was noised abroad, the multitude came together, and were confounded.' Confounded by what? Something quiet, non-spectacular, unobtrusive? No! 'because that every man heard them speak in his own language. And they were all amazed and marvelled, saying....' This is a phenomenon, a spectacle, not something hidden, quiet, or restrained. There is an ebullience, a vitality, a joy, an exuberance, a power, it is here on the very surface.

Later on we read in verses 12 and 13: 'They were all amazed, and were in doubt, saying one to another, What meaneth this? Others mocking said, These men are full of new wine.' Why did they say that about them? Well, because of their behaviour and appearance, because of what they were doing. Everything is indicative of a phenomenon, something experimental, something that is not only obvious to the man himself but obvious to those who are looking on.

And indeed you virtually get the same at the end of Acts 2: 'And all that believed were together, and had all things common; And sold their possessions and goods, and parted them to all men, as every man had need.' Cannot you see the picture? Is this a quiet, unobtrusive something in an ordinary church just going on from week to week? Do they sell their possessions and goods and so on? 'They continuing daily with one accord in the temple, and breaking bread from house to house, did eat their meat with gladness and singleness of heart, Praising God, and having favour with all the people.'

Now the nearest you will ever get to that in church history is when you read of revivals of religion.

Then we must consider the evidence in Acts 4. This is ultimately a biblical question: what is the teaching of the Scripture? We read in Acts 4:8: 'Then Peter, filled with the Holy Ghost' – remember he had been filled on the day of Pentecost but here he is now with John standing before the court, the authorities, and, because he is in a predicament he is given another filling – 'Peter, filled with the Holy Ghost, said unto them...' And again you get this great characteristic that we have seen in Elisabeth and Zacharias and even in our Lord himself. But still more striking, of course, is what you find in 4:31: 'And when they had prayed, the place ws shaken where they were assembled together; and they were all filled with the Holy Ghost, and they spake the word of God with boldness.... With great power gave the apostles witness of the resurrection of the Lord Jesus: and great grace was upon them all.'

Restrained! Quiet! Unobtrusive! My dear friends, why not listen to the evidence? This is the kind of thing that happens when the Spirit 'comes' upon man, even the building was shaken, and this tremendous uplifting took place in the experiences of the apostles and the other believers.

You find it really, also, in the sixth chapter where we read about the question of the appointing of deacons. 'Wherefore, brethren,' say the apostles, 'look ye out among you seven men of honest report, full of the Holy Ghost and wisdom, whom we may appoint over this business.' How could they tell whether a man was filled with the Holy Spirit? They had not only got to pick out men who had wisdom, and were good men, and of honest report, but they had to be 'filled with the Holy Spirit.' How do you tell that if it is something that cannot be observed, if it is something that is not known? Of course it is known, otherwise they could never have been given these instructions. You find it in verse 5 too: 'The saying pleased the whole multitude: and they chose Stephen, a man full of faith and of the Holy Ghost, and Philip....' and the rest of them of whom the same thing was true. You have it also in verse 8: 'Stephen, full of faith and power, did great wonders and miracles among the people.' Verse 10: 'And they were not able to resist the wisdom and the Spirit by which he spake.' That is not natural spirit, but the fullness of the Holy Spirit.

The evidence is still more explicit in chapter 8 where we are told how Peter and John went down to Samaria. In verse 17 we read 'Then laid they their hands on them, and they received the Holy Ghost.' Now, this is interesting, the next verse reads like this: 'When Simon saw that through laying on of the apostles' hands the Holy Ghost was given' – it was something that he could see – 'he offered them money.' He drew the wrong deduction but the point is that this able man saw that as a result of the laying on of the apostles' hands something had happened to these people; they had received the Holy Spirit. So he said in effect, 'Can I be given this gift? What do I have to pay for it?' In other words it is clear that it is something absolutely evident, not only to the consciousness of the individual making him aware of it, but also to other people who are looking on.

The same thing is true of the apostle Paul himself, in Acts 9: 'Immediately there fell from his eyes as it had been scales: and he received sight forthwith, and arose, and was baptized. And when he had received meat, he was strengthened.... And straightaway he preached Christ in the synagogues, that he is the Son of God.' He who had been persecuting, breathing out threatenings and slaughter ... an entire turnaround! He is aware of it, everybody else is aware of the same thing.

I have already given the most notable instance of this, in Acts 10: 'While Peter yet spake these words the Holy Ghost fell on all them which heard the word. And they of the circumcision which believed were astonished, as many as came with Peter, because that on the Gentiles also was poured out the gift of the Holy Ghost.' How did they know? They must have seen something. Of course they did! 'For they heard them speak with tongues, and magnify God.' It was obvious to these Jewish believers who had accompanied Peter that the Holy Spirit had fallen upon these people and Peter himself saw it. 'Peter answered, Can any man forbid water, that these should not be baptized, which have received the Holy Ghost as well as we?' They knew it had happened, Peter knew it had happened, Peter's companions knew that it had happened. This thing is clear.

Then, you remember, a dispute arose about all this – was Peter right in admitting Gentiles into the church? So they had a Council about it, described in Acts 11. The essence of

Peter's argument is in verses 15-18: 'And as I began to speak, the Holy Ghost fell on them, as on us at the beginning. Then remembered I the word of the Lord, how that he said, John indeed baptized with water; but ye shall be baptized with the Holy Ghost. Forasmuch then as God gave them the like gift as he did unto us, who believed on the Lord Jesus Christ; what was I, that I could withstand God?'

That is the argument, and it is all indicative of the fact that this is something obvious, experimental, manifest – a phenomenon. Now there are degrees of it but the main emphasis is there in all the instances. It is the same in Acts 19, when Paul asked: 'Did you receive the Holy Ghost when you believed?' clearly indicating that he was aware of the fact there was something lacking, but could not get his evidence. So he put the question and then discovered that he was right to do so. He then, you remember, laid his hands upon them and the evidence was very soon produced.

To complete this particular argument, take again Galatians 3:2, 5: 'This only would I learn of you, Received ye the Spirit by the works of the law, or by the hearing of faith?' Paul is not talking about their becoming Christians, but about this peculiar special thing of receiving the Spirit. If he had meant simply believing on the Lord Jesus Christ he would have said, 'Did you believe in the Lord Jesus Christ as the result of your circumcision, or as the result of faith?' But that is what he has already dealt with in the first two chapters. This is a further argument and a very powerful one, and so he repeats it in verse 5: 'He therefore that ministereth to you the Spirit, and worketh miracles among you, doeth he it by the works of the law, or by the hearing of faith?' What he is saying is this – As you were justified by faith, so it is in this faith realm, in exactly the same way that you have received the gift of the Spirit. It is a phenomenon, something external to which he can therefore appeal for the sake of evidence.

There, then, is essentially the biblical evidence with regard to this matter, and I would again remind you of the fact that the same thing exactly is always true in all accounts we have of the great revivals in the church. It is always something that can be recognized. Now I am old enough to remember the revival in Wales in 1904-5 and I remember hearing people say of somebody else, 'He has "had" the revival'. What did they mean by that? Well, they were referring to an experience. The man had been a Christian, he had been a church member and so far in the revival, he had remained untouched and unaffected. No longer. 'He has had the revival!'

In revival, you see, something happens. It is a phenomenon. The Spirit comes, falls upon people and upon congregations; they are transformed, and it is obvious to them and to other people, so that others can say about a man, 'He has had the revival.' How do people know that? Well, the man has given evidence of it, and the evidence, of course, can be strange and wonderful.

I do not want to go into this too much at this point but I knew for many years a man who died several years ago, a minister of the gospel, who used to describe how he, to use the phrase, 'had the revival'. All he knew was that initially he was very much opposed to it. He wanted to be a musician and had gone to his usual practice on a Saturday night, and on returning he was very annoyed to find nobody there.

'They have gone to this [with an expletive] Revival Meeting,' he said. 'I'm going to see what all this is about.' And he went off in a temper. The place was so crowded that he just managed to squeeze into the back seat. There were people standing in the aisles, which were all blocked, but the next thing that the man remembered was getting up from his knees in the big seat immediately beneath the pulpit, where he had been praying in a most amazing manner.

In telling you all this I am simply emphasizing that we must be very careful in these matters. What do we know of the realm of the Spirit? What do we know of the Spirit falling upon people? What do we know about these great manifestations of the Holy Spirit? We need to be very careful 'lest we be found to be fighting against God', lest we be guilty of 'quenching the Holy Spirit of God'. A revival is always something plain and obvious. When a revival breaks out in a church or in a district it is known, it becomes a topic of conversation, it arouses great curiosity, exactly as it did on the day of Pentecost, and people come crowding, out of sheer curiosity to see what it is that has happened.

Now to support this and show you that what happened at the beginning is that which has continued to happen, let me give you some quotations. Everybody is familiar with what happened to John Wesley in Aldersgate Street here in London on the 24th May 1738. He had been convinced for several weeks of the doctrine of justification by faith only. He saw it quite clearly, was preaching it, and believed it. But still there was something lacking.

He describes what happened in this way:

> About a quarter before nine while he [the man who was reading the Preface to Luther's Commentary on Romans] was describing the change which God works in the heart through faith in Christ, I felt my heart strangely warmed. I felt I did trust in Christ alone for salvation, and an assurance was given to me that He had taken away my sins, even mine, and saved me from the law of sin and death.

John Wesley had believed that before. He is now given a tremendous assurance of it. But this is what is interesting. That happened on May 24th 1738. Read John Wesley's Journal for the 1st January 1739:

> Mr. Hall, Hinching, Ingham, Whitefield, Hutching and my brother Charles were present at our love feast in Fetter Lane with about sixty of our brethren. About three in the morning as we were continuing instant in prayer the power of God came

> mightly upon us, insomuch that many cried out for exulting joy and many fell to the ground. As soon as we were recovered a little from the awe and amazement at the presence of His Majesty, we broke out with one voice, "We praise Thee O God, we acknowledge Thee to be the Lord."

Now you notice what happened – the power of God came mightily upon them at three o'clock in the morning. They had prayed many times before, they had had love feasts very regularly, but it was on this occasion it happened in that way. It is not the only one but it is a perfect instance and illustration of what I am trying to say. He says here, 'He came mightily upon us, insomuch that many cried out for exceeding joy, and many fell to the ground.' Have we any right when dealing with these matters to talk about its being restrained and quiet? My dear friends, what do we know about the Holy Spirit?

Another example is the great Anglican clergyman and friend of Charles Simeon, Henry Venn, who had a remarkable ministry in Huddersfield and afterwards at Yelling. Look at the way in which he writes to Lady Huntingdon. He had just buried his dear wife, and says:

> Did I not know the Lord to be mine, were I not certain His heart feels even more love for me than I am able to conceive, were not this evident to me, not by deduction and argument but by consciousness, by his own light shining in my soul as the sun doth upon my bodily eyes, into what deplorable situation should I have been now cast.

You see what he is talking about? He is talking about an inner mystical experience, about the love of God 'shining' by the light of the Spirit into his own soul just as the power of the sun shines upon his external body.

Let me close with quotations from Charles Simeon, the famous clergyman at Cambridge at the end of the eighteenth and the beginning of the nineteenth century, the man who really is the ultimate father of the Evangelical Christian Unions, the IVF [now UCCF] and all the rest. This is how he speaks about these matters:

> This is a blessing which though not to be appreciated or understood by those who have never received it ... [and that is what is so clear to me in so many writings. Men are writing about things they do not know, they have never received, they do not understand] ... is yet most assuredly enjoyed by many of God's chosen people. We scarcely know how to describe it because it consists chiefly in an impression on the mind occasioned by manifestations of God's love to the soul

– a highly experimental matter which Simeon himself had experienced. Then he goes on again: 'An unbeliever cannot possibly be sealed ...' You see he says this is only for believers. He means 'sealed with the Holy Spirit' or 'receive the baptism of the Spirit', or 'being filled', or 'the Spirit falling upon him', this assurance in its highest form – why? 'Because the Holy Spirit would never mark those as God's property who do not really belong to Him. Nor are persons usually sealed on their first believing in Christ'.

That is the distinction I have been drawing between believing and becoming regenerate on the one hand, and later receiving the baptism or the sealing or this full assurance. Simeon puts it like that –

> Nor are persons usually sealed on their first believing in Christ. It is reserved for those who having believed have maintained a close walk with God. They must first be "in Christ", then for Christ's sake this benefit shall be vouchsafed to them.

Let us leave it there. I will go on to consider even more directly what exactly this baptism with the Holy Spirit is. May God give us grace to examine these things, to examine the Scriptures, and to read the history of the church. Keep your mind and your heart open to the gracious leadings and influences of the Spirit of God.

Chapter 4

Filled with the Spirit

We have seen that it is possible to be a Christian without being baptized with the Spirit, and that the experience of baptism is something that happens to us. Furthermore, it is something experimental, which is clear and unmistakable both to us and to those around us.

That then brings us to the point at which we can come closer and more directly to a definition of what exactly the baptism with the Spirit is. Here, again, confusion arises mainly, I think, for the following reason. In Acts chapter 1:5 we read that our Lord told the disciples that they should 'be baptized with the Holy Ghost not many days hence'. Then in Acts 2 we get the fulfilment of that: in ten days or so it did happen. But the interesting thing is that in Acts 2, where we are given the account of how the first disciples and apostles were baptized with the Holy Spirit, the term 'baptism' is not used; we are told that 'they were all filled with the Holy Ghost', and that is the term that is generally used afterwards.

Now that tends to lead to confusion in this way – people jump to the conclusion that every time you come across the phrase 'filled with the Spirit' it must of necessity mean exactly the same thing. They say, 'Filled with the Spirit is filled with the Spirit.' And so it is that so many people are utterly confused by what we read in Ephesians 5:18, 'And be not drunk with wine, wherein is excess; but be filled with the Spirit.' 'Now there it is,' they say, "be filled with the Spirit". And the disciples were filled with the Spirit on the day of Pentecost.' So these people tend to fall into the error and confusion of imagining that these two things are identical.

Now the trouble here is a failure to understand the New Testament teaching concerning the work and the operation of the Holy Spirit. He has a number of functions which he serves; they include conviction, and particularly, of course, regeneration. But he also does the work of sanctifying us. It is the Spirit who sanctifies us through the truth. But in addition to that he has a great work in the matters of assurance, of certainty, and, with that, the matters of witness, of testimony, of ministry and of work. Now these functions of the Holy Spirit must be differentiated, otherwise there will be endless confusion.

So it seems to me (and it has always been recognized by the great classic treatments of this subject in the doctrine of the person and the work of the Holy Spirit) that his work can be divided up like this: his regular work and his exceptional work – or, if you prefer it in different language, his indirect work and his direct work.

Now this division in the work and operations of the Holy Spirit is of very great importance. Perhaps I can best illustrate this to you again by talking about revivals of religion. The Holy Spirit is in the church today and he does a regular work in it, though these are the days of small things. But we must not despise these days because, after all, what is happening is the work of the Holy Spirit. That is what I mean by his regular work. But the moment you begin to look at revivals of religion, you see them stand out in the history of the church. They are still the work of the Holy Spirit, he is still the operator but he is now operating in an exceptional, an unusual manner.

Or, to take my other classification, which is perhaps, for

our immediate purpose, the more important of the two – the Holy Spirit normally works through means. That is what I have in mind when I say that his work is 'indirect'. It is the Holy Spirit who has given us the Word, and his regular ministry, his ordinary (if one may use such a term with regard to the Holy Spirit) work is to deal with us through the Scriptures. He enlightens the mind, gives us understanding, opens the Scriptures to us, uses the teacher or the preacher, and so on. Now that work is more or less indirect; but it is plain and clear – and this is the very nerve of this whole doctrine of the baptism with the Spirit: that the Spirit also works and operates in a direct manner.

I want to try to show you, therefore, that the way to avoid this confusion of assuming that every time you find the expression 'filled with the Spirit' it means exactly the same thing, is to observe the context and to see what the writer is talking about. In Ephesians 5:18, as I want to show you, he is dealing with sanctification. That is more or less his regular work. And therefore it has really nothing to do directly with this whole matter of being able to define what is meant by the baptism with the Spirit. In both instances you are filled with the Spirit. A man is baptized and filled with the Spirit at the same time. But I want to suggest that a man can be filled with the Spirit in terms of Ephesians 5:18, and still not be baptized with the Spirit. However, let me try to make that plain and clear to you.

The baptism with the Spirit belongs to the category of the exceptional and direct. This brings us to the characteristics of the baptism with the Spirit. I must remind you again of the terms that are used with respect to this act of baptism with the Spirit. The great term is 'poured out'. This, of course, suggests at once a great profusion – and this is what we must emphasize. The Spirit came upon them as he came upon our Lord. He came upon those people who were assembled together in the upper room. If you like, you can describe it almost as a kind of 'drenching with the Spirit'. This, I have long believed, is very clear from Ephesians.

People seem to think that this is some strange new doctrine. It is very old indeed, as old as the New Testament, and it has received prominence in the church throughout the centuries. There is an illustration which may help to bring out this point. You may be walking along a country road and there may be a slight drizzle, but because you haven't got an overcoat you go on walking through this drizzle and eventually you get thoroughly wet; but it has taken some time because it was only a slight drizzle. But then you may be walking along the same road at another time and suddenly there is a cloud-burst and you are soaking wet in a matter of seconds. It is raining in both cases, but there is a great difference between a gentle drizzle, which you scarcely observe, and a sudden cloud-burst which comes down upon you.

Now what is described here in Acts is comparable to the cloud-burst. Poured out! Coming with a kind of 'drenching'. Peter, you observe, in addressing the people on that day, quotes from the prophecy of Joel, and the very point of doing that is to bring out and to emphasize this aspect. 'Peter, standing up with the eleven, lifted up his voice, and said, Ye men of Judaea, and all ye that dwell at Jerusalem, be this known unto you, and hearken to my words: For these are not drunken, as ye suppose, seeing it is but the third hour of the day. But this is that which was spoken by the prophet Joel; it shall come to pass in the last days, saith God, I will pour out my Spirit upon all flesh: and your sons and your daughters shall prophesy, your young men shall see visions, your old men shall dream dreams: And on my servants and on my handmaidens I will pour out in those days of my Spirit; and they shall prophesy.'

Now the thing that is being emphasized there is this 'gushing forth', this tremendous profusion. Indeed, it can be said that this is the marked and greatest difference between the work of the Holy Spirit in the Old Testament and the New. He came occasionally upon certain people, certain chosen people, in the Old Testament for some special, immediate function – people like the prophets for instance. He came upon them and they were taken up into some kind of ecstasy – there is no question about that. There was a kind of 'divine afflatus'. 'Holy men of God spake as they were moved', carried along, by the Holy Spirit. It was not merely that he was working quietly in them and heightening their powers a little bit. No, there was something well beyond that – there was the giving of the revelation, the consciousness of the power, and they knew it was happening. Indeed, there were certain means and methods that were sometimes employed in order to encourage this. Other men, for certain functions, were given the Spirit for that particular purpose. But now, says Joel – it was given to him to see – there is a time coming when it is not going to be like this, and the big difference will be not only the variety of people who are going to receive this, but also the profusion, the amount, the overwhelming character of it. And of course this is something that has been substantiated so frequently in the history of the church, particularly in times of revival. But even apart from that, it is true – and thank God for this – of individuals also. It does not only come to certain able, intellectual people, it can also come to anybody for the most humble soul can know and experience it, too.

That, then, is what we must emphasize, and, of course, the apostle Paul makes exactly the same point in Romans 5:5 where, having pointed out how we are enabled to glory in tribulations also, he says, 'And hope maketh not ashamed; because the love of God is shed abroad in our hearts by the Holy Ghost which is given unto us.'

Now if you believe at all in the inspiration of the Scriptures you must believe that these men were guided to use the particular terms that they used, and the apostle Paul was not content with saying that the love of God is sent into our hearts, he says the love of God is 'shed abroad' in our hearts, and he means what he says. It is a kind of gushing forth. It is a very strong term and it is the one that the apostle under divine inspiration was led to use, and we must not minimize these terms.

We agree that no man can be a Christian without knowing something about the love of God, of course; we have emphasized that a man cannot be a Christian at all without having the Spirit in him. Romans 8:9 reminds us of it: 'If any man have not the Spirit of Christ, he is none of his.' But there is a difference between knowing the love of God in that general sense and being overwhelmed by the knowledge of the love of God. 'Shed abroad'! – in abundance, in profusion.

Now indeed take the very word that is used in Acts 2: the word 'filled'. Now 'filled' means filled. It does not merely mean that the Spirit was in them, they were 'filled with the Spirit' to overflowing; or 'drenched'. He came upon them and in them and it was because they were so filled that the visible results, that we considered earlier, took place and happened amongst them. There then is something that you must hold in the very forefront of your mind, that you are not dealing here with the regular, you are not dealing here with the customary, you are dealing here with the unusual. The second great characteristic is the directness of the Spirit's work in this matter. No longer indirect, but direct. Now there are many examples of this. Let me just take one, from Romans 8:16 where the apostle says, 'The Spirit itself beareth witness with our spirit, that we are the children of God.' Now I wish I had the time to expound the rich teaching of these two verses 15 and 16, but we must press on 'For ye have not received the spirit of bondage again to fear,' says the apostle, 'but ye have received the Spirit of adoption, whereby we cry, Abba, Father.'

We will deal later with some of the results of baptism with the Spirit but I am concerned here with the particular point which we find in verse 15. Paul's word 'cry', again, is a very strong word. It means something elemental. The term originally meant the croaking of a certain kind of bird, the noise that birds can sometimes produce with great intensity. That is the term: 'We "cry" Abba, Father.' We not merely believe that God is our Father. We all believe that as Christians. But here it wells up within us. Paul, then, says in addition to that, 'The Spirit itself beareth witness with our spirit.' The first, you see, verse 15, is 'our spirit', but, he says, on top of that 'The Spirit itself beareth witness "with" our spirit.' Our spirit is crying 'Abba, Father', but the Spirit now confirms this, 'beareth witness with it [together with it] that we are the children of God: And if children, then heirs of God, and joint-heirs with Christ.'

The point I am making is that this is most important, because this is entirely the action of the Holy Spirit – not our action. This is the peculiar differentiating thing about it. This witness of the Spirit with our spirit is not dependent upon what we do, but, as I will show you, Ephesians 5:18 is entirely dependent upon what we do. It is a command and an exhortation. But here the thing that is stressed is that the Spirit is bearing witness with our spirit. There is a witness in our spirit, but he now bears witness with that – together with that, right upon that; seals that and makes it absolutely certain to us. Occasionally he may use means, but speaking generally he does this without means.

Let me put it to you like this. Some people try to expound this by saying, 'Ah yes, that is what happens, of course, when we read the New Testament and especially the epistles and their teaching.' But, you see, the people to whom the apostle Paul wrote had neither got that teaching, nor a New Testament. This is something that happened to the first Christians at once, before they had any of the books of the

New Testament at all, which shows that it was direct and immediate. I am not going to the extent of saying that he never uses any means at all, because there are many testimonies to the effect that sometimes he may take a verse. Not necessarily when a man is reading, even, he may bring a verse to a man's mind. But generally speaking it is something which happens directly.

Again, I commend you to go through all the instances that we have in Acts. You will find in each case that when the baptism with the Spirit takes place it is the Spirit who is acting. He is sent by the risen Lord, he baptizes us with the Spirit, and the Spirit immediately does something, and this is the experimental, phenomenal aspect which we were emphasizing earlier. It is his action, and his direct action. It is not his slow work of sanctification, his regular work in us; it is exceptional and it is very direct.

Let me give you some clear statements from the Scriptures concerning this operation of the Holy Spirit. I want to try to show you that this is something which has been taught and recognized in the Christian church throughout the centuries and by men belonging to various and varied theological schools. That is what to me is so interesting and glorious about all this – that it cuts right acros the various theological distinctions such as Arminianism and Calvinism and so on.

I will start by quoting a statement from Dr John Owen, one of the great (some would say the greatest of the) intellects amongst the Puritans of three hundred years ago. It is from his *Treatise on Communion with the Holy Ghost*. He says, referring to Romans 5:2 –

> That rejoicing in hope of the glory of God ... which carries the soul through any tribulation, even with glorying, hath its rise in the Spirit's shedding abroad the love of God in our hearts. Now there are two ways whereby the Spirit worketh this joy in the hearts of believers: (1) He doth it immediately by Himself

> without the consideration of any other acts or works of his or the interposition of any reasonings or deductions and conclusions. As in sanctification He is a well of water springing up in the soul immediately exerting His efficacy and refreshment, so in consolation [which means assurance] He immediately works the soul and the minds of men to a joyful rejoicing and spiritual frame, filling them with exultation and gladness. Not that this arises from our reflex consideration of the love of God, but rather gives occasion thereunto. When He so sheds abroad the love of God in our hearts and so fills them with gladness by an immediate act and operation (as He caused John the Baptist to leap for joy in the womb upon the approach of the Mother of Jesus) then doth the soul even from hence raise itself to a consideration of the love of God whence joy and rejoicing doth also flow. Of this joy there is no account to be given but that the Spirit worketh it when and how He will. He secretly infuseth and distils it into the soul, prevailing against all fears and sorrows, filling it with gladness, exultations, and sometimes with unspeakable raptures of the mind.

Now if ever there was by nature an intellectual and a calm and controlled man it was Dr John Owen, but that is how he describes this – 'unspeakable raptures of the mind'; 'gladness'; 'exultations' – something which is beyond description.

Let me quote to you his contemporary, Dr Thomas Goodwin, another bright shining star in this spiritual firmament, a man like John Owen. Owen taught at Oxford, Goodwin taught at both Cambridge and Oxford. He writes:

> There is a light that cometh and overpowereth a man's soul and assureth him that God is his and he is God's, and that God loveth him from everlasting.... it is *a light beyond the light of ordinary faith*.

That is the point I am making: this is not the ordinary, this is the unusual. Now a man cannot have what he calls ordinary faith without the work and the operation of the Holy Spirit.

'If any man have not the Spirit of Christ, he is none of His.' You cannot be a Christian at all without that, but Goodwin calls it 'ordinary faith', and he is absolutely right, because it is so different from this which he is describing. He puts it like this: 'This is the next thing to heaven, you have no more; you can have no more till you come there.' According to Thomas Goodwin this is an experience which brings you nearer to heaven than anything else can possibly do, it is a real foretaste of heaven. You will never know anything beyond it, he says, until you are in heaven itself. 'It is faith aided and raised above this ordinary rate.'

It is at this point that I must again give a solemn warning. There seems to me to be a tendency today on the part of some to reduce everything to the ordinary and to talk about restraint. This is not the ordinary, this is the extra-ordinary, the unusual, to be at the very gateway of heaven, as it were. There is only one thing beyond it, and that is the glory everlasting itself.

Thirdly, let me quote you a man very different from the other two in many ways but especially different in his theology – John Wesley. Here is a man belonging to the eighteenth century, who is neither classified as a Puritan, nor as Reformed or Calvinistic, but who was well known as a teacher of an Arminian doctrine. But he says exactly the same as the other two. He writes:

> This is something immediate and direct, not the result of reflection or argumentation.... There may be foretastes of joy and peace, of love, and these not delusive but really from God long before we have the witness in ourselves.

You see what he is saying? He says a believer can have foretastes of joy and peace and love, which are quite genuine, not delusive but really from God. But you may have those, he says, 'long before we have the witness in ourselves, before the

Spirit of God witnesses with our spirit that we have redemption in the blood of Jesus, even the forgiveness of sins.'

Now there you have both the teaching and the interpretation of the scriptural teaching by three outstanding men in the history of the church. They all three refer to these great characteristics – the immediacy, the directness, and the overwhelming character of the experience. To confuse that with the regular operation of the Holy Spirit in the life of the individual and the church is really to misunderstand the Scriptures in a most serious respect and to come very near to being guilty of what is called 'quenching the Spirit'. It is interesting that people who do not agree with what I am teaching never expound the phrase 'quench not the Spirit'. But that is the test you must keep in your minds.

Our greatest danger, I feel today, is to quench the Spirit. This is no age to advocate restraint; the church today does not need to be restrained, but to be aroused, to be awakened, to be filled with a spirit of glory, for she is failing in the modern world. God knows, as I shall go on to show you, there is a control about the Spirit always, and the teaching of the New Testament is here for us, to teach us and to warn us against everything that is false and spurious, everything that the devil may try to counterfeit.

I am hoping to come to all this later, but this is such a large and a vital subject that you cannot rush it, you must establish your doctrine point by point.

Let me come finally, to the third aspect and here again we will see how it is so essentially different from what I am describing as the regular work of the Spirit. The baptism with the Spirit is always associated primarily and specifically with witness and testimony and service.

Now here again is an all-important point. Go through Acts and in every instance when we are told either that the Spirit came upon these men or that they were filled with the Spirit, you will find that it was in order to bear a witness and a testimony. Of course, that is clear in Acts 2. But remember the two instances I quoted to you earlier from Acts 4 when Peter and John were before the authorities – 'Peter, filled with the Holy Ghost said'. Then the room was shaken, they were all filled again with the Holy Spirit – the people who had already been filled – in order to strengthen them and enable them to stand and to go on bearing their witness and testimony in spite of the threatenings of the authorities; and we are told that 'with great power gave the apostles witness of the resurrection'. Now go right through Acts and you will find that that is always the case.

This is so important that I must put it negatively as well. You will find that some would have you believe that this is mainly a matter concerned with 'moral qualities and character'. But it is not. That is sanctification. That view is sheer, utter confusion. This is not primarily concerned with moral qualities or character; this is primarily concerned with witness, testimony, and efficiency in operation.

There is a very simple way of proving this. Look at the case of the church at Corinth. The apostle has to say very serious and solemn things to them about their moral character and qualities. They were very deficient in that respect, but he says they are deficient in no respect in this matter of the gifts of the Spirit and the power of the Spirit amongst them. This is a most important point. The fact that a man is filled with the Spirit, baptized with the Spirit in this sense, does not mean of necessity that you can guarantee the moral qualities of his life. It should do; but it does not. That is why you always need the further exhortations. This is primarly a matter of witness and of testimony.

So you see the apostle is able to say something that we generally seem to forget, because we are carried away by the magnificence of his language in 1 Corinthians 13: 'Though I speak with the tongues of men and of angels, and have not charity' – you can speak with the tongues of angels, speak in tongues if you like, without having charity – 'I am become as sounding brass, or a tinkling cymbal. And though I have the gift of prophecy' – this is not anything ordinary; he says you may have that – 'and understand all mysteries, and all knowledge; and though I have all faith, so that I could remove mountains, and have not charity' – have not love – 'I am nothing' – and so on.

Now there is a clear enunciation of this all-important distinction. This is not primarily concerned about character – moral quality and character, nor primarily with the fruit of the Spirit. Let us put it as plainly as that: you can be baptized with the Spirit and not show the fruit of the Spirit, for you can be baptized with the Spirit immediately at the point of conversion. We have seen an instance of that – the household of Cornelius. But that does not guarantee the fruits. Fruit means growth. That is development, that is sanctification, that is something quite different.

The first result of the baptism with the Spirit, therefore is not the fruit of the Spirit, but experimental evidence of the direct work of the Spirit upon us. That is the 'baptism of the Spirit' – this thing that happens to us, that comes upon us, this direct work of the Spirit, when the believer is taken up even into a state of ecstasy, and witnesses and manifests that this has happened to him.

The fruit of the Spirit, on the other hand, is a process. This is the result of the indirect, constant, regular work of the Spirit within us as he uses the word and the teaching and example of others and fellowship with others – thus the fruit of the Spirit is produced in us. Not suddenly; that is a whole gradual process of sanctification, and it is of course that to which Ephesians 5:18 refers.

Ephesians 5:18 deals with how Christian people behave together in the fellowship of the Christian church and it is concerned not with what the Spirit does to us but what we do. It is a command, an exhortation to us. It is something that we control: 'Be not drunk with wine, wherein is excess; but go on being filled with the Spirit.' How do you control it? Well, he has already told us in the prevous chapter. You can 'grieve', 'quench' or 'resist the Spirit', and he is telling them not to do that but to go on being filled with the Spirit.

The whole essential difference is this: in Ephesians there is an exhortation to us to do something, whereas in every single instance of the baptism with the Spirit it is something that happens to us, which we do not control. You can pray for the baptism of the Spirit, but that does not guarantee that it happens, as many of you know. You can live a good life, surrender yourself, do all you are told to do, but still you are not baptized with the Spirit.

Why not? It is he who does it. It is in his control. He is the Lord. He is a sovereign Lord and he does it in his own time and in his own way, as Dr John Owen reminded us.

But as far as Ephesians 5:18 is concerned I could show you that there is a grave danger that we may misunderstand even what the apostle is saying there, and reduce it to our old level of church life at the present time. He tells us to 'speak to one another in psalms and hymns and spiritual songs', and if you interpret that to mean our kind of service where we may sing a psalm and a hymn – well, you are making a big mistake. What is a spiritual song? What is a spiritual psalm? What does he mean by 'Speaking to one another in psalms and hymns and spiritual songs'?

If you want the answer to that, you go to 1 Corinthians 14 and there you find the type of meeting they had in the early church – 'One hath a psalm, one hath a testimony, one hath an experience, one hath a tongue' – and so on. The whole thing was alive with a pneumatic spiritual power; and 'spiritual songs' means 'songs in the spirit'. The apostle says, 'I will pray with the spirit, and I will pray with the understanding also: I will sing with the spirit, and I will sing with the understanding also.' It is a type of singing about which the majority of us know nothing at all. So be careful lest you reduce even what was the normal regular life of the early Christian church down to the level of what has become customary in our churches.

However, we cannot deal with that in detail now, but I am simply trying to put before you this big, vital, radical distinction that the baptism with the Spirit is the action of the Spirit within us given by the Lord Jesus Christ.

So finally, shall I just 'stir up', to use a scriptural expression again, 'your spiritual minds' by giving you just an instance or two of what happens when a man is baptized with the Spirit? Think about it and work out your doctrine to account for something like this. This is again a Puritan, John Flavel who was on a journey one day:

> Thus going on his way his thoughts began to swell and rise higher and higher like the waters of Ezekiel's vision, till at last they became an overwhelming flood. Such was the intention of his mind, such the ravishing tastes of heavenly joys, and such the full assurance of his interest therein, that he utterly lost all sight and sense of the world and all the concerns thereof, and for some hours he knew no more where he was than it had been in a deep sleep upon his bed. Arriving in great exhaustion at a certain spring he sat down and washed, earnestly desiring that if it was God's pleasure that this might be his parting-place from the world. Death had the most amiable face in his eyes that ever he beheld, except the fact of Jesus Christ which made it so, and he does not remember though he believed himself dying, that he ever thought of his dear wife and children or any other earthly concernment. On reaching his Inn the influence still continued, banishing sleep, still the joy of the Lord overflowed him and he seemed to be an inhabitant of the Other world. He many years after called that day one of the days of heaven, and professed that he understood more of the life of heaven by it than by all the books he ever read.

Do you know anything about things like that? Be careful in

what you say about the baptism with the Holy Spirit. That is what is possible to a man here on earth.

Then consider Jonathan Edwards:

> As I rode out into the woods for my health, in 1737, having alighted from my horse in a retired place, as my manner commonly has been, to walk for divine contemplation and prayer, I had a view that was for me extraordinary, of the glory of the Son of God, as Mediator between God and man, and His wonderful, great, full, pure and sweet grace and love, and meek and gentle condescension. This grace that appeared so calm and sweet, appeared also great above the heavens. The Person of Christ appeared ineffably excellent with an excellency great enough to swallow up all thoughts and conceptions, which continued, as near as I can judge, about an hour; such as to keep me a greater part of the time in a flood of tears, and weeping aloud. I felt an ardency of soul to be, what I know not otherwise how to express, emptied and annihilated; to lie in the dust, and to be full of Christ alone; to love Him with a holy and pure love; to trust in Him; to live upon Him; to serve Him and to be perfectly sanctified and made pure, with a divine and heavenly purity.

And finally, an entirely different man from Jonathan Edwards, the genius, the brilliant intellect, perhaps the greatest philosopher America has ever produced – another American, but a most ordinary man intellectually, the great evangelist, D. L. Moody.

> I began to cry as never before, for a greater blessing from God. The hunger increased; I really felt that I did not want to live any longer. [He had been a Christian, and not only a Christian but a minister, and in charge of a Mission for some time; he was getting conversions, but still he wanted more.] "I kept on crying all the time that God would fill me with His Spirit. Well, one day in the City of New York – oh! what a day, I cannot describe it, I seldom refer to it. It is almost too sacred an experience to name. Paul had an experience of which he never

> spoke for fourteen years. I can only say, God revealed Himself to me, and I had such an experience of His love that I had to ask Him to stay His hand."

It was so overwhelming, he felt as if he was going to be physically crushed. The love of God! That is what is meant by 'the love of God shed abroad in your hearts'. That is the baptism of the Spirit. That is what turned D. L. Moody from a good, regular, ordinary minister, into the evangelist who was so signally used of God in this and in other countries.

Chapter 5

The Sense of His Presence

We are living, let us remind ourselves in an age hopelessly below the New Testament pattern – content with a neat little religion. We need the baptism with the Spirit. We have already seen that this is not something that takes place at conversion, it is something that happens to us, and is clear and unmistakable. Lastly we have seen that it is the direct and unusual action of the Holy Spirit (Romans 8:16) and that it is not primarily a matter of character or moral qualities – it is not, in other words, to be confused with the continuous process of sanctification as outlined in Ephesians 5:18.

That, then, brings us to the point of saying again that the primary purpose and function of the baptism with the Spirit is beyond any question to enable us to be witnesses to the Lord Jesus Christ and to his great salvation. So if we bear this in mind I think it will help to clear up the error that people get into in confusing this with sanctification. This is primarily a matter of witness.

Let me give you some proofs of what I am saying. Take, for instance, what our Lord himself told the disciples before his ascension. Our Lord had appeared to the disciples in the upper room and in Luke 24:45-47 we read: 'Then opened he their understanding, that they might understand the scriptures. And he said unto them, Thus it is written, and thus it behoved Christ to suffer, and to rise from the dead the third day: And that repentance and remission of sins should be preached in his name among all nations beginning at Jerusalem.'

That is the teaching and they have now got it and understood it and grasped it. Then the Lord continued: 'And ye are witnesses of these things.' And they were of course. They had been with him, they had heard the preaching, they had seen him crucified, buried, risen from the dead, with the empty grave, and here he is, actually speaking to them in the room. But he goes on and says, 'And, behold, I send the promise of the Father upon you: but tarry ye in the city of Jerusalem, until ye be endued with power from on high.' They have the facts, they know and believe them, but before they can be effective witnesses they must receive this baptism with the Holy Spirit.

Then, of course, you find virtually the same thing stated again in Acts 1: 'And, being assembled together with them, [he] commanded them that they should not depart from Jerusalem, but wait for the promise of the Father, which, saith he, ye have heard of me. For John truly baptized with water; but ye shall be baptized with the Holy Ghost not many days hence.'

Then verse 8: 'But ye shall receive power, after that the Holy Ghost is come upon you.' Power! What for? Well, 'and ye shall be witnesses unto me both in Jerusalem, and in Judaea, and in Samaria, and unto the uttermost part of the earth.'

That is the main purpose of the baptism with the Spirit, to make us powerful witnesses to the Lord Jesus Christ and his salvation. Go on through the New Testament and you will find that this fact is repeated. Take, for instance, the apostle Peter standing before the authorities: 'Then Peter and the other apostles answered and said, We ought to obey God rather than men. The God of our fathers raised up Jesus, whom ye slew and hanged on a tree. Him hath God exalted with his right hand to be a Prince and a Saviour, for to give repentance to Israel, and forgiveness of sins. And we are witnesses of these things, and so also is the Holy Ghost, whom God hath given to them that obey him' (Acts 5: 29-32).

Now the coming of the Holy Spirit, the baptism with the Holy Spirit, is a witness to these things. A witness is not something secret but public, something that is evident. And you see this on the day of Pentecost at Jerusalem when the Holy Spirit descended upon these disciples and the others – upon the 120 gathered in the upper room. The whole of Jerusalem was stirred and disturbed and the crowd came together. 'What meaneth this?' they said. 'What is this?' The coming of the Holy Spirit and his effects upon the Christian people is a tremendous witness. The apostles therefore say, 'We are witnesses of these things; and so is also the Holy Ghost, whom God hath given to them that obey him.'

And, as I have reminded you more than once already, that was the witness that convinced the apostle Peter that Gentiles should be admitted into the Christian Church. He took some convincing. Peter was a Jew and even though he had had a vision, he was not quite clear about this. The vision had convinced him that he must go with these people to preach in the household of Cornelius, but he was not clear about it even then. Then when he saw that the Spirit had descended upon these people, even as it had upon him and the others at the beginning, he said, 'Who was I that I could gainsay this, or refuse them water?' The witness of the Spirit, obvious, external, convinced the apostle.

Now there is another very interesting statement of all this in Hebrews 2. The writer is exhorting the people to take heed lest they slip away from these things. He says, 'How shall we escape, if we neglect so great salvation; which at the first began to be spoken by the Lord, and was confirmed unto us by them that heard him....' Then notice this, the writer continues – 'God also bearing them witness' – How? – Well, 'both with signs and wonders, and with divers miracles, and gifts of the Holy Ghost, according to his own will'.

That is another way in which this is stated. The purpose, the main function of the baptism with the Holy Spirit, is to witness, to enable God's people to witness in such a manner that it becomes a phenomenon and people are arrested and are attracted. And in Hebrews 10: 14-15 we have the same thing. 'For by one offering he hath perfected for ever them that are sanctified. Whereof the Holy Ghost is a witness to us.' That carries exactly the same meaning there.

How does he do it? Well, that leads me to what I would call the fifth big division of this whole subject. What are the marks and signs, or, if you prefer it, the results of this baptism with the Holy Spirit? There is no difficulty about this. It is seen very clearly in all the accounts that we have of various people being baptized with the Spirit. You find it perfectly, in Acts 2, in the case of the disciples themselves and you see the difference that the baptism with the Spirit made to them. But then you get it in all the other examples and illustrations given everywhere in the New Testament. You find it, as we have seen, in the epistles, where it is implicit, and at the back of all of them. You do not begin to understand them unless you know something about this doctrine of the baptism with the Holy Spirit. As I mentioned earlier, how many churches do you know today to whom you need to write the first letter to the Corinthians, where there were excesses because of this?

It is also in the testimonies and lives of innumerable saints throughout the long history of the Christian church. I have quoted some examples to you and shall quote more, in order that people may see that this is not 'some strange new doctrine'. This is New Testament Christianity! This is what has been true of the church especially in all the great revivals that she has been privileged to experience and to enjoy.

What, then, are the marks, the signs and manifestations of baptism with the Spirit? I am going to give you general principles. Obviously there are variations from case to case: that is common sense, for not all experiences are identical. They are identical in their character but not in their degree; and this again is a most important point, because it works in two ways. Some people tend to think that unless you have had the maximum experience as it were, you have had nothing at alll. Well obviously that is wrong, it can depress people. There are people who may feel that they have never received this baptism with the Spirit because they have not had certain particular experiences. That is quite wrong, quite false. We must look at the principle, at the various manifestations as a whole. And then, having looked at them as a whole, and bearing in mind that there is variation in the degree, we shall be able to test ourselves and to examine ourselves.

These principles can be divided up in two ways: certain things which are in us, certain subjective experiences, and then the objective, the things that become evident and obvious to those who know us and who are outside us. I think that is the most convenient classification.

Let us start with the personal, subjective, experimental consciousness of the individual. What is it that inevitably happens when one is baptized by the Lord Jesus Christ with the Holy Spirit? Well, first and foremost I think we must put this – a sense of the glory of God, an unusual sense of the presence of God. This is something, it seems to me, that stands out in all the instances in the New Testament itself and in the subsequent history of God's people. What the Holy Spirit does is make real to us the things which we have believed by faith, the things of which we have had but a kind of indirect certainty only. The Holy Spirit makes these things immediately real. The account of Jonathan Edwards, which we have already considered, brings out particularly clearly the great sense of the glory of God – the Father, and the Son, and the Holy Spirit. Now Jonathan Edwards had believed these things but, as he says, it was extraordinary. It is possible for us to have an immediate awareness of the glory of God. Customarily we walk by faith and not by sight, we believe the testimony of the Scrpture and the Spirit applies it to us and we know that these things are true. But here there is something over and above that; you just know that you are in the presence of God. It is almost impossible, as he says, and as others have said, to put these things into words.

I have quoted Jonathan Edwards, an outstanding American genius. Now let me quote a man called Thomas Charles Edwards, the Principal of a college in Wales in the last century. I mention him because he is the same type of man: someone unusually brilliant. He had the best education that was available and was a great scholar. Some of you may know his commentary on the first epistle to the Corinthians. He tells his own experience, which happened to him in a revival in 1859. He was away from home as a student and had been reading books on philosophy and theology that had got him into a state in which he was filled with doubts and questionings. His father was a great man before him and the Principal of a theological seminary. But still this young man was in trouble, uncertain, almost, he says, 'of the very being of God.'

Then he went home on vacation and heard it announced in the chapel that one night in the following week two comparatively simple preachers from another part of Wales were due to preach in that chapel. These two men were very much involved in the revival that was then sweeping the country; one of them was the instrument, if I may use such a term, whom God used to start the revival, and the other was his companion. So this young man decided that he would go to the meeting, and he describes how he went and sat in the gallery. And there he was, full of doubts and expecting nothing – after all, these men were two simple men. One had been a carpenter and the other a tailor, while he had been reading, and listening to the great lecturers, the leading philosophers of the last century. So he went in a somewhat patronizing spirit.

Then he tells us how he left that meeting. He does not remember all the details, but the main thing that he does know is that when he left that meeting 'he was more certain of God than he was of even the things he could see with his naked eye.' He had met with God, he had felt the present of God. He knew that *God Is*. The glory of God had appeared to him through the ministration of these simple men in that meeting. That, you see, is a time of revival. The Holy Spirit was outpoured and this man was carried not only from doubt to belief but to certainty, to awareness of the presence and the glory of God.

And inevitably accompanying this sense of the glory of God and of his presence is also a sense of awe. You read of people in the Bible who have either a vision of God or have been given something comparable to what I am talking about, and immediately they are all filled with a sense of awe. Isaiah describes, in the sixth chapter of his prophecy, how 'In the year that king Uzziah died he saw the Lord sitting upon a throne, high and lifted up.' This vision! And he felt immediately that he was a man unclean.

Is not this our trouble, my dear friends, that we talk about God and we believe in God but do we know God, the glory of God? You get illustrations of this in the Bible. Think of Moses and the burning bush: the glory which made him stand back, the voice that spoke. It is there everywhere. John in the Book of Revelation describes the same thing. 'He fell down as one dead.' The apostle Paul had a glimpse of the risen Lord on the road to Damascus, and falls down, blinded. But when the Spirit comes, when we are baptized in this way with the Spirit, he makes all this thing vital and real to us, and there is a kind of luminosity and an immediacy. It is the great characteristic of being baptized with the Holy Spirit.

Let me remind you again of D. L. Moody, whose experience I have already quoted to you. Here is a man who was as converted as a man could ever have been and who had a knowledge and an assurance of a kind. But in the light of what happened to him in New York City, in Wall Street, it almost becomes nothing. 'God', he says, 'revealed himself to me, and I had such an experience of his love that I had to ask him to stay his hand.' And, as those of you who know his story are aware, it was after that that Moody began to be used in the way that we know of in Britain, and in the United States, and other places. It was the turning-point in his whole career. This is the thing that made him the witness that he became. But notice how he describes it; he puts his emphasis there upon this sense of awe and of majesty; and accompanying it inevitably again is a sense of being humbled. This is most important.

I will come back later to deal with how we should differentiate between the baptism with the Spirit and the counterfeits – there are counterfeits to everything. The devil is subtle and able; he can transform himself into an angel of light. He is so subtle as almost to be able to deceive the very elect, says our Lord himself. When we come to that, this will be a most important point – that the baptism with the Holy Spirit always has the effect of humbling you, because it is a manifestation of God, an extraordinary and immediate realization of God's presence. This is inevitable.

Let me put this in terms of a statement which you will find in the Journal of George Whitefield for November 5th 1740. He says:

> Mr Gilbert Tennant preached first and I then began to pray and to give an exhortation. In about six minutes one cried out, "He is come! He is come!" and could scarce sustain the manifestation of Jesus to his soul.

This was just an ordinary member of the congregation, remember. This was not Whitefield himself nor Gilbert Tennant, who was also a mighty preacher and used of God. It was a member of the congregation who suddenly cried out like that. Whitefield continues:

> But having heard the crying of others for the like favour obliged me to stop, and I prayed over them as I saw their agonies and distress increase. At length we sang a hymn and then retired to the house, where the man that received Christ continued praising and speaking of Him until near midnight. My own soul was so full that I retired and wept before the Lord, and had a deep sense of my own vileness, and the sovereignty and greatness of God's everlasting love. Most of the people spent the remainder of the night in prayer and praising God. It was a night much to be remembered.

Now George Whitefield was one of the saintliest men that has ever trod the face of this earth; he was outstandingly so. But the effect of this experience upon him there was just a repetition of what he had had previously – a deep sense of his own vileness and the greatness of God's everlasting love.

My friends, if you say and if you argue that every Christian has been baptized with the Holy Spirit, well then I ask you this question: how often have you had that sort of experience? Have you ever had it? Be careful. If you postulate that every Christian of necessity has been baptized with the Holy Spirit, I am afraid you will have to come to the conclusion that there are very few Christians in the Christian church. This is what happens when a man is baptized with the Holy Spirit – this immediacy. This is not reason, or faith; but action taking place upon us and to us. It is a manifestation, God – Father, Son, and Holy Spirit – making themselves real to us and living in our very experiences.

Another pronounced characteristic that always accompanies it is an assurance of the love of God to us in

Jesus Christ. This is most important and remarkable. On the one hand you have such a conception of the glory and the greatness and majesty of God, and of your own vileness and filthiness and foulness and unworthiness. 'Well,' you say, 'it must be a most depressing experience.' It is not, for at the same time you have an overwhelming knowledge given to you of God's love to you in our Lord and Saviour Jesus Christ. Now I would say personally that this is the greatest and most essential characteristic of the baptism with the Spirit. He makes us witnesses because of our assurance.

I once read in a paper a story which I must confess searched me to the very depth of my being. It was an account of a meeting held in the St Andrew's Hall in Glasgow a number of years ago and the report of the meeting was given by Alexander Gammie, who was well-known as a religious writer, but he also went to political meetings and so on. He had been listening to two men speaking, and speaking on the same theme, and he later wrote: 'They were both excellent speakers, very eloquent, able men, able to marshall their arguments, state their case and so on, but,' he said, 'I felt there was one great difference between the two men.... The first man spoke as an advocate, the second man spoke as a witness.'

That is the difference! The first was like a barrister, with his brief – an advocate. He stated the case – and stated it so well because he believed in it. But the second man had got something additional, a plus – he was a witness.

Now the thing that makes a man a real witness is his assurance of these things. You can be a Christian without that. You can have believed the Scriptures, you can have read it, you can have heard it preached and believed it and you can have a kind of certainty with respect to it; but that is not the thing that made the apostles witnesses. Our Lord tells them, 'Ye are witnesses of these things.' Of course they were. They had been with him, and he is there with them in the upper room; but in Luke 24 he says, 'Ye cannot be witnesses for me until....' This absolute certainty! And, of course, this is the thing that is so evident and obvious in their whole life and experience after the day of Pentecost.

You notice that even in Acts 1 these men, though they had had such instruction and such opportunity, are still a bit muddled; in Acts 1:6 we read that they say, 'Wilt thou at this time restore again the kingdom to Israel?' – still that old materialistic thinking. There was a kind of uncertainty. But all this disappears after the Baptism with the Holy Spirit; they are different men, and speak with assurance and certainty.

So the baptism with the Spirit is that which gives us the highest form of assurance. There are in the word of God three types of assurance possible to the Christian. The first type of assurance is the assurance that we get by deduction from the Scriptures. This is the commonly recognized form of assurance. You have all heard it and it has probably been said to you. You have been troubled as to whether you are a Christian or not and you go in your trouble to a minister or to some Christian friend.

'Wait a minute,' they say, 'you should not be confused like this. The thing is quite simple.' They ask, 'You believe the Scriptures to be the word of God?'

'Yes,' you reply, 'I do.'

'Well,' they say, 'this is what the Scriptures say – "God so loved the world, that he gave his only begotten Son, that whosoever believeth in him should not perish, but have everlasting life." Do you believe that?'

'I do.'

'Very well, then, you shall not "perish", but you have "everlasting life." "For God sent not his Son into the world to condemn the world: he that believeth in him is not condemned." Do you believe that?'

'I do.'

'Well, you are not condemned then. "But he that believeth not is condemned because he believeth not in the name of the only begotten Son of God."'

Then they conclude, 'Well, there you are. If you believe the Scriptures you must believe that. The Bible says that because you believe, you are not condemned, you are saved, you must be saved. Do not worry about your feelings, believe the bare word of God.'

And that is right. Perfectly right. That is something we must all do. But I venture to describe that as the lowest form of assurance. It is a form of assurance but still the lowest.

The second form of assurance is the kind that is dealt with in the first epistle of John. John tells us there in chapter 5:13 that his whole object in writing to those people was 'That ye [who believe on the Son of God] might know that ye have eternal life' – assurance.

How, then, does he give it them? Well, he says that there are various tests which you can apply to yourselves. Some people have described these tests as the 'tests of life'. The familiar one, the commonest of all is: 'We know that we have passed from death unto life, because we love the brethren.' This is a better test than the first one. While the first one is valid, the danger is that you may say, 'Ah yes, but is this only an intellectual assent that I am giving? Am I only doing it with my mind?'

Now here is a more thorough test because it examines your total reaction to the truth you claim to have believed. You love the brethren? You can say honestly that you would sooner be with the brethren than with anybody else, that you have found that people whom you do not like by nature you can love as Christians because they are, with you, children of God? If you do find yourself loving the brethren, you can be sure that you are a child of God. You know that. You will know that nothing else would make you love such people and enjoy their company but this fact that it has happened to them and to you, and you are aware of this thing that you are sharing together – common participation in the life of God.

And you apply the other tests as well such as: his commandments are no longer grievous; he has given us of his Spirit; we have an unction, and an anointing, and an understanding, and so on. We must work them out for ourselves.

But there is a third type of assurance, which is the highest, the most absolute and glorious, and which differs essentially from the other two. How? Like this. You notice, in the first two types of assurance, that what we are doing is to draw deductions, as we read the Scriptures, perhaps. We arrive at the assurance by a process of reading, understanding, self-examination or self-analysis. It is a deduction that we draw from the premises given; and it is right and true. But the glory of this third and highest form of assurance is that it is neither anything that we do, nor any deduction that we draw, but an assurance that is given to us by the blessed Spirit himself.

Now if you like, it is again the whole difference between Romans 8:15 and Romans 8:16. Romans 8:15 reads like this: 'For ye have not received the spirit of bondage again to fear; but ye have received the Spirit of adoption whereby we cry, Abba, Father.' Then verse 16: 'The Spirit himself beareth witness with our spirit' (RV). Our spirit has been crying 'Abba, Father', but over and above that the Spirit now bears witness with our spirit – he confirms ours saying to us: 'You are right.' The Spirit does it. Now this is neither our action, nor our deduction, but the immediate witness of the Spirit, and that is why it is both so absolute and so certain. What the Spirit does is this: he tells us in the most unmistakable manner that we are the children of God, that God loves us with an everlasting love, and that it was because he so loved us that Christ gave himself for us.

The Spirit does this in many ways. Sometimes he will do it through a verse of Scripture, a verse you may have read a thousand times before but which suddenly seems to stand out – it is for you, he is speaking to you. Sometimes it is without even a verse of Scripture; it is an impression upon the mind and in the heart. You do not hear an audible voice, or see anything, but you just know with an absolute certainty. That is the Spirit bearing witness with our spirit, that we are the children of God.

Let me finish on this particular point by putting it to you once more in the form of the experiences of certain people. Let us start with an old Puritan who died in 1623 – Edward Eltham. He says:

> I take it therefore that the witness and testimony of the Spirit he has spoken of is an inward secret and unspeakable inspiration of the Spirit; the Holy Spirit of God inwardly, secretly, and in an unspeakable manner informing our hearts and inwardly persuading us that God is our Father, and pouring into our heart a secret, wonderful and unspeakable sweet sense and feeling of God's love to us. Not of God's ordinary or common love, but of his special and Fatherly love, that God loves us with such love as He bears to His only begotten Son Christ Jesus, in Whom we are adopted to be His children. As the Lord Jesus Himself speaks in that excellent prayer of his [John 17:23] that God loves us, we believing in Christ as He hath loved us. And to this purpose the Apostle speaks plainly [Romans 5:5] the Holy Spirit of God given to us doth infuse and pour into our hearts a sense and feeling of God's love to us in Christ.

Let me also quote from the journals of a man called Howell Harris, who was mightily used of God two hundred years ago. Here was a man who was convinced on Good Friday in 1735, went through an agony of conviction and uncertainty, and then, on Whit Sunday the same year was given the knowledge that his sins were forgiven, so that he believed and rejoiced. Three weeks later, after his conversion, after he had received a quiet assurance of salvation he received a further experience. He had gone to retire to the Clock Tower of the church in Llangasty. He went there in order that he might have peace to read the Scriptures and to pray. His biographer tells us what happened next: 'After two to three weeks that love burst forth into a flame which melted his whole nature.'

His experience of forgiveness which he had received earlier 'was doubtless sweet, nevertheless it left in his heart an indefinable sense of some further need, but while he was engaged in secret prayer in the church at Llangasty, that sacred place where he had given himself to God, God now gave himself to him' – and there he scarcely knows how to describe what happened.

He piles the richest biblical phrases one on top of the other in an attempt to give adequate expression to what he felt and experienced that day; that was when his heart was cleared from all idols, and the love of God was shed abroad in his heart. Now he had received the Spirit of adoption whereby we cry Abba, Father, and he began to desire to depart and to be with Christ. All fears were cast out for months, and perfect love took their place. And he never forgot that day. It was from that day that Howell Harris began to be such a remarkable and outstanding witness, and testified to the grace and love of God. And he describes how this love of God came upon him in wave after wave after wave.

Another man called Christmas Evans does exactly the same thing. Those of you who have read the autobiography of Charles Finney will know that he says exactly the same thing again.

Now this is what I mean by this highest form of assurance, the Spirit bearing witness with our spirit, that we are the children of God. It is direct, immediate. Not our deduction but his absolute certainty, the Spirit telling us that we are children of God.

Let me finally tell you again what I regard as one of the most beautiful ways in which this matter has ever been put. It is by Thomas Goodwin, one of those great Puritans again of three hundred years ago, the President of Magdalen College at Oxford during the commonwealth, and a brilliant scholar and preacher. This is the difference between what I call, the customary assurance of the child of God, and this extra-ordinary assurance. He describes a man and his little child, his son, walking down the road and they are walking hand in hand, and the child knows that he is the child of his father, and he knows that his father loves him, and he rejoices in that, and he is happy in it. There is no uncertainty about it all, but suddenly the father, moved by some impulse, takes hold of that child and picks him up, fondles him in his arms, kisses him, embraces him, showers his love upon him, and then he puts him down again and they go on walking together.

That is it! The child knew before that his father loved him, and he knew that he was his child. But oh! this loving embrace, this extra outpouring of love, this unusual manifestation of it – that is the kind of thing. The Spirit bearing witness with our spirit, that we are the children of God.

This is the outstanding characteristic of the baptism with the Spirit. God give us grace to examine ourselves in the light of these things. I take it you have all got the first and the second types of assurance: do you know anything about the third? Do you know anything of the glory of God, this immediacy, this certainty, this absolute assurance given by the Spirit that banishes all doubt and uncertainty and you know that God loves you in particular with an everlasting love in Jesus Christ?

Chapter 6

Joy, Love and Understanding

We have seen that when Christians are baptized by the Holy Spirit, they have a sense of the power and presence of God that they have never known before – and that this is the greatest possible form of assurance. A Christian is not so much an advocate, as a witness, and this witness is not effective without assurance. The certainty that comes with assurance – 'I know in whom I have believed' is the obvious and greatest necessity in connection with witnessing.

We now go on to consider further aspects of this matter. Let me say again, that, according to the teaching of the Scripture and according to the subsequent history of the church, this is not something, which is confined to certain people. It is not only something experienced by great preachers or leaders, it is not confined to the apostles, or to some notable persons in the history of the church, but is something which has been experienced by ordinary people, so-called, throughout the centuries – and again I want to emphasize that.

I have been quoting people from different centuries simply that you may see that this is something which is to happen at all times. The apostle Peter said on the day of Pentecost, 'The promise is unto you, and to your children, and to as many as are afar off', but there are some foolish, ignorant people who seem to think that because this is the twentieth century, this kind of thing is no longer to be expected. That is just a denial of the gospel. This is what God's people are offered at all times in all places; there is no limit placed upon it at all.

Now I trust that that is clear, and I go on giving these illustrations in order to bring out that particular point. And thank God there are witnesses to these things in this day and generation as there have been at all other times in the history of the church.

We proceed, therefore, to consider other aspects and other manfestations of this glorious, wonderful experience which is offered to the children of God – and I trust that we all have not only our minds open, but our hearts open too, and a longing to know something of the riches of his grace. Take the hymn:

> Jesus, the very thought of Thee
> With sweetness fills the breast.

Does it? It should! There is something wrong with Christian people who cannot sing or say that honestly and truly. That is how we should be. And so, you see, we are considering what it is that brings a man into the position of being able to say that.

You may know the date of the author of that hymn. Some people say, 'Ah, he lived in the eleventh century.' Christianity is apart from time, it happens in every century. And it seems to me that we are confronted with one of two possibilities. We either get to know something of this experience or we stop singing such hymns. The question of honesty is involved here and of truth. So, then, what can be more important than that we should be looking into this glorious matter together. Thank God we have such a matter to consider.

The next manifestation, therefore, and I think you will agree that it follows quite inevitably from all that we have been seeing, is, of course, the element of joy and of gladness. Here is something that you find running through the New Testament. There is no more exhilarating book extant today than this and in particular, perhaps, this is true of Acts. What a thrilling book it is! And this is the one great note, 'And they', we read in chapter two, 'continuing daily with one accord in the temple, and breaking bread from house to house, did eat their meat with gladness and singleness of heart'. That is it! Now these were not only the apostles, but also the three thousand people whose names we do not know; ordinary people if you like, but people who were filled with this same spirit of joy and of rejoicing.

To me it is very wonderful to notice the way in which these things are stated, as if it is quite ordinary, something just to be expected. The apostle Paul, writing to the church at Thessalonica to remind them of how the gospel came to them, puts it like this: 'Our gospel came not unto you in word only, but also in power, and in the Holy Ghost, and in much assurance; as ye know what manner of men we were among you for your sake.' Then, notice this: 'And ye became followers of us, and of the Lord, having received the word in much affliction, with joy of the Holy Ghost.'

You see these people, when they became Christians, were subjected to the most terrible persecution on the part of their relatives and friends, and of society in general; the persecution was grievous and yet we are told that though they were thus afflicted, there was, accompanying the affliction, this joy in the Holy Ghost.

Paul also reminds the Roman Christians of these things. In Romans 5 he writes: 'Being justified by faith, we have peace with God through our Lord Jesus Christ: By whom also we have access by faith into this grace wherein we stand, and rejoice in hope of the glory of God. And not only so' – not only so! – 'but we glory in tribulations also.' We rejoice in the midst of our tribulations – 'knowing that tribulation worketh patience; and patience, experience; and experience, hope: And hope maketh not ashamed' – why is all this? – ' because the love of God is shed abroad in our hearts' (Romans 5:1-5). The inevitable result of a knowledge and an assurance of the love of God towards us is to fill us with this great joy.

And then take 1 Peter 1:8: 'Whom having not seen, ye love; in whom, though now ye see him not, yet believing, ye rejoice with a joy unspeakable and full of glory.'

To whom is he writing? Let me nail this foolish idea that this is only for certain people at certain times or in certain special circumstances. The letter was addressed 'to the strangers scattered abroad throughout Pontus, Galatia, Cappadocia, Asia, and Bithynia.' The apostle does not even know their names, or who they are – most ordinary people. Yet he does not hesitate to say that about them. They rejoice in the Lord Jesus Christ whom they have not seen and whom they cannot see; but they rejoice in him with a joy which is 'unspeakable'. It is so marvellous that they cannot express it. Indeed he says 'full of glory', which probably means that it is a part of the joy and the rejoicing which is known by the saints in glory who actually see him as he is. 'Joy unspeakable and glorious.' A foretaste of the joy and the rejoicing and the happiness of the glory everlasting.

Peter said to these ordinary people – and again, remember, he tells us that they were passing through a time of tribulation and of trial, their faith was being tested very severely – and yet, he says, I know that that is your position, that you are rejoicing in him and loving him with a joy which is 'unspeakable and full of glory.'

Now this is what we are meant to be as Christian people. The apostle John – and I quote him again just to show that it is the universal teaching of all these New Testament apostles and writers – says in 1 John 1:4: 'These things write we unto you, that your joy may be full.' They had it but he wanted it to be a full joy, an abounding, abundant joy. Our

Lord had promised this to his followers before he went, and he had promised it in connection with his sending of the Holy Spirit.

There, then, is something which is always associated with the baptism of the Spirit. It leads to a joy and a rejoicing which is quite exceptional.

Once more we find that the history of revivals illustrates and demonstrates what is here stated so plainly in the New Testament itself. You always get, as the chief characteristic in every revival, a great spirit of rejoicing and of singing. Singing generally is a part of a revival – not a worked up singing, but a spontaneous bursting forth into song. You will always find that the really greatest hymns of all – I do not mean these almost maudlin, sentimental hymns that are rather characteristic of the last century, but the great, strong hymns such as you get in the eighteenth century – all these hymns are, in a sense, saying something like these words of Charles Wesley:

> O for a thousand tongues to sing
> My great Redeemer's praise

At that time, as in all times of revival, it was not an exceptional poet like Charles Wesley who says a thing like that; it was the feeling of the most ordinary people, and Wesley was just given a gift to express for them, to put into words on their behalf, emotions that they all really felt in the depths and profundities of their own being. There has been nothing which has been more characteristic of all the great revivals in the history of the church than this desire on the part of God's people to give expression to the joy, the happiness, the peace which they have experienced.

And again – let us keep our eye on this fact – you will generally find that there were phases in all this. The first effect, always, of a revival is to humble people and to convict them, to cast them into an agony of soul, to make them wonder whether they had ever been Christians at all. Then suddenly from the very depths they are lifted up to the heights, and the joy and the rejoicing correspond to the former sense of desolation and unworthiness and condemnation.

Now all I am trying to establish is this, that this is what Christian people are meant to be. This is the whole message of the New Testament, that the Son of God came into this world to deliver us. It is a salvation; he is a Saviour who sets us free from the guilt, the power and the pollution of sin. And no man can be aware of that really without rejoicing. The Christian is not meant to be a man who is just managing to hold on and who is miserable and unhappy and forcing himself to do these things, dragging himself, as it were, to the house of God, as so many foolish people are saying at this present time.

What an utter denial it is of the whole of the New Testament, this foolish suggestion that one service a Sunday is enough, one that takes place at nine o'clock in the morning, to get rid of it, as it were, in order that you can then really go and enjoy yourselves and have real happiness in looking at the television or in rushing to the seaside or in playing golf!

But what happens when people are baptized with the Holy Spirit – as you read throughout Acts – is that they want to keep together, to get together as often as they can – they continued daily, steadfastly, talking about these things, singing together, praising God together. This was the thing that was first above everything else. Everything else came second; even their work was something they *had* to do. It was right that they should do their work, of course, but this was the thing that meant life to them, and joy and salvation.

What I am trying to put to you is this: I am certain that the world outside is not going to pay much attention to all the organized efforts of the Christian church. The one thing she will pay attention to is a body of people filled with this spirit of rejoicing. That is how Christianity conquered the ancient world. It was this amazing joy of these people. Even when you threw them into prison, or even to death, it did not matter, they went on rejoicing; rejoicing in tribulations.

I am commending this to you, not merely that you may have the experience of the joy of salvation, but also, I hope, as a matter of duty. I am exhorting you in this evil world in which we find ourselves that if you really are concerned about it, if you really do feel what you say about the daily evidence in the newspapers of the moral rot that is setting in in this country, if you feel that we are facing ruin economically and industrially, because people are worshippers and lovers of pleasures rather than lovers of God, if you really believe that and mean it and feel it, then it will be your duty to become a person such as is depicted here, because this is the only thing that is going to persuade men. They say, 'Oh we know your teaching and preaching, we have had it all before', but when they see it in operation they will listen because they are miserable and unhappy. When they see this quality they will begin to pay real attention. So there is nothing more important than for us to understand this teaching and to experience it in our own personal and daily lives.

Now I am putting before you the teaching of the New Testament but I am also anxious to bring this home, and sometimes practical stories and illustrations help; and at the same time I am again able to show you how in all ages this same thing happens.

Take an account written by Dr Isaac Watts, whose hymns we are so fond of – 'When I survey the wondrous Cross', for example. In writing about this extraordinary witness of the Spirit he quotes the case of the Rev John Howe, who was chaplain to Oliver Cromwell for a period in Whitehall in London in the 1650s. John Howe was a particularly intellectual man, a judicious and scholarly man, and yet, as Watts says, he was someone whose name commanded respect, and who confirmed what he (Watts) has been teaching. Howe is important for this reason: people say, 'Ah well, of course, I know there are certain types. I know these effervescent types, these emotional people, these unstable people, they claim all sorts of wonderful things, but an intellectual man, a man who ... that's different.' Watts tells us that when John Howe died they found that he had written some paragraphs on the blank leaf of his Bible. Notice what he writes:

> December 26th 1689 – After that I had long seriously and repeatedly thought with myself that besides a full and undoubted assent to the objects of faith, a vivifying, savoury taste and relish of them was also necessary, that with stronger force and more powerful energy they might penetrate into the most inward centre of my heart, and there being most deeply fixed and rooted govern my life.

That is what he wanted. He believed these things intellectually and they were true to him and in a sense he had assurance of salvation – but he wanted something more:

> ... and that there could be no other sure ground whereon to conclude and pass a sound judgment on my good estate Godward. And after I had in my course of preaching been largely insisting on 2 Corinthians 1:12. 'This is my rejoicing, the testimony of a good conscience etc.' This very morning I awoke out of a most ravishing and delightful dream, that a wonderful copious stream of celestial rays from the lofty throne of the Divine Majesty did seem to dart into my open and expanded breast. I have often since with great complacency reflected on that very signal pledge of special Divine favour vouchsafed to me on that noted memorable day, and have with repeated fresh pleasure tasted the delights thereof. But what of the same kind I sensibly felt through the admirable bounty of God and the most pleasant comforting influence of the Holy Spirit on October 22nd 1704 ... – this is another experience of the same thing; first 1689, now 1704 – '...far surpassed the most expressive words my

> thoughts can suggest. I then experienced an inexpressibly pleasant melting of the heart, tears gushing out of mine eyes for joy that God should shed abroad His love abundantly through the hearts of men; and that, for this very purpose, mine own heart should be so signally possessed of and by His blessed Spirit, Romans 5:5.

Let me give another helpful example, this time a statement by William Guthrie, a Scotsman from the same century, a typical Scot, the extreme opposite of the effervescent, emotional, unstable type; a great brain, and a theologian. He says:

> It is a glorious divine manifestation of God unto the soul, shedding abroad God's love in the heart. It is a thing better felt than spoken of. It is no audible voice but it is a ray of glory filling the soul with God as He is Life, Light, Love and Liberty, corresponding to that audible voice 'O man, greatly beloved', putting a man in a transport. With this on his heart it is good to be here, it is that which went from Christ to Mary when He but mentioned her name. 'Jesus saith unto her, Mary. She turned herself, and saith unto him, Rabboni; which is Master.' He had spoken some words to her before and she understood not that it was He, but when He uttereth this one word 'Mary', there was some admirable divine conveyance and manifestation made out unto her heart by which she was so satisfyingly filled that there was no place for arguing and disputing whether or not that was Christ and if she had any interest in Him. That manifestation wrought faith to itself and did purchase credit and trust to itself, and was equivalent with 'Thus saith the Lord'.
>
> This is such a glance of glory that it may in the highest sense be called the 'earnest' or the 'firstfruits' of the inheritance (Ephesians 1:14) for it is a present and as it were, sensible discovery of the Holy God, almost wholly conforming the man unto His likeness, so swallowing him up that he forgetteth all things except the present manifestation. Oh how glorious is this manifestation of the Spirit! Faith here rises to so full an assurance that

> it resolveth wholly into the sensible presence of God.
>
> This is the thing which doth best deserve the title of 'Sensible Presence' and it is not given unto all believers, some whereof are all their days under bondage and in fear; but here 'Love (almost perfect) casteth out fear'. This is so absolutely let out upon the Master's pleasure, and so transient or passing or quickly gone when it is, that no man may bring his gracious state into debate for want of it.

A third, remarkable example is the great Blaise Pascal, one of the great geniuses of all times. Again, he belonged to that seventeenth century but, of course, lived in France, and he was a Roman Catholic. Here was a man who developed a great concern about his soul and about his salvation. He was a brilliant thinker and philospher, who used to read and talk a lot; also he conducted mathematical experiments and gave mathematical lectures: he was the lion of scientific circles in Paris in those days. When he died they found he had written something on a bit of paper and had sewn it inside his shirt – an amulet in which he describes a remarkable experience that he had:

> This day of Grace 1654;
> From about half past ten at night, to
> about half after midnight,
> Fire.

Now here you have not got one of these obvious 'psychological types', always seeing visions and imagining things. You have got one of the greatest mathematicians of all times.

> Fire
> God of Abraham, God of Isaac, God of Jacob,
> Not of the philosophers and the wise.
> Security, security. Feeling, joy, peace.
> God of Jesus Christ

Thy God shall be my God.
Forgetfulness of the world and of all save God.
He can be found only in the ways taught
in the Gospel.
Greatness of the human soul.

He just put these things down as best he could recollect them, these things that came upon him in such profusion.

Greatness of the human soul.
O righteous Father, the world hath not known Thee,
but I have known Thee.
Joy, joy, joy, tears of joy.
I have separated myself from Him.
My God, why hast Thou forsaken me?...
That I be not separated from Thee eternally.
This is life eternal: That they might know Thee
the only true God, and Him whom Thou has sent, Jesus Christ,
Jesus Christ,
Jesus Christ.
I have separated myself from Him; I have fled, renounced,
crucified Him.
May I never be separated from Him.

He is mixing his past with his present. He is made to feel by what was given to him what he had been in the past.

May I never be separated from Him
He maintains Himself in me only in the ways taught
in the Gospel.
Renunciation total and sweet.

And of course that is precisely what he did after this astonishing experience.

From thenceforth he retired from the world and all his mathematical interests and pursuits and joined himself to a religious body at Port Royal, the Jansenists of that time.

There he began writing his famous works: the *Provincial Letters* and the *Thoughts (Pensées)* which are so profound and moving. He was a brilliant philosopher and scientist, yet it was in this one experience that he really came to knowledge and understanding.

But what he emphasizes above everything else, is 'joy, joy, joy, tears of joy'.

Now this is the 'joy unspeakable and full of glory' to which the apostle Peter refers in that first chapter of his first epistle.

All I want to convey to you, my dear friends, is that we all ought to know something like that. And that is the question: do we know it? This is not something you work up. Pascal was not in a meeting; they had not been singing endless hymns and choruses and working themselves up into an excitement. No. When the Holy Spirit is operating you do not need to work it up, you do not need to organize it; he does it all. It is the vision of him, the knowledge of him, this immediacy, and this is the inevitable result – a joy which is unspeakable and full of glory, though we do not see him. The people to whom Peter was writing had never seen him at all, they were 'strangers scattered abroad'. Peter had actually seen the Lord physically, they had not. It is not necessary. The Spirit is sent in order to bring him to us and this is the result of this knowledge of him and experience of him.

Then, of course, the next we mention is 'love to God'. 'We love him,' says John in his first epistle, 'because he first loved us' – and this is again quite inevitable, and does not need any demonstration. You cannot know the love of God to you without loving God in return. The one follows the other as the night follows the day; and when we know this our love to God rises as a response to his love to us. It is a love which, as John puts it, 'casteth out fear'. William Guthrie made that point, and he is just repeating the teaching of the apostle John. It is a love that casts out a craven fear, the 'fear that hath torment'. It does not get rid of the awe, it increases that. But it removes fear. We realize we are no longer under law, but under grace; that we are the children of God and therefore we cry 'Abba, Father'. There is the love mentioned in Romans 8:15, but this other is beyond that – look at it even in terms of this love that is in us that cries 'Abba, Father'. How do we approach God? How do we pray to God? Is he someone in the vast distance? Or do we approach him as 'Father'? Do we know anything of a love rising up within us, a desire to know him more and more, and a desire even to be with him? These are the things that are testified to in the Scriptures and by the saints throughout the centuries. I leave that just as a question with you.

Let me go on to the next thing because this is more practical and it is a test of our love. It is the desire to glorify him, to glorify God the Father, to glorify the Lord Jesus Christ, and in doing that we glorify the Holy Spirit at the same time. But it is important also to remember that our Lord Jesus Christ, in promising all this, said of the Spirit, 'He shall glorify me.' The Holy Spirit has been sent particularly to glorify the Lord Jesus Christ, not himself. The Lord Jesus Christ said that he was sent to glorify the Father, and so he did always, he pointed people to the Father. He would disappear and they would not be able to find him. He did not want personal glorification. He had come to glorify the Father, and he says, 'The Spirit is sent to glorify Me.' So one of the greatest tests of the work of the Spirit and especially in the baptism, is the desire to glorify the Lord Jesus Christ.

Now when you read Acts you find that this is what always happened. The first thing that happened when the apostles were baptized with the Holy Spirit was this – 'They began to speak and tell forth the wonderful works of God.'

A recent writer on 'the fullness of the Spirit' tries to say that 'the first sign of being filled with the Spirit is that we speak to one another'. He is there countering the tendency to speak in and pray in tongues to God and he thinks he disposes of that by saying that in Ephesians 5:19 you find the phrase, 'Speaking to one another in psalms and hymns and spiritual songs.' He says, 'The man who is filled with the Spirit is not a man who as it were speaks to himself, but he speaks to other people.' But actually, that is not so. The first thing a man who is filled with the Spirit does is to speak to God, he praises God, and his first desire is to glorify the Lord Jesus Christ. So these men filled with the Spirit, begin 'to tell forth the wonderful works of God'.

This, I repeat, is something that is surely quite inevitable. Here it is again – 'Praising God, and having favour with all the people.'

'They continuing daily with one accord in the temple, and breaking bread from house to house, did eat their meat with gladness and singleness of heart, Praising God, and having favour with all the people. And the Lord added to the church daily such as should be saved' (Acts 2:46,47). That is what a man does when he is filled with the Spirit – he wants to praise God, to glorify him, to tell others about him, and to glorify the Lord Jesus Christ in particular.

Read again in Acts 4 where they are again filled with the Spirit, the same men who had been filled on the day of Pentecost. Peter and John had been arrested, you remember. They had been severely reprimanded by the court, and were set at liberty only on condition that they should neither preach nor teach any more in the name of this Jesus. So they went back and reported all this to the Church. Then they all with one accord began to pray, and this is what happened. 'When they had prayed, the place was shaken where they were assembled together; and they were all filled with the Holy Ghost.' This means the Holy Spirit 'came upon them' again – 'and they spake the word of God with boldness.... And with great power gave the apostles witness of the resurrection of the Lord Jesus: and great grace was upon them all.'

You remember, too, how when the apostle Paul was

converted, Ananias visited him and he was baptized with the Holy Ghost. Then, this is what we read in Acts 9:20: 'And straightway he preached Christ in the synagogues, that he is the Son of God.' Now that is the result always, the immediate result of the baptism with the Spirit. He did not talk about himself nor his experiences, 'he preached Christ in the synagogues, that he is the Son of God'. But I am emphasizing that he did it 'straightway', immediately. This is the desire of a man who knows these things: he wants to tell forth his praise. So you will find that when the authorities tried to prohibit them doing this they had only one answer to give, 'We cannot but speak' – 'we must! – 'the things which we have seen and heard.'

The next result, of course, is light and understanding, and the Spirit always gives this. He is the Spirit of truth, and when a man is baptized with the Spirit he knows the truth as he has never known it before. I am not interested in the experiences of a man who is still wrong in his doctrine. The test of the baptism with the Spirit is that it leads a man to the truth and to an understanding of the truth. Why is this? Well, he cannot witness without that. You cannot be a witness unless you know. You must have something to say, to be 'ready at all times to give a reason for the hope that is in you'. So the Spirit does this. He gives a kind of luminosity, a clarity of understanding and of apprehension.

Let me, therefore, finish by giving you some examples and illustrations of this. Now this is to me a most remarkable thing. Would you know the Christian truth, would you know the Christian doctrine? Would you have a firm grasp and understanding of God's great and glorious purpose? The highway to that is the baptism with the Holy Spirit. It gives greater light and knowledge and instruction than anything else, and it does so in order that we may be witnesses. I have already quoted the experience of John Flavel, how on a journey he sat by a well and had that astonishing experience. But this is what is interesting.

> He many years after called that day one of the days of heaven, and he professed that he understood more of the life of heaven by it than by all the books he ever read or discourses he ever entertained about it.

He was a great student and reader, a thinker, but in that one experience he had got more knowledge than he had had in the whole of his life.

The same was true of Pascal, whom I quoted earlier, who says, 'God, the living God, not of the philosophers and the wise'. Now he was a philosopher and he had been grappling with great thoughts and understanding. Yet suddenly; in the space of two hours, illumination! And he learned so much there. He felt he had got to give the rest of his life on earth, with his most precarious health, to teaching people and telling people, and so he wrote his *Letters* and his *Pensées*.

But to me in many ways the most extraordinary illustration of this particular point is none other than the man who is honoured by the Roman Catholic Church by the name of St Thomas Aquinas. In 1879 the Pope issued an official proclamation to the effect that Thomas Aquinas is the thologian and teacher of the Holy Catholic Church. He had been regarded as that for many centuries. He lived in the twelfth century, and most Roman Catholic teaching is based upon the teaching of Thomas Aquinas. It is interesting that at the present moment his famous work is *Summa Theologica*, a 'Summary of Theology, or of the Knowledge of God', in a number of volumes. It has always been the standard work of the Roman Catholic church.

Aquinas was a great thinker, a brilliant philosopher. From our standpoint as Protestants he did great harm because he took the philosophy of the Greek philosopher Aristotle, and he harnessed that to the Christian faith – something that cannot be done; but with his brilliand mind he satisfied most people that he had been able to do it.

The essence of his teaching was this – that it is impossible for a mortal man to have any direct experience of God. 'Your position,' he says, 'rests mainly on reason, things that you can sense and see and feel, and then reason applied to them.' So he has his famous 'Proofs of God' – how you can prove the being of God: cause and effect, and so on; good – better – best, etc. – five great proofs of the being of God.

Now that is the essence of Thomas Aquinas's teaching, but here is an authentic history about him. I quote to you a man who puts it very well. (You can read it in most biographies of him and find it in most of the references to him.)

> Then after spending the whole of his life demonstrating how man has no direct contact with immaterial reality, Aquinas shortly before his death had such an overwhelming direct experience of God that he wrote no more. Urged by a friend to complete his great work, *The Summa Theologica*, he answered, 'I can do no more; such things have been revealed to me that all I have written seems as straw, and I now await the end of my life.'

That is it! The genius and the brain of Thomas Aquinas demonstrating, proving, then he suddenly has one experience of God that makes all the *Summa* 'straw'. He knows, he has experienced; God through the Spirit has given it to him. He writes no more.

This is something beyond understanding, beyond reason, indeed beyond comprehension, and yet it is absolute certainty, it is light, knowledge, the truth itself, for it is God; Father, Son and Holy Spirit. Such is the light and the knowledge and the understanding that is given to a man who is baptized with the Holy Spirit of God. As the apostle Paul puts it: 'Which none of the princes of this world knew: for had they known it they would not have crucified the Lord of glory.... But God hath revealed them unto us by his Spirit: for the Spirit searcheth all things, yea, the deep things of God' (1 Corinthians 2:8, 10).

Chapter 7

Bold to Speak

Now the implications of all these things, of course, are obvious and self-evident. The church has fallen into the error of thinking that a man can get this knowledge by academic teaching and learning. I am not here to decry these things; academic teaching and learning are of importance. But they are not all-important, and the tragedy of the last hundred years has been to put a premium on such things, men boast of their degrees and diplomas and their passing of examinations, and so on. That is all very well, but it is not the way to know God more fully. It is through the Spirit, through the baptism of the Spirit that one comes to this fuller knowledge. I quoted to you the cases of Pascal and Thomas Aquinas which surely should put us right on this matter once and for ever. When Christianity becomes a subject in a seminary or in a university, well then I say we have really departed from the faith. These things are aids, they are helps, but we have lost our sense of proportion. The knowledge is given by the Holy Spirit, and thus it has often happened that people like Priscilla and Aquila, as we have seen, are able to put right a brilliant, learned man like Apollos and others; and that has been repeated endlessly throughout the centuries.

We have, then, been looking at the evidences or the marks of the baptism of the Holy Spirit within us ourselves. They can all, more or less, be subsumed under the category or the heading of 'subjective evidences'.

We now turn to the external evidences, those that are apparent to those who are outside and looking on, and these are equally important. It is dealt with in the Scriptures so we must therefore deal with it. It is always a matter which is clearly of prime importance, because if the object of the baptism with the Spirit is to enable us to bear witness, it is to other people that we bear it and therefore there must be something about this which becomes evident and obvious to others. In defining the meaning of the baptism with the Spirit we must put considerable emphasis on the fact that it is not only something a man himself knows for certain but other people also know.

Now anybody who is familiar with Acts will know at once, of course, that this is something very striking. As we have seen, the moment the apostles and the company who were assembled in the upper room were baptized with the Holy Spirit, it became evident and obvious to all who were round and about them, and a great stir was created in Jerusalem and people came gathering together to look into this matter. There it is at once.

We shall have to go again into this in detail but the point that I want to establish is that the thing was patent and evident. Peter makes use of this in his sermon on the day of Pentecost when he puts it like this in Acts 2:33 – 'Therefore, being by the right hand of God exalted, and having received of the Father the promise of the Holy Ghost, he hath shed forth this, which you now see and hear.' So he is appealing to this external, obvious evidence of that which had taken place in them and to them.

But perhaps the most striking example of this is what happened in the house of Cornelius which is described in Acts 10. We read in verse 44 that 'While Peter yet spake these words, the Holy Ghost fell on all them which heard the word.' And if your doctrine of the Holy Spirit does not include this idea of the Holy Spirit falling upon people, it is seriously, grievously defective. This, it seems to me, has been the trouble especially during this present century, indeed almost for a hundred years. The whole notion of the Holy Spirit falling upon people has been discountenanced and discouraged, and if you read many of the books on the Holy Spirit you will find it is not even mentioned at all, a fact which is surely one of the prime explanations of the present state of the Christian church.

Then you go on to read, 'And they of the circumcision which believed were astonished, as many as came with Peter, because that on the Gentiles also was poured out the gift of the Holy Ghost. For they heard them speak with tongues, and magnify God. Then answered Peter, Can any man forbid water, that these should not be baptized, which have received the Holy Ghost as well as we?'

Now you will remember that, in the next chapter, the apostle Peter is called to book by the authorities up at Jerusalem for having admitted the Gentiles into the Christian church. The Jews could not understand this, so Peter falls back on this argument. 'As I began to speak,' he says, 'the Holy Ghost fell on them, as on us at the beginning. Then remembered I the word of the Lord' – and then he quotes the statement of John the Baptist. Then he says, 'Forasmuch then as God gave them the like gift as he did unto us, who believed on the Lord Jesus Christ; what was I, that I could withstand God?' He appeals to the evidence. It is obvious to those who were outside. And so, of course, you go on reading right through this book, and it is there by implication in the epistles and it is something that is substantiated by the subsequent history of the Christian church.

What, then, are these external manifestations? The first is one that may come as a surprise – it is facial appearance! Look at the account given in the Old Testament of what happened to Moses when he was up on the mount with God receiving the Ten Commandments and receiving instructions about the construction of the tabernacle and the forms of worship and so on. We read that, when he was coming down the mount at last the people rushed forward to meet him, they suddenly stood back in terror and alarm. The explanation given for this is that the face of Moses was shining – although Moses did not know it himself – because he had been in the presence of God and something of the glory of God was being reflected back from his face. This is a great mystery, a wonderful thing.

You get the same idea in the account of our Lord's transfiguration. He was transfigured before them and there came a kind of brightness upon him, a glory, which the apostles had not observed in him before.

Well now that is the kind of thing to which I am making reference, and what seems so clear is that because the baptism with the Holy Spirit does bring one into this presence of God and into a living and an active realization of God and his glory, it is not at all surprising that one of the inevitable concomitants is that something happens even to the physical facial appearance of people who receive this baptism.

You particularly get the evidence for this in Acts, and you find it there in the second chapter. It was evident at once to the populace of Jerusalem that something had happened to these men. This was not only because they spake with other tongues, with other languages, but everything about them – their very appearance, their conduct and various other things, to which we shall be referring later. And again I would emphasize that statement in Acts 2:33: 'which you now see and hear'. They were hearing the tongues, the languages, all speaking 'the wonderful works of God, in their own languages; but in addition to what they heard, they saw.

Now this is something that is very much neglected but which is very important. You 'see'. It was evident by looking at these people that something had happened to them.

Let me give you another example to show you the same thing. Consider what we are told about the martyr Stephen in the last verse of Acts 6. Here was a man, we are told, filled with the Holy Spirit and with faith, and because of his preaching and teaching and his other works he fell foul of the authorities, so they arrested him and they put him on trial. Verse 13 tells us, 'They set up false witnesses, which said, This man ceaseth not to speak blasphemous words against this holy place, and the law: For we have heard him say, that this Jesus of Nazareth shall destroy this place, and shall change the customs which Moses delivered us. 'Then: 'And all that sat in the council, looking steadfastly on him, saw his face as it had been the face of an angel.'

Now this is sheer history, and the explanation is the one that I am giving you. This again is nothing but some reflection of the glory of God. 'Like the face of an angel' – and the angels are in the realm of glory, in the presence of God, and everything in that realm reflects something of the glory of God. That is why I am emphasizing this, because if you read the accounts of the great revivals in the history of the church you will find that this is something that has been frequently noticed and has been the means of the conversion of many people. They have just beheld the face of certain people who have suddenly been filled with the Spirit in the revival, and they have been amazed at the glory, the wonder, something luminous in the face.

Lest you may think that I am only describing exceptional people, one of the most extraordinary and wonderful personal testimonies that I think I have ever had the privilege of listening to was the experience of a woman, still alive, in a very humble calling in life, if you can draw such distinctions. (But that is what the world does. I have put it like that that you may know what I am saying. I am not talking about some highly cultured or erudite person, I am talking about somebody who performs very menial tasks.) And I had the privilege of hearing her tell me of how she became a Christian, in a revival that took place in the Island of Lewis before the last war. We have not heard much about it, but there was a visitation of the Spirit of God in the Island of Lewis from April to September 1939, during which meetings were held in a house, not even in a chapel.

She was not very interested in these things but a friend of hers was, and, at last, she was persuaded to go to one of the prayer meetings that was held in the house. She failed to get in once or twice because of the crowd but eventually succeeded in getting in. And the thing that led to her conversion was the sight of the face of a little child in that house. The woman suddenly saw the face of this child shining, and that was the means of her conviction of sin, her need of a Saviour, her salvation and her being filled with the Holy Spirit.

So here is something, I feel, which we have tended to neglect. People concentrate only on the tongues in Acts 2, but there are evidences quite apart from tongues and in many instances where there have been no tongues at all, there have been things like this. And in the accounts of revivals I have often heard it from people whom I have known well and intimately, who experienced something of the Revival in Wales in 1904/5. It was frequently said, too, about Mr Evan Roberts who was so signally used in that revival – people were amazed when they just saw his face and this 'shining' quality.

Then we are told about the saintly Robert Murray McCheyne in his church in Dundee in the late 1830s and early 1840s. It has been authenticated so many, many times, that Robert Murray McCheyne had simply to enter the pulpit and before he had opened his mouth people used to begin to weep and were convicted of sin. He had not uttered a word. Why? Well, the explanation was that this man had come from the presence of God and the Spirit was poured forth. One of the results is something that can be seen even externally.

I am emphasizing this because I am convinced that the main trouble with most of us and with the church in general is that we seem to have forgotten the presence of the Spirit and the power of the Spirit. We have become so formal, with everything so set, so organized, all in the control of man – and have forgotten this other evidence, the power and the glory of the Spirit and the sanctity and the holiness. I am convinced that the greatest need of the church is to realize again the activity of the Holy Spirit. You see, we organize – organize meetings, organize campaigns, but that is because very largely we have forgotten this element that I am trying to emphasize to you. When the Spirit comes his evidence is unmistakable and the results are amazing and astounding.

The next thing that I hasten to emphasize is the effect of the baptism with the Spirit upon the speech of men, by which I really mean preaching. Not only public preaching, but personal conversation, too. (I am not yet dealing with the question of tongues. That is to be dealt with as we consider the gifts.) I am discussing here the effect of the baptism with the Spirit upon men's speaking in what we regard as the ordinary meaning of that term. Here, again, this is something that has been promised of course. You remember how the promise is given there in John 7: 37-39: 'In the last day, that great day of the feast, Jesus stood and cried, saying, If any man thirst, let him come unto me, and drink. He that believeth on me, as the scripture hath said, out of his belly shall flow rivers of living water. (But this spake he of the Spirit, which they that believe on him should receive: for the Holy Ghost was not yet given; because that Jesus was not yet glorified.)'

That is a universal statement and it is true that when people are baptized with the Spirit they discover certain things happening in this matter of testimony and of speaking to others, either in private conversation or in a more public manner. And then our Lord, as I have reminded you already, tells the disciples, 'Tarry ye in Jerusalem' – stay where you are 'until ye be endued with power from on high' – then you will really be able to speak.

Now one must again reiterate this point and emphasize it because it is obviously crucial. Here were men who had been with him during the three years, had heard his preaching and seen his miracles; who had seen him crucified and die, who had seen the body taken down and buried in a grave: and had seen the empty grave. Not only that, they had seen him with their naked eyes as he had appeared to them in the upper room and in various other places, and they had received his teaching and his exposition of the Old Testament, and here he was with them at this moment as they were standing together on the Mount of Olivet. Well, you would have thought, what more do you need, here are men who have obviously had the best training conceivable in order to make them preachers. They have got all the facts, they have even witnessed them, what more can be needed? Yet our Lord says, 'Stay where you are, you need something, you need power.' And that is, of course, what happened to them on the day of Pentecost.

Now it is there and when you look at it like that, that you see how utterly ridiculous it has been for the last hundred years for us to put all our emphasis upon academic teaching and learning, as if that is the thing that is most essential to make a preacher. Of all the people that I have read of in the course of history I know of no people who have such a responsibility at the bar of eternal judgement as the people from roughly 1850 until today. The change took place somewhere in the 50s of the last century; until then the great impact of the Evangelical Revival of the eighteenth century still persisted and there had been other revivals and people knew about the power of the Spirit.

But suddenly we all became so respectable and so learned and people said, 'Ah, that old type of preaching is no longer good enough, the people are now receiving education. They are beginning to read and becoming learned and so on. 'And the middle classes were becoming prosperous and wealthy. Then followed that most devastating thing that has afflicted the life of the church – Victorianism. It entered into the churches, particularly the Free Churches, which now began to imitate other forms of worship and the great word became 'dignity'. Dignity! Formality! Learning! Culture!

Now it is easy, perhaps, for me to criticize; the temptation to such men must have been very great. But oh! Why did they not keep to the New Testament? Why did they make this fatal error? And so the whole notion of preaching became increasingly academic and removed from the Old Testament and a man was judged in terms of his degrees and his diplomas, not his anointing with the Holy Spirit.

Now I do not want to make an either/or issue of this, but I do wish to say this, that if you neglect this element all the rest will avail you nothing. In a sense this neglect has emptied the churches. And there is no hope until we return to the New Testament, the primitive pattern. Here it is – this which happens even in the speaking.

What is it? Well, the great element that stands out at once, of course, is the power and the liberty. This is most striking, as it has always been, in all the subsequent history of the Christian church.

You get foreshadowings of this in the Old Testament – take the prophets. Some of them were unusual men, but some were very ordinary. Amos tells us that he was a most ordinary man: 'I am neither a prophet, nor the son of a prophet.' He was a man who looked after cattle, but he was enabled to speak, as were all these prophets. And what happened was that they received a kind of 'divine afflatus' – they were filled not only with knowledge, but also with an ability to speak which astonished them themselves. Jeremiah, you remember, refers to 'a fire burning in his bones'. He decided not to speak any more, because every time he spoke he got into trouble. He had an unpopular message and said, 'I will never speak again.' But the fire was burning in his bones. The Holy Spirit does that. And you get these suggestions of it there in the Old Testament.

And then let me remind you again of how you get a kind of foreshadowing of the day of Pentecost in the Gospels. In Luke 1:41, for instance, where we read, 'And it came to pass, that, when Elisabeth heard the salutation of Mary, the babe leaped in her womb and Elisabeth was filled with the Holy Ghost: And she spake out with a loud voice, and said....' There it is. And you get the same thing about Zacharias in verse 67: 'And his father [the father of John the Baptist] Zacharias was filled with the Holy Ghost, and prophesied, saying, Blessed be the Lord God of Israel; for he hath visited and redeemed his people.' The preaching of John the Baptist can only be explained in the same way. We are told of him that 'he was filled with the Spirit from his mother's womb' and thus he spoke with the power and liberty that made him a phenomenon.

And as you go on reading then in Acts after the day of Pentecost, you are at once struck by this same thing. The apostle Peter is able to stand up in Jerusalem, though he is just a fisherman. He can expound the Scriptures, and speak with authority, with great power and with unusual liberty. This is what always happens. We read of this in Acts 4:31 – 'they spake the word of God with boldness.' Then again in 4:33 – 'With great power gave the apostles witness of the resurrection of the Lord Jesus, and great grace was upon them all.' And so it goes on right through the New Testament.

Take the apostle Paul, this outstanding genius, this most learned Pharisee, this erudite man. One of the most amazing things he ever said is that statement in 1 Corinthians 2 where he reminds these Corinthians who were interested in philosophy and so on – 'And I, brethren, when I came to you, came not with excellency of speech nor of wisdom, declaring unto you the testimony of God. For I determined not to know anything among you, save Jesus Christ, and him crucified.' Let us not forget that this was his message. He did not talk about himself, nor his experiences, nor his gifts; he preached Jesus Christ, and him crucified. 'And I was with you in weakness, and in fear, and in much trembling. And my speech and my preaching was not with enticing words of man's wisdom, but in demonstration of the Spirit and of power.'

That is it! Power of God! Not the wisdom of men. He was dismissed by the learned as being a 'babbler'. They said, 'His presence is weak, and his speech is contemptible' (2 Corinthians 10: 10). It was not their idea of speaking, but there was power there, and the power manifested itself in what happened to the people who listened to him. And then we have already seen how he reminds the Thessalonians of how the gospel came to them: 'For our gospel came not unto you in word only, but in power, in the Holy Ghost, and in much assurance.' That is the thing, it runs right through the New Testament.

You get the apostle Peter saying exactly the same thing. In 1 Peter 1:10-12 he talks about this great salvation: 'Of which salvation the prophets have inquired and searched diligently, who prophesied of the grace that should come unto you: Searching what, or what manner of time the Spirit of Christ which was in them did signify, when it testified beforehand the sufferings of Christ, and the glory that should follow. Unto whom it was revealed, that not unto themselves, but unto us they did minister the things, which are now reported unto you by them that have preached the gospel unto you with the Holy Ghost sent down from heaven; which things the angels desire to look into.'

Now there it is in the New Testament, and the evidence is so perfectly plain and clear.

When you come to the history of the church you get exactly the same thing, and that is why I have always said that there is nothing next to the Bible which is more encouraging than to familiarize oneself with the great history of the church. There is a feeling and a teaching abroad that says about all this: 'Oh yes, that was New Testament; it was only the beginning but nothing like that happens afterward; this is only the beginning.' My dear friends, the answer to that is the history of the church, and especially the history of revivals; and the story, of course, is a glorious one. How at periods when the church had become dead and lifeless, God would suddenly take hold of a man and pour his Spirit upon him and raise him up and transform his preaching.

I have not the time to go into this in detail, but it has been happening throughout the running centuries. Let me just mention one or two which are striking because of the very age in which it happened to them, in the so-called dark middle ages, in the darkness and the ignorance which Roman Catholicism had produced.

There was a man upon whom God laid his hand in Germany, John Tauler, He was a Roman Catholic priest preaching in a great cathedral but God suddenly took hold of this man and filled him with his Spirit and his whole preaching was transformed. You can read books about him, and certain others of these so-called mystics of that time, who even in the darkness of that era were burning and shining lights. Everybody was aware that something had happened to them and they became phenomenal. It is the only explanation of a man like Savonarola. You cannot explain him – or Martin Luther either – except in terms of being baptized and filled with the Spirit.

Do you remember something of the story of John Knox? It was said that Mary Queen of Scots used to say that she 'was more afraid of John Knox's prayers than she was of many battalions of English soldiers.' And he certainly was so filled with the Spirit that when he used to preach in Edinburgh and she was present listening, she was made to tremble, as Felix trembled while he was listening to the apostle Paul.

Now this is nothing but the power of the Spirit, for it is no human ability nor human speech; it is this other, this power. Hugh Latimer used to preach at St Paul's Cross and it had exactly the same effect; he was possibly the greatest preacher of all the Protestant Fathers.

But it is true of all these men. Have you ever heard, I wonder, the story of a man called John Livingstone, who was a minister in the Church of Scotland in the first half of the seventeenth century? John Livingstone was a very able man and a very good minister, who in writing the account of his life for his grandchildren towards the end of his life, refers to one day in his ministry and to an experience which he never forgot, and it is just a perfect instance of this thing that I am holding before you. They used to have 'Communion seasons' in those days, (they still have them in certain sections of the Christian church in Scotland – Communion season twice a year only). It used to begin on a Thursday and there would be meetings on Thursday, Friday, Saturday, Sunday, and then final meetings on the Monday.

Now in the month of June, 1630, John Livingstone and others were present at a Communion season in a place called Kirk-'o-Shotts, and it was decided that John Livingstone should be one of the preachers, the main preacher, in fact, on Monday June 21st. He was always a good, what they called solid, preacher, a man who expounded the Scriptures, knew the doctrines, was an able divider of the Scripture, and so on. And here he was, due to preach on this Monday. He tells the story of how between eight and nine o'clock in the morning he went out into the fields to pray and he was attacked by the devil who told him to go home, to disappear. Who was he, the devil asked, to preach to a great crowd of people? He was a good minister in an ordinary way but not the man for such an occasion. Livingstone was seriously tempted to go home or to get out of sight somewhere because he was afraid of this ordeal of preaching to such a number of people.

However, he overcame the attack of the devil and then the time came for him to preach and he took for his text, Ezekiel 36:25-26, on this very matter of the Holy Spirit. And he goes on to say that he preached for an hour and a half, and then he came to his application, which he had intended to be brief. An hour and a half of exposition outlining the doctrine, then application. But he suddenly found that there was something happening to him and the application which he had intended to be brief went on for another hour; and as it went on, astounding things were happening. People were falling to the ground, others breaking down weeping.

The end of the story was that it was estimated that at least five hundred people were converted as the result of that one sermon. When I say converted, I do not mean that they just came forward at the end. They did not do things like that in those days, there was no need, I do not mean that they signed some form. No, they were converted in the sense that their whole lives were changed and remained changed and they joined the Christian church with no pressure to decision brought upon them, none of the usual machinery that we have become so accustomed to – nothing like that at all. All that only began about the middle of the last century. But this was the power of the Spirit!

And what is so remarkable is that Livingstone never had a service like that again. It was the one and only time in his life. He lived many years afterwards but he never forgot that day and he constantly refers to it in his account of his life.

That is the kind of thing I mean. Here is a man, you see, taken up and suddenly enabled to speak with a power that he had never known before and that he never knew again. There is only one explanation of that – that is the Holy Spirit, that is the baptism of the Holy Spirit enabling a man to speak and to preach with power. I have already quoted some of the testimony of how Howell Harris, two hundred years ago in Wales, was baptized with the Spirit in that church tower, and you see it was as the result of that that this man began to speak with power.

This is what is so fascinating to me. Harris was a schoolmaster. He never intended being a preacher at all but was satisfied to continue teaching. But then, as you remember, he was converted and then after his conversion, and even after he had had assurance, about three weeks' later he had this great baptism which he always called his baptism with fire. Fire! The fire and the power, it does not matter which you call them. Call it power, call it fire, call it liberty.

Now this is how it worked in his case. He at once began to feel a concern for men and women who lived round and about him, his own mother and brothers and the people living in the neighbourhood, and he did not know what to do. He suddenly felt that he could at any rate go and visit the sick so he began to do so. Then he thought that was not enough, that he must try and help them in some way. He had got certain good pious books and he thought, well I will just go to these people and I will read these books to them. And he began to do it.

But the power of the reading of somebody else's book, somebody else's writing, was so great that people were convicted of sin and converted; and whenever it was heard that he was going to visit a sick person with one of his books, everybody crowded round, and they just sat and listened to this man reading, not even looking at the people, not preaching – reading out of books. And the power came upon them, and this was the thing that led eventually to his becoming a preacher and an evangelist.

We are all familiar with the power that from the very

beginning attended the preaching of George Whitefield. He knew that he had been called and sealed with the Spirit. He was aware of power, so that when he preached that first sermon of his in his own town, in the city of Gloucester, tremendous things took place and a complaint was made that fifteen people had been driven insane. And he was not preaching an evangelistic sermon, but preaching on the value of Christian fellowship; but such was the power.

Everybody knows the story of John Wesley, who could not be more learned but was so hopeless a preacher that he was no good at all. He was a miserable failure when he went out to Georgia in America, and he came back utterly disconsolate. Of course, he could always give a learned sermon but it was quite useless. But after that experience in Aldersgate Street, this man suddenly began to preach with power, he became an evangelist. Like the author of the epistle to the Hebrews he could say, 'Time would fail me…' but I am simply holding these things before you, my dear friends, to remind you of one thing only – the power of the Holy Ghost, this living power of the Holy Ghost.

You may have read the autobiography of Charles G. Finney where you will find the same thing. But let me tell you one other story. In 1857-59 there was a religious movement, a religious revival. It was in America in '57, in Northern Ireland in '58 and came over to Wales in '59. How do you explain a thing like this: this is a proof to you again of the power of the Spirit coming upon a man. There was a man, again a most ordinary preacher in Wales, of the name of David Morgan – and when I say ordinary I mean ordinary. He was a man of little ability and had had practically no training at all, but he was a good and godly man, who had started preaching when he was a carpenter and had eventually been set aside for the work of the ministry. This was the man who was used above all others in the Revival of 1859 in Wales, and this was his story.

He was in a meeting one night and was very moved, but he said to a friend later, 'I went to bed that night as usual, David Morgan. I had felt power in the service but I went to bed at night David Morgan. But,' he said, 'you know when I woke up the next morning I realized I was a different man. I felt like a lion, I felt great power.' He began to preach with tremendous power and it went on for two years.

Then he said to this same friend, 'One night I went to bed filled with this power that had accompanied me for two years, I woke up the next morning and found that I was David Morgan once more. 'And he continued to be David Morgan until he died about some fifteen years or so later.

Now there is only one way of explaining a thing like that. You see, that is the Holy Spirit coming upon a man and filling him, and then leaving him where he was before. It does not mean he had done anything wrong, it just means that the Spirit is Lord, he can give this power, and he can withdraw it.

I have referred several times to the story about D. L. Moody. That man was made what he was by the baptism that came to him on the street in New York City. Dr R. A. Torrey tells us exactly the same thing. His great missions were entirely the result of this. And if you have ever read the life of a man called Dr A. B. Simpson who started the Christian and Missionary Alliance you will find precisely the same thing there: again, an able and a learned man conscious that there was something ineffective about his work and ministry, who was then suddenly filled with the Spirit, with the result that his whole ministry was transformed and led to incalculable results.

You may say, 'Ah well, but all these men you have been dealing with have been exceptional men.' I grant that in certain ways they all were exceptional men by nature; but the point I am trying to establish is that that is not the thing that accounts for the fact that we know about them. We would never have heard of them were it not that the power of the Spirit had come upon them.

But I will tell you something much nearer to our own level. I do not believe I have ever stated this in public before but I do it to the glory of God and I do it in order to warn you beforehand against certain criticisms that people may make and comments like, 'Ah, this is only for exceptional people.' It is not.

I was in a prayer-meeting once which those of us who were in it will never forget. I remember very well that it was in the month of June. It was a Monday evening prayer-meeting which we had regularly in that church where I was then minister. We had had a remarkable Sunday in many ways, but we came to the meeting as usual and I had called upon somebody to open by reading Scripture and prayer: the meeting started at seven-fifteen. And this man had read the Scripture and had prayed, and another man had got up and prayed in the same way.

Then a third man got up to pray, a man we all knew very well, a simple man, a very ordinary man from the intellectual standpoint. Indeed I must say this, and he would not have resented it; he is no longer alive and his family would not mind. He was a man who had certain defects – as we all do – certain striking defects; a self-important little man, and a man whom we did not in any sense regard as either unusually spiritual or in any other way unusual, and I had heard this man pray many times.

However on this particular evening this man had not uttered more than two or three sentences before I was aware, and everybody else became aware, of something most extraordinary. He was normally halting, humble, pedestrian, ordinary; let me even use the word boring. But suddenly this man was entirely transformed; his voice deepened, a power came into it, even in his speech, and he prayed in the freest most powerful manner I think I have ever heard in my life.

And you can imagine what happened. The prayer-meeting continued without any intermission, and the freedom that had accompanied this man's prayer was given to all the others. And that went on until nine-fifty. I had not said a word, there was no hymn-singing, there was nothing. It was just this tremendous free power in prayer. One felt that one was outside time, that one was in heaven; one was really lifted up to the spiritual realm. And here I was listening to people whom I knew so well, praying with freedom and power and assurance; people who had never prayed in public in their lives before, and who had been terrified at the very thought of it, found themselves praying.

Well there it is. All I am concerned to put to you is this: do you know anything about this spiritual power, this spiritual realm? Is not this the thing that the church has lost? Is not this the thing that explains the state of the Christian church with all the talk about organizing and amalgamating and learning and this and that, how 'we' are going to put it right? You know when the Spirit of God comes even upon the most ordinary man he can make a giant out of him that can shake a meeting and pass on an inspiration to others and transform them. That is God's way; that is the Christian church; that is New Testament Christianity. It is the only Christianity that is worth talking about at all. This is the thing that is needed, and this is one of the manifestations of the baptism of the Holy Spirit.

Chapter 8

Gifts that Authenticate

The words to which I should like to call your attention are to be found in John 1: 26, 33 – 'John answered them, saying, I baptize with water: but there standeth one among you, whom ye know not.... And I knew him not: but he that sent me to baptize with water, the same said unto me, "Upon whom thou shalt see the Spirit descending, and remaining on him, the same is he which baptizeth with the Holy Ghost."'

The subject we are dealing with is this great matter of the baptism with the Holy Spirit. I am trying to show that this is what enables us as Christian people to represent our blessed Lord and Saviour, and God our Everlasting Father, in this world of sin and shame. We believe that this gospel of salvation is the supreme need of the world today, the supreme need of every individual, the only hope for the world at large. We are living in a world which is full of trouble and confusion; a world which has been trying to deal with and to solve its own problems throughout the centuries, and which is no nearer to solving them now than it was at the beginning; a world which, we believe, according to the teaching of Scripture, is under the wrath of God; a world which has turned away from God and brought down calamity and trouble upon itself; the only hope for such a world is in the gospel. And Christians are people who are called to be representatives of God's kingdom in that world. Endless statements to that effect can be found everywhere in the Bible.

The children of Israel, the Jews, were God's people and they were given the oracles of God. God gave the revelation to them in order that they might represent him before the nations of the world. And that is true of the Christian today; this is the business of the church, to tell the world as it is of this great and glorious salvation which is in Christ Jesus. He is the only hope of the world. There is no hope in men. The only hope is in the Son of God, and our business is to represent him, to glorify him among the people of the world, to magnify his name, to show them the excellencies of his person and of his great salvation; that is our business, we alone do that in this world. The church is to preach Christ, and him crucified, as the only hope, the only Saviour of the world; to declare that 'there is none other name under heaven given among men, whereby we must be saved' (Acts 4:12), and Christian people alone have that message, and they alone can present it to the world. The world does not know this message, it does not believe – that is the cause of its trouble. So we are called uniquely to bear witness to Jesus Christ and to magnify him.

But the question is: how can we do that? We are aware of the facts concerning him but he himself has taught that that is not sufficient. Christ tells even those trained apostles, his disciples who had been with him throughout his earthly ministry and had seen his death and burial, and were witnesses of his resurrection with their naked eyes, he tells them: 'Tarry ye in the city of Jerusalem until ye be endued with power from on high' (Luke 24:49). And on the day of Pentecost he sent that power upon them in a baptism of the Holy Spirit. And so we are trying to show that the central, main object of the baptism with the Holy Spirit is to enable us with the power to be witnesses to the Lord Jesus

Christ, to his person, and to his work. And therefore there is nothing more important at the present hour than that we should understand this teaching.

We shall now spend some time considering what are the evidences of this baptism with the Spirit. I have divided them into two main categories: those which are more or less internal and subjective, known mainly to the man or woman himself or herself; and those which are more objective in their character and therefore visible to others. Obviously the objective evidences of the baptism are of vital importance in this whole matter of witness and of testimony.

One of the objective results of the baptism with the Spirit is at times seen even in a person's facial appearance, a kind of transfiguration, some reflection of the glory of God. As the face of Moses shone when he came down from the mountain having been with God, so there is something of this in the Christian. 'We all,' says Paul in 2 Corinthians 3:18, 'with open face beholding as in a glass the glory of the Lord, are changed into the same image from glory to glory, even as by the Spirit of the Lord.'

Let us next consider the evidence of the baptism with the Spirit as it shows itself in speech. The first great characteristic here is the power and the ability that is given not only in preaching but in ordinary conversation and in prayer. There are still people, I find, who seem to think that what we are talking about is only for certain special people. Now, that is a complete fallacy, for the New Testament offers this to all and indicates clearly that this is possible to all. We must be clear about this. This baptism is not only for certain special people, and the Bible gives no such teaching. 'For the promise is unto you, and to your children, and to all that are afar off (Acts 2:39). There are many illustrations, as we have seen, which show that ordinary unknown people can know this glorious experience in the same way as outstanding and distinguished people can. The devil would rob us of the most glorious aspects of the Christian faith. Let us therefore concentrate with all our powers as we study this together, lest he rob us of something that God is offering to us.

A further evidence of this baptism is the note of authority. Now this, of course, was the thing that struck people about our blessed Lord himself, though he was a carpenter and though he was, as judged by the world, a mere nobody. Yet when he began to speak they were struck at once by the way in which his teaching differed from that of the Pharisees and scribes. They said, 'This man speaketh and teacheth with authority, not as the Pharisees and scribes', and that was the great characteristic of his ministry.

But, do not forget, even the Lord, the Son of God incarnate, was not able to commence his ministry until he had been baptized with the Spirit at his baptism with water in the Jordan by John the Baptist. That is why the apostle John puts it here. John the Baptist had been told: 'He that sent me to baptize with water, the same said unto me, Upon whom thou shalt see the Spirit descending, and remaining on him, the same is he which baptizeth with the Holy Ghost' (John 1:33) – And you remember what our Lord did when he went back after that to his home town of Nazareth, and went into the synagogue on the Sabbath day. He was given the Book to read and he began to speak. The passage which he read was that famous passage from Isaiah 61: 'The Spirit of the Lord God is upon me; because the Lord hath anointed me to preach good tidings unto the meek.' The anointing took place when the Holy Spirit descended upon him in the form of a dove at his baptism in the Jordan, and from that moment this authority appeared and it was evident to all.

This authority is something that was equally clear and evident in the apostles after their baptism with the Spirit. The contrast in the case of Peter is so striking. Read his sermon on the day of Pentecost, as recorded in Acts 2, and you are struck by the authority with which he spoke and taught that congregation and expounded the scriptures. There was no hesitation, no fumbling; yet this is the same man who, with the other disciples, could not at first even believe the report about the resurrection. Read the last chapter of Luke's gospel and you will find that when the women who had gone early to the tomb came back and reported to these very disciples the fact that they had found that tomb to be empty, they met with this reaction: 'Their words seemed to them as idle tales, and they believed them not' (Luke 24:11). The apostles were clearly muddled in their whole understanding of the Old Testament scriptures. But here is one of those men now speaking and expounding the scriptures with authority. This is always one of the results of the baptism with the Spirit.

And you get exactly the same thing in the case of the apostle Paul. There are such endless examples of this that one scarcely knows which to select. Let me give you one example from Acts 13 concerning the apostle Paul, on his first missionary journey in Cyprus. Paul began to preach and the chief man of the island was listening to him, but he had another man with him called 'Elymas the sorcerer'. Sergius Paulus, a prudent man, the governor, was very ready to listen, 'But Elymas the sorcerer withstood them, seeking to turn away the deputy from the faith. Then Saul, (who also is called Paul), filled with the Holy Ghost' (Acts 13:8-9). Now that was something that happened at that moment to him. It does not mean that he was always so filled with the Holy Spirit. He was given special authority and power.

You find that being repeated right through the book of Acts. We are told of the disciples and others that they were 'filled with the Spirit' on the day of Pentecost. Then in chapter 4 Peter and John were on trial and had been commanded 'not to speak at all nor teach in the name of Jesus' (Acts 4:18). Threatened with extermination, they went back and they prayed to God, and God again sent the Spirit upon them, and they were filled again. And in the passage in

Acts 13 Paul was given a special filling, another baptism, if you like, of power and authority. So you read this (verses 9-11): 'Then Saul, (who is also called Paul), filled with the Holy Ghost, set his eyes on him, And said, O full of all subtilty and all mischief, thou child of the devil, thou enemy of all righteousness, wilt thou not cease to pervert the right ways of the Lord? And now, behold, the hand of the Lord is upon thee, and thou shalt be blind, not seeing the sun for a season. And immediately there fell on him a mist and a darkness; and he went about seeking some to lead him by the hand.'

Now there, you see, is the authority, there is no hesitation. The Apostle knew. And all these men always knew. They had this authority in speech, they had this authority in performing miracles: it is always a characteristic. And as you read again the subsequent history of the church you will find that this authority invariably characterizes these people. You get it in every revival, you get it in great reformations. What was it that enabled Martin Luther to stand alone – alone against fifteen centuries of tradition with all the ecclesiastics against him? To stand alone and say, 'Here I stand, I can do no other, so help me God'? That is authority, and it has always characterized men who have received the baptism of the Spirit. And this is true not only in public declaration; the same assurance is evident in all people who know this experience.

The last thing I mention under this heading of objective evidence is boldness and fearlessness. This is very striking, and is again seen perhaps most perfectly in the instance of the apostle Peter himself. Peter was by nature a very impulsive man. He had a kind of boldness, too, but it was a natural boldness with a good deal of the braggart in it. When our Lord was taken captive and set on trial, and a serving maid recognized Peter and said, 'You were one of them; you were with this Galilaean', Peter you remember denied him; he denied him three times.

Why did he do that? Well, he was afraid, he was a coward trying to save his own skin, he did not want to be put to death. So he denied his Lord whom he had heard and whom he had seen performing these mighty miracles; he denied him in order to save his own life. And yet the moment he is baptized with the Spirit, you see him standing up and addressing that crowd at Jerusalem with fearlessness and boldness, charging them with sin, bringing the message home to them, afraid of no one and of nothing. What a contrast!

Again, we read in Acts 4 that Peter was himself on trial – the very thing he was so afraid of before the baptism with the Spirit. We are told that the authorities 'laid hands on them, and put them in hold unto the next day' (verse 3). Here are Peter and John they are on trial, and then in verse 8 you read: 'Then Peter, filled with the Holy Ghost' – now that was another enduement, that was something special, the Spirit came upon him again with unusual power – 'said unto them, Ye rulers of the people, and elders of Israel, If we this day be examined of the good deed done to the impotent man, by what means he is made whole; Be it known unto you all, and to all the people of Israel, that by the name of Jesus Christ of Nazareth, whom ye crucified, whom God raised from the dead, even by him doth this man stand here before you whole' (verses 8-10). Boldness! Fearlessness!

This is what the Holy Spirit does to a man. And you find the same thing later on in that chapter, when again the authorities 'commanded them not to speak at all nor teach in the name of Jesus. But Peter and John answered and said unto them, Whether it be right in the sight of God to hearken unto you more than unto God, judge ye. For we cannot but speak the things which we have seen and heard' (verses 18-20). Now this is obviously one of the great characteristics of the baptism with the Spirit, it gives this boldness and fearlessness.

Let me give you one other example because, my dear friends, if we are not thrilled by this kind of thing, if we do not feel that there is something wrong with us, that we know nothing about this quality, well then, I say, we are almost beyond hope. Read on... 'Then Peter and the other apostles answered and said' – and they are before the court again – 'We ought to obey God rather than men. The God of our fathers raised up Jesus, whom ye slew and hanged on a tree. Him hath God exalted with his right hand to be a Prince and a Saviour, for to give repentance to Israel, and forgiveness of sins. And we are his witnesses of these things; and so is also the Holy Ghost, whom God hath given to them that obey him' (Acts 5:29-32).

Well there it is in the Scripture, and in the long annals of the Christian church is there anything comparable to the way in which the saints of God have been given this same boldness and fearlessness? We know of some of the great notable examples, and for myself these are the things in which I glory, these heroes of the Christian faith defying kings, emperors, princes, the great ones of the world, speaking the truth of God and the truth concerning the Lord Jesus Christ. Think of those early martyrs and confessors, think of those men who were not afraid of a Nero. They would not be subjugated and subdued, they defied him and were ready to be cast to the lions in the arena, praising God that at last they had been accounted worthy to suffer for his name's sake. And down the ages they come, these glorious men, standing up, fighting, defying the 'lion's gory mane' and every principality and power.

But let us not forget this. Among them were large numbers of ordinary common people. As Gray puts it in his 'Elegy in a Country Churchyard', 'Some village Hampden, some unknown Milton' – nobody knows their names. But there have been ordinary men and women who have had to do this very thing and have been threatened with losing their work turned out of their cottage homes where they and their ancestors had lived for centuries – turned out for one reason only, that they had become Protestants. The annals of the church are full of stories of such people. We do not know their names but we know of them – the common people.

This has been one of the most glorious things in the long history of the Christian church. Boldness! Fearlessness! Not foolhardiness remember, not being ridiculous, but always being ready to give a reason for the hope that is in you, with confidence, with assurance; not allowing yourself to be intimidated by any earthly human power. Your loyalty is to him, and you have been given such a knowledge of him and of his love to you that you are ready to declare it with boldness and fearlessness whatever the consequences may be.

And this is still happening today, even in our own age. We thank God for the martyrs in the Congo, many of whom went through this very experience. It was their boldness, their fearlessness that was such an offence to others. There are endless illustrations which one could give. I have known such people myself, friends who passed through a similar experience with the Communists in China in the 1920s. As long as I live I will never forget hearing Mr and Mrs Porteous of the China Inland Mission telling how with guns facing them and expecting certain death they asked that they might just be allowed to sing before they died. Their request was granted and they sang, 'And I shall see Him face to face, and tell the story, Saved by grace'. God in his mercy used that opportunity to lead to their release and their freedom.

These then are some of the external signs of the baptism in the Spirit and they are clear and obvious to all. I have considered them each in turn so that we all may examine ourselves and ask the question: Is there something about me that makes this impression upon men and women? I am a Christian, as these people were, but is there that quality about me which makes such an impact, leading men and women to consider these matters?

We come now to another division of the work of the Holy

Spirit. I confess freely that it is beyond any question the most difficult aspect of the whole subject, and yet we must deal honestly with it because it is in the Scriptures. It is the question of the gifts of the Holy Spirit which result from the baptism with the Spirit. The issue is not an easy one mainly because it is controversial. It has certain inherent difficulties, which often arise because of our ignorance of the spiritual realm, but at this time it is a very important matter for two main reasons. The first is that we need some supernatural authentication of our message; and secondly, it is important because of the danger attending it, because of the enemy, who can counterfeit to such an extent as almost to deceive, according to our Lord and Saviour, 'even the very elect themselves'. This is our Lord's own teaching and warning in Matthew 24:24. He says: 'They shall shew great signs and wonders' – lying signs and wonders, which are so clever and subtle – 'that if it were possible, they shall deceive the very elect' themselves.

On the first point, it is becoming clear to everybody – at least it should be – that the Christian church today is failing, and failing lamentably. It is not enough even to be orthodox. You must, of course, be orthodox, otherwise you have not got a message. People are not going to listen to our speculation; they can speculate themselves. People want a word of authority. This has always been so through the ages and we have seen how people recognize this authority. We need authority and we need authentication. It is not enough merely that we state these things and demonstrate them and put them logically. All that is essential but it is not enough. Is it not clear that we are living in an age when we need some special authentication – in other words, we need revival.

Indeed, we are not only confronted by materialism, worldliness, indifference, hardness, and callousness – but we are also hearing more and more, both directly and in the media, about certain manifestations of the powers of evil and the reality of evil spirits. It is not merely sin that is constituting a problem in this country today. There is also a recrudescence of black magic and devil worship and the powers of darkness as well as drug taking and some of the things it leads to. This is why I believe we are in urgent need of some manifestation, some demonstration, of the power of the Holy Spirit.

In the New Testament and, indeed, in the whole of the Bible, we are taught that the baptism with the Spirit is attended by certain gifts. Joel in his prophecy, quoted by Peter on the day of Pentecost, foretells this: 'And it shall come to pass in the last days, saith God, that I will pour out my Spirit upon all flesh: and your sons and your daughters shall prophesy, and your young men shall see visions, and your old men shall dream dreams: And on my servants and on my handmaidens I will pour out in those days of my Spirit; and they shall prophesy: And I will shew wonders in heaven above and signs in the earth beneath' (Acts 2:17). Joel, and the other prophets who also spoke of it, indicated that in the age which was to come, and which came with the Lord Jesus Christ and the baptism with the Spirit on the day of Pentecost, there should be some unusual authentication of the message.

And as we see in John 14 our Lord himself prophesied this. In reasoning with the unbelieving, he said: 'If you do not believe me, if you do not believe my words then believe me for the very works' sake.' The Lord's miracles were signs, for that is the term used in the gospel of John with respect to them. The miracles were not only done as acts of kindness. The main reason for them was that they should be 'signs', authentications of who he was.

Our Lord makes this clear when he says: 'Believe me that I am in the Father, and the Father in me: or else believe me for the very works' sake.' And then he goes on: 'I say unto you, He that believeth on me, the works that I do shall he do also;

and greater works than these shall he do; because I go unto my Father' (John 14:11-12).

Our Lord constantly used this very argument. For instance, when John the Baptist sent two of his disciples to him asking: 'Art thou he that should come, or do we look for another?, Jesus answered and said unto them, Go and shew John again those things which ye do hear and see: The blind receive their sight, and the lame walk, the lepers are cleansed, and the deaf hear, the dead are raised up, and the poor have the gospel preached to them. And blessed is he, whosoever shall not be offended in me' (Matthew 11:3-6).

It is clear, then, from all the teaching leading up to the book of Acts that this was to be expected. And as soon as you look at Acts itself, you find the evidence there in great profusion. From the opening chapters we read of 'cloven tongues as of fire', visible signs, miracles of various descriptions, prophetic utterances and so on. Such manifestations of the Spirit run right through the book of Acts. But what is interesting is that they are not confined to Acts. You find exactly the same thing being taught in the various epistles. Take, for instance, the famous passage in 1 Corinthians from chapter 12 right to the end of chapter 14. These chapters deal exclusively with this great matter, showing that in the church at Corinth, as in all the other churches, this kind of thing was taking place and so the apostle has to deal with the situation.

And, indeed, in 2 Corinthians 12:12 where the whole question of his being an apostle has been raised by certain enemies and detractors, Paul writes: 'Truly the signs of an apostle were wrought among you in all patience, in signs and wonders, and mighty deeds.' The apostle's ministry was authenticated in that way.

And then in Galatians 3:2 he says: 'This only would I learn of you, Received ye the Spirit by the works of the law, or by the hearing of faith?' And then in verse 5: 'He therefore that ministereth to you the Spirit, and worketh miracles among you, doeth he it by the works of the law, or by the hearing of faith?' Now the apostle says that the Spirit came upon those who had believed by faith. It is to believers that the Spirit is given in this way in baptism. The result was that God ministered the Spirit to them and miracles were being worked among them, and the apostle uses the same argument in that respect.

Let me give you a final illustration of what I am trying to show from Hebrews 2:3-4. The author talks about the gospel 'which at the first began to be spoken by the Lord, and was confirmed unto us by them that heard him; God also bearing them witness, both with signs and wonders, and with divers miracles, and gifts of the Holy Ghost, according to his own will?'

I am simply trying to establish the point that it is perfectly clear that in New Testament times, the gospel was authenticated in this way by signs, wonders and miracles of various characters and descriptions. And you cannot begin to understand the New Testament, the epistles as well as the book of Acts without holding that fact in your mind and seeing that that is clearly the case.

Now I believe I am right in saying that everyone who is a Christian in any sense at all is prepared to believe and to accept that these things happened, but it is here that the vital question arises – do we accept it as being only true of the early church? Was it only meant to be true of the early church? This is the question to which we must now address ourselves. There are many people who teach that. They say, 'Of course I accept the whole of that evidence' – though they may try to water even that down. I have known people who have tried to explain away things that are clearly miraculous – the cloven tongues of fire, and the speaking in other languages on the day of Pentecost. I have heard men using the greatest ingenuity to try to explain it all away, claiming some knowledge which they have just received about some odd dialects and so on.

But I am not wasting my time with that kind of argument. I am dealing with people who say, 'Of course I accept everything that I find in the New Testament. I am sure it is historical and that these things actually happened. But that really does not apply to us now, it was only meant for that time'. They may also suggest that all this was really meant as a sign to convince the unbelieving Jews. Take our Lord's answer to John the Baptist. John was a typical Jew and our Lord says to him, 'Look the signs that were prophesied are taking place, there is your answer.' And this leads those people to say that all these signs and miracles in the New Testament period were solely designed to appeal to the Jews and to convince them.

For example, one writer actually says that after our Lord's own failure in his teaching – he came to found the kingdom and hoped he would persuade the Jews to follow him, but he did not succeed and they put him to death – the church was a kind of afterthought and God then made his last effort on the day of Pentecost in the sending of this miraculous power among the apostles. It was the final appeal to the Jews.

As a result of accepting this interpretation, when they come to the disciples in Acts 19, whom Paul came across at Ephesus and to whom he put the question: 'Did you receive the Holy Ghost when you believed?', they have to say, 'Of course, these again were obviously Jews', although there is not a word to support this assumption. In fact, most authorities are agreed that these people almost certainly had some connection with Alexandria in Egypt. Certainly that was the case, as we know, with regard to Apollos. However, they do not hesitate to state quite dogmatically that these people were Jews, and that because of that they were given the particular sign of tongues in order to convince them.

Another way in which the argument is put is to agree that those extraordinary signs were given then, but that was because it was the beginning of the Christian church, and God, as it were, did the unusual to get the church going. They say that the same kind of thing happened in the Old Testament at the beginning of the great line of prophets, in Elijah and Elisha, where you read that they performed certain miracles. These expositors maintain that you always tend to get this sort of thing at the beginning of a work, but that of course you do not expect it to go on. It is like a father setting up his son by giving him a farm or a business. He puts a sum of money in the bank for him and then says, 'get on with it'. He does not go on giving him these gifts, after setting him up, this is something unusual and exceptional at the beginning of a work. So they say that these things did happen, but it was only meant to mark the beginning of the dispensation.

Another argument is that these things happened, these signs were given and so unusual powers and manifestations did occur, but only until the New Testament canon was completed. When the church began Christians did not have the New Testament epistles. But we have them, we have the full truth in the words of Scripture, which we can read, study, expound, and understand. The early church could not do that, so God gave revelations to apostles and to prophets and to certain other people at certain times; they were dependent upon this direct message and teaching. But the moment the church was given the Scriptures, all that was no longer necessary. We have got the truth so you do not need anything miraculous or supernatural.

These expositors are particularly fond of arguing that point in terms of 1 Corinthians 13. One writer actually puts it like this: 'After the Scriptures were completed these supernatural signs ceased.' He makes a dogmatic pronouncement, and says that they ceased because they were no longer necessary once we had the Scriptures. The argument which they try to put forward is as follows: Paul says in 1 Corinthians 13:8-10: 'Charity never faileth: but whether there be prophecies, they shall fail; whether there be tongues, they shall cease; whether there be knowledge, it shall vanish away. For we know in part, and we prophesy in part. But when that which is perfect is come, then that which is in part shall be done away.'

They argue that 'that which is perfect' is the giving of the New Testament Scriptures and once they were given 'that which is in part shall be done away.' 1 Corinthians 13:11 continues: 'When I was a child, I spake as a child, I understood as a child, I thought as a child: but when I became a man, I put away childish things' – such as prophecy and speaking in tongues and miracles and things like that – 'I put away childish things.' 'For now', Paul goes on, 'we see through a glass, darkly; but then face to face.' That is, they maintain, when you get the Scriptures: 'Now I know in part; but then shall I know even as also I am known.'

For the proponents of this view all this means that until the Scriptures came knowledge was very partial and the apostle is quite clearly saying here that all these partial supernatural manifestations belong to the realm of childish things which will vanish away when the perfection and the fullness comes, and that did come when the New Testament canon was completed. Added to this they produce a subsidiary argument and go so far as to say that even in the New Testament itself you have clear evidence that these things were already passing away. They cite the fact that Paul could not heal Timothy and has to tell him to take a little wine for his stomach's sake, that Trophimus was left sick and ill at Miletum, that Gaius was not healed, and that Epaphroditus was desperately ill, 'nigh unto death', but that the Lord had had mercy upon him and that he had got well again. They say therefore that even in the New Testament itself you see these things passing—starting on the day of Pentecost in great fullness, but gradually disappearing as you go on in the New Testament.

And so they come to a final conclusion, which they state with the utmost confidence and dogmatism, that after the coming of the New Testament canon all these gifts were entirely withdrawn.

There, then, is an outline of the argument that is being put forward at the present time, and which has been put forward very largely during this present century. Let me begin to answer it by giving you just one thought at this point. It is this: the Scriptures never anywhere say that these things were only temporary – never! There is no such statement anywhere. 'Ah but', says somebody, 'what about that passage from 1 Corinthians 13?' Well, I would have thought that that chapter is sufficient answer in and of itself to this particular criticism. You see what we are asked to believe by that kind of exposition? We are told that the coming of the New Testament Scriptures puts us into a place of perfection; whereas if you look at verse 12 it actually says: 'For now we see' – that is the apostle and others. The apostle is included with all other Christian believers before the New Testament canon, much of which was written by Paul himself, had been completed. We read: 'Now we see through a glass, darkly; but then' – when the Scriptures have come and are complete – 'face to face: Now I know in part; but then' – which they say means the completion of the Scriptures – 'shall I know even as also I am known.'

You see what that involves? It means that you and I, who have the Scriptures open before us, know much more than the apostle Paul of God's truth. That is what it means and nothing less, if that argument is correct. It means that we are altogether superior to the early church and even to the apostles themselves, including the apostle Paul! It means that we are now in a position in which we know 'face to face' that 'we know, even as also we are known' by God because we have the Scriptures. It is surely unnecessary to say more.

What the apostle is, of course, dealing with in

1 Corinthians 13 is the contrast between the highest and the best that the Christian can ever know in this world and in this life and what he will know in the glory everlasting. The 'now' and the 'then' are not the time before and after the Scriptures were given, because that, as I have said, puts us in a position entirely superior to the apostles and prophets who are the foundation of the Christian church and on whose very work we have to rely. It is inconsistent, and contradictory – indeed, there is only one word to describe such a view, it is nonsense. The 'then' is the glory everlasting. It is only then that I shall know, even as also I am known; for then we shall see him as he is. It will be direct and 'face to face'. No longer, as Paul puts it again in 2 Corinthians 3:18 – as an image or a reflection, but direct, absolute, full and perfect knowledge.

So you see the difficulties men land themselves in when they dislike something and cannot fully understand it and try to explain it away. All things must be judged in the light of the Scriptures, and we must not twist them to suit our theory or argument. Let me finish with this general statement – there is nothing in the Scripture itself which says that these things are to end, and further, every attempt to make the Scriptures say that leads to the same dismal, impossible conclusions that we have already seen in the case of 1 Corinthians 13.

My friends, this is to me one of the most urgent matters at this hour. With the church as she is and the world as it is, the greatest need today is the power of God through his Spirit in the church that we may testify not only to the power of the Spirit, but to the glory and the praise of the one and only Saviour, Jesus Christ our Lord, Son of God, Son of Man.

Chapter 9

'As the Spirit Wills'

We have been considering those words of John the Baptist when he proclaimed the One who would baptize with the Holy Spirit. In these verses John the Baptist indicates what is to be the outstanding characteristic of the age of the Lord Jesus Christ and of his ministry. It is, therefore, something which we should be clear about in our minds as it obviously controls the whole of the New Testament teaching. And so we have been looking at it and examining the teaching that we have here concerning it which is abundantly confirmed in the subsequent history of the Christian church.

Now this is of importance to us for so many reasons. Primarily I would suggest that we must be concerned about this, because we as Christian people are to be concerned about the state of the world in which we live and the state of the church. The church seems so weak and ineffective in this modern world, and so filled with troubles that the problem of what we can do about the situation should be uppermost in the minds of all Christian people.

We read the New Testament and we see the great power that was given to the early apostles and disciples. Their world was very similar to ours: we recognize the sin and aberrations, the perversions and the foulness, the moral degradation that we read of in parts of the New Testament. And yet we find that just a handful of simple, unlettered, ignorant men and women were able, not only to make an impact upon that world, but to influence it and to influence it profoundly. The explanation is, of course, that they were baptized with the Holy Spirit. What John the Baptist prophesied, what our Lord himself prophesied, literally came to pass. And the only explanation of the New Testament church and the astounding things that she was enabled to do in later centuries is this power that was given by the baptism with the Holy Spirit. As we have seen it is essentially something that is given to enable us to witness: 'Ye shall receive power…', says our Lord, 'and ye shall be witnesses unto me' (Acts 1:8). Its primary object is to make us witnesses, people who testify to God and his redeeming grace in and through our blessed Lord and Saviour. Our Lord said of the Spirit, 'He shall glorify me.' Not himself. And the business of the witness is to bear witness to the Lord Jesus Christ as the Son of God and the only Saviour. And now we have come to this great question of the gifts, the spiritual gifts which are given by the Spirit to men and women in order to enable them to become witnesses.

This is not only a great subject, it has, alas, also become a controversial one, and that is why we must examine it very carefully. There is teaching about this in Scripture and it is our business to know the Scriptures and to expound them. We must not side-step anything taught in the Scriptures as being too difficult or controversial. We must examine it in the Spirit, not to prove our case or our point, but to arrive at a knowledge of the truth that we may glorify our Lord and, through him, glorify God, the Eternal Father.

At the present time there is a new interest in this matter in the United States and in this country, and in many other parts of the world, and it behoves us as Christian people to clarify our minds, to seek a true understanding in the light of the scriptural teaching. That is what we are now trying to do, and we are endeavouring to do it thoroughly. I do not believe in short cuts or glib answers; they are never satisfactory. They always leave something out of account. So let us go on quietly, and let us pray God to give us the spirit of understanding that we may lay hold on these things which clearly are difficult. That is why they had to be dealt with in epistles in the first century, and it is still as essential today that these matters should be understood at the present time.

We saw earlier that some people believe that the gifts were withdrawn when the New Testament canon was complete. Some of them go so far as to say that church history shows clearly that these gifts were withdrawn; and some say quite dogmatically that they have never occurred since – that there has literally been no miracle since these New Testament times. And there are those who actually go further – I have read a number of their booklets recently – and say beyond any question that what are claimed to be manifestations of the gifts of the Spirit are nothing but the manifestations of 'devilish power'. And they say that in cold print! Christian people actually write and publish these things.

But they base it on this argument and in this they are quite logical. They say all this was only meant for the time of the New Testament church and finished then, therefore anything that may appear to be a supernatural gift since then must of necessity be 'of the devil', a counterfeit, something to be avoided as the very plague itself, and indeed, something which is extremely dangerous.

We have already dealt with the wrong interpretation of 1 Corinthians 13 but we must go on with this argument so that this most important point may be made very clear. If these people are right and these gifts were only meant for that particular time and that can be proved, then there is no need to say any more. However, I want to suggest to you that that is not the case. Take the argument that the gifts were meant only for the Jews. It seems to me that the book of Acts is sufficient in and of itself to give us an answer – an answer that is also supported in the epistles.

Let me explain.... The book of Acts shows very clearly that many miracles were performed among the Gentiles as 'signs'. Indeed, reading Acts I cannot see how anybody can come to any conclusion but this – that generally speaking when he was dealing with Jews the apostle Paul 'reasoned with them from the scriptures'. For instance, there is a perfect illustration of that in Acts 17, where we are told how Paul, when he arrived at Thessalonica, went into the synagogue of the Jews. Then we read: 'And Paul, as his manner was, went in unto them, and three sabbath days reasoned with them out of the scriptures, opening and alleging, that Christ must needs have suffered, and risen again from the dead; and that this Jesus, whom I preach unto you, is Christ' (verses 2-3).

That is obviously a very reasonable procedure. Here were Jews who boasted in their Old Testament Scriptures, so the Apostle simply shows them 'out of the scriptures' that Jesus is the Christ, and that it was prophesied that the Christ was not going to be a great military conqueror, but that he was going to be one who was going to suffer, be 'led as a lamb to the slaughter'. The Apostle almost invariably approached Jews in this way. It was what our Lord himself had done after his resurrection with the disciples themselves. They had been stumbled by the cross, so our Lord took them through the prophets and Moses and the Psalms, and demonstrated to them from the Scriptures.

When dealing with a Jew who has got the Scriptures and who knows them, that is obviously the procedure to adopt, and that is what the apostles did. But when you are dealing with Gentiles you cannot do that, because they do not know the Scriptures, and do not have the same background. You can only begin to do that with them after a while, after you have given them instruction concerning the Old Testament

Scriptures. So what we find is that when the apostles work amongst the Gentiles they generally work large numbers of miracles.

There are many examples of this such as Acts 14 when Paul is in Lystra and Acts 16 where Paul at Philippi ministered to the girl with a spirit of divination. Then in Acts 19 there is a most interesting phrase which is used about Paul at Ephesus: 'God wrought special miracles by the hands of Paul' (verse 11). Now that was in a Gentile community, so this idea that such signs were only for the Jews seems to me to be something that simply cannot be substantiated at all from the book of Acts – indeed it is almost the exact opposite as one would expect. It seems that this great profusion of miracles was wrought among Gentiles, who could not be reasoned with out of the Scriptures because they did not know them. Without the authority of Scripture they needed this other authentication. And indeed we read further about Paul: 'So that from his body were brought unto the sick handkerchiefs or aprons, and the diseases departed from them, and the evil spirits went out of them' (verse 12), and it led to that trouble which ended in a riot in Ephesus.

Then take another statement which is based upon the fact that these things are not mentioned in the pastoral epistles or in what are regarded as the later epistles of the apostle Paul. Some people deduce that they are not mentioned because they had already disappeared. Now this, it seems to me, is a most dangerous argument. It is what is called the argument from silence. Because the apostle, in the pastoral epistles and in epistles like that to the Colossians, does not deal with the question of the gifts as he does in 1 Corinthians, it is presumed that these gifts had already been withdrawn even before the end of the New Testament canon.

Let me give you just one illustration of what I mean. I read an article on this very subject recently which shows how men with a bias and a prejudice are so governed by it that they read things into the Scriptures which are not there and so draw their false deductions. Let me quote from that article: 'St. Paul indeed hardly mentions the gift' – the writer is dealing with 'tongues' in particular – 'except to try to regulate the behaviour of those who possess it and to check its misuse.' Then he goes on: 'It was no doubt this that led him to relegate the gift to the bottom of the list of charismata and to urge his readers to try and get it in perspective.' All right. But then he says, 'To him it was permissible rather than desirable.' 'Permissible rather than desirable!' But the Apostle says himself quite clearly in 1 Corinthians 14, 'I would that ye all spake in tongues.' Now that is not merely permissible; that is desirable! The writer goes on to say this: 'Is there any significance in the fact that the Corinthian Church, where alone it appears that the practice prevailed....' You see, he is assuming, because it is not mentioned concerning the other churches, that it did not occur there. Now that is nothing but argument from silence. It is deduction. But let us go on. 'Is there any significance in the fact that the Corinthian Church, where alone it appears that the practice prevailed, was morally and spiritually the least mature in the early Christian communities?' There is no evidence at all for saying that. We do not know that the Corinthian church was the 'least mature'. There is evidence to suggest that the churches at Thessalonica and in Galatia were equally immature.

This is all pure conjecture; it is reading into the Scriptures in order to substantiate your particular prejudice. The writer proceeds, 'I know St. Paul said, "Thank God I am more gifted in ecstatic utterance than any of you"' – but Paul did not actually say that, he said 'speak in tongues' (1 Corinthians 14:18). Some would say that it is not 'ecstatic utterance'. I happen to agree with the interpretation, which says that it is ecstatic utterance but it should not be used as if it were a translation. The writer is now putting in 'ecstatic utterance' in the place of 'other tongues' – he goes on: '...but was the inference not simply that he knew what he was talking about when he urged his readers not to set great store on this gift?' I suggest that it means much more than that and I hope to deal with that later on.

'I do not know', this man continues quite honestly, 'I would not like to dogmatize' – and yet that is what he has been doing, for this is what we all tend to do – 'but at least I have never had these questions answered in a really satisfactory way.'

It seems to me that the answer is in the Scriptures themselves – and that if you take them as they are, you find that you are not entitled to make these statements. 'I would that ye all spake in tongues.' Not permissible only but even desirable! Again, 'Forbid not', Paul says, 'to speak in tongues.' I suggest, then, that when he says: 'I thank God, I speak in tongues more than you all', he is not merely claiming that he knows more about this than they do in a sense of having knowledge about it, he is in fact claiming something experiential and experimental.

So we must beware that we do not try to avoid these things or get rid of them merely by making assumptions. It is always most dangerous to deduce something merely from silence. The epistles were all written for a specific purpose. In Corinth there was a great deal of confusion because of the gifts and the Apostle deals with it at great length. In other churches the gifts were present with equal profusion as suggested by 1 Corinthians 1:47 and 1 Thessalonians 5:19-21, but because they were not being misunderstood and because people were not getting too excited about them there was no need to deal with the question. So the explanation of why these things are not mentioned in other places is probably that they did not constitute problems.

We must get one thing clear in our minds. These epistles were not written as textbooks on theology or on the doctrine of the church. They were all written to meet some particular situation. Take for instance the epistle to the Colossians. Now there the big problem was the philosophical speculations that were coming in. So the Apostle deals with that. He does not set down on paper a complete treatise on the whole of church doctrine. The apostles were busy men, travelling and evangelizing and they wrote their letters to deal with particular problems as they arose; and if you bear that in mind, you will have a new and a fresh understanding of all these epistles. In Galatia the great question was that of circumcision, but it was not the only problem. As I have already quoted from Galatians 3:2,5, the apostle refers, just in passing, to the fact that miracles were being worked there. But whereas there were problems in the Corinthian church over gifts, Paul does not have to deal with any problems arising from the miracles, as far as the churches in Galatia were concerned.

So the principle is, be careful lest you base your argument solely on this argument from silence. It is a notorious trap. It has accounted for many heresies throughout the centuries. We must take the Scriptures as a whole, and, as I have been trying to remind you, the background to the whole of the New Testament writings is the history of the Acts of the Apostles. You must not found your doctrine on the epistles only. The epistles are to be read in the light of the history that is given us so plainly in Acts.

Let us, then, go on to another argument. We read that Timothy is exhorted to 'take a little wine for his stomach's sake' instead of being miraculously healed, that 'Trophimus was left sick at Miletum', that 'Epaphroditus had been desperately ill so that they had even despaired of his life and feared that he was on the verge of death'. The argument based on these facts is that miracles had obviously been withdrawn, or these men would have been healed at once; there would have been no need to give medical advice to Timothy and this kind of prescription would have been quite unnecessary.

Now that is the assumption. But the New Testament nowhere tells us that sickness must always be healed, and always be healed miraculously. Some people who believe that these gifts are permanent and who claim miraculous healing today go so far as to say a Christian should never be ill and that he should always be healed miraculously. The other extreme is to assume that the fact that these men were not immediately healed is proof that the miraculous was immediately withdrawn.

Both these views are guilty of the same error, which is to assume that in the New Testament any Christian taken ill should be healed miraculously. But the New Testament never teaches that. A miracle is an exceptional thing, which only happens sometimes.

The real answer to this whole question is the apostle's statement in 2 Corinthians 12 where he deals with his own thorn in the flesh. The apostle himself tended to fall into this error. He was taken ill and could not do his work, so prayed that God should take it away. But it was not taken away. He prayed three times and was most urgent about it. Here is a man who had performed tremendous miracles and had seen astounding things and yet when he is ill himself he has to endure his illness. But he was taught the reason for this. He was taught that there is something more important than physical healing, and that is one's knowledge of God. This great lesson, 'My grace is sufficient for thee.' He had not known that before as he should have done.

The Bible teaches that illness is sometimes permitted for the good of our soul. God permits things to happen to us for our good. Now that does not mean that every sickness is always permitted by God for our good; there are secondary causes – the world is a world of sin and disease has come in. All I am saying is that sometimes this is true. That is all the Apostle says. In his particular case the thorn in the flesh was not removed in order that he might learn that 'When I am weak, then am I strong'.

So the principle is established that you must not argue that because some men in the New Testament were not miraculously healed, that the miraculous power had therefore been withdrawn. The miracles, including the power of healing, were always something occasional, determined by the Spirit. It did not happen automatically that every Christian was immediately healed. Some men were healed, some were not. God has a purpose in all these matters. All these gifts, as I shall be emphasizing, are under the sovereignty of the Spirit. He decides when and how and where. We must never think of it as automatic, that you just pull a lever and there it is, it has all happened. That is entirely foreign to the New Testament. A power was given, a commission was given on particular occasions, and then the miracles happened.

But let me take you on to another argument which to me is a very important one. It seems that this idea that these things belong only to the New Testament period and have nothing to do with us is really guilty of the error known as 'higher criticism'. This is the error which sits in judgement on the Scriptures and says, 'Of course, yes, that was only temporary, that does not apply to us.' You decide what is acceptable and what is not. You pick and choose. This argument is exactly the same.

In other words that whole section of 1 Corinthians, we are told, has nothing to do with us because that was a temporary position. But in that case, was not the whole of the New Testament church a temporary position? It was a church that was filled with the Spirit; 'miracles and signs and wonders' were taking place. We have considered the quotation which demonstrates that fact in Hebrews 2:4 and again I would remind you of the statement in Galatians 3:5. The New Testament church was a pneumatic church that was filled with the Spirit and these things were happening. The whole of the New Testament church was in that condition. So then to be logical, these friends ought to say that the whole of the New Testament does not apply to us at all, that it has nothing to say to us, because the position is now quite different since we have got the Scriptures. But the argument turns back upon itself. The Scriptures which we have are those which deal with the New Testament church, and therefore if they have any relevance to us we must be essentially in the same position as the New Testament church itself.

We must beware, then, of a teaching which judges the Scriptures and says, 'This applies to us, that does not'.

Having thus dealt with the arguments in a purely scriptural manner, let me adduce history. Take this idea that all miraculous gifts and manifestations ended with the apostolic age. Now here, surely, is something that we have no right to state dogmatically, because there is clear historical evidence that many of these gifts persisted for several centuries. There are authentic records in the lives and writings of some of the great Fathers of the church – Tertullian and others – which leave us in no doubt that these things did persist.

But more than that – and this to me is very important – there is great evidence of these things even at the time of the Protestant Reformation. Have you ever read the life story of that great man and scholar John Welsh, the son-in-law of John Knox? There are amazing things which appear to be well authenticated in connection with him. There is a tradition, which has been repeated by the most sober-minded historians, that on one occasion, when he was living in exile in the south of France, John Welsh actually raised someone from the dead. Now I do not know, I just put the evidence before you. All I am trying to say is that I would not dare to assert that these things ended with the apostolic age and that there has never been a miracle since. Indeed, I do not believe it! There is evidence, from many of those Protestant Reformers and Fathers, that some of them had a genuine true gift of prophecy – I mean by that foretelling events. And you find among the Scottish Covenanters people like Alexander Peden and others who gave accurate, literal prophecies of things that subsequently took place.

Let me put it at its very lowest to you. I feel that what needs to be said to this generation in which we are living is this: 'There are more things in heaven and earth, Horatio, than are dreamt of in your philosophy.' Our danger is to quench the Spirit and to put a limit upon the power of God, the Holy Spirit. Have you ever read the life of Pastor Hsi of China? Can you deny the miraculous in that story? – the manifestation of some of these same gifts that were so clear in the history of the early church? Throughout the centuries books have been written on this great theme. Horace Bushnell, a preacher and theologian in America in the last century, dealt with this very thoroughly and marshalled a great deal of evidence. There is further evidence in the Woodrow collection of biographies mainly connected with Scottish worthies and in *Men of the Covenant* by Alexander Smellie.

I commend you to read these books and there you will find this gift of prophecy that was given to men to see the future, the power of speech that was given to them, and the occasional miracle. Anyone who is prepared to say that all this ended with the apostolic age, and that there has never been a miracle since the apostles, is making a most daring statement. Not only is there nothing in the Scripture to say that all these miraculous gifts had to end with the apostolic age; the subsequent history of the church, it seems to me, gives the lie direct to this very contention.

I say once more, therefore, that to hold such a view is simply to quench the Spirit. And surely, we must deduce from the Scriptures that if you say that the Holy Spirit was given to the early church to start it off, then these things are necessary, indeed essential, at all times when the church is down in the depths and the world is loud and strong and powerful. Surely that is just the time when you would expect a manifestation of some such power. If the apostles were incapable of being true witnesses without unusual power, who are we to claim that we can be witnesses without such power?

There then is the main argument. There are also certain trivial arguments which I mention merely in order to dismiss them. Many people at the present time say: 'You mustn't touch this subject, because it is only producing strife and division among Christian people.' This I find really very pathetic; that is the charge that has always been brought against Evangelicals, it was the charge that was brought indeed against Martin Luther, indeed it was the charge that was brought against the Puritans – 'Why wouldn't they keep the ranks, why must they be separatist and claiming....?' It is the argument that was brought against the Methodists, that has indeed been brought against Evangelicals whenever they have been called to witness for God in a special manner. Down through the ages they have been accused of causing division and strife and separation. Be careful, though, for if you press that argument we shall all be back in Rome, for it is ultimately the Roman argument against the whole of Protestantism – these separated 'Brethren' who made the mistake of going out.

But then there is another minor argument. It is said that people who are concerned about these things manifest a feeling of superiority, despise others and look down upon those who do not have these gifts or who have not received the baptism with the Holy Spirit. Again the answer is exactly the same; that has always been the argument of a traditional dead church against anybody who receives new life from the Spirit. It is invariable. It was, indeed, the argument of the Pharisees against our Lord.

So far we have been dealing with the attempt to dismiss the whole of this question on the basis that it only belonged to the New Testament period and therefore has nothing to do with us. Now I want to deal with the exact opposite position. It is interesting to notice how you always get the extremes.

The second position is that of those who assert that the full and miraculous gifts of the Holy Spirit ought always to abide in the church, and that it is only from want of faith that we do not possess them now. Some of them go further and say that we ought to 'claim' these gifts. These people maintain that these gifts were meant not only for the New Testament church but for the church at all times and the church today, they say, would be thrilling with all these gifts were it not for our lack of faith. They ought always to be present even as they were in the early church.

I want to suggest to you that this position is also unscriptural and once again finds no warrant in the Scripture itself. The teaching of the Scripture is that these things are to be considered in terms of the lordship of the Spirit. It is he who decides. 'He giveth to every man severally as he wills.' It is he who chooses. That was the whole trouble in Corinth, where they were all claiming 'all the gifts', as it were. And the answer to them is that he gives one this and the other one that. It is all entirely within his control. He decides when, how, to whom, and where.

Let me put this argument in the way which has always been most helpful to me. This is exactly the same as the question of revival. A revival by definition is not something permanent. It is something that comes, and goes, and comes, and goes. The history of the church has been the history of revivals. There have always been people who have taught that you can get a revival whenever you like. All you have to do is to pray, or to do certain things and to claim it, and you get revival. But the simple answer is, You cannot! I have known some of the best, most honest and saintly men who have fallen into that error; *you* cannot decide when revival comes. It always comes in the sovereignty of the Spirit. It often comes when you least expect it. It can come in the most unlikely quarter, and the man used can be the most unlikely sort of man.

The same principle applies to the gifts of the Spirit. Wc must not legislate on one side or the other. We must not say 'only' for New Testament times nor must we say 'always'. The answer is, 'as he wills', as the Spirit wills. It is always right to seek the fullness of the Spirit – we are exhorted to do so. But the gifts of the Spirit are to be left in the hands of the Holy Spirit himself.

Finally, I should like to draw your attention to three further points. In the light of the teaching of the sovereignty of the Spirit we are entitled to deduce, firstly, that gifts may be withheld as well as given in the sovereignty of the Spirit. He can withhold them as well as give them. We must never forget that for it is an essential part of this whole notion of sovereignty.

Secondly, we must never use the word 'claim'. It is incompatible with sovereignty. People say, 'Claim this gift; claim healing.' You cannot claim healing. The Apostle himself claimed healing three times and did not get it. Never claim; never even use the word. We are to submit ourselves – it is the Spirit who gives. The claiming of gifts, or claiming even the baptism of the Spirit, is something that is clearly incompatible with the whole of the New Testament emphasis. No, no, he is Lord, he controls and he gives. You can supplicate but you must never claim. Never!

Then, thirdly, a variation is clearly seen in the New Testament, as I have already shown you. Things do not always happen even when the apostles expect them to happen. And the variation again is to be explained solely in terms of the sovereignty of the Spirit. This is supported and substantiated by the history of revivals, and, indeed, beyond that. There is very clear evidence, it seems to me, that generally at the beginning of any new work, something unusual does happen. I have mentioned the period of the

Reformation, and the beginning of missionary work in China and so on.... The unusual happened and this is again in entire accord with the doctrine of the sovereignty of the Spirit.

But I also want to say this – and here is something that is very frequently forgotten. We have noted the argument of people who say: 'These things stopped at the time of the apostles. You do not get these things going on in the history of the church, therefore they were not meant to go on.' But there is another very important side to that question. It is historically true that as you read the history of the church in the first five or six centuries you find less and less evidence of these supernatural powers. And inevitably the question arises, 'Why was that?' These people assume, 'Obviously, they were withdrawn; they were not meant to continue.' I suggest to you that there is a much better answer, which lies in what happened to the life of the church herself. In the second century the church, as she was spreading increasingly amongst the Greeks, wanted to present her gospel in a learned, philosophical manner. There were men called Apologists, who tried to show that the gospel was not incompatible with Greek philosophy and with Roman law. They did so very largely because of persecutions and misunderstandings, and although they set out with good motives they were actually quenching the Spirit by turning the gospel into a 'reasonable' philosophy.

To make matters worse, the Emperor Constantine in his 'wisdom' decided to become a Christian and to bring the Roman Empire into Christianity. The church now became an institution, where everything was controlled; a kind of higher monarchical system came in, and metropolitans were introduced. In other words, the church by the end of the third or fourth century was a church that one simply cannot identify with the church of the New Testament. Not because God had withdrawn the gifts but because man had taken charge of the church and the Spirit was not given opportunity but was being quenched. The institutional church in time gave rise to the Roman Catholic Church of the Middle Ages.

And what is so interesting is that the bogus church always produces bogus miracles. They deny New Testament gifts but they produce bogus miracles, generally in terms of the virgin Mary. How easily we can go astray. We say, 'If you read your history, you will find that these supernatural gifts did not happen for a few centuries.' But we do not ask, 'Why did they not happen?' Or if we do, we give the wrong answer. It is not that God withdrew, it is that the church in her 'wisdom' and cleverness became institutionalized, quenched the Spirit, and made the manifestations of the power of the Spirit well-nigh impossible.

So my final conclusion is this: in the sovereignty of the Spirit these things are always possible. Always possible! I am saying no more. That does not mean that every claim is right. All I am arguing is that on the basis of the teaching of the Scriptures plus the history of the church, these things are always possible. They are especially needed in times of declension, and they have generally characterized some new work on the part of the Holy Spirit of God.

You must not say, 'They never can happen, they were only for the New Testament church....' Nor must you say they should always be present in their fullness. Both views are wrong. But they are always possible! And therefore when we are confronted by something that claims to be a revival or a new giving of such gifts, we must not reject it out of hand, but we must prove it, we must test it. And thank God we are not only exhorted by the Scriptures to do so because of the terrible danger of counterfeits, we are even told and instructed as to how we are to conduct the test.

Chapter 10

Test the Spirits

At this point in our consideration of the gifts of the Holy Spirit, I want briefly to support the conclusion at which we have arrived by adducing again the evidence of history, the history of the church, and particularly the history of revivals.

A revival of religion is nothing but a great outpouring of the Spirit of God upon the church, a kind of repetition of what happened on the day of Pentecost. A revival, in other words, is a number of people being baptized with the Holy Spirit at the same time. You hear or read of Christian people who were doing their best to live the Christian life. They had the assurance of their salvation, which they deduced by examining themselves in the light of the Scriptures, and, indeed, they possessed a spirit within themselves that enabled them in a measure to say 'Abba, Father'. But suddenly the Spirit of God descends upon them. Suddenly they are lifted up to a new height and a new level. They are given an assurance such as they never had before, and they see things with great understanding and luminosity.

Now that is what we mean by revival and, as I have reminded you, there are always certain phenomena attendant upon such visitations of the Spirit of God. We need not go into the details, but there is this new power, and sometimes a kind of prophetic gift is given. Yet it is interesting to observe that in the great revivals in the church throughout the centuries, there has not been very much by way of manifestation of some of these particular gifts, such as the gift of tongues or evidence of miracles.

That is to me a most important point. I am not saying that such gifts are altogether absent, but that they are uncommon and unusual. I am thinking, for instance, of the revivals of 1859 in Northern Ireland, 1857 in America and in other countries, and of the great Evangelical Revival of the eighteenth century in Britain. They were undoubtedly revivals, but there was very little by way of miracles, practically nothing by way of gift of tongues and prophetic utterances. Now these are simply facts that I am putting before you – facts that are well attested and well established.

Why do I make this point? Well, I do so for this reason, and to me it is a very vital one. It is, indeed, my main purpose in this whole series of sermons. It seems to me that the teaching of the Scripture itself, plus the evidence of the history of the church, establishes the fact that the baptism with the Spirit is not always accompanied by particular gifts.

Those who are interested in the contemporary discussion will realize the importance of that statement. There are people today, as there have been now for a number of years, who say that the baptism with the Spirit is always accompanied by certain particular gifts. It seems to me that the answer of the Scripture is that that is not the case, that you may have a baptism with the Spirit, and a mighty baptism with the Spirit at that, with none of the gifts of tongues, miracles, or various other gifts. No one can dispute the baptism with the Spirit in the case of men like the brothers Wesley, and Whitefield and many others, but none of these things happened in connection with them.

Now that, I feel, establishes this all-important principle, that you must draw a distinction between the baptism with the Spirit itself and its occasional or possible concomitants. We must keep these things distinct in our minds. There is great confusion at this point. In my earlier sermons I have already drawn attention to the way in which people get confused between the baptism with the Spirit and sanctification, which leads to great trouble. This confusion between the baptism and the gifts of the Spirit leads to equally great trouble. I am very anxious to bring out this point with great clarity that the baptism of the Spirit itself may be present in great power and yet none of these gifts may be manifest as such.

That is, of course, because of the sovereignty of the Spirit. He chooses to give them at times, and equally not to give them at others. And we must submit to that and be ready for that. We must not say that gifts cannot happen, nor must we say that they should always happen. The scriptural position, substantiated by the history of the church, is that they may or may not happen, and therefore we must not lay down these dogmatic positions on the one side or on the other. So, then, the main conclusion stands – that this question of gifts is entirely within the sovereignty of the Spirit and that because of that we should always be open, in mind and in heart, to anything that the Spirit of God may choose to do in his sovereignty.

It is very important that we should be concerned about the truth about the baptism in the Spirit for one main reason and that is the state both of the world in which we are living, and that of the church. If you, my friend, as a Christian are not concerned at this moment more than anything else with the need of the power of the Holy Spirit in the Christian church, I am afraid I do not understand your Christianity. Never was there such need of the proclamation of the truth with authority and power, and nothing but a baptism with the Spirit will enable the church to do this. It is God's way at all times. Never was there greater need of our being clear on the doctrine of the baptism with the Spirit, or revival of religion if you like to take it collectively, than at this present time.

As this question of gifts is involved with it, we must examine it, because there are many people who reject the doctrine of the baptism, because they reject the gifts. Again, there are others who, rejecting the false 'coalition', as it were, of sanctification and the baptism, reject the baptism because they feel the claims to entire sanctification cannot be verified or substantiated. What should be of concern to us is the power of the Holy Spirit upon individuals and upon the church in general; and it is in order that we may be clear about this that we should consider this question of gifts. Obviously, if the Spirit chooses to give them, it is a wonderful attestation of the truth. But it remains in his sovereignty and we must not lay down any rules of our own.

Are we to assume, then, that everything that claims to be a reappearance or a revival of such gifts in the church is of necessity true? That is the immediate and urgent practical question. We are open; we have no longer shut our minds to the possibility in terms of a false understanding of the scriptural teaching; we are clear about that. And suddenly we hear reports of the appearance of the gifts. Are we therefore to accept them immediately as being the gifts and the manifestations of the Holy Spirit?

At this point there are two main dangers which confront us. The first is the danger of quenching the Spirit. I put that first because I believe it is the more common of the two. There are people who automatically discount anything that is reported; their whole bias of mind, their whole prejudice is against it. History demonstrates that the greatest opposition to a true revival in the church, or to the work of individual men who have been baptized with the Spirit, has almost invariably come from the church herself. It is a startling, frightening truth, and it is all due to quenching the Spirit. The Roman Catholic Church persecuted the Reformers for this very reason; and, alas, the Protestant Church has often in her turn persecuted men upon whom the Spirit of God has come.

Why? Well, the danger is institutionalism and the fondness for decorum, order and pomp and ceremony with everything being controlled and ordered. So that if anything different happens it is immediately frowned upon and disliked. It is the same as the objection to the personal emphasis in the gospel. I have quoted elsewhere that remark of Lord Melbourne, Queen Victoria's first Prime Minister, who said, 'Things are coming to a pretty pass if religion is going to start becoming personal.' How typical that is! We want a dignified religion which never disturbs us, nor anybody else. There must be no liberty and freedom of the Spirit – the very thought is almost indecent. Fancy upsetting the clocklike, mechanical perfection of a great service with an outpouring of the Spirit! The thing is unthinkable! Now that is quenching the Spirit, and so you find the Apostle saying, 'Quench not the Spirit.'

Temperament undoubtedly comes into this. Some people have the temperament which leads to their liking order and discipline and decorum and so on; and they have to watch that. Their danger is to quench the Spirit, and this is a very real danger. And so there are many people in the Christian church who, the moment they hear of anything unusual, condemn it. 'There must not be anything unusual. We have never had anything like this before,' they say. That has always been the opposition to revival; that is why the saints have always been persecuted by people who like the ordinary, the drab, the uneventful and the dead. And remember it can be true of orthodox people quite as much as others. You can have a dead orthodoxy as well as a dead formality. The great danger confronting the majority is that of quenching and resisting the Spirit, thereby standing against the sovereignty of the Holy Spirit.

The other danger is the exact opposite and it is interesting to see how the one extreme or the other predominates: it is the danger of an uncritical acceptance of everything. Again temperament comes into this. Some people are credulous. It is very interesting reading the history of the church to see this element coming out in some of God's great servants. There are some men who are always anxious for the unusual – it is the thing they have to watch. Each of us has got to know himself or herself. We all have certain weaknesses and tendencies and we must watch them. It is the most difficult thing in the world: 'Know thyself!' And we have to be on our guard lest our natural temperament should become a prejudice and we may be found fighting against God.

This uncritical acceptance is often the result of a spirit of fear. You see, the first people are never afraid of quenching the Spirit at all; they just have their set fixed opinion in which everything different is condemned. But then there is this other type, who are terrified of quenching the Spirit. And that can become 'a spirit of fear' which interferes with their critical faculties, so that they are ready to believe anything and everything. They are so afraid of standing against a work of God that they pass things that they should not pass.

This, of course, is what always leads to fanaticism, or what the Bible calls a false fire. Here again not only does the Bible give us great teaching, but history also confirms the danger of fanaticism, wild fire, of another spirit simulating the Holy Spirit. Fanaticism is always to be condemned and it has often caused great havoc in the life of the church. Even an uncritical acceptance of anything purported to be the manifestation of the gifts of the Spirit may well lead to manifestations of certain excesses. Again, anybody who has ever read the history of revivals will know this danger and also that of a false emphasis, a lack of balance, the kind of thing that was obviously happening in the church at Corinth and which necessitated that section which the great Apostle devotes to it.

We proceed now to the next big principle. Why must we not accept uncritically everything that claims to be a manifestation of the power of the Holy Spirit? The answer is, first and foremost, that the Scriptures themselves warn us against uncritically accepting everything that is put before us. This is for the simple reason that there is such a being and person as the devil, that there are such entities as evil spirits, foul and malign spirits. You remember the great word of the apostle in Ephesians 6:12, 'For we wrestle not against flesh and blood, but against principalities, against powers, against the rulers of the darkness of this world, against spiritual wickedness in high places.' The beginning of this matter is to realize that we are living in a spiritual realm, a spiritual atmosphere. This world is not only a material one – there is the spiritual element surrounding it and there are forces and spirits which are evil and malign, set against God and everything that is holy. That is why by contrast the third person in the Trinity is designated the 'holy' Spirit.

If we do not begin by realizing that there are these two kinds of spiritual powers and forces, we are doomed to disaster because the teaching of Scripture is that these evil powers and spirits are always there and they have tremendous power. You see it even in the Old Testament. You remember how Moses, the servant of God, was given power in order that he might have means to attest his claim to his God-given leadership. He was sent by God to rescue the children of Israel, but Moses foresaw the difficulty. He said in effect, 'When I go and say this to them they will turn to me and they will say, Who are you, why should we listen to you? You are asking us to take a great risk. All right, said God, I will tell you.... I will tell you what to say.... say that I AM has sent me'. But God said beyond that, 'Look at that staff you have in your hand; I will enable you to do things through that.' He gave him certain miraculous powers. But that alone, you remember, was not sufficient, because the magicians of Egypt were able to repeat and to counterfeit many of the things that were done by Moses. So the apostle Paul, in writing his second letter to Timothy, referring to those magicians, and comparing them with the evil teachers of his day, says, 'As Jannes and Jambres withstood Moses, so do these also resist the truth: men of corrupt minds, reprobate concerning the faith' (2 Timothy 3:8). There, then, we have a great instance of this very thing in the Old Testament.

Unfortunately, things are not, therefore, quite as simple as some people seem to think. We are always surrounded by these evil spirits as well as by the 'holy' Spirit and their one object is to ruin the work of God. The devil rebelled against God, and his great ambition is to bring God's work into disrepute. There is nothing that he is more ready to do, therefore, than to confuse Christian people, especially those who are most spiritual, and the havoc that the devil has wrought in the history of the church is quite appalling to consider. Because of this, Scripture not only gives us the history and its teaching about the devil and his followers, but it also goes so far as to tell us to 'try the spirits', to 'prove the spirits'. 'Try the spirits whether they are of God', says John in his first epistle chapter 4:1. Now that is a commandment. 'Believe not every spirit', he says. Do not believe every spirit, but prove them and try them to see whether they are of God, or 'of the world' as he puts it, and that is an actual injunction to us. We are not therefore to accept everything that is reported. No; the Bible tells us to exercise our critical faculties and to prove and test them.

Writing to the Thessalonian church, Paul says, 'Prove all things; hold fast that which is good' (1 Thessalonians 5:21). Do you notice the context? He started by saying, 'Quench not the Spirit'. There is the rebuke to that first group – do not quench the Spirit. There were people who were doing that, but you must not, says Paul. But then, he says, do not go to the other extreme, 'Prove all things.' Do not be uncritical because I have told you not to quench the Spirit and not to despise prophesying. Do not act hastily and say, 'All right, I will believe everything....' 'Prove all things; only hold fast to that which is good.' You will have to reject a lot, but 'Hold fast to that which is good.' Now there it is as plain as anything could be.

Let me sum up this point by putting it like this. The trouble in the church at Corinth was entirely due to their failure to do this very thing that the Apostle exhorts the churches to do. They were confused about spiritual things because they had not learnt this all-important lesson.

In addition to Scripture we have exactly the same warning from the history of the Christian church – and you notice that I keep on putting these two things together. We must do so. The church is one. The church is the church of God, and essentially the same throughout the ages. There is an amazing continuity, and the principles taught in Scripture are worked out in the history of the church. And because we are in the flesh, we are helped by examples and illustrations, hence the great value of history. I know of nothing next to the reading of the Scriptures themselves that has been of greater value to me in my own personal life and ministry than constant reading of the history of the church. I thank God for it more than ever, for the way in which, by illustrating these things, it has saved me from pitfalls and has shown me the right way to assess these matters.

So we turn to history and we find that very early in the Christian church great difficulties arose owing to this very matter. This is a very difficult subject. There was a movement towards the middle of the second century called Montanism. I want to be careful about this because I believe that Montanism has been wrongly judged on many occasions. The official church was against it, because the official church was tending to become institutional and the Montanists were concerned about life and power. But there is no doubt that the Montanists went too far in this; they violated certain biblical principles such as, that women should not be teachers in the church, and that in itself showed that they had already gone wrong somewhere. And with that certain excesses tended to come in at the same time.

Then as you come on down the centuries you will find that the Roman Catholic Church began to report almost endless miracles; they began doing this in the fourth century. And, of course, it increased by leaps and bounds. They were claiming the most amazing miracles – healings and various other forms of miracles. Generally they happened in connection with what are called the 'relics of saints'. A bone was claimed to be from the body of Peter or some other 'saint' and this had miraculous qualities; or it was the 'grave' of a saint, or some such site, where endless miracles were reported. You will even find great men like Saint Augustine and Chrysostom and others reporting them and believing in them; by the Middle Ages it had become not only widespread but very profitable for the church herself.

What are called the miracles of the Roman Catholic Church, such as you get at Lourdes at the present time, are another fact and phenomenon in connection with the history of the church. Many people – credulous, uncritical people – are prepared to believe any wonder or sign by which they may be confronted and immediately to attribute it to the work of the Holy Spirit. Many people have done this and become 'converts to Rome', directly as the result of this kind of thing. There, then, is one great warning from history. We shall be dealing with these things again later on.

Coming down the centuries you find the same thing in Protestantism. It is very interesting when reading about the great Revival of two hundred years ago, connected with men such as Whitefield and the Wesleys, to consider the story of what were called 'The French Prophets', particularly in London. Many of the Huguenots had come over to this country at the end of the seventeenth century and this kind of connection was kept up. There had been certain phenomena in some parts of France and they gradually came over to this country. It is very interesting to notice how even a discriminating, intellectual man like John Wesley, was for a while captivated by this. Whitefield was not, as he was always more fearful of these matters. But John Wesley, who for so long had clung to his own intellect and understanding, tended as such men often do to swing too far to the other extreme. He became credulous and was greatly impressed by the manifestations of these so-called French prophets. But eventually he came to see that at the very least it was very doubtful whether all these manifestations were of the Spirit of God and not rather of the evil spirit.

In other words, I am simply trying to make this point. You hear a great deal at the present time about the revival of these gifts and so on, but this is not the first time this has been reported, nor the first time it has been claimed. It is a repetition of something that has happened frequently in the history of the church.

Let me move on to the last century and to the whole episode known under the name of Irvingism, in connection with Edward Irving. This man was a brilliant Scot, a one time assistant to the great Dr Thomas Chalmers, who subsequently came down to London and began to preach in the Scottish Church near Hatton Garden. He became the sensation of London in the 1820s. People flocked to hear him, including society people. He had many things which attracted – his personality, his appearance, eloquence and so on – and he became one of the most popular men in the whole of London. But the story ended in great tragedy and it all arose from the claim that the gifts of the Holy Spirit were being renewed and were being repeated under his ministry. I must not take you through the history; there are books which have been written on this, which are most instructive to read. But I have had the privilege of reading a little booklet called *Narrative of Events* by Robert Baxter, which I should like to refer to at this point.

Robert Baxter was a barrister who lived in Doncaster. He was an able, godly, spiritually minded man, who for a while became the very centre of the movement round Edward Irving, and their leading prophet. He claimed to be receiving messages direct from God, messages concerning the truth to be delivered, and what he was to do. He was told, he claimed, by the Spirit of God that he must leave his wife and family and his profession, and go and deliver this message. He was told, he claimed further, to go into the law courts and to get up and interrupt a case and address the judge and deliver this message from the Spirit of God, if he felt the impulse while he sat in court. Actually he did not feel the impulse, and did not do this, but he had taken steps to leave his wife and family, having been told that he was not to bid them farewell even, but was to go at once.

All this was reported and was regarded as the leading of the Spirit. Men claimed to be speaking in other tongues and Robert Baxter, who was at the very heart and centre of this, was regarded as an 'oracle', as an unusually spirited man. He testified that his love of the Lord was greater than ever and so was his happiness. Yet this man came to see that all this was not of the Spirit of God. Exact prophecies had been given to him but they were not verified, and did not happen. And then he began to realize that some of these things he was told to do were not in accord with the plain teaching of Scripture. But he had thought, and he was as honest as the day, that this was all the Spirit of God. Eventually his understanding was restored to him and he continued the rest of his life a godly, saintly man in the church. It was to warn others that he wrote that book long since out of print called *Narrative of Events*.

Now, my dear friends, we must not discount such things. Irvingism collapsed, though they did establish what they called the Catholic Apostolic Church. But the whole thing ended in disaster, including the death of poor Irving who was overwrought and even suffered physically, eventually dying a broken man. There were certain prophetesses who even denounced one another while some of them later admitted and confessed that they had invented facts at certain points. Do not misunderstand me – I am not saying all this in order that you may say the moment you hear of any claim, 'Obviously nonsense! A repetition of Irvingism; have nothing to do with it.' That is not my object. All I am saying is do not believe everything uncritically. 'Prove all things; hold fast that which is good.'

I could recount at length stories about the freak religious sects that arose in the United States in the last century. A book was written once on these called *Group Movements and Experiments in Guidance*. Now the point about them all is that there was no doubt about their sincerity. They all really believed that the things they experienced were the acts of the Spirit of God, but the story ends in disaster.

Let me move on to a third bit of evidence which is equally important and which illustrates the danger of evil spirits counterfeiting to mislead 'if it were possible even the very elect'. The third evidence is that from spiritism and from psychology. Here again the thing is quite clear if you take the trouble to examine it. I have never understood those people who say that all that is claimed for spiritism should be rejected. A man like the late Sir Oliver Lodge was not a fool, neither was the late Sir Arthur Conan Doyle. I know that there is a lot of dishonesty in the realm of spiritism and a lot of fictitious evidence has often been presented. But – and I think that the Society for Psychical Research has established this – there is always a residuum which simply cannot be explained away in terms of trickery and dishonesty. There are such things as phenomena belonging to spiritism. I have no difficulty in believing this, because I believe the whole of spiritism is the manifestation of the work of evil spirits. There are evil spirits who can produce phenomena and can do amazing things.

In other words there is no question – and it has been reported and established many times over – that in spiritism you have people who can speak in tongues. Evil spirits can make people speak in strange tongues and languages that people do not understand. They can counterfeit the speaking in tongues produced by the Holy Spirit. To all appearances they appear to be identical. Not only that, but there is no question that healings can happen in the realm of spiritism This again has been checked by careful observers and people who do not believe in spiritism at all. You cannot say that the whole of the work of a man like the famous Harry Edwards is all dishonesty and fraud. There are certain cases of healings which are as genuine as anything that can be reported by Christian faith healers. It is ridiculous to deny the facts. The danger is that the practitioner claims that he is the medium of the spirit of a dead person.

I am putting this evidence before you as a warning – spiritist phenomena can be amazingly like these other phenomena, so that if you are going to believe anything that is put before you uncritically, you are obviously exposing yourself to the deceit of spiritism and all that belongs to that realm.

This is, also, true of psychology. All this is being discovered more and more and it is receiving a good deal of attention of course. You may have seen programmes on the television, or read the book by Dr William Sargent, *Battle For the Mind* where the intention is to discount the Christian faith and to explain it all away in terms of psychology. What they can demonstrate is that under hypnotism you can make people speak in other languages which they know nothing about and of which they have never heard. And there are people who can hypnotize themselves and make themselves do this without invoking the spiritual realm at all. Purely on the level of psychology, you can reproduce certain spiritual phenomena, such as speaking in tongues by auto-suggestion and auto-hypnosis or by the reviving of something that is deep down and lost in the memory, something of which the man is no longer conscious can be brought to the surface again. There are extraordinary phenomena along that line.

Then there is the whole realm of hysteria where almost anything can happen. You will hear people say, 'Now look, if you are going to base your Christianity upon the presence of these phenomena, here they are for you,' and they will produce them by using hypnotism, hysteria and trance conditions. They will give you pictures which they have taken in certain odd sects in various parts of the world where you can see the thing happening psychologically. There it is, they say, and that is the whole of your Christianity – Christianity is nothing but that.

These are some of the reasons why you and I must pay close heed to the exhortations of Scripture. 'Prove the spirits'; 'test the spirits'; 'prove all things; hold fast only to that which is good'. It is our bounden duty as we value the doctrine of God and as we are concerned about the state of the church. God forbid that people should confuse the phenomena, the manifestations, with the baptism of the Spirit itself, because if they do people who reject the phenomena will reject the baptism with the Spirit also. These two things must be kept distinct and separate.

How do we test the spirits? It is vital that we should know how to test, especially those of us who really know something of the burden of the times in which we live. God forbid that there should be anybody sitting back in smug satisfaction and contentment at this point and saying, 'Of course, at last he has said it, I have been waiting for it all the while. I have always said there is nothing in this, lot of nonsense – some even say it is of the devil.' God have mercy upon you if you can be smug in the Christian church at a time like this!

No, I am speaking particularly to those good, honest,

spiritually-minded men and women of any age whatsoever, who are longing for revival and reawakening, longing to see the church speaking with power in this evil age, addressing governments if necessary, doing something that will arrest the moral declension that is happening round and about us and believing that this is what we need. It is to such people that I address these words in particular. For it is your very anxiety to know the fullness and the baptism of the Spirit that constitutes your danger and exposes you to this possibility of not using your critical faculties as you should.

At this point I will give you the negative only: Do not rely only upon your inward feelings. Many have done this and have found themselves in grievous difficulty. What I mean is that they make decisions entirely on their own inner feeling. They say, 'You know, I have a feeling that this is right. I don't like that other possibility.' But that is entirely subjective, and while I do not discount the subjective altogether, I say it is not enough. You must not rely solely upon some inner inward sense, because that is the very thing the devil wants you to do. That means you are not using your full critical faculties; deciding in a purely emotional and subjective manner.

Let me add this: do not be swayed even by the fact that something reported to you makes you feel wonderful. You may say, 'Well now surely anything that makes me feel greater love to God must be right.' Robert Baxter, to whom I have already referred in connection with the Irvingite movement, used to say that he had never felt so much love, the love of God in his heart, or so much love in himself to God as he did at this period. He was ready to leave his wife and family for God's sake. He was filled with a sense of the love of God, he said, that he had never known before, but he came to see that it had all been misleading him.

So we must not judge even in terms of such feelings. You may say, 'I have never known such love, I have never known such peace, I have never known such joy.' The people who belong to the cults will often tell you exactly the same thing. So we must not rely upon our own subjective feelings. Do not dismiss them or discount them, but do not rely upon them. Do not say, 'I feel this is right, everything in me says this is right, all my Christian spirit.' It is not enough. The devil is as subtle as that. Remember our Lord's word – 'if it were possible, they shall deceive the very elect.'

Lastly, do not base your judgement on the people who are speaking to you and making their report to you. The tendency is to say, 'Well now, I know this man to be a good Christian man, an honest soul, and a most devout person – therefore anything he says must be right.' He may be wrong! He is not perfect, the devil has brought down greater and stronger men than he. So the mere fact that the report is brought to you by good people who may say to you, 'My whole experience has been transformed by this', is not enough. It may be right, it may be wrong.

Once again, you have these warnings not only in Scripture but in the continuing history of the Christian church. It is often some of the best, most honest and sincere people who can be most seriously led astray. The cynics sit back and say, 'Of course, I knew that that was false.' Exactly! They say that about everything. They say that about the true as well as the false. They down everything, they condemn everything. God have mercy upon them. Are they Christian at all, I wonder? No, it is the good and the honest and the true soul that the devil tempts most of all because this person is the nearest to the Lord. The devil does not waste any of his time and energy with your smug formalist – he is safely asleep, already under the drug of the devil, though he is sitting in a Christian church. The devil does not waste time with him. But the man about whom he really is concerned is the man who is anxious to follow his Lord all the way.

So I say that you must not decide merely in terms of the

character of the people giving the report, nor even in terms of their experience, whatever they may say to you. Be open, be ready to listen but never be uncritical, 'Prove all things; hold fast that which is good.'

Chapter 11

Understanding and the Word

As we resume our studies, I would again remind you that our reason for looking into this great matter of the baptism with the Holy Spirit and the gifts of the Spirit is not *only* that it is in the Scriptures. It is our business always to investigate and to study everything that is in the Scriptures; we do not pick and choose. If we believe that this is the word of God, well it is all the word of God and we are to be familiar with the teaching of the entire Bible. We have no right to ignore teaching simply because we do not happen to like it or because we think it may involve us in difficulties and problems. That is the first and main reason for studying this subject.

But in addition the whole state and condition of the Christian church at the present time makes this study imperative. We are witnessing a world in sin and chaos, and it is surely by now evident to everybody that nothing but a great outpouring of the Spirit of God upon the church can be of any avail in such a situation. We have tried everything else, and I am not disparaging the efforts of men, but it is quite clear that human organizations and attempts are really not touching the true situation as it exists in this and in other lands. God's method throughout the centuries has been to send a revival among his people, to pour out his Spirit again upon his church. For this reason, it is urgently important for us to examine the teaching concerning this and to look at it especially in the light of the subsequent history of the church. And so we will continue our study of the gifts of the Spirit.

In our last study we began to consider how we should test the phenomena and I offered the negative advice not to trust feelings. Now I should like to consider the positive ways of testing and examining each phenomenon. Firstly, we should use our reason and understanding. Now some may be surprised that I start with this and not with the Scriptures. My reason for doing so, of course, is that in the early church they did not have the Scriptures as we have them. The question arises: how could they test? How could they prove the spirits? So I start with reason and understanding and this, I think, is a most important matter. Let me show you what I mean. I would lay down as a proposition to be found in the Scriptures themselves that we must never abandon or jettison our minds, our reason, our understanding. Let me put it in the phrase that is most commonly used. We must never 'let ourselves go'.

Those of you who are interested in these matters, and especially in the new interest that is being taken in these things at the present time in this country, in America and in other parts of the world, will know exactly what I mean. There is a teaching which comes to us and says, 'Now if you want this blessing, let yourself go, and especially your mind.... If you want this you have got to abandon yourself, to let yourself go.'

I am trying to show that that is always wrong, but I want to make this point clear. Someone may say to me, 'But surely you are contradicting the plain teaching of the Scriptures, which you yourself are never tired of emphasizing, namely, that a man does not reason himself into Christianity, that a man by mere intellectual understanding and effort will never make himself a Christian', to which the answer is quite simple – that is perfectly right. We never can 'reason' ourselves into Christianity. We can never by means of an intellectual process bring ourselves into the truth and into the kingdom of God. That is true. But it is equally important that we should remember that Christianity is not unreasonable and never irrational – never! You cannot reason yourself into it, but the moment you are in it you find that it is the most reasonable and rational thing of all.

At no point, then, are we deliberately to abandon our intellects. There is never instruction in the Scriptures for us to do that. Deliberately to stop thinking and to let ourselves become blank, as it were, and to surrender ourselves to other forces – that is never advocated in the Scriptures. How, then, does one become a Christian? It happens like this: the Holy Spirit enlightens the understanding. He does not make us Christians apart from the understanding. What he does is to lift the understanding up to a higher level. There is nothing wrong with reason except that it is governed by a sinful disposition, and that is why it can never bring us into Christianity or into the kingdom. But the Spirit can lift up the mind and the reason. A man is never saved against his reason and his understanding – never! What happens is that his understanding and his reason are enabled to see the truth which he formerly rejected. 'But the natural man,' says the Apostle, 'receiveth not the things of the Spirit of God: for they are foolishness unto him: neither can he know them, because they are spiritually discerned.' Quite right. But the answer is not to commit intellectual suicide, nor to stop thinking, nor deliberately to let yourself go and abandon the powers that God has given you. The answer is to trust yourself to the illumination and the guidance of the Spirit. As you do that so the Spirit will illumine the mind. As the Apostle puts it in 1 Corinthians 2:10 – 'But God hath revealed them unto us by his Spirit: for the

Spirit searcheth all things, yea, the deep things of God.'

I trust this point is clear. Intellect alone cannot enable us to grasp the truth, but when the revelation is given through the Spirit, the intellect and the reason do grasp the truth, rejoice in it and apprehend it.

There is my first answer to this, but let me give you a second one which is still more important. The whole presupposition behind the argument in 1 Corinthians chapters 12, 13 and 14 is the exercise of the understanding, and reason, and that is the same with all the other New Testament teaching. Why was the church at Corinth in trouble over the exercise and manifestation of these gifts? Because they were not employing their reason and their understanding, they were abandoning themselves.

Let me work this out with you. Take that injunction in the first epistle of John: 'Beloved, believe not every spirit, but try the spirits whether they are of God: because many false prophets are gone out into the world' (1 John 4:1). Now how can you possibly prove or try the spirits unless you are using your mind and reason and understanding? The thing is impossible. The position represented is this. Here is man with the Holy Spirit on the one side and the evil spirits, and the spirit of antichrist on the other side, and they are both trying to possess us and to influence us. How do we know which is which? If you 'abandon' yourself, or let yourself go, or stop thinking, or cease to reason and apply your understanding, how can you test? It is impossible! And it is because they were not doing that, or refusing to do that, that trouble arose in the church at Corinth.

But there is another way in which we can look at this. In 1 Corinthians 14 the Apostle deals – and I hope to come back to this later – with the whole question of the misuse of the gift of speaking in tongues. They were tending to misuse it or at any rate wanting to exercise it the whole time when they gathered together, and so the Apostle warns them of the effect that would have on a possible outsider coming in: 'If therefore the whole church be come together into one place, and all speak with tongues, and there come in those that are unlearned, or unbelievers, will they not say that ye are mad?' (1 Corinthians 14:23). Now that is the position that the Apostle had to deal with. The Corinthians wanted to spend the whole of the time in their church meetings in speaking in tongues that other people could not understand.

Now what is the Apostle's advice to them, what is his exhortation and his teaching? It is that this must be controlled, and that you cannot at one and the same time abandon yourself, let yourself go, and still be in control. The verse which puts it all in a nutshell is 1 Corinthians 14:32 – 'And the spirits of the prophets are subject to the prophets.' Now that settles it surely once and for ever! You are not to let yourself go, because if you do, you will expose yourself to the other spirits, you will not be able to test, and still more, you will not be able to control. So Paul ends that chapter with the injunction: 'Let all things be done decently and in order', which is impossible if you abandon your thinking, your reason, and your understanding.

Now there is a problem here and I am going to deal with it later on. It is to me one of the most wonderful aspects of this truth – how at one and the same time you can be gripped and lifted up by the Spirit and still be in control. But that is the glory of Christianity, that is what differentiates it from everything that is false and spurious. So I argue that the first thing we have to do is to use our reason and understanding, the very powers that God has given us. Indeed I want to put this as a positive assertion, that it is the very central glory of the Christian salvation that it takes up the whole man. It takes up his mind, his heart and his will. Any teaching that tells you that you are only going to get the blessing if you stop thinking is contrary to the teaching of the gospel itself. Here is something that enlightens the eyes of our understanding. The mind is at full stretch, the intellect is involved, it is taken up and the whole man is involved.

So, then, we are right to be suspicious of anything that tries either by its methods or by suggestion to stop us thinking. I mean by that the employment of certain well-known psychological techniques such as putting out the lights and having a rhythmic repetition of music or of phrases. You must have seen and read about the kind of thing that happens amongst the more primitive races, how they slowly work themselves up by these means into a condition in which they are no longer thinking and have lost the power of reasoning and understanding. Anything that does that should be suspect. There is nothing approaching it in the New Testament, indeed you find the exact opposite.

What is this message which we believe? Well it is called the truth, and that is patently something that comes primarily to a man's mind; so that any suggestion that you 'let yourself go' already indicates that there are at the least very good grounds for suspecting such a teaching.

Let us now move on to the second great principle as to how we should test the spirits and that is the Scriptures themselves. I have already reminded you that the early church had not got the Scriptures as we have them. The churches were in being, these problems had already arisen and that is why the apostles had to write their letters. But these people were obviously in a position, before that, to apply certain tests. But today, thank God, we have the Scriptures and it is therefore our business to use them. 'The church,' says the Apostle Paul, 'is built upon the foundation of the apostles and prophets' (Ephesians 2:20) and it is through these men that we have the Scriptures. Here is authoritative teaching – here is all the teaching that we need. There is no need of a supplement to the Scriptures, because everything we need has already been given to us here.

Now we shall consider the way in which we should apply

these tests. We must realize that there is no greater danger than that of putting the Spirit against the Scriptures. All who are at all familiar with the history of the church will know exactly what I mean. This is always the characteristic of the false movements, of heresies if you like; especially those that are concerned with spiritual gifts and manifestations. They always tend to put the Spirit against the word, and eventually arrive at a position where they do not hesitate to say that the Scriptures are no longer necessary. Why, they ask, do you need the Scriptures if you have got the inner light? If you are receiving direct messages from the Spirit, where is the need of the Scriptures?

This is a most important matter and it is one of the first tests that we must apply to anything that offers itself to us as a new manifestation of the Holy Spirit, particularly in this matter of gifts. Watch the place that is given to the Scriptures. You will often find in the history of such movements that, while they start well, there is an increasing tendency on their part to use Scripture less and less and to attach greater and greater significance to what they call 'prophetic messages'. They talk more about them, pay more attention to them, and begin to print them instead of expositions of the word of God; that is always a most dangerous sign.

In Scripture is all the truth we need, and what we need is the illumination of the Holy Spirit upon our minds to enable us to understand it and to expound it. So I would lay it down as a valuable and general rule, that if you see an increasing tendency to base a position less and less upon the Scriptures, and to spend less and less time in expounding them, but more and more time in what are claimed to be direct messages from the Spirit, then you are entitled to have all your suspicions aroused and it is your duty to be on guard.

Again I can illustrate this quite simply from the history of the church. There were movements that arose in the early church, that is in the first three centuries, which fell into this very error. It was one of the great dangers with Montanism and other similar movements. But perhaps one of the most striking examples of this was immediately after the Protestant Reformation. For centuries the Roman Catholic Church had been governing everything with its iron, rigid system, and its own interpretation of the Scriptures. The Protestant Reformers saw through that error. They grasped the whole truth of the universal priesthood of all believers; they saw that every man with the Spirit is entitled to come and to read the Scriptures, and people were liberated as the result of that. But, you see, the enemy came in and tried to press this too far to the other extreme. The exact opposite of Roman Catholicism, in a sense, is what is called the Anabaptist movement. You can read about the movements which arose in the sixteenth century and which caused such trouble to people like Martin Luther, Zwingli, John Calvin and others.

Let me say quite frankly that I think those great Protestant Reformers were too severe on them and went astray themselves in their condemnation; but what they were facing was the danger that these wild movements – which said you did not need the Scriptures at all, that the Spirit gave you direct guidance on everything – were likely to wreck the Reformation altogether; they put the Catholics into the position of being able to say, 'The moment you leave us what do you get? – chaos and utter confusion.' So it is interesting to see how these men calling themselves 'prophets', claimed, not so much that they were expounding the Scriptures, but that they had immediate and direct guidance.

A still more well-known example, of course, is that of the Quakers. George Fox and others started with the Scriptures, and all they claimed was that they had the light within them to enable them to understand. But very soon they had left that position and were saying more or less that you did not need Scriptures at all. You had this inner light or guidance and all you did was to look to the Spirit and he would tell you. And so they increasingly turned their backs upon the Scriptures, and that has persisted as a characteristic of that movement even until today.

You find the same thing in the history of Irvingism, to which I have already referred. They again left the Scriptures and looked more and more to these prophetic utterances. When Robert Baxter was present, all they did was to sit and listen to what he had to say claiming, as he did, to be speaking under the power and the influence of the Spirit, and getting a direct message. He did not preach, or expound the Scriptures, but just gave these prophetic messages, as they were called. And, as I reminded you, it not only led to confusion but finally it ended in tragedy and Baxter himself came to see that it was not the Spirit of God at all as he had thought, and he was mercifully restored to a Christian and scriptural position.

These, then, are the two main principles involved in testing the spirits. We must use our minds and our understanding, and must never 'let ourselves go'. We must not abandon ourselves for in doing so we lose the ability to be critical, to evaluate, to prove and to control. Above all, we must apply the Scriptures. We have the Spirit in us, our mind is enlightened and we have the Scriptures. We must put these things together. Nothing is more dangerous than to put a wedge between the word and the Spirit, to emphasize either one at the expense of the other. It is the Spirit and the word, the Spirit upon the word, and the Spirit in us as we read the word.

How do we carry out these principles in detail? I am going to put before you a number of general principles which seem to me to be helpful. I put them forward as the result of reading the Scriptures, together with my own experience over the years. They are also the result of my reading of church history and of movements in connection with the life of the church. Here are some of the conclusions at which I have arrived and which I would put to you as general principles which you can apply.

To begin with, always be suspicious of – indeed, I would go further and say, be ready to condemn and to reject – anything that claims to be a fresh revelation of truth.

I am sure you know what I mean by that. People in this state and condition claim that something has been revealed to them. There are certain well-known movements, even at this present time, which were started by people claiming to have had a special revelation.

One of the most common revelations of all concerns the second coming of our blessed Lord and Saviour. They claim that it has been revealed to them that our Lord is coming again in a given year. Seventh Day Adventism, as it is called, started in that way. A man called Russell and a woman called Mrs Eleanor White claimed that the Holy Spirit had revealed directly to them the exact year when our Lord was going to come. It did not happen of course, but it does not matter and the movement goes on. The point I am establishing is that the whole thing was based upon what is claimed to have been a direct and immediate revelation concerning a particular truth.

How do you test a thing like that? What do you say if someone comes to you and says that it has been revealed to them, in a spiritual state, that the Lord is going to return, let us say in 1970?* Well, I suggest that what you should not do is to start working through the figures and the numerics of the Scriptures, which so many do. I should have thought that it is quite sufficient to take just one scripture which tells you that you are not to be concerned about the times and seasons; and, therefore, if you are given an exact date you should reply that the Bible tells us that we are not to know the exact date: 'But of the times and the seasons, brethren, ye have no need that I write unto you'. Why? Well you know that the Lord

*These sermons were preached in 1965.

will so come 'as a thief in the night' (2 Peter 3: 10). Our Lord himself said when he was in this world that even he did not know the exact date, that it was only known to God. Therefore this is a claim to a fresh revelation and it is contrary to scriptural teaching. You are entitled on those grounds alone to reject it.

But, alas, people have not done this. They have said, 'but look at this person, this Mrs White, what a godly woman she was,' and there have been others who have claimed exactly the same thing. In connection with the Irving movement again, there was great concentration on the second coming – indeed it was the very centre of the teaching that seems to have been particularly popular in America and in this country just at that time.

But let me give you a still more interesting illustration of this, one which is not so well known. There has been a teaching which has gained great popularity in evangelical circles, concerning what is known as 'the secret rapture of the saints'. It teaches that the Lord at his second coming will appear only to his saints, and that they will be raptured into the heavens secretly with nobody seeing it, nobody knowing anything at all about it; all they will know is that suddenly the saints will have gone.

I wonder whether you know the history and the story of that teaching? The people who hold it seem to assume that this has always been the teaching of the church, that it is truly biblical teaching, but do you know its history? The answer is that this teaching was first put forward in 1830. It had never been heard of before.

How then did it start? The answer is most interesting; again we must bring in the name of Edward Irving. In about 1830 the people who had become known as the Plymouth Brethren, including such names as J. N. Darby, B. W. Newton and S. P. Tregelles, and others of the early first leaders of the Brethren movement, began to gather together with Edward

Irving and some of his followers to hold what they called Prophetic Conferences. They became interested in the whole doctrine of our Lord's second coming, and they said, 'This has been neglected and we must look into it and we must examine it.' So they held conferences at a place called Powerscourt. And it was in connection with those conferences that this whole idea of the secret rapture of the saints came in. We have the authority of S.P. Tregelles, a great and famous biblical scholar, who tells us how it happened in a book he wrote called *The Hope of Christ's Second Coming*. In it he says, 'I am not aware that there was any definite teaching that there should be a secret rapture of the Church at a secret Coming until this was given forth as an "utterance" [notice his inverted commas] in Mr. Irving's church from what was then received as being the voice of the Spirit. But whether anyone ever asserted such a thing or not it was from that supposed revelation that the modern doctrine and the modern phraseology respecting it arose.' Tragelles attended these conferences, so he speaks with authority.

In Edward Irving's church they claimed that the gifts of the Spirit had all been restored, prophetic utterances among them, and it was through one of these supposed utterances of the Spirit that this idea of the secret rapture of the saints came in. So this was something that they claimed the Spirit had given as a direct revelation, and they accepted it. What is amazing is that a man like J. N. Darby accepted it, but he did, and he continued to teach it, and it has been taught very commonly ever since then. Tregelles would not accept it, neither would B. W. Newton. It was the first cause of a division amongst the Plymouth Brethren. (Incidentally, J. N. Darby very soon saw the dangerous tendencies in Edward Irving and entirely broke with him, but he continued to accept the secret rapture solely as the result of what claimed to be a prophetic utterance.)

The principle I am laying down, therefore, is that one

should be most cautious in accepting anything that claims to be a new teaching or a fresh or additional revelation. That should always be regarded with the profoundest suspicion, because, as I say, it is unnecessary, and because so often you will find that it contradicts something that is clearly taught in the Scripture itself. That leads us to a second principle. Obviously, if what someone claims is a message from the Spirit, contradicts quite patently a teaching of the Scripture, again you reject it.

Let me illustrate what I mean by this. It is quite astonishing to notice the credulity of people, including Christians, which leads them to expose themselves either to charlatans or to men who are mentally deranged. I referred earlier to a book reprinted in the 1930s called *Group Movements and Experiments in Guidance*, which is an illuminating account of various freak religious movements in the United States in the last century. Now is it credible to you that sane Christians, godly spiritual people could accept a thing like this. A certain teacher claimed that he was so filled with the Spirit that you had only to touch him in order to receive a blessing. We read in Acts 19 of special miracles wrought by the Apostle Paul, whereby if sick people sent their handkerchiefs and put them on Paul's body they could be healed by putting those handkerchiefs on their own bodies. So those Christians applied that and said, 'Yes, this man is the same.' They thought he had been so filled with the Spirit that just physical contact with him would give the blessing. So people went in large numbers in order to do this. It ended in a most tragic manner. I think the man was mentally deranged, but it ended in his claiming that this blessing was obtained at its maximum if people actually slept with him in the same bed. I need say no more. Both men and women did that and it ended, of course, in a grave scandal.

The point I am trying to establish, my dear friends, is simply that this was a trap into which good, godly, spiritually-minded people fell, people who really wanted the full blessing of God. Of course, the formal church members did not fall into the trap; they just sat back and said, 'We told you so, every time you get this talk about the Spirit that is where it is going to end.' God have mercy upon them! God have mercy upon them! It is better to be too credulous than to be carnal and to be smug and dead. No, this is something, I say, that constitutes a danger to the best people. For the moment you abandon your tests and let yourself go, the moment you stop thinking, 'Where is there anything like that in the Scriptures', you fall a prey to such things as I have just quoted.

Let me give you another example. I personally have known at least two ministers, who as the result of great experiences which they had in the Welsh Revival of 1904/5 stopped preparing their sermons. They argued that it was no longer necessary, because the Spirit gave them the message. Indeed, I once heard a godly Christian praising a man who was visiting this country at the time to hold meetings, and this was the highest praise he could give him. He said, 'You know it is most wonderful, I have never known anything like it, he never has to prepare an address or a message at all, it is all given to him sometimes as he is walking into the meeting.' Well, that is the kind of thing which one hears said, and these two ministers whom I knew stopped preparing their sermons, because they said, 'We read in Scripture: "Open thy mouth wide, and I will fill it" (Psalm 81:10), and doesn't the Scripture say: "Take no thought beforehand what ye shall speak ... but whatsoever shall be given you in that hour, that speak ye" (Mark 13:11)?'

The only answer to that is that Scripture must always be taken in its context, and 'Open thy mouth wide and I will fill it' is in a psalm which has nothing to do at all with preaching, but rather it has to do with eating and with food. With regard to the other quotation, it is what the disciples are told to do when they are on trial in court, suddenly arrested and apprehended, and again has nothing to do with preaching and teaching.

In other words, this is not the way to use Scripture. Notice, too, and this to me is most important, that the two ministers, who stopped preparing their messages and would go into the pulpit waiting to receive the message, were godly, honest and sincere men; but I need not tell you that their ministry was completely ruined and their churches disappeared almost under their very hands.

Also, of course, the whole thing is so contrary to the teaching of Scripture itself, which is given in order that it might be expounded. That is why it was written and why there were teachers in the early church, who gave instruction in the Scriptures, who were set aside in order to do so, and who were said to be worthy of double honour.

And as you come down the running centuries, you find that when men had been baptized with the Spirit – men such as Whitefield, Wesley, Moody, Finney – they all expounded the Scriptures, they studied them, they prepared their messages from them and then relied upon the Spirit to give power to it and to apply it to the hearers.

Let me give you a final piece of advice under this general heading. Anything that is merely spectacular should always be regarded with suspicion, or anything that we perceive with our minds and reasons to be foolish should always be under suspicion. In other words, let us always be on the look-out for fanaticism, the hall-mark of which is that it not only overstretches itself but always introduces the element of the ridiculous. Oh how difficult these matters can be!

I am going to give you two examples of this, not to amuse you, for again I am going to refer to two godly men who suffered very much for their faith, and whom I know are now in the glory everlasting. I did not know the first man very well but I knew people who did. This man thought that he was being led of the Spirit to have all his teeth extracted so that a new set might grow. This would be a great and glorious testimony to the work and the power of the Spirit. He said he had been given an assurance about this, it was going to happen, and he actually had his teeth extracted.

I say that this comes under the heading of fanaticism because that man was expecting a new act of creation. You do not get that in the miracles of the Bible. You get healing and restoration but you do not get a new creation. I have heard of people who have prayed for a man who has lost a limb for a new limb to grow; it has never happened. That involves creation. But this is where the counterfeit comes in.

Let me tell you about the second man whom I knew very well indeed. Again he was a minister who was greatly and marvellously used of God in the Welsh Revival of 1904/5, and who was given intimations by the Spirit in a most astonishing manner. He lived at a place about four miles from the sea and one day he announced that it had been revealed to him by the Spirit that he would be enabled to walk on the sea. So he actually went down to the shore in an attempt to do so, which of course ended in nothing but complete failure. And that man, godly saint as he was, was very often depressed and unhappy. Why? Because an evil spirit had, I think, come in and tried to counterfeit and had pressed him too far; this would have been a mere spectacle, with no spiritual benefit.

You remember the kind of thing that the devil suggested to our Lord in the three famous temptations; that he should set himself up on the pinnacle of the temple, and throw himself down, and so on. Now that was just a spectacle and you will find in the history of these matters that the devil often overreaches himself just in that way, by trying to persuade good Christian people to do something that has no value, that is merely spectacular. That is always indicative of a tendency to fanaticism. Indeed the main tendency of the other powers is to press us too far and to urge us in the direction of credulity and an uncritical attitude until the whole thing becomes ridiculous and indeed at times even tragic. And, of course, that is what the devil is ultimately concerned about, that the work of the Spirit and the work of the Lord, shall be brought into ridicule and into contempt.

Well, there we are – we have begun to consider how we carry out the injunction of the Scriptures to 'test the spirits', 'to prove all things' and 'to hold fast that which is good and that which is true'. May God therefore keep us all humble, and guard some against quenching the Spirit. It is a terrible sin to quench the Spirit. And may he guard others from abandoning the gifts which God has given them of reason and understanding, from abandoning even the Scriptures and exposing themselves to the errors, the dangers and the tragedies of fanaticism.

Chapter 12

Safeguards against Error

There are still certain other matters, it seems to me, under this general heading of proving spirits, where great caution is needed. The New Testament exhorts us to be cautious, to prove and to test, not to believe everything that we hear or see. Nothing is more vital than that we should realize that we are in a spiritual realm and that there are principalities and powers and spiritual wickedness even in heavenly places with which we have to contend. The devil himself can transform himself even into an angel of light and deceive almost the very elect themselves if it were possible. Therefore we need great caution. Scripture exhorts us to it, history proves the necessity of it.

The first area where Scripture and church history show the need for extreme caution and wariness is the prophesying of future events. Now I have already partly dealt with this earlier when we considered the tendency to fix the exact date of our Lord's second coming and things like that. That has always been a trap which has been set by the devil, and it is really sad and pathetic to notice how good people have been caught in that way in spite of the exhortation of the Scriptures not to be concerned about the times and the seasons. The devil knows us so well and he knows our curiosity – one of the most prominent characteristics of all of us – how we want to 'know' these things even though we are not meant to know them. The date and time is known only to God.

But this propensity is not confined to our Lord's second coming. You will always find in the history of these aberrations from the New Testament pattern that other particular events have often been prophesied, or a statement made that something particular was going to happen on such and such a date. Robert Baxter did this on several occasions. But I do not want to stay with this. All we need say about it – and we must keep the balance – is that the foretelling of the future is possible, for the Holy Spirit can enable a man to do this. In the annals of some great Scots worthies you will find this very thing. John Welsh and others were enabled to predict accurately certain events which subsequently took place. We must not rule this out, it is always possible. As God gave the gift of prophecy to the prophets in the Old Testament, there is always this possibility which we must not exclude.

All I am saying is that we must be very careful because this is a rare phenomenon. It does occur, but it is a rare phenomenon, so that when you find people doing it freely and without any hesitation you should always be extremely cautious. The ultimate test of the prophet is the one taught us in the Old Testament itself: Does what he has prophesied actually come to pass or not? In the Old Testament, you remember, there was that great struggle going on almost constantly between the true and the false prophets, and both were making prophecies. So the teaching is that, ultimately, you test the truth of the prophet and his claims by that test. You have to wait. If what he says does not happen, then you know he is not a true prophet, and that it is not a word from God.

So when people confidently prophesy that this and that is going to happen on such and such a date and it does not happen, you are made to think. It was largely through this that Robert Baxter eventually came to find that the spirit which was in him, which he had hitherto thought was the Holy Spirit, was clearly not. When a prophecy is given by the Holy Spirit, it does come to pass – it is infallible. So failure is clearly indicative of the fact that it is another spirit.

It would be easy to enlarge on these things, but I must not do so. There is much interest at the present time in what is called extra-sensory perception, an odd ability that some people seem to possess to foretell the future up to a point. Now this should make us see the need of being cautious here. We must realize that in the light of all these things we must be careful lest we too readily ascribe or attribute to the Holy Spirit something which really does not come from him.

Another point where very great caution is needed is the question of 'personal leadings'. Here again is a most extraordinary subject, and indeed a very fascinating one, and, from many angles, a most glorious one. There is no question but that God's people can look for and expect 'leadings', 'guidance', 'indications of what they are meant to do'. There are many examples of this in the Scriptures and I take one at random. You remember the story in Acts 8:26ff of how Philip the Evangelist was told by the angel of the Lord, 'Arise, and go toward the south unto the way that goeth down from Jerusalem unto Gaza which is desert'. Philip went and, of course, found that he had been sent there in order that he might meet the Ethiopian eunuch and preach Christ to him. Read the story again for yourselves.

Now there are leadings such as that. You get a still more specific one at the beginning of Acts 13, where we are told, 'There were in the church that was at Antioch certain prophets and teachers.... As they ministered to the Lord, and fasted, the Holy Ghost said, Separate me Barnabas and Saul for the work whereunto I have called them.' 'The Holy Ghost said'! They knew that it was the Holy Spirit speaking and they acted upon his instructions. Saul and Barnabas were obedient, because they realized it was the leading of the Spirit.

Again if you read the history of the saints, God's people, throughout the centuries and especially the history of revivals, you will find that this is something which is perfectly clear and definite – men have been told by the Holy Spirit to do something; they knew it was the Holy Spirit speaking to them, and it transpired that it obviously was his leading. It seems clear to me that if we deny such a possibility we are again guilty of quenching the Spirit.

But once more that is not the only thing we have to consider; there is another side to this. Leadings do and can happen. I am sure that many of you who have ever had a specific leading in this respect will not only always thank God for it but look back with a sense of awe upon it as one of the most wonderful and amazing things that has ever happened to you. But we cannot leave it at that, because it does seem to be quite clear in the Scriptures that even the greatest men of God have not habitually lived in a kind of direct, constant leading of the Spirit.

I am going to give you one example which, it seems to me, puts this matter quite clearly – and that is in the case of the apostle Paul himself. Here is one of the most spiritual men the church has ever known, a man baptized with the Spirit, and that, it seems, many times over; the Spirit came upon him and filled him on special occasions. And yet it is interesting to notice that the Apostle obviously did not live perpetually under immediate and direct leadings and guidance of the Spirit. He used his mind and reason and the powers that God had given him, now enlightened and quickened by the Holy Spirit. Let me give you just one example from Acts 16 which is very important in this connection, especially verses 6 and 7: 'Now when they had gone throughout Phrygia and the region of Galatia, and were forbidden of the Holy Ghost to preach the word in Asia, After they were come to Mysia, they assayed to go into Bithynia: but the Spirit suffered them not.'

The two important phrases, of course, are they 'were forbidden of the Holy Ghost to preach the word in Asia', and again, 'they assayed to go into Bithynia: but the Spirit' – 'the Spirit of Christ' as some of the manuscripts have it – 'suffered them not'. The only conclusion we can come to from this is that the Apostle had decided to preach in Asia, because it seemed to him the right thing to do. He was determined to do it, and the Holy Spirit had to intervene in a special manner to stop him. That, I say, shows that he did not wait until he had some special leading to go into Asia. He had decided to go there, but it was not the will of the Holy Spirit at that point, and so he was hindered. Then in exactly the same way 'they assayed', they attempted, 'to go into Bithynia', and they were proceeding to do so 'but the Spirit suffered them not'.

Now you can draw many conclusions from that, but to me the main one is that clearly the Apostle did not wait for some special leading, even with this great and all-important work. He used his reason and his understanding to reach a decision and when it was not the will of the Spirit, the Spirit would intervene and restrain him and hold him back.

So I would lay down the principle that if we find people beginning to claim special and immediate guidance over practically everything they do, I think we are entitled to have our suspicions aroused. You will find that it comes into their talk. They say that they have been 'led' to do this or that. I have sometimes heard preachers do this and they obviously regarded it as being a mark of unusual spirituality; they prefaced the giving of the text by saying, 'The word to which the Spirit has led me'. Now one should not say that for this reason – a man who is called to the office of the ministry should always submit and subject himself to God, he should always seek the guidance of God in everything and then use the powers that God has given him. But he will sometimes find that he is hindered, and at other times that he has been given a message directly. Thank God that does happen. But when a man gets into the state and condition in which he always waits for that and will do nothing without it, then I say he is on the verge of fanaticism.

This again can be abundantly illustrated from the history of the church. The Quakers, of course, were particularly noticeable in this respect, putting the emphasis as they did upon the 'inner light'; and, with this emphasis upon immediacy and direct leading and guidance increasingly at the expense of the Scriptures, they clearly became open to this particular attack of the devil. Read the story of the early Quakers – it is something worth reading because they bring out an aspect that tends to be forgotten at the present time. But observe it closely, and even as you read it you will find that there was an increasing tendency in some of them to attribute everything to the guidance of the Spirit. You find it in the life of George Fox himself, a man who certainly had many direct leadings and guidance, but not always, as he himself had to discover.

Another notable instance of this and a somewhat surprising one is no less a person than Oliver Cromwell – surely one of the greatest Englishmen who has ever lived. Now here again was a man who, because he was a spiritual man, was a little bit subject to this tendency. He would sometimes hold up parliament or the army council for a day or two and would not give his answer, or judgement, because he was waiting for a direct leading. Nothing is more interesting in the life of the great Lord Protector than the way in which he sought immediate and direct guidance – the term they used then was 'leading'.

Now the danger always is that once you have any experience of such direct leading, you get into the condition in which you cease to function with your normal faculties because you are always waiting for some immediate guidance.

I use my next illustration with considerable fear and

trembling, and yet I feel confident that what I am going to say is right. In the history of the 1904-5 revival in Wales, I always feel that the man who was so signally used of God in that revival, the late Mr Evan Roberts, definitely crossed the particular line that I am trying to draw, and got into a state in which he would do nothing without an immediate direct leading of the Spirit. For instance, he might have been announced to preach in a chapel. The people would be there and even he would be there, but he would sit and not speak a word because he said that the Spirit had not led him to do so even though the meeting had been announced and the fact that he was to be present at it. And thus it became increasingly the case with him that he would not take even some of the smallest decisions without some immediate direct guidance. Eventually, of course, he had a breakdown in health and in his nervous constitution. And that has happened to many others who have gone in this particular direction.

I trust I am making this point clear. God forbid that I should say that we should discount everything that appears to be a personal leading. That is just to quench the Spirit. No, it can happen; but beware lest the devil should come and press you so far in that direction that you ultimately become guilty of fanaticism in such a way that you will not do anything without a leading of the Spirit, or regard everything that comes to you as an idea as of necessity being the leading of the Spirit. There are many things attributed to the Holy Spirit which should not be so attributed.

Let me end this subject by telling you the famous story of Charles Haddon Spurgeon which, because it is Spurgeon, has its amusing side. I do not give it to entertain you, however, but to show you a principle enunciated by that great preacher. It is about a man who came to him one day telling him that the Spirit had told him that he (this man) was to preach in Spurgeon's Tabernacle on the following Thursday night. Mr Spurgeon simply replied: 'Well, it seems very odd to me, the

Spirit has not told me that.' And so the man did not preach in Spurgeon's Tabernacle. This principle is a very sane one. This is where reason and common sense come in. If the Holy Spirit had meant that man to preach in Spurgeon's Tabernacle, he would also have told Mr Spurgeon, because it was Mr Spurgeon who habitually preached there and who had been announced to preach that evening.

In other words, quench not the Spirit, but prove all things. Do not assume that everything that appears to be a leading of the Spirit *is* a leading of the Spirit. There are ways and means whereby these things can be tested. And there is nothing more dangerous for godly, innocent people, who always want the best, to believe such a man and to accept everything that he says as being of the Holy Spirit because he claims that it is.

We are not, I think, far from the truth if we put it like this: that normally guidance is given to us through the general teaching of the Scriptures and through our own faculties and powers. If we are Christians, the Holy Spirit is in us and he affects, influences and heightens all our faculties. That, plus the teaching of the Scripture, is the normal way of guidance. Anything beyond that by way of direct leading is exceptional and, indeed, there is good scriptural ground, as I think I have shown you, for saying that the exercise of this direct leading is often as negative and restraining as it is positive and indicative.

This is not an easy subject which is why all this attention to it is so necessary. And as you find people claiming this kind of thing more and more, you have to be cautious with regard to them and, as brethren, you must warn them to be equally cautious also. Any increasing tendency to attribute everything to the Spirit, or this perpetual direct leading, is something that we should always carefully examine.

I go on now to the next principle, which follows on from the last. Anything which makes self prominent or great should always be regarded with the greatest possible suspicion. It is not surprising and yet how difficult it is. A man in the Spirit, anxious for the glory of God and of our Lord, finds that the devil comes to him and tells him, 'Now you are the one who is going to do this for God.' And his mind is chiefly on the glory of the Lord and so he does not see the subtlety of the devil's temptation which is really to put him in a position of prominence.

The history of the church is strewn with tragedies in this respect. Some of the great heretics started by being most godly and great men, but this subtle tendency came in and pride with it. The apostle Paul is constantly warning the early churches against this; for example, in 2 Corinthians 11: 'Would to God ye could bear with me a little in my folly: and indeed bear with me. For I am jealous over you with godly jealousy: for I have espoused you to one husband, that I may present you as a chaste virgin to Christ. But I fear, lest by any means, as the serpent beguiled Eve through his subtilty, so your minds should be corrupted from the simplicity that is in Christ.' That is it! And what Satan played on with Eve and Adam was their pride, of course; pride was the cause of the fall of the devil himself, and the devil always uses this as one of his greatest weapons.

Now this is obvious, but it is tragic to notice how slow people are to see it. And when you yourself are the victim, it is especially difficult to do so. But there are such extraordinary cases in history that the thing should be quite clear to us. One of the early Quakers, called James Naylor, a true man of God, was so pressed by the devil on this point that eventually he was to be found riding a horse into the City of Bristol claiming that he was the Messiah, with a crowd of innocent women and children surrounding him and acclaiming him – a kind of imitation of our Lord's triumphant riding into Jerusalem. Poor Naylor, he was completely led astray at this point. Quite innocently, there is no question. He did not see that it was all self and magnifying Naylor.

And, again, the same thing can be seen very clearly in the story of Robert Baxter, who, poor man, thought that he was to be the messenger of God sent to address the whole country about its future: the message was to be given directly to him. Everything was making Robert Baxter great. But at last, as I have told you, he awakened to a realization of what was happening to him.

Let us now consider the fourth danger point in these matters. This happens when the physical element in connection with the experience is unusually prominent. Here again is a subject that I feel very much needs investigation. By this expression 'physical element' I mean an emphasis upon physical sensations. If there is a lot of talk about the physical aspect of the experience or excitement about it, we should always be extremely suspicious. For example, you get some people describing how they received the baptism of the Spirit in terms of an electric current passing through them, or a great sensation of heat, or seeing a ball of light, or some vision, or something like that.

This kind of thing comes into the question of healing too. Once again, of course, we must remember that the evil spirits can also heal – there is no doubt about that. For every case that you can produce of spiritual healing as the result of the influence of the Holy Spirit, the spiritists, or spiritualists, whichever you like to call them, can produce an equal number of cases. If you go merely in terms of appearances, and show people who have been crippled and who suddenly find that they can stand and walk and jump and dance – well, the spiritists can show you as many cases as you can show them. How then do we tell the difference?

I think it is just at this very point that what I am putting to you becomes important. You will find in the case of the spiritist healings that there is always emphasis on the physical element. People will testify to a feeling of heat as the hand of the healer came upon them, or of a sensation like an electric shock or something like that – the physical is always very prominent.

I put it like this for this reason. I know I must handle this argument carefully because you must never build a case on the argument from silence, but there is nothing corresponding to that in the New Testament. When men and women were baptized in the New Testament era, they testified to their joy and to the love of God shed abroad in their hearts, and this has been the characteristic of God's people throughout the centuries. They do not talk much about their physical sensations but about their Lord and his love for them and their love for him. Likewise, there is nothing in the case of people healed in the New Testament which tells us anything about this sensation of heat or of electric thrill or current or anything like that. It is just not there. And I feel that it is not there because it is something which is unimportant.

But here, you see, the devil once more falls into the same trap. He always overdoes things, making it spectacular – too spectacular – and he calls attention to the physical concomitants. I am not saying the people in the New Testament did not feel anything physically, they may have done. We are not told, that is all. All they knew was that they were healed, they were whole, they were well, and they attributed the praise and the glory unto God. So if you find people always talking about the sensation of heat or what they felt or the thrill, or the light, or the vision, I say that surely in meeting with something so unlike the pattern of Scripture, you are entitled to regard it with great caution, and are indeed not wrong to be suspicious. It is one of the points that differentiates the spurious from the true.

Let us now move on to another consideration – and here again it is a most important and a very difficult one. This is the whole danger connected with the power of suggestion. With all that is being taught at the present time, and all that has really been brought into prominence during the last hundred years, in particular in the realm of psychology, we can see, perhaps with an especial clarity, the need for caution. The Bible is again proved to be a contemporary and up-to-date book. Its writers did not have the scientific knowledge that we have, but they were aware of the facts. The Holy Spirit knows all, and in New Testament language he tells us to beware of some of these most modern things; not in modern terminology, but in words meaning exactly the same thing.

The power of suggestion is a very real and definite thing. It is always one of the dangers with a crowd, or a mob – we speak of mob or mass psychology. Hitler would never have come to power but for this. He may not consciously have realized what was happening but he was certainly illustrating this very point. He had a kind of hypnotic power; clearly he could make suggestions, and by repetition he could get people to accept them. The people addressed were not conscious of what was happening, but it was the power of suggestion. Now this phenomenon can come into the realm of things spiritual and we are but tyros in these matters unless we realize this. Everything that appears to be conversion is not conversion. You will often find people responding to a call forward in a time of excitement or in a highly organized campaign with large numbers. If you ask them afterwards, 'Why did you go forward?', they will often say, 'I don't know'. And that is the truth – they do not know. It was the power of suggestion; seeing others going forward, they felt an impulse to go and to do the same thing.

Now this can be illustrated, as I say, in many realms. In the political realm it can often be seen in meetings, addressed by someone who is anxious to propagate a doctrine. It is one of the things of which we have to be most wary, and is surely one of the things the Apostle has in his mind when he says in 1 Corinthians 2 that he did not preach in Corinth 'with enticing words of man's wisdom, but in demonstration of the

Spirit and of power'. It is because one realizes these dangers that one should avoid them. Far from using psychological techniques and so on, you should avoid them. We all know and have read about these things. You dim the lights and perhaps put a cross, one red cross only, above the pulpit light, and tremendous things can be done. We are all gullible, all liable to these things. And, again, the history of the church tells us a great deal about this – how men, unscrupulous men sometimes, for very mercenary reasons, have used and employed all these things in order to serve their own unworthy purposes.

But what I am anxious to deal with is one particular aspect of this matter that has had a certain amount of prominence recently. It is the phenomenon of speaking with tongues, and one cannot help noticing that this only tends to appear when it is talked or preached about, or when it is suggested in some shape or form. There is a most interesting piece of evidence on this very matter. Some of you may remember a book published several years back called *This is That*. It was an account of the remarkable revival that broke out in the Congo. (Incidentally one cannot but feel that God blessed those people at that time in that way because of what happened to them afterwards. Revivals often come like that to prepare people. It was given in Korea in exactly the same way.) This book tells how this great revival broke out, but there was no manifestation of speaking in tongues except in stations where the subject had already been mentioned and dealt with. In stations where the people had never heard about speaking in tongues, there was no speaking in tongues. This fact was confirmed to me by one of the men most involved in the revival, Mr Ivor Davies. He confirmed that tongues only appeared where they were spoken about.

Surely our suspicions should already be aroused. Or put it another way. If we find that people tend to speak in tongues only as the result of contact with a particular person, preacher or teacher, our suspicions should once more be aroused, because you again have this possibility of suggestion and hypnotic power.

You may be thinking, 'Why do you say this?' I do so because as you read the book of Acts you find that the apostles had this gift of laying their hands upon others who received the Holy Spirit and spoke in tongues, but it is something that seems to have been confined almost entirely to the apostles. I have not forgotten the one exception – Ananias, who was sent, you remember, to the apostle Paul to lay his hands upon him 'that [he] might receive [his] sight and be filled with the Holy Ghost' (Acts 9:17). But that seems to me to confirm the point that this was a gift that was confined to the apostles. Ananias was given a special commission. He was particularly commanded to do what he did, and he obeyed. So that this very exception tends to prove the rule.

Here is a point, I think, that is really beyond any discussion. Let me put it like this to you. If – and it is indeed the teaching of 1 Corinthians 12 that this is the case – if the gift of speaking in tongues is something that is given by the Holy Spirit himself in his sovereignty and in his Lordship, if he is the giver, then he can give it whenever he likes, and he can withhold it whenever he likes. And when it does happen, What will be prominent and evident is not that some particular 'person' has suggested it or taught it, but that it is in truth the gift of the Spirit.

Now why was it that this only happened in the Congo where it had been spoken about, if it is the gift of the Spirit? Why was it confined only to that one particular station and area, if it is all in the sovereignty and the gift and the power of the Spirit?

The answer to that question is perfectly clear to me and I would put it in this form – that if you find this particular phenomenon only occurring as the result of some suggestion or teaching or as the result of the activities of certain particular individuals, then you are fully entitled to be cautious and even suspicious. It is in the sovereignty of the Spirit and he can give and withhold as he pleases. But obviously, if the suggestion is made that all who have the baptism of the Spirit must speak in tongues and this is repeated and repeated, it is not surprising that people begin to speak in tongues. But the question then arises as to what they are doing. That is a question which we shall have to go into later, but all I am concerned about at the moment is that we should never forget the power of suggestion.

What strange creatures we are! It is not even a matter of intellect. You will find that if highly intellectual people get into a spirit of fear they can become very gullible and can therefore mislead many others. We are all subject to these things. But the Scriptures tell us to be careful, to prove, to test, to examine, not to believe every spirit, to remember that there is a power that can counterfeit in a most subtle and brilliant manner so as almost even to deceive the very elect themselves.

I have finished now my list of the particular danger points which I feel we should always keep in the forefront of our minds. The next step is to examine the direct scriptural teaching on this matter. I thank God we are not left in any doubt! There are certain tests which are taught here very plainly and very clearly – specific and explicit tests. I have not dealt with them so far, for we have been considering the 'implicit' tests. We have found in the Scriptures warnings of this great need for caution. We found them there with the use of our mind and reason, and we find them illustrated in the history of the church and the history of particular persons. Oh may God give us balance and wisdom and sanity with respect to these matters!

Let me say again, 'Quench not the Spirit.' To dismiss everything out of hand is not to exercise discrimination; it is to quench the Spirit. If you come to an end of this particular study saying, 'I am not going to touch it. I am not interested in any of it. I am just going on living my Christian life', my dear friend you are quenching the Spirit, and it is a terrible thing to do. No, we must follow the Scriptures. These things are possible and we must always be open. But we must not believe every spirit but 'try the spirits whether they be of God'. Let us thank God for the Scriptures and the illustrations we find in them; let us thank God for the history of the church preserved for us by godly men; let us pay heed to the warnings; and as we see the dangers on the two sides, let us with great humility hold to that simplicity which is in Christ. That, as I hope to show you, is indeed the ultimate test in all these matters.

Chapter 13

Jesus is Lord

Perhaps it would be good, at this point, to recapitulate on what we have been considering so far. We have seen that it is very important that we should test everything that purports or presents itself to us as being gifts or manifestations of the Spirit. The Scriptures themselves tell us to do that, they urge us to 'Jesus is lord'. The Christian is not just some credulous person who believes everything he is told; he is meant to test and to examine. The Scriptures tell us why we must do that: because certain false evil spirits are abroad. That is the great theme of the Bible. In a sense the Bible is a record of the great conflict between God and the devil worked out in various ways. Well, here is this conflict in the very centre and heart of the New Testament. The early church was immediately confronted by this great problem. The devil always tries to ruin the work of God. He ruined the first creation and he tries to do the same with the new creation, so that all who become Christians are immediately special targets of the 'evil one', the 'adversary of the brethren'.

The devil does this work of his in many ways, and one way is to confuse the children of God. He does that by counterfeiting as best he can the manifestations of the work of the Holy Spirit in the believer, and that is why we are told so constantly to 'prove' and to 'try' and to 'test' the spirits.

And we have seen that the way to do that is to use our reason and understanding. They have been given to us by God, and the Holy Spirit enlightens and sharpens them, so that the Christian is to be a highly intelligent person. He is not just an emotionalist, he does not just 'work himself up' emotionally. He is a man who is to use his mind. The great New Testament epistles tax our minds and our understanding. We are meant to use our minds, enlightened as they are by the Spirit. The natural mind does not help here, for it does not even understand what these things are talking about. But given the enlightenment and the unction and the anointing of the Spirit, we are to use our minds and understanding. And then on top of that we are given the clear instruction of the Scriptures themselves.

Now I have put to you a number of general principles derived from the Scriptures – understanding, reason, plus – and very important, not more important than the others, but very important – the history of the church throughout the centuries. Fortunately, we are not the first people who have been engaged in this battle, and there is nothing which can be of greater help to us, next to the Scriptures, than the history of the church. We can see how men and women like ourselves reacted in the same situation, how they fell to temptations at certain points, and all these things are written for our understanding. So we must use them all together to try to arrive at this position in which we can prove and test the spirits. Nothing is more dangerous than to say 'No, I am not interested in what has happened in the past, I am only interested in direct spiritual experiences, I want nothing else.' I have heard people who say that. They are not interested even in the Scriptures; they get it all directly. And there are others who are not interested in church history. They are the people who are most likely to end in some sort of a disaster.

Having considered some of these general principles, which seem to me to be quite obvious, and which guide us in this matter of testing, we come now directly to the particular teaching in Scripture itself.

The first test, which we must always employ, is the one suggested to us in 1 Corinthians 12:3: 'Wherefore I give you to understand, that no man speaking by the Spirit of God calleth Jesus accursed: and that no man can say that Jesus is the Lord, but by the Holy Ghost.'

At once we are brought face to face with the supreme test, and it is interesting to note that when the Apostle deals later in that chapter with this question of the gifts, and the confusion that had arisen in Corinth because of their misuse, he puts this test at the very beginning. When you are dealing with spiritual gifts, he says, you must always put this first.

1 John 4, you remember, says precisely the same thing 'Beloved, believe not every spirit, but try the spirits whether they are of God: because many false prophets are gone out into the world. Hereby know ye the Spirit of God: Every spirit that confesseth that Jesus Christ is come in the flesh is of God: And every spirit that confesseth not that Jesus Christ is come in the flesh is not of God: and this is that spirit of antichrist, whereof ye have heard that it should come; and even now already is it in the world.'

Those two statements confirm, of course, what our Lord himself said, as it is recorded in John 16. You remember how just at the very end of his ministry and before his death upon the cross, our Lord taught the disciples concerning the Holy Spirit and his work. They were crestfallen because he had told them that he was going to leave them, and they wondered what was going to happen to them. The answer was that the Holy Spirit was to come. And our Lord instructed them about him and told them what he was going to do.

The crucial statement is in verse 14: 'He shall glorify me: for he shall receive of mine, and shall shew it unto you.' Now that is absolutely basic. 'He' – the Holy Spirit when he comes – Christ says, 'shall glorify me.' This is the supreme test of anything that claims to be the work of the Holy Spirit. Indeed, our Lord had already said much the same thing earlier on in that same chapter, beginning at verse 7: 'Nevertheless', he tells them, 'I tell you the truth; It is expedient for you that I go away: for if I go not away, the Comforter will not come unto you; but if I depart, I will send him unto you. And when he is come, he will reprove the world of sin, and of righteousness, and of judgment: Of sin' – why? – 'because they believe not on me' – always pointing to him – 'Of righteousness, because I go to my Father, and ye see me no more; Of judgment, because the prince of this world is judged.' And he judged that enemy by dying upon the cross.

There then we have our Lord himself laying down the great principle that the supreme and outstanding characteristic of the work of the Holy Spirit will always be to glorify him. The Spirit will not speak out of or from himself, or even call attention to himself. He will always – if I may use such an expression – focus a light upon the Son of God.

This is a most wonderful thought. You remember how our Lord himself kept on saying about his own ministry that he had come to glorify the Father. There are many Christian people who forget that. There are many Evangelicals who very rarely speak about the Father, but only about the Son; whereas the Son himself said so often that he had come to glorify the Father and to bring us to him. And in exactly the same way there are people who seem to talk only about the Spirit and forget that the Spirit has come to glorify the Son. This, therefore, is the test of all tests which we must apply to anything that claims to be the work of the Holy Spirit of God.

Now what does this mean exactly? What is this test as put by Paul to the Corinthians and by John in his epistle? It means acknowledging the truth about the Lord Jesus Christ and his person. 'Jesus is Lord!' That is the great confession! It was the great confession of the early church. 'Jesus Christ is

Lord!' And it was in terms of this test that so many of the early Christians were martyred. They were being asked to say, 'Caesar is Lord', but they would not. No, Jesus is Lord and he alone is 'the Lord'.

To glorify him means that we believe the truth concerning his person, that he is indeed the only begotten Son of God. If a man does not believe in the unique deity of the Lord Jesus Christ, nor in his eternal Sonship; if he does not believe in his co-equality and co-eternity with the Father, nor in the great doctrine of the incarnation, then this man is simply not a Christian and he has not got the Spirit of God in him. He may claim to be a Christian, he may even be a so-called Christian preacher, and have prominence in the church, but if he denies that Jesus is God, he has not the Holy Spirit in him.

This is essential – 'that Jesus Christ is come in the flesh' as John puts it in 1 John 4. Notice, too, that the two sides of his nature are prominent – his eternal Godhead and the reality of his human body. There were men appearing in the churches who taught that the incarnation was not really a fact, that Jesus, the 'Lord of Glory', had taken on a kind of phantom body, and that he was not really man. Others were saying that he was *only* man. Both are denounced in the New Testament. So we have to assert, and the Holy Spirit makes us do so, that 'Jesus is Lord', that 'Jesus Christ is truly come in the flesh'.

There is a tradition concerning the apostle John in his old age that as he was entering a certain bath house, he was told that Celsus, one of these heretics who denied the reality of our Lord's manhood, was there having a bath. The moment John heard this he turned away and would not even be in the same building with such a man. And that is of course right. How much more terrible it is that such men are to be found in the Christian church; men who deny the reality of the incarnation, or who deny one or the other of the two natures in the one person of the Son of God.

And then the Holy Spirit enables one to understand not

only the person but also the work of Christ. It is the Holy Spirit alone who can enable one to understand the bread and wine of the communion table and why we observe this sacrament, and what it means. People deny this, they ridicule it or explain it away, calling Christ a pacifist or just a good man. But the Holy Spirit brings a man to see that there on the cross he is bearing our sins and their punishment. 'God was in Christ, reconciling the world unto himself, not imputing their trespasses unto them' (2 Corinthians 5:19). It is the Spirit alone that can bring a man to see these things, and denial of any one of them means that it is neither Christianity, nor the Christian message.

I want to add another test to this first one. It means not only that you believe these things about the Lord, but that you give the central place to him. That is why I am emphasizing this aspect of the matter, that the Holy Spirit is to glorify him. And it is enlightening to notice that in the remainder of the New Testament following the gospels it is still the Lord Jesus Christ who dominates the situation. There are some people who try to persuade us to call the book of the Acts of the Apostles, the book of the Acts of the Holy Spirit. But that would be quite wrong. Luke himself makes that perfectly clear at the beginning of the book: 'The former treatise have I made, O Theophilus, of all that *Jesus* began both to do and to teach.' It is Jesus who goes on doing it. There you see the great activity of the Spirit. It is the Lord Jesus Christ who stands out, who dominates the scene. Acts is the continuing story of his work. The Spirit leads men to glorify the Lord Jesus Christ.

Thirdly, this term 'Jesus is Lord' means, of course, that we surrender ourselves to him. You may think that when the Apostle says, 'No man can say that Jesus is the Lord, but by the Holy Ghost' what he means is that if a man gets up and says, 'Jesus is Lord', he is automatically a Christian. But it does not mean that. This is a very profound statement. If you said, 'Jesus is the Lord', in the ancient world of the first century, it might very well mean martyrdom for you. If you were a Jew, it would certainly mean that you were ostracized from your family and your name expunged from the family tree. A man who says, 'Jesus is Lord', and means what he says, is one who has surrendered his life to him, who has joined the church, and who is often exposed to persecution and ridicule and misunderstanding. So the confession that 'Jesus is Lord' is not just repeating a phrase; anybody can do that. The empty repetition of a phrase does not mean that a man is guided, led, moved and indwelt by the Holy Spirit. This is the profoundest statement of all. It is the ultimate; not only the acceptance of the faith, but commital of oneself to it, casting all one's hopes and fears and everything upon him, taking up the cross and following him.

Here, then, is the first and the greatest test, one which obviously excludes many things that offer themselves to us and claim to be Christian. It is, therefore, an excluding test, and most valuable in that respect. I mentioned earlier some of the history of the Quakers, and they are particularly interesting in this respect. Having started as fully orthodox Christians, like the other Puritans in the seventeenth century, the Quakers, by putting their emphasis increasingly upon the inner light and discounting the teaching of the word began to go astray in their doctrine. I am not being at all critical of them or unfair to them when I assert that by today the vast majority of them are unitarians.

Now this is no accident, it is the kind of thing that happens. People may come to you, they may give every appearance of being very spiritual, highly moral people, who may do excellent works – they may be the greatest philanthropists in the country – but that is not enough. The question we want to know is this – and here is our most valuable excluding test – what do they say about this Jesus? What is their confession with respect to him? Is he just the great teacher, just the supreme mystic, or is he the Son of God incarnate, who saves by his death upon the cross, by his body being broken and his blood being shed? These are the tests, and if you apply them you will discover the interesting result.

This test does not only apply to the Quakers, but also to many of the cults that are current at the present time, as well as those that have had their day and their vogue in past centuries. You will find that this preliminary test is always of great value. You may get people coming to you and using very wonderful language and professing great idealism. They may talk to you about miracles of healing, wonderful guidance and various other things. It all sounds so Christian, and they seem to be offering most of the things listed in the gifts of the Spirit. But you must not accept all that at face value. It may sound like the Christian position but that is where the subtlety comes in. You have got to 'prove', and to 'test', and the test you apply is this: what do they say about the Lord Jesus Christ? They may well have miracles to offer you, or wonderful experiences to give you; they may be able to put people forward to give their testimony and say, 'I used to be miserable and unhappy, now I am happy all the day and I have got no troubles and problems and all is bright and glorious.' But you listen to them, and listen for one thing only – where does the Lord Jesus Christ come in? And you will generally find that he does not come in at all. If he is mentioned, it seems he is just the first propagator of this particular teaching – Christ, the first Christian Scientist, for instance. He had the right view of life, they say, the true science, philosophy and understanding of life; he is just the first propounder and exemplar of this or that, and no more than that. He is not the Son of God. He is not eternal and he does not save by dying on the cross – there is no atonement

In other cases, you find he is not mentioned at all. It sounds like the real thing: people feel much better; they have had a wonderful experience or a great deliverance; they have been healed physically. Surely, you say, this is Christianity, the very thing we want; indeed it is so much better than what the churches offer, we do not find these things in the churches. This is real Christianity. Be careful, my friend, be careful! Apply the first great excluding test, what do they say about the Lord? Where does he come in in all their teaching and their scheme? Is he the eternal Son of God? Does he save by shedding his blood? Is he central, is he essential, is he all-important?

But having said all that and emphasized all these things, I have now to say that even that important test is not enough! You notice that I have kept on referring to it as essentially an 'excluding' test, and I have been doing that very deliberately, because it is not enough. You might interpret these statements as meaning that if a man comes and tells me that he believes that Jesus is Lord, then obviously I must accept everything he says and everything he does. You might think that because he says, 'Jesus is Lord', he must be right in every respect. But that does not follow, and this is where this whole necessity for testing becomes so subtle and so delicate.

Now on what grounds do I say that? Well, let me give you my evidence. I am not here to give voice to my own opinions; God knows we all have to be careful; so let us listen to Scripture. Read what our Lord says in Matthew 24:23 – 'Then if any man shall say unto you, Lo, here is Christ, or there; believe it not. For there shall arise false Christs, and false prophets, and shall shew great signs and wonders; insomuch that, if it were possible, they shall deceive the very elect.' What a statement! False Christs! People will say, 'Here is Christ, or there is Christ.' Do not believe them. Read that passage again. Those are the words of our blessed Lord himself, and he says that this is going to become particularly true towards the 'end of the world', the 'end of this age'.

Look at a comparable statement in 2 Thessalonians 2:8-9 –

'And then shall that Wicked be revealed, whom the Lord shall consume with the spirit of his mouth, and shall destroy with the brightness of his coming: Even him, whose coming is after the working of Satan with all power and signs and lying wonders.' Exactly the same thing is being prophesied and it is because of these things that we have to exercise such great care.

All these warnings are addressed to the church, not to the world. It means that all these things are going to happen in terms of the Christian message. Look again at 2 Corinthians 11. This was the great problem in Corinth: they got so excited about the different gifts and so on that they were losing their balance, and so Paul has to keep on repeating the warning to them. He begins like this: 'Would to God ye could bear with me a little in my folly: and indeed bear with me. For I am jealous over you with godly jealousy: for I have espoused you to one husband, that I may present you as a chaste virgin to Christ. But I fear, lest by any means, as the serpent beguiled Eve through his subtilty, so your minds should be corrupted from the simplicity that is in Christ (2 Corinthians 11:1-3). There is the warning. The moment we get away from this central simplicity that is in Christ we are already doing something that is extremely dangerous.

Paul continues with this theme later in the same chapter. He is talking about certain other teachers who were going round the churches as Christian teachers. Now this is so important. They were not going round as people denying the Christian faith, but as Christian preachers, and they were confusing the churches. Paul says of them, 'Such are false apostles, deceitful workers, transforming themselves into the apostles of Christ. And no marvel; for Satan himself is transformed into an angel of light. Therefore it is no great thing if his ministers also be transformed as the ministers of righteousness; whose end shall be according to their works' (verses 13-15). Could anything be plainer? They appear as apostles of Christ, and yet they are false teachers.

So these warnings go on. Another is given to us by our Lord early in his ministry, even in the Sermon on the Mount itself. Matthew 7:21-23 tells us: 'Not every one that saith unto me, Lord, Lord, shall enter into the kingdom of heaven; but he that doeth the will of my Father which is in heaven. Many will say to me in that day, Lord, Lord, have we not prophesied in thy name? and in thy name have cast out devils? and in thy name done many wonderful works?' And he does not deny that they have done them. 'Then will I profess unto them, I never knew you: depart from me, ye that work iniquity.' He does not deny that they have had the power to do the works when they claim that they have done some wonderful thing, and done it in his name.

You see, this is where we have got to be so careful. You may say, 'Oh yes, with regard to the cults it is plain enough. We have applied your test, and as they do not believe about our Lord as we read in the New Testament – indeed many of them do not even mention him – then that is perfectly clear. But surely when a man comes along and says he has done it in the name of the Lord, he must be right.' No! it does not follow. Read the passage again. Is this point not very plain, my friends? It is not enough that people should 'say' that Jesus is the Lord.

Let me give you further proof of what I am saying, and show you further the importance of applying these tests, because these evil spirits can make most extraordinary statements in order to delude us. Read Mark 3:11 – 'And unclean spirits, when they saw him, fell down before him, and cried, saying, Thou art the Son of God.' Here are evil spirits falling down before him in the persons of their victims and making the confession, 'Thou art the Son of God.' So it is obviously not sufficient that people should say, 'Jesus is Lord'; evil spirits may say that. Here they were, according to the record, doing that in the very days when our Lord was here in this world. You get the same thing reported in Luke 4:41 – 'And devils also came out of many, crying out, and saying, Thou art Christ the Son of God. And he rebuking them suffered them not to speak: for they knew that he was Christ.' As James reminds us, 'The devils also believe, and tremble' (James 2:19). So the mere statement of an orthodox view does not guarantee that the work that is being performed is of necessity the work of the Holy Spirit.

Let me give you one final example from Acts, which shows how the apostles in turn put this very teaching into practice. It is the famous incident in the ministry of the apostle Paul when he and Silas were at Philippi. In Acts 16:16, we read: 'It came to pass, as we went to prayer, a certain damsel possessed with a spirit of divination met us, which brought her masters much gain by soothsaying: The same followed Paul and us, and cried, saying, These men are the servants of the most high God, which show unto us the way of salvation.' Would you not have expected Paul to have added her immediately to his evangelistic party as just the very thing he needed? Here is a girl obviously possessed with some wonderful powers. She points at them day after day as they go by and continues to make these statements about them. What a wonderful advertising agency, you might have thought, for the preaching of the gospel. No, no! Verse 18 continues: 'And this did she many days. But Paul, being grieved, turned and said to the spirit, I command thee in the name of Jesus Christ to come out of her. And he came out the same hour.'

Now I trust that these pieces of evidence are more than sufficient to convince us that even if the confession is made of the name of Christ, it does not guarantee that everything that is being done is of necessity the work of the Holy Spirit. The Scriptures warn us.

Let us see how history again confirms all this. I could give you many examples. The history of the church is strewn with examples of people who have been misled at this very point. Most of the heretics went astray just here; and most of the aberrant, fanatical movements, which have caused such trouble, went astray in exactly the same way. Let me give you just one example – Robert Baxter. I use him again because I have already mentioned him earlier. The same thing was true, of course, of Edward Irving himself and of all the people who used to worship together. These people were true Christians. You could not wish for a more orthodox Christian than Robert Baxter, whose great desire was to exalt the name of the Lord Jesus Christ. There was no doubt about that. He unquestionably passed the test of 1 Corinthians 12:3 and of 1 John 4:1-3. He did confess that Jesus Christ was come in the flesh. He was very much concerned to do that. And yet, as I have already mentioned, poor Robert Baxter made the terrible discovery that the spirit that was in him, which he had thought was the Holy Spirit, was clearly not the Holy Spirit, and he thanked God for delivering him from a possibly terrible fate.

Here, then, is the very essence of this problem. We cannot rest on that one test, although we are tempted to do so. We all, I suppose, have done this at some time or another. Someone comes along and speaks in a certain way, tells you of a certain experience he has had, or reports to you certain things that have been happening. You have various hesitations, but you say that the man is patently a fine Christian and utterly orthodox in his belief. Because he is genuine, sincere, and all out for the glory of God and of Christ, we feel that what he says must, therefore, be right. So you overrule your desire to test and to prove; in fact you feel it is almost wrong to do so, that you would almost be sinning against the Holy Spirit or guilty of blasphemy even to question and to query such a person. And yet I trust I have demonstrated to you that you must test such a person. 'Believe not every spirit; but test and prove and try the spirits whether they be of God or not.' Some of the most genuine people are the ones who have gone most grievously astray, simply because they have not realized that this one test is not enough. You will find, indeed, in the history of Robert Baxter that when questions did arise in his mind, and especially when his wife expressed her concern about what was happening to him and what he was doing, and reasoned with him out of the Scriptures – the only answer he kept on giving was, 'I don't know, but all I know is that Christ is more real to me and I am more concerned for his glory, and I love him more than I have ever done.' That seemed to answer everything. But it is not enough. We must go on testing and proving and trying the spirits.

What then do we do in the light of all this? Well, thank God that in the New Testament there are still more specific tests, which we must examine. If the Apostle had felt that merely to say that 'Jesus is Lord' was enough, he would never have written the rest of 1 Corinthians 12, or chapters 13 and 14. He would have said, this alone matters. But he knew better and so he had to go on and deal with the subject in detail. And I would like to do that with you.

Let me say again that my reason for doing so is not some theoretical or academic interest. I have but one concern. To me the one thing that should be uppermost in our minds at this moment is the need of the Christian church for a baptism of the Spirit, to lift her out of her formality and lethargy and deadness. Nothing is more urgent than a great revival of religion. You see the moral declension. It is no use just condemning it – I hope to show how futile that is. What is needed is this power of the Holy Spirit upon the word, the authentication of the message, the orthodox message of the Christian church, a sifting of the true from the false, and then for God to come down upon this word of truth. It is the supreme need, and all who are concerned about that are, in my opinion, following directly the leading of the Spirit himself.

But the moment we do that the other spirit will come in. He will try to spoil it by counterfeiting it or pressing us too far along certain lines; he will get people to confuse the baptism of the Spirit with the occasional gifts of the Spirit, and people will reject both together, and the great need of revival will be forgotten. That is why I am dealing with this matter and it has got to be done in detail. The apostle Paul was a very busy man, a traveller and an evangelist, who did not have time just to sit down in a study and write letters to churches. No, he never wrote a letter unless he had to do so, and he was concerned and troubled about the church at Corinth. He says he was 'jealous over them with a godly jealousy'. He wanted to save them from themselves and their own errors, to save the reputation of the church because she was the church of Christ, of God, and he wanted to save the reputation, as it were, of God the Father, the Son and the Holy Spirit. So we too must be imbued with the same desire.

Let me, then, just introduce this subject to you now, and then we will go on to look at it and to consider it in detail. The great trouble I often find with 1 Corinthians 12, 13 and 14 is that people become so interested in the details over particular gifts that they miss the whole message of these three chapters. Nowhere is the danger of missing the wood for the trees greater than just at this point. In other words, the first thing you must do is to ask a question. Why did the Apostle write this section? What is his ultimate object? What is he really trying to do? Is he trying to tell us about tongues or about healings? No, he is not; he assumes these things. What he is concerned about is that we should get all these things into the right perspective and balance. He did not write these chapters in order to give a disquisition on the gifts of the Spirit. That is not his object at all! There was trouble and confusion and even division in the church at Corinth over these matters, and the Apostle's one object is to straighten that out and to put it right.

So we must not be over-concerned about the details. We must grasp first and foremost the overriding principle, the grand objective. Here you are, he seems to be saying, dividing up and vying with one another. Listen: 'I give you to understand that no man speaking by the Spirit of God calleth Jesus accursed: and that no man can say that Jesus is the Lord, but by the Holy Ghost.' Have you forgotten about Jesus? *That* is what he is really saying. And then, of course, he works it out in terms of his analogy of the body and so on, showing that a true balance with regard to these things has an essential unity, which all focuses in the person of the Lord Jesus Christ.

Now that is the great leading principle which we must have in mind as we follow the Apostle as he works it out in detail. I am not going to do anything but expound to you in a very general way the teaching of these three chapters. It is no part of my object – indeed, it is unnecessary that we should take these nine gifts in detail and say what each one means. I think if we do that we are likely to fall into the very error against which the Apostle is trying to safeguard us. The central principle is to have a balanced and true view of the purpose and place of all these things in the life of those who truly believe that Jesus is the Lord. And as we follow the teaching, I think we shall be saved from many of the dangers that beset us, and have beset the church at many different times. Notice the last verse of chapter 14, just to finish with this general principle. Here is the object: 'Let all things be done decently and in order.' Paul writes these three chapters because the church at Corinth had become 'indecent and disorderly' in a spiritual sense. This is the error he is seeking to redress.

Chapter 14

Seeking the Gifts

In our consideration of this subject of the baptism with the Holy Spirit we have come to the point where we are considering the matter of the spiritual gifts. The baptism with the Holy Spirit, as we have seen, is essentially designed for witness. Our Lord told the disciples, 'Tarry ye in the city of Jerusalem until ye be endued with power from on high' (Luke 24:49), and then he tells them that they would be 'witnesses unto him'. As they were they were not yet fit to be witnesses. Let us never forget that these words were uttered to the disciples who had been with our Lord during the three years of his ministry. They had heard his sermons, they had seen his miracles, they had seen him crucified on the cross, they had seen him dead and buried, and they had seen him after he had risen literally in the body from the grave. These were the men who had been with him in the upper room at Jerusalem after his resurrection and to whom he had expounded the Scriptures, and yet it is to these men he says that they must tarry at Jerusalem until they are endued with power from on high. The special purpose, the specific purpose of the baptism with the Holy Spirit is to enable us to witness, to bear testimony, and one of the ways in which that happens is through the giving of spiritual gifts. That is why we must consider this subject in dealing with the general doctrine of the baptism with the Holy Spirit.

We have already seen that it is possible for one to be baptized with the Holy Spirit without having some of these special gifts. That is made clear in this passage in 1 Corinthians 12-14 and it is made equally clear in the long history of the Christian church. There have been men raised up of God, baptized with the Spirit – and I am thinking of men such as Whitefield and the Wesley brothers, Finney and D. L. Moody and others – clearly and patently baptized with the Holy Spirit as a separate experience, but they never spoke in tongues and they did not work miracles. It is vital that we should keep these things distinct and clear in our minds.

Now that does not mean to say that there are to be no manifestations of gifts at the present time. We have seen that we must be open to this. We disagree with those who say that these things were confined to the apostolic period; we disagree equally with those who say that all these things should always be manifest in the church. We say that it is a matter for the sovereignty of the Spirit, and clearly throughout the centuries in revival in various times in the church the Spirit has manifested this sovereignty. He has given power of utterance, power of speech, power of preaching oftentimes without some of these particular gifts.

However, it is vital that we should consider these things because at any time, at any moment, the Spirit in his sovereignty may decide to give these gifts again. That is why we should be familiar with the teaching for we have seen that there is great cause for spiritual caution in these matters. We are exhorted to test and to prove the spirits, and that is what we are now trying to do. We see that we do so by the employment of our reason and understanding, particularly with regard to the Scriptures, and that the Holy Spirit will enlighten our minds as we read them. And we have seen so far that the first and the greatest test of all is the place given to our blessed Lord.

But we have also seen that even that is not enough in and of itself. It excludes a lot, but it is not enough to exclude various other counterfeits that may be worked by the devil. So we come now to consider the teaching of these three great chapters, 1 Corinthians 12, 13 and 14. Now Paul, you remember, makes it particularly clear that he was not writing to the Corinthians just for the pleasure of it, but for one reason only, and that was because it had become essential. The church had become divided up into groups and sects and divisions. They were a carnally minded church, divided up amongst themselves even with regard to their teachers and preachers – I am of Paul, I am of Apollos, I am of Cephas – divided again about whether they should eat meat offered to idols or not. These things had become matters of division and they were particularly in trouble over this question of spiritual gifts, which is why the Apostle writes to them. If they had not abused these gifts, he probably would never have written about this matter; but they had, and so Paul's whole object in this passage is to correct this abuse. Confusion had arisen among the Christians in Corinth owing to the fact that they were suffering from a lack of proportion in their understanding of these spiritual gifts.

The Apostle writes to them almost with a sense of astonishment. He tells them that they should be children in malice, but to be men in understanding. 'Brethren, be not children in understanding: howbeit in malice be ye children, but in understanding be men' (1 Corinthians 14:20). They were behaving like children, and he writes to them in order to give them a right sense of proportion with regard to these matters.

So, then, what is Paul's teaching? I have tried to classify it by picking out the principles. I am not concerned to go into the details of the particular gifts. That is a right thing to do, but it is not really essential for the present purpose, because what is true of any one gift is true of all the gifts, since they are all given by the one and the selfsame Spirit, as he keeps on emphasizing – indeed that is his main point, as we shall see. The first and foremost principle concerns the place and the purpose of these gifts in the life of the individual Christian and in the life of the church. Here the Apostle's teaching is surely quite plain, namely that they must never be regarded as ends in themselves – never! That is the danger that people regard these gifts as ends in themselves and forget their whole object and purpose. The moment we do that, we have got them out of proportion. They must be considered in their setting, in their object, and in their whole purpose, and that is what the Apostle proceeds to show these people.

In other words, the gifts must never be put in the centre. They were becoming central in Corinth, occupying the very centre of the stage as it were, and that is why the Apostle has to rebuke the Corinthian church. He says, You have got this out of proportion, they are not meant to be central. In other words, we must never be constantly talking about the gifts. There is a place for them, but not in the centre of our conversation, or our preaching and teaching.

Now this is what is so interesting. Take the New Testament itself and you cannot but see that what dominates the New Testament in the central position is the Lord Jesus Christ himself, and everything points to him. There are many other things that are incidental, including this question of the gifts. But it is not the gifts that are central to the New Testament; it is the Lord.

Again you will find that in the great periods of reformation and revival in the church, when remarkable things have happened and phenomena have been evident, it is not the wonders that have been at the centre, but the Lord himself. These things have simply pointed to him. So that the moment we find ourselves constantly talking about gifts, any one of them or all of them together, and putting them in the centre of our teaching and preaching, we have already lost the balance and proportion. They are never meant to occupy the centre of the stage. It is still worse, of course, when they become the cause of division or when they divide a church up into sects as they had done at Corinth. It is because of this that Paul writes his letters and he reprimands them. They are very wrong in doing this. So it seems to me that to form movements with respect to the gifts of the Spirit is utterly unscriptural.

But let us be fair in this matter. This does not only apply to spiritual gifts. The way in which people have formed movements with respect to particular matters never ceases to amaze me. For instance, I cannot see in the New Testament itself any possible justification for a movement in connection with holiness. I cannot see any justification for a movement just to teach prophetic teaching or concerning the second advent of our Lord. We should not form movements with regard to particular aspects of the faith or of doctrine. No; the moment you do so you lose your balance. All these things should always be taken together; in the same way there must be no movement in connection with the gifts of the Spirit. Why? Because these are to be manifested in the church, and the church is a whole and her doctrine is a whole. You do not 'specialize' on doctrines in the Christian life.

This is something, of course, which one could illustrate from many other realms. Over-specialization is always a danger. For what it is worth it seems to me that this is what is happening in modern medicine, and it is a very dangerous thing. You get men who specialize exclusively on the chest, while others only know about abdominal conditions, which is very dangerous because you may have a disease in your chest, but your pain may well be in your abdominal area. They are parts of a body and you should not divide the body up like that. And it is exactly the same with the various aspects of Christian teaching or of the various manifestations of the life and the power of the Holy Spirit in man. The moment these things are isolated and are put in a special position, with all the attention focused on them, you have already lost your New Testament balance and sense of proportion. So I say that it is surely evident that when an individual or a number of individuals are always talking about gifts, and never talking about anything else, and while they are always preaching and teaching this, they have already gone into the Corinthian position.

That does not mean to say that the gifts themselves are wrong, but it does mean that this attitude towards them is wrong and that these people are already in a position which is contrary to the teaching of Scripture, They are too excited about them. They were very excited in Corinth about these things. As you read these chapters you can feel the tension and the excitement. The whole church was in a condition in which the Apostle had to reprimand them and write the great thirteenth chapter on love in order to bring them back to a right sense of balance with regard to these matters.

Then another obvious thing about them was that they were lacking in a sense of discipline with respect to the gifts, and they were guilty of a certain amount of disorder and, indeed, of causing a riot. Paul emphasizes, 'Let all things be done decently, and in order.' They were so undisciplined that he has to say to them: 'If therefore the whole church be come together into one place, and all speak with tongues, and there come in those that are unlearned, or unbelievers, will they not say that ye are mad?' (1 Corinthians 14:23). When the Church gives the impression to the outsider that she consists of a number of maniacs, she is doing the exact opposite of what our Lord intended her to do. There was great disorder here, simply because they were not viewing these gifts in the right way; gifts had become everything and they all wanted to show that they had got the gifts, and they were all doing it at the same time. And so a stranger coming in and hearing all these people speaking in tongues at the same time, would say, 'They are mad!'

Another terrible thing that had arisen was that a spirit of competition had come in with respect to the gifts. That is the burden of the middle section of the twelfth chapter. Paul writes, 'The body is not one member, but many. If the foot shall say, Because I am not the hand, I am not the body; is it therefore not of the body?' (verses 14-15). You see these gifts differ. Paul lists nine different gifts, some of which are more spectacular than others. Because they had got the whole subject out of proportion, they became jealous of one another, and the men with the greater gifts tended to despise the others, so that the whole church was in a state of turmoil. As well as showing an utter lack of discipline, the Corinthians were literally filled with envy of one another. The whole condition of the church was a most unhappy and a most unfortunate one.

This sense of competition had led to the tendency to 'display' the gifts. The Christian life is a very wonderful life, it is a new life; but we are still in the body, and not yet made perfect. There are infirmities that remain, and there is the devil, the adversary, who is always ready to upset the work of God. When these gifts are given, the devil comes in and gets us to view them in the wrong way, and so we begin to display ourselves and show off the gift.

I need not expand on these things, they are always important. They are important, for example, in prayer meetings, as I have often had to point out. The ideal prayer meeting is one in which almost everybody present takes part, but sometimes some people pray at such length that there is no time for anybody else. But Paul teaches here that we should think of one another, and not be making a display. They were guilty of doing that in Corinth and it is always one of the dangers that tends to creep in.

Then, finally, under this heading the thing that the Apostle emphasizes is the importance of putting the gifts into the right order. There is no doubt at all that the main trouble in

Corinth was that the gift of tongues was being given too much prominence. That is the main thrust of the three chapters. Paul always puts it last on the list.

Now let us be clear about this. Paul says quite specifically 'prohibit not to speak in tongues'. We must not do that. But it is equally clear that he says, Do not put it first, do not monopolize the whole of the life of the church in speaking in tongues as that is not its place. He says, 'Covet earnestly the best gifts'; adding later on in chapter 14, 'Follow after charity, and desire spiritual gifts, but rather that ye may prophesy.' To show the importance of prophecy over and against tongues, he gives us this teaching with regard to the respective merits of prophesying and speaking in tongues. Indeed, the whole of that fourteenth chapter is designed to show that tongues must never be the one thing to be talked about; it must not be the one thing that everybody covets nor must it monopolize all the attention – that is what he condemns. The gifts must be put in the right order. The gift of tongues is a very spectacular and exciting one, and that is exactly where the devil sees his opportunity. He gets people to lose their sense of balance and proportion, so that this becomes the centre. It should not be; it is always put last in the list, and seems to be the least of the gifts. It is a spiritual gift; 'I would that ye all spake with tongues', says Paul. Obviously they did not all do so, otherwise he would not say that. He says that he himself speaks in tongues, and thanks God for it, but he keeps it in order and in its right place. Paul says, 'In the church I had rather speak five words with my understanding … than ten thousand words in an unknown tongue.'

So we see how these things can be abused because people forget the place and the purpose and the object of all these gifts, which is to glorify the Lord. That is the thing that people will keep on forgetting. They stop at the gifts themselves. 'Isn't it wonderful,' they say, 'isn't it marvellous.' But where is the Lord, my friend, where is he? All these things are meant to glorify the Lord! How is it that we can so often forget the pattern and the example which is set for us by the apostles themselves?

Look at that great incident in Acts 3 when Peter and John went up to the temple at the hour of prayer. They saw the lame man laid daily at the Beautiful gate and were enabled to heal him. Here was a man who had never walked in his life and Peter said to him, 'Silver and gold have I none; but such as I have give I thee: In the name of Jesus Christ of Nazareth rise up and walk.' In the actual performance of the miracle Peter is careful to put the Lord at the very centre. He had been given this gift, this is the gift of miracles being exercised. But notice the way in which the Apostle performs the miracle.

It becomes still more interesting when Peter addresses the crowd that had gathered together. They were filled with wonder and amazement, 'And when Peter saw it, he answered unto the people, Ye men of Israel, why marvel ye at this? or why look ye so earnestly on us, as though by our own power or holiness we had made this man to walk?' He will not let himself be placed in the centre, nor have attention focused on himself. He says, 'The God of Abraham, and of Isaac, and of Jacob, the God of our fathers, hath glorified his Son Jesus; whom ye delivered up, and denied him in the presence of Pilate, when he was determined to let him go.... His name through faith in his name hath made this man strong, whom ye see and know: yea, the faith which is by him hath given him this perfect soundness in the presence of you all.' Peter goes on preaching Jesus Christ. He does not give them an address on gifts, he manifests the gift. The purpose of the gift is to call attention to the Lord. You do not stop with the gifts, and attention should not be focused on them. You should not be always preaching and teaching about the gifts. No, you are to preach Christ! You are to preach what he does, how he sends the Spirit, and how the Spirit in turn may or may not give the gifts.

You do not found a movement on gifts, because if you do you will find that you are saying very little about the Lord. And any teaching or preaching which does not keep the Lord central and vital and overruling everything is already wrong teaching. That kind of teaching always leads to trouble and eventually to disaster. Let us not forget that this is what happened to the Irvingite movement. What a contrast all this is to the mighty preaching that has always characterized the great revivals in the history of the church. They preached Jesus Christ as Saviour and as Lord. He was the centre of all the preaching. This emphasis is even reflected in the hymns that we have in our hymn books, the great hymns. They are all focused on him. And once we cease to realize that the object of all the gifts is to glorify him – the moment we forget that, we have already gone wrong.

The second object of the gifts is evangelistic. The Apostle makes this quite plain, for instance, with regard to this gift of tongues, 'Wherefore tongues are for a sign, not to them that believe, but to them that believe not' (1 Corinthians 14:22) – and it is quite clear from the book of Acts that this is so. We must test anything that claims to be a movement of the Spirit in terms of its evangelistic power.

This is important, because it is rather a subtle point. All the great movements of the Spirit as recorded in the Scriptures and in the subsequent history of the church, have always been great evangelistic movements. Revival, of course, always starts in the church but it does not stop there. God's way has been to revive his people and then, because they are revived, his power is manifested in their preaching, their witness, their testimony, and in the whole of their lives.

That is the characteristic of a true movement of the Spirit – it always has an outreach. On the other hand, the tendency of the counterfeit is to be a small, inward movement where you get a little coterie being formed, and where they just share wonderful experiences among themselves, but nobody else gets any benefit. This is, of course, always characteristic of the cults, which tend to be inward-looking with no outreach in that sense. But the great characteristic of the work of the Spirit is invariably this evangelistic consequence.

Watch the order. It must start in the church, which is then empowered to witness and testify boldly of the Lord. The Holy Spirit is not given that we may have wonderful experiences or marvellous sensations within us, or even to solve psychological and other problems for us. That is certainly a part of the work of the Spirit, but it is not the primary object. The primary object is that the Lord may be known. So you are entitled to judge anything that claims to be a movement of the Spirit – I am not here referring to an organized movement in connection with the Spirit or one concerned to teach about the Spirit – I am talking about a movement of the Spirit himself, the action of the Spirit. You are entitled to test that by applying to it this vital evangelistic test.

In other words, you see, such a movement of the Spirit is going to affect the whole church. It moves the whole church forward and does not merely gather together people who are interested in experiences and sensations and who are always turning round in a little circle. That is the cause of division. This is more general in its operation.

The next point I would emphasize is the one made by the Apostle when he says that these gifts are given in order that we may profit. 'The manifestation of the Spirit is given to every man to profit withal' (1 Corinthians 12:7). Now this again is a most important point. There is to be profit for the man himself and also for the whole church. Let me put it to you as you have it in 1 Corinthians 14:12 – 'Even so ye, forasmuch as ye are zealous of spiritual gifts, seek that ye may excel to the edifying of the church.' Now here is the great rule that the Apostle lays down: there must always be profit and edification. The moment we lose that again we have gone astray.

The devil, of course, will tempt us, as he has always tempted people throughout the centuries, to be interested merely in phenomena and experiences. We are all in the flesh, and we are all anxious to have certainty and assurance. The danger is that that may be turned inwards in such a way that we are only interested in sensation and experiences, and so forget the profiting; there are undoubtedly people, who go to meetings not that their minds may be enlightened or that they may be profited in their understanding, but because they want a thrill, they want to feel something.

Now this happens not only in connection with the doctrine of the baptism of the Spirit, it is also true of every church service. You will know full well of great rallies where some people just go from meeting to meeting waiting for some feeling, some thrill or excitement. They do not grow, they do not profit, nor do they increase in understanding, for they are not interested in those things. All they want is the excitement of the experience. The Apostle's teaching shows that this attitude is quite wrong. 'The manifestation of the Spirit is given to every man to profit withal', and it is to be always to the edifying of the church.

Now I come to the second heading, which again is a vitally important one – it concerns the way in which we seek the gifts. The Apostle says, 'Covet earnestly the best gifts' (1 Corinthians 12:31). It is at this point that the enemy once more tends to take advantage and to come in. Let us be clear about this; we are exhorted to seek the gifts and to desire them, and to do so earnestly. But here is where the danger enters. There are wrong ways of seeking the gifts. Well, let me note some of them.

First and foremost, of course, the spirit in which we seek them is vital in and of itself. If we seek these things with a selfish motive or merely with the desire to make ourselves important, so that we can speak and be prominent in giving testimony, rather than for the edification of the church, then we are already wrong.

We have to start by asking ourselves this first question – why do I desire these gifts? What is my motive and my object? And you will find that that will help you. Do you want it in order to have some thrilling and exciting experience? You are already wrong. The Holy Spirit is sent to glorify the Lord Jesus Christ and we must never forget that. Our motive should always be to know him so that we may minister to his glory and to his praise.

Having examined your motives, the second point I would make is this, and I do this in the light of some teaching that I have been reading recently. There is a teaching popular today which tells us that the quickest way of obtaining the baptism with the Holy Spirit is to get the gift of tongues which, they say, is very wonderful. If you want the baptism with the Spirit, start with tongues, and then that will probably lead you to the baptism with the Spirit. Now this is almost incredible because it cuts right across the whole of the teaching of the New Testament, which says that the gift of tongues is one of the manifestations of the Spirit. So you do not start with the tongues and go to the Spirit, you have the Spirit and the gift of tongues is one proof of it. But now the exact opposite is actually being taught. This is over-anxiety, of course, this is man coming in with his methods.

What does the New Testament describe? The apostles, and the hundred and twenty, met together in the upper room, the Holy Spirit came down upon them and they began to speak; they were first baptized with the Spirit, then began to speak in tongues. And so it is in all the other instances in Scripture. But the new teaching says start with tongues, it is the easiest and simplest way; and via tongues you arrive at the baptism of the Spirit. Well, there is no need to say more! It is just sheer lack of scriptural understanding, it is the flesh intruding and trying to do for us what the Spirit himself alone can do.

Let me put that still more plainly. There is nothing, it

seems to me, so wrong and so dangerous as to try to induce or produce in ourselves the gifts of the Spirit. Again it is almost incredible that people should go astray on these matters. But people have always tended to do so and it is happening extensively at the present time. Their teaching is an attempt to help the Spirit to do his own work. Now Scripture teaches that the Holy Spirit is given to us, the risen Lord baptizes us with the Holy Spirit. 'The one upon whom thou shalt see the Spirit descending, and remaining on him', said God to John the Baptist, 'the same is he which baptizeth with the Holy Ghost.' And he alone does it, nobody else. He needs no assistance, the Spirit needs none of our help. The moment you try to help the Spirit you are already asking for trouble.

Take, for instance, a teaching which is well known at the present time as to how one can be baptized with the Spirit. Here we are, Christian people, anxious to receive the best that God has to give us, and to receive the baptism with the Spirit in order that we may glorify the Lord and witness to him. We may feel we have not received this, so how do we do so? 'Quite simple,' we are told. 'Do you want the baptism of the Spirit? Well, all you need do is stay to an after meeting.' Then you sit on a chair and relax yourself as much as you can, relax your body. Then we are told that our Lord in the upper room 'breathed' the Holy Spirit upon the disciples and said, 'Receive ye the Holy Ghost'. So the next step in the teaching follows thus: 'Now remember he has breathed out the Holy Spirit; do you want to be baptized with the Holy Spirit? Well, this is all you have to do – in this relaxed condition, breathe in deeply, and as you are doing so you are breathing in the Holy Spirit into yourselves, and are receiving the baptism of the Holy Spirit. So relax and breathe in deeply and go on doing so, and as you are doing so you are breathing in the Holy Spirit.'

Now that is actually being taught! Where do you find anything approaching that in the New Testament? My dear friends, this is sheer psychological teaching and nothing but the power of suggestion. It is typical of the methods of psychology and you may have seen leading psychologists demonstrating on the television. And it is because Christian people teach this kind of thing that the critics are able to make their attacks while the world laughs in derision. But I am saying here that that teaching is not only unscriptural, it is purely carnal, not to say anything worse about it. Where do you see a man in the New Testament being told to relax and to breathe in deeply, or to do anything? No, what you find is that Christians are gathered together, praying to God, and suddenly he comes upon them; the household of Cornelius were sitting, listening to the preaching of Peter, and the Holy Spirit came upon them. In Ephesus Paul lays hands upon them and the gift is received; they do nothing by way of relaxing and deep breathing. That is psychology. And yet there are innocent people who follow this teaching and who fondly imagine that they have been baptized with the Spirit. They have not! They have either been hypnotized by another, or hypnotized themselves, or else they have entered into a state of hysteria; and, as I have already reminded you, psychological conditions can produce these phenomena as can spiritism. The moment you begin to do something like this in order to help the Spirit, you have already opened the most dangerous door you can ever open in your Christian life.

Let me give another illustration of the same thing. Take this question of speaking in tongues. When a man comes to me and tells me of some great occasion in his life when, while praying, the Holy Spirit suddenly came upon him and he was lifted up out of himself and found himself speaking in a strange tongue, I am ready to believe him and to accept him, especially if he tells me either that it has never happened to him again or that it has only happened very infrequently. I will accept it as being an authentic experience.

But when I read something like this (as I do so often in various journals) I am in an entirely different position. This is the teaching: 'Do you want to speak in tongues? 'Very well,' they say, 'this is what you have got to do; surrender your jaw and your tongue – let them go.' This is no laughing matter, my friends, the thing is too serious. There are people being led astray by such teaching today. 'Then,' they continue, 'then begin to utter sounds, any sort of sound, it doesn't matter whether it has sense or meaning or not; utter any sound that offers itself to you and go on doing that. And if you keep on doing it you will find yourself speaking in tongues.' And the simple answer is you probably will, but it will have nothing to do with the Holy Spirit. I do not hesitate to say that. Where is there any suggestion whatsoever that we have to do things like this in the New Testament? It is just not there at all. What happens in the New Testament is that a man is baptized with the Spirit and finds himself speaking in tongues. This is the gift of the Spirit and he is all-powerful. He does not need your help. But psychology does. If you want to be hypnotized, you have got to yield and surrender yourself, you have got to behave in an automatic manner, and do what you are told to do. That is exactly what these people are teaching.

Now I am not querying their motives; I know they are honest, and that their motives are good; what I am saying is that they are not only unscriptural, they are also putting themselves into the hands not only of the psychologists but perhaps even of evil spirits. You must do nothing at all. The Spirit gives these gifts 'severally to every man as he will'. That is the statement: 'All these worketh that one and the selfsame Spirit, dividing to every man severally as he will' (1 Corinthians 12:11). If I am going to give somebody a gift, I do not want any help from them. But that is what people are being taught to do at the present time, as if the Holy Spirit cannot decide, and cannot do it in and of himself. He does not need your help! The moment you begin to try to induce a gift you are acting psychologically; indeed, as I have said, you may be handing yourself over to evil spirits. That is exactly what happens to those who become 'mediums' in connection with such work; they just hand themselves over and they are used by evil spirits. There is nothing more dangerous than this, but what amazes me is how anybody who is a Christian can believe such teaching. Where is it, I ask, in the New Testament? It is not there at all! According to the New Testament it is the gift of the Spirit, it is in the sovereignty of the Spirit, and we must leave it entirely to him and do nothing ourselves in order to try to help or to induce it or to produce it.

I am expounding this to you in its extreme form because that is how it is being popularly taught today. There have been meetings in which they have tried to work up an excitement by clapping their hands or by repeating a chorus or a hymn. All that is pure psychology, and not needed. No! The way of the New Testament is the exact opposite; it is to go to him, to seek it of him. He is the giver. Do not do anything else. The Holy Spirit does not need our help, my friends, or our psychological aids. He does not need us to reduce the lights and to put up an illuminated cross over the pulpit. He does not need all our help with all our singing and all our preliminaries and working up of emotions.

I am not only speaking now, you see, about the baptism with the Spirit, I am thinking of popular evangelism also. If the Spirit is Lord – and he is – he does not need these helps, and anything that tries to help the Spirit to produce a result is a contradiction of New Testament teaching. 'Not with enticing words of man's wisdom', says the Apostle, 'but in demonstration of the Spirit and of power.' Go to him! Speak to him! Ask him! Pray to him! That is what they did in New Testament times, and that is what they have done in all the greatest and best periods in the subsequent history of the Christian church.

Let me end with this note. The best way of all, according to the apostle Paul, is the way that he outlines in 1 Corinthians 13. Look at that last verse in chapter 12: 'But covet earnestly the best gifts: and yet shew I unto you a more excellent way.' There is no passage of Scripture that has been more frequently abused and misinterpreted than just that. The common way in which the quenchers of the Spirit use it, of course, is this: 'Yet shew I unto you a more excellent way,' they say. 'Do not talk about or get interested in gifts; gifts are all right, but they are nothing. Go in for the graces.' They interpret it like that because they base their teaching upon the Authorized Version translation of that statement, which is incorrect. 'Yet shew I unto you a more excellent way', says the Authorized Version, but the translators had no right to translate it like that. There is no comparative at all in the original. The way it should be translated is: 'Moreover I show you an excellent way.' That is all. You might translate it like this: 'And yet I show you a way according to excellence.'

What does Paul mean by that? I agree with Charles Hodge when he interprets it like this: 'Covet earnestly the best gifts; and moreover I show you the way par excellence to obtain the gifts.' You see it is the exact opposite of those who say that this is to dismiss and to belittle the gifts. It cannot mean that because when the Apostle takes up the subject again at the beginning of chapter 14 he says, 'Follow after charity, and desire spiritual gifts.' He has not dismissed them, he is not contrasting the spiritual gifts with the graces. No, no, he says. If you really want the gifts, seek the graces. The best way to get the gifts is to seek the love of the Lord, his love to you and yours to him. If you are filled with this love then you are likely to get the best gifts. It is the way par excellence of obtaining them.

Without any question this is the New Testament way, as it

has been the way of the saints throughout the centuries. Do not seek the gifts directly, seek them indirectly. Seek him! Seek his love! Seek his glory! Seek the knowledge of him! Seek the power to witness and to testify unto him! Be filled with a love to him and then you will get your gifts. If you do not, what will happen to you will be this. You may speak with the tongues of men and of angels, but because you have not got charity you will 'become as a sounding brass, or a tinkling cymbal'. Remember, that means that you will be able to speak in tongues but it will be of no value. 'And though I have the gift of prophecy, and understand all mysteries' – you have been seeking them directly – 'and all knowledge; and though I have all faith, so that I could remove mountains, and have not charity, I am nothing.' It is no good.

In other words the prescription is – seek him! Seek his love, seek his life, seek to know him in the very vitals of your being; seek that you may be filled with love to him, and you will receive the gifts. Not talking about them always, not having meetings about them. No! Have meetings about him! Preach about him! Preach about him in the glory of his person and his divine saviourhood and all he has done. Preach him! Seek him! Love him! And he will give you the gifts to enable you to witness to him and to bear testimony to him and to the glory of his praise!

We must leave it at that, but these matters, as you can see, are of the most vital and urgent importance. Keep the balance, my dear friends. Keep your sense of proportion. And above all be wary lest in your anxiety to get gifts you may hand yourself over either to the psychologist or else to the evil spirits that are able to counterfeit even these choice and precious gifts of the Holy Spirit given by the risen Lord. May God give us all a spirit of understanding, and a spirit of wisdom with respect to these matters.

Chapter 15

Control of the Tongue

We have seen that Paul emphasizes above everything else that the purpose and the object of the gifts is to glorify the Lord. The Spirit himself has been sent to glorify the Lord Jesus, not to call attention to himself but always to point to the Lord. We must ever keep that in the forefront of our minds. We have seen too, that the next thing the Apostle takes up – and it is to this indeed that he gives most of his attention – is the whole question of balance and order. Finally, we considered briefly the way in which we seek these gifts. Paul tells us to 'Covet earnestly the best gifts', and we saw that there are certain false mechanical, psychological ways in which people can attempt to do this and so get themselves into trouble and ultimately bring the whole doctrine concerning gifts into disrepute.

We must continue to examine this whole question of gifts as the Apostle does. You notice that in 1 Corinthians 12-14 he gives the greatest prominence to the whole question of what is called 'speaking in tongues', because that was clearly the main cause of trouble in Corinth and the issue which was causing confusion. The object of the three chapters is really to put the question of speaking in tongues into its right place, to give the Corinthians a due sense of proportion with respect to it. They were putting it in the first place, talking about it and all trying to show that they possessed the gift. Thus the disorder to which he refers had entered into the life of the church.

There is no doubt whatsoever that this is the main object which the Apostle has in his mind, because he keeps on repeating it. The whole of the fourteenth chapter is virtually given over to this one thing, and it is interesting to notice the way in which he handles it. In the two lists he gives, he deliberately puts speaking in tongues last and he does this because the Corinthians were putting it first. That is his way of correcting them. And then he goes out of his way to repeat it several times, to show that prophecy is the greater gift and that this is the one they should seek. In other words, he deals with tongues by contrasting it with the gift of prophecy, thereby showing that the exaggerated importance which the Corinthians were giving to this speaking in tongues was entirely wrong.

We are dealing with it here because it is our duty to expound the Scriptures. If there is anybody who says at this point, 'I am not interested in the gift of tongues, or in 1 Corinthians 12-14', then I have to say to you that what I want to discuss with you is not the gift of tongues but your whole view of the Scriptures. Anyone who cuts out portions of Scripture is guilty of a very grievous sin. It is the business of all of us as Christians to understand the whole of the Bible, and unless we are making an effort to do so we are very poor Christians; quite apart from the fact that we are at the same time probably quenching the Spirit and are just desirous of going along in our undisturbed, self-satisfied, smug kind of formal Christianity. I have nothing to say to that except to warn such people that they will have to stand before God in the judgement and give an account of themselves, including how they have paid attention to the word that he has provided for them, and for their growth and development. That, then, is our main reason for considering it.

Another very good reason for considering this whole matter is that this question has received a great deal of prominence in this present century. A movement broke out in 1906, particularly in America, but also to some extent in this country, in connection with speaking in tongues. This movement has become known as Pentecostalism. We need not here go into the history of the movement but this subject has received a good deal of prominence ever since, and it behoves us, therefore, to know something about it. In recent years there has been a revival once more of interest in this, again starting mainly in America but also spreading to this and other countries. There is at the present time amongst many good, excellent Christian people a great deal of interest in the whole matter of speaking in tongues. It is, therefore, our business to be aware of the teaching of Scripture with respect to it in order that we may know what attitude to adopt.

Thirdly, and lastly, my reason for calling attention to this gift is that it is quite obviously, of all the spiritual gifts the one that is most likely to be misused and abused by believers. That is the whole thrust of this passage in 1 Corinthians. I do not know why this should be. It may be that it was the gift that was distributed most freely; it may well be because it is the least of the gifts. The trouble in Corinth was that they all wanted to speak in tongues and many of them wanted to do so at the same time. It tends to lend itself to exhibitionism and to promote selfishness.

Now the wonderful thing about the Christian life is that we are born again – but we are not made perfect. That is why we are liable to go astray, and to listen to the attacks of the enemy, the adversary of our souls. That is why these New Testament letters ever came into being, because Christian people were being led astray in these various ways. And so I say there is no gift perhaps that is more liable to be abused than this one, none that is more liable to attract the carnal part of our being and so lead to excess and to abuse. And certainly it is true to say that there is no gift of the Spirit that has lent itself so much to the counterfeit of the devil in various forms than this particular gift.

I think I have already reminded you that it is quite possible for spiritists to speak in tongues – there is no question about that. There have been endless recorded cases of it. Not only that, people under certain psychological states and conditions can be made to do this under the influence of spiritists. I think of a certain lay pastor, who came to me in considerable distress over the case of a girl who was clearly devil-possessed and was able to speak in tongues. These things are well-established facts. Therefore I say, because of this, it behoves us to be unusually careful as we approach this subject. So we do so along the lines that I have already been indicating to you. We must avoid the two extremes, one of which is to dismiss the whole thing and refuse even to consider it.

I am amazed at some of the things I have read recently on the subject – certain Christian people have issued booklets and pamphlets, and in one of these the writer did not hesitate to say that 'all speaking in tongues today is of the devil'. How a man ventures to make such a statement I simply cannot understand. I would not dare to do so. No, we must be very careful in all we say and we must be open in this matter. The Apostle tells us, 'Wherefore, brethren, covet to prophesy, and forbid not to speak with tongues' (1 Corinthians 14:39). We have already dealt with the argument that says this belonged only to the early church. If you once go along that line you will soon find that the New Testament has practically nothing to say to you at all, you will have to say it was all for the early church. But clearly it was not, it is for us.

We start then by saying that it is always possible that the Holy Spirit may give this gift to certain individuals. So that when we hear of any reported case, we do not dismiss it, nor do we condemn it. We must examine it. In the sovereignty of the Spirit he can give any one of these gifts at any time; we must therefore be open. But for the reasons we have already adduced we must also always be cautious and careful, we must 'prove all things', and only 'hold fast to that which is good.

Now what is the teaching in Scripture with regard to speaking in tongues? In the first place, speaking in tongues is not the invariable accompaniment of the baptism of the Spirit. I put it like that because there is teaching which has been current for a number of years and still is today, which says that speaking in tongues is always the initial evidence of the baptism with the Spirit. It therefore goes on to say that unless you have spoken in tongues you have not been baptized with the Holy Spirit. Now that, I suggest, is entirely wrong. In 1 Corinthians 12:30 the Apostle asks, 'Have all the gifts of healing? do all speak with tongues?' Again in 1 Corinthians 14:5 he says, 'I would that ye all spake with tongues, but rather that ye prophesied'. And when he says that he would that they all spake in tongues, he is clearly saying that they all did not. That, it seems to me, should be sufficient in and of itself.

But in addition to that there is other great evidence. When we were dealing with the question of the baptism with the Spirit in general I gave you a number of quotations of some of the greatest and most saintly men the church has ever known, some of the greatest preachers and evangelists. These were men who had received the baptism with the Holy Spirit after their conversion in a most unmistakable manner and who gave proof that they had received this by being used so mightily of God in evangelism and in revival; but none of them spoke in tongues, not one of them.

Now these are sheer facts and they surely should indicate to us how wrong it is to make these dogmatic assertions. But let me be quite fair; not all who belong to the Pentecostal church teach this: some do and some do not. It is very interesting to note that at the European Pentecostal

Conference, which was held in Stockholm in 1939, it was admitted that tongues might occur apart from the Spirit's action. Now these men are honest men of God who were ready to admit in a world conference that powers other than the Holy Spirit can enable people to speak in tongues; they then went on to say that a Christian could be filled with the Spirit without the sign of tongues. Quite so! They would have been flying in the face of the facts of history as well as in the plain teaching of the Scriptures had they not made that admission and concession.

Now I am concerned about all this for this reason. When people are told that unless they speak in tongues they have not been baptized with the Holy Spirit, many who have been baptized with the Holy Spirit are made to feel very unhappy. They say, 'But I have never spoken in tongues, and I am told that because of that, I have never been baptized with the Spirit.' But they had thought that they were, they had every reason for thinking that they were, and thus they are made unhappy.

But still more serious is the fact that having been made unhappy in this way by this false teaching, they then, of course, become much more open than they were before to psychological pressure, let alone the influence of evil spirits. They are so anxious to have this 'essential' evidence that they do everything they can to speak in tongues and, of course, after a while some of them begin to do so. But the question is – what has made them do so? Others remain unhappy and miserable, which is quite wrong and false. It is all due to this one teaching. It is to fly in the face of the Scriptures and the history of the church to say that unless a man has spoken in tongues, he has never been baptized with the Holy Spirit.

Let me say again that one of my main objects in this whole series of sermons is to safeguard the doctrine of the baptism with the Holy Spirit. There is a tendency on the part of some, because they dislike the gifts and the manifestations and the excesses, to throw out the doctrine of the baptism of the Spirit with it. Let me underline this important fact – you must differentiate between the two. It is possible for a man to be baptized with the Holy Spirit without ever speaking in tongues, and, indeed, without having some of these other gifts which the Apostle lists in this great passage that we are examining.

Let us come to the second matter. What is speaking in tongues? This is helpful again to throw light upon the present discussion. How do you define speaking in tongues? There is a difficulty that arises here because of what we are told in Acts 2 of what happened to the apostles and to those also who were gathered with them in that upper room on the day of Pentecost. We are told, 'And there appeared unto them cloven tongues like as of fire, and it sat upon each of them. And they were all filled with the Holy Ghost, and began to speak with other tongues, as the Spirit gave them utterance.'

Now the tendency in some is to identify that with what the apostle is speaking about in 1 Corinthians 12-14. And yet it seems to me that that is sheer confusion. I say that because it is perfectly clear from what happened on the day of Pentecost that the apostles were speaking in known languages. We prove that by pointing out how the different people who were there were astonished that they were all hearing these men speaking in their own languages. 'They were all amazed and marvelled, saying one to another, Behold, are not all these which speak Galileans? And how hear we every man in our own tongue, wherein we were born?' (Acts 2:7-8). They were clearly speaking in their languages.

There are some who say that what happened was that the apostles were speaking the normal language of Galilaeans, but that the gift of understanding them was given to the other people. That is wrong for this reason: if that were so, it would be the other people on whom the Holy Spirit had descended. The miracle would have happened in the listeners But the account tells us that the miracle had taken place in the speakers, in the apostles, who were enabled to speak these various languages, and the people were able to hear them. In other words, there was no need of an interpreter. The people knew the languages and they understood what was being said.

Now the whole point in 1 Corinthians 14 is that interpretation is an absolute necessity and that without interpretation the gift of tongues should not be exercised. There is this emphasis on the need for an interpreter in verses 2, 4, 14 and 15. It is clear to me, therefore, that in the Corinthian passage we are not dealing with 'known languages' as we were in Acts. There is a very good reason, which we need not go into here, why what happened on the day of Pentecost did happen. It is the answer to the Tower of Babel. It is the indication of the universality of the gospel.

But here we are dealing with something different. It is quite clear that in a cosmopolitan city, a seaport like Corinth, there would have been people from different parts speaking different languages. It is quite clear that if these Christians were speaking in various languages that there would have been people present who could have understood. The apostle Paul himself was a man who clearly could speak several languages, but he says that when he spoke in tongues there were times when he did not understand (see 1 Corinthians 14:14); as the gift of tongues was given so there was the gift of interpretation also. Therefore, it seems to me quite clear that in Corinthians we are not dealing with known languages. In any case there seems no point or purpose in a man in private prayer praying in some other known language. What is there to be gained by that? There does not seem to be any object or any purpose in it.

I want to suggest to you now that a lot of the trouble has arisen, because people have not given the full significance to the word 'tongue' – 'in an unknown tongue' or 'in a tongue', the 'unknown' is generally supplied. What is the basic meaning of this word 'tongue'? Now I am not giving my own opinion here, but the opinion of the experts in these matters and there is no doubt but that the Greek word means 'speaking tongue', or if you prefer, 'the tongue in action'. It is not referring to dialects or languages.

What the Apostle is talking about here, therefore, is 'the tongue speaking as it is moved by the Holy Spirit'. Normally when a man speaks, his tongue moves as the result of his understanding and the direction of his will; but when a man speaks in a tongue, the tongue is in action as the result of the operation of the Spirit. All these gifts are gifts of the Spirit, and therefore the very word that is employed rejects this whole notion of languages or dialects, and is indicative of the fact that it is speech, the tongue in action, the tongue speaking as the result of the propulsion or direction or control of the Holy Spirit himself.

This seems to me to be made perfectly clear by the Apostle in verses 14 and 15 of chapter 14 where he says, 'If I pray in an unknown tongue, my spirit prayeth, but my understanding is unfruitful. What is it then? I will pray with the spirit, and I will pray with the understanding also: I will sing with the spirit, and I will sing with the understanding also.' You see the contrast is between 'praying in the spirit' and 'praying with the understanding'. In the one case it is the Spirit – the Holy Spirit – acting upon the man's spirit and moving his tongue. In the other it is the man himself with his understanding speaking through his tongue.

These are crucial verses and those who are familiar with Charles Hodge's commentary will know how he finds himself in considerable difficulty at this point. The only way in which he can get himself out of it is to say that what the Apostle is actually telling us is this: 'If I pray in an unknown tongue my spirit prayeth, but I am not giving understanding to other people.' But that is not what the Apostle says. Paul is talking about his own spirit and about his own understanding; not about giving understanding to other people. Indeed that is precisely what he is not saying, and that explanation, therefore, does violence to the whole text. There are other commentators who entirely agree with what I am saying. Paul is referring to something that happens in himself.

Verse 2 confirms this: 'He that speaketh in an unknown tongue speaketh not unto men, but unto God: for no man understandeth him; howbeit in the spirit he speaketh mysteries.' And he says in verse 4, 'He that speaketh in an unknown tongue edifieth himself. This is the whole mystery with regard to this gift. It seems to me that we can only interpret it by saying that to speak in a tongue means that for the time being a man has been taken up by the Spirit. The Spirit has come upon him and has lifted him up into the spiritual realm and he finds himself speaking in a language that he does not understand. It is an extraordinary language. Though he does not understand it, it is yet edifying to him as verse 4 says. He does not understand the words but he knows what he is doing – he knows that he is glorifying God. That is the real meaning of verse 2: 'He that speaketh in an unknown tongue speaketh not for men, but for God.' It is better to translate it 'for' rather than 'unto'. He is not helping men as it were, he is not doing anything for men, but he is doing something for God. He is glorifying God, worshipping him, and magnifying him. He knows he is doing that, but he cannot identify the actual words that he is using. The whole thing is a mystery.

But, you see, we are dealing with the realm of the Spirit, a realm which is miraculous and which is supernatural. This is the theme which the Apostle has in mind throughout this whole chapter. These are *spiritual* gifts. This is not man's natural faculties being heightened; this is a gift, something new, something which is given. And so the Apostle says that what happens when a man speaks in tongues is that the Spirit is controlling him, by-passing his understanding for the time being. Instead of it coming through the understanding to the tongue, it goes directly through the man's spirit to the tongue.

The final proof of what I am saying is, of course, found when he contrasts tongues with prophesying. Prophesying means that a man again is enlightened by the Holy Spirit, but it is his understanding that is enlightened. So we read in the third verse, 'He that prophesieth speaketh unto men for edification, and exhortation, and comfort.' The operations of the Spirit are almost endless. The Spirit does enlighten a man's mind and his understanding. Thank God for this! We have all known this and preachers in particular know how the understanding can be heightened. But a man knows that it is coming through his understanding and the tongue is moved by the understanding enlightened by the Spirit. But in 'speaking in tongues' the understanding is not involved. It is something that happens directly through the Spirit acting upon the spirit of man moving the tongue.

Now I was very interested in turning up this definition in an excellent Lexicon by Arndt and Gingrich. They say that beyond any question at all the 'speaking in tongues' referred to in these chapters means 'broken speech of persons in religious ecstasy'. That is precisely what I am trying to say – that when a man speaks in tongues he is taken hold of, he is lifted up above himself and he speaks in a language that he does not understand. I am very ready to agree with those who say that he is probably speaking in the language of paradise, the language of the glory itself. I have always felt that this is similar to what we get in 2 Corinthians 12 where the Apostle says that, fourteen years before, he was lifted up into the heavens where he heard things that were inexpressible I cannot prove this to you. But it seems to me to be the inevitable exposition here. So that this is not some kind of gibberish; it is a man possessed by the Spirit, lifted up into a condition of ecstasy in which he speaks in this language of glory, not understanding what he is saying, and yet knowing that it is the language of glory, and that he is glorifying God.

But let me add one qualification. Though I say that the man is in a state of religious ecstasy, it does not mean that he is unconscious; it does not mean that he has lost control of himself, as I will demonstrate to you later.

The next principle we come to is that speaking in tongues is not something that can be initiated by us. Or if you prefer it, a man cannot speak in tongues whenever he likes. Now this is to me perhaps the most important point of all. You will generally find with people who claim today to speak in tongues that most of them say that they can do so whenever they like. Ask them, 'Can you speak in tongues whenever you like?' They say, 'Yes, whenever we like', and they will do it for you there and then. I suggest that that puts them in a category outside the teaching of 1 Corinthians 14. This is to me one of the crucial points in the differentiation of true speaking in tongues from the counterfeit.

How do I substantiate this? I do so by calling attention to what the Apostle says in 1 Corinthians 14:18 where we read, 'I thank my God, I speak with tongues more than ye all.' Now that to me is a most crucial statement. Let us be careful to observe exactly what he does say. He does not say 'I speak with more tongues than you all.' I underline that because people who reject the whole of the supernatural and the miraculous in these chapters say that all the apostle Paul is claiming here is that he knew more foreigu languages than the Corinthians did. They say the whole question refers to speaking in other languages and that the Apostle says 'Well, I happen to know more foreign languages than any of you.'

I reject that because it is wrong even grammatically. What he says is that he speaks more in tongues. It is an adverb; he means 'more frequently'. 'I thank my God, I speak in tongues more frequently than do you all.' Now if it is true to say that a man can speak in tongues whenever he likes, what is the point of the Apostle's statement? If it is true of all who have the gift of speaking in tongues that they can do so whenever they like at will – what is the point of the Apostle saying that he speaks in tongues 'more frequently' than they all do? It would simply mean that he decides to do so more frequently than they do. There is no purpose in saying that, and, indeed, in the next verse he makes such an explanation impossible for this reason: 'Yet in the church I had rather speak five words with my understanding, that by my voice I might teach others also, than ten thousand words in an unknown tongue.'

No, it seems to me that there is only one explanation of this statement which is that the Apostle is saying, 'I think I know more than any of you what it is to be taken up by the Spirit.' This is not something ordinary, but something remarkable, glorious and exceptional. He is saying, 'The Spirit comes more frequently upon me than any of you.' He tells them in effect, 'You are boasting, you are making me boast, and I am telling you that I know more frequently than any of you do what it is to have the Spirit taking hold of me and lifting me up into this realm.' It is the only conceivable explanation. Indeed, I suggest that verses 29 and 30 support this. He says, 'Let the prophets speak two or three, and let the other judge.' Then he goes on: 'If any thing be revealed to another that sitteth by, let the first hold his peace.' What does that mean? Well it means this. Suppose there is a prophet speaking; now, Paul says, if a message is given to another prophet, let the first stop in order that the second may speak. But you notice what it says, 'If a message is given to another prophet.' A prophet is not filled with messages which he can speak whenever he likes. No; the message is 'given'.

All the gifts are given. What applies to tongues applies also to miracles. Is there any evidence in the New Testament that a man who has the gift of miracles can work a miracle whenever he likes? Of course there is not. It is the exact opposite. It is the same with all these gifts. The prophet is not always filled with messages which he can turn on or give out whenever he likes. No, the message comes to him, it is given to him.

I think that this is the most important matter of all, because I suggest that if a man tells me that he can speak in tongues whenever he likes, it is probably something psychological and not spiritual. The spiritual gifts are always controlled by the Holy Spirit. They are given, and one does not know when they are going to be given.

Let me prove this to you by illustrating it in the case of miracles. Look at the apostles in Acts. They had the gift of miracles, but what is so interesting to observe is that the apostles never made experiments, or tried to heal somebody, wondering whether it would happen or not. No, there were no trials, no experiments and no failures. What is still more interesting is that the apostles never made an announcement that they would work miracles on such and such a day. They never put up a poster saying, 'Come on Thursday, there will be miracles performed'. Never! Why not? There is only one answer – they never knew when it was going to happen. What clearly happened was that they were suddenly confronted by a situation and the commission was given to them.

Take the first instance of this in Acts 3. We read that 'a certain man lame from his mother's womb was carried, whom they laid daily at the gate of the temple which is called Beautiful, to ask alms of them that entered into the temple; Who seeing Peter and John about to go into the temple asked an alms.' Then notice this: 'And Peter, fastening his eyes upon him with John, said ...' Now that is a clear indication that he was given a commission. This is not an experiment, he is not just trying to see what may happen. He knew. He said, 'Look on us. And he gave heed unto them, expecting to receive something of them. Then Peter said, Silver and gold have I none; but such as I have give I thee: In the name of Jesus Christ of Nazareth rise up and walk. And he took him by the right hand, and lifted him up: and immediately his feet and ankle bones received strength'. And Peter then turned to the gathered crowd and gave the explanation: 'The God of Abraham, and of Isaac, and of Jacob, the God of our fathers, hath glorified his Son Jesus ... and his name through faith in his name hath made this man strong, whom ye see and know.' In other words, Peter was clearly given this very definite commission, and so what he says happens.

You can find numerous examples of this. Take Acts 13 and the miracle that the apostle Paul worked upon the man Bar-Jesus, who was with Sergius Paulus, a great man in the island of Paphos. We are told, 'But Elymas the sorcerer (for so is his name by interpretation) withstood them, seeking to turn away the deputy from the faith. Then Saul, (who also is called Paul,) filled with the Holy Ghost, set his eyes on him ...' This is not a man able to work miracles whenever he wants to. No, he is given a commission, and filled with the Holy Spirit, he says: 'O full of all subtilty and all mischief, thou child of the devil, thou enemy of all righteousness, wilt thou not cease to pervert the right ways of the Lord? And now, behold, the hand of the Lord is upon thee, and thou shalt be blind, not seeing the sun for a season.' The apostle Paul could not do that sort of thing whenever he wanted to; he is given a commission, and so what he says happens. It is absolutely certain.

It is the same with his healing of the man at Lystra in Acts 14:8 where you find the same expression again. 'The same heard Paul speak: who steadfastly beholding him, and perceiving that he had faith to be healed, Said with a loud voice....' Can you not hear the authority? Can you not hear this note of commission? It is the Spirit who gives it. It is not a permanent possession in a man.

Then here is another striking example in Acts 16:16 in the case of the girl with a spirit of divination. 'And it came to pass, as we went to prayer, a certain damsel possessed with a spirit of divination met us, which brought her masters much gain by soothsaying: The same followed Paul and us, and cried, saying, These men are the servants of the most high God, which show unto us the way of salvation.' Now take note – 'And this did she *many days*.' If the Apostle permanently had the power of exorcism, why did he not deal with her the first day? He knew it was a spirit of divination and that she was devil-possessed. He was not given his commission straightaway. 'This did she many days. But Paul, being grieved, turned and said to the spirit, I command thee in the name of Jesus Christ to come out of her.' He knew. There was no failure, there was no experimentation. Paul was given a commission and the evil spirit 'came out of her the same hour'.

I am saying all this to establish the fundamental point that what applies to miracles, exorcism and all the gifts applies equally to the gift of tongues. It is not something, therefore, that a man can do whenever he likes. No. 'I thank God that I speak with tongues more than ye all.' In other words, 'I know what it is', says the Apostle, 'to be dealt with by the Spirit in this matter more frequently than any of you.' He is not just saying, 'I decide to do this more often than any of you do.' No, that is not what he is saying – he says it happens to him. All these things are the gifts of the Spirit. They happen to us, they are given to us. And, therefore, I say that if we possess some gift which we can handle or use or employ whenever we like, it seems to me that that puts it out of the category of the spiritual gifts of 1 Corinthians 12-14. But it very definitely does put it into line with what we know about the realm of the psychological. Self hypnotism is something that one can do whenever one likes; that is its very characteristic.

I know a man, a missionary for years in China, who tells me that on one occasion when alone in his room, he was baptized with the Holy Spirit and found himself speaking in tongues. He has never done so since. Now he was often worried about this and spoke to me about it. I shall never forget his sense of release and of joy when I expounded 1 Corinthians 14:18 to him. I said, 'My dear friend, the fact that you tell me that it has only happened to you once makes me say that it was genuine and authentic. If you told me that you could do it whenever you liked I would be really troubled.' No, my friends, these things are spiritual gifts; they are in the control of the Holy Spirit, not in the control of man. They are gifts given to the church. He is the Lord, he gives to whom he will, he gives when he will. Let us therefore be very careful, lest we be deluded by the counterfeit in various shapes and forms. Consider again carefully the evidence of 1 Corinthians 14.

In order that I may conclude this, let me expand on what I said earlier that though the man who speaks in tongues is in a state of ecstasy he is still rational; he has not lost self-control. I prove that by 1 Corinthians 14:27-32. 'If any man speak in an unknown tongue, let it be by two, or at the most by three, and that by course; and let one interpret.' He could not say that if we were not able to control these things. 'But if there be no interpreter, let him keep silence in the church; and let him speak to himself, and to God.' You see, there is to be control. 'Let the prophets speak two or three, and let the other judge. If any thing be revealed to another that sitteth by, let the first hold his peace. For ye may all prophesy one by one, that all may learn, and all may be comforted.' Here is the crucial verse – verse 32: 'And the spirits of the prophets are subject to the prophets. For God is not the author of confusion, but of peace, as in all churches of the saints.'

So here is this marvellous and wonderful thing that though the Holy Spirit possesses us when he wills and lifts us up into this realm, yet we have not become irrational. You cannot initiate this, but you can control and stop it. That is the teaching of these chapters. It is the movement of the Spirit; yes, and he may come upon any number of people at the same time. But, the Apostle says, you are still rational and therefore there must be no confusion; there must be a limit to the number making public utterances and it must be done in order. Speaking generally of the church Paul says let it be prophecy rather than speaking in tongues. 'Wherefore, brethren, covet to prophesy, and forbid not to speak with tongues.'

But the teaching seems to be that you should exercise this gift, if you truly have it, on your own when you are in private prayer. The Apostle here is contrasting what happens in the church and what happens when you are in private. To make his meaning clear he takes a hypothetical case. He says, in effect, 'Imagine what the position would be if you all spoke in tongues at the same time.' Take verse 23: 'If therefore the whole church be come together into one place, and all speak with tongues, and there come in those that are unlearned, or unbelievers, will they not say that ye are mad?'

So here he clearly teaches this extraordinary thing that while he is lifted up into a realm even beyond understanding yet he retains perfect self-control. You will find in the counterfeit that self-control is often lost. You are encouraged to let yourself go and even to abandon your reason. You must not do that. We are never to put our minds out of action – never! If the Spirit chooses to do something directly to us above the understanding, well, praise God for it; but you must never surrender your understanding or 'let yourself go'. That is always to open the gate to false evil spirits, to the psychological, to suggestion, and to various other things. This is the glory of the way of the Holy Spirit – above understanding and yet the understanding can still be used. And so the Apostle can end his discourse by saying, 'Let all things be done decently and in order.' A prophet cannot initiate, but he can control: 'The spirits of the prophets are subject to the prophets.'

May God grant that we may meditate more and more upon this great teaching of the baptism with the Holy Spirit and his gifts so that we may be able to discriminate and to differentiate in these days in which we live. 'Prove all things; hold fast that which is good.'

Chapter 16

Baptism with the Spirit and Sanctification

We have been concentrating on the fact that the great purpose of the baptism with the Spirit has been to enable us to witness and to bear testimony to the great salvation that God has granted us through Jesus Christ our Lord. And as I have said, my great concern is that we should understand the essence of this teaching concerning the baptism with the Holy Spirit. That, according to John the Baptist, is to be the outstanding characteristic of the ministry of our blessed Lord and Saviour. 'I,' he says, 'I baptize with water; he shall baptize with the Holy Ghost and with power.'

I repeat again, therefore, and am concerned to emphasize that that is the primary object and purpose of the baptism with the Holy Spirit.

There are, however, one or two other matters which we must deal with before we leave this great subject, in order that we may help those who have particular difficulties. One question is: what exactly is the relationship of the baptism with the Holy Spirit to various other aspects of the Holy Spirit's work? Now there is often a good deal of confusion about this. It is quite clear from the teaching of the New Testament that the Holy Spirit has many manifestations and activities. It is he, of course, who convicts us of sin. No man can convict another of sin. We can point out to one another that we may be wrong, but that is a very different thing from conviction of sin. It is the Holy Spirit alone who can do that. It is also he alone who can give us an understanding of the Scripture.

The apostle Paul tells us that 'the natural man receiveth not the things of the Spirit of God: for they are foolishness unto him: neither can he know them, because they are spiritually discerned' (1 Corinthians 2:14). Well that, you see, is an operation of the Spirit who quickens us, and who regenerates. We are born 'of the Spirit'.

There are many other operations of the Spirit. We read about the unction of the Spirit, the enlightenment, and the anointing, and the sealing. There are different terms used to describe his various activities and because of that, it is not a bit surprising that there is occasionally some amount of confusion in people's minds with regard to the relationship of these things to one another; and as one or two of them are particularly important, it seems to me that we must address ourselves to them.

The first is the relationship of the baptism with the Holy Spirit to sanctification. Here there is (and has been) much confusion in the minds of people. Now this is not at all surprising. I think the trouble arises in the following way or for the following reasons. One thing is that the term 'filled' is used. In Ephesians 5:18 the apostle says, 'Be not drunk with wine, wherein is excess; but be filled with the Spirit.' And then when you read the account of what happened on the day of Pentecost, which is the account of the baptism with the Holy Spirit. What we are told about the disciples and the others with them in the upper room is, 'they were all filled with the Holy Ghost'. The same term as is used in Ephesians 5:18. So it is not at all surprising that people should therefore tend to identify the two things. The very terminology, in and of itself, is liable to lead to this confusion.

But there is a second thing which tends to exaggerate this

tendency, and that is the experience of people as they undergo the baptism with the Holy Spirit. The very nature of the experience, as I am going to show, is such that it is not surprising that people do regard it as something which essentially denotes sanctification. And, of course, there has been very definite teaching given along this very line, teaching which originates in many ways with the brothers John and Charles Wesley, and which has been repeated, more or less, ever since then in the Christian church by certain sections and groups of godly, spiritually-minded people.

Those, then, are the reasons why the confusion almost inevitably tends to take place and it seems to me that there are two main tendencies, therefore, in regard to this whole question of the relationship between the baptism with the Holy Spirit and sanctification. The first tendency is to regard the baptism with the Holy Spirit as meaning entire sanctification; or to use the term of the Wesleys, 'perfect love'; or, to use another term, 'sinless perfection'. And there are those who therefore teach that when a man is baptized with the Holy Spirit he is entirely sanctified, and that should be our essential definition of the baptism with the Holy Spirit – that our heart is cleansed and that we are delivered from sin. Some talk about 'eradication' of sin. The terms do not matter; it is the main teaching that is of importance.

But then there is a second tendency which, as usual, is the exact opposite of this. (We always tend to go from one extreme to the other.) This is that there are some people who ignore sanctification in this matter altogether – they do not speak about it, and are always talking about the manifestation of the gifts. That was obviously the tendency in the church at Corinth, as it has been in many sections of the church throughout the running centuries – the danger of being taken up entirely with the gifts and becoming excited about them and only thinking about them. And as you are doing so, the life and the living are not only ignored but tend to degenerate, and so you get the exhortations that the apostle has to address to the members of the church at Corinth.

Now both these tendencies have been manifest through the centuries, but particularly in the last two or three centuries, and are very obvious today. There has been much disrepute brought upon the whole doctrine of the baptism with the Spirit because of this; people claiming great gifts and wonderful experiences but patently failing in their Christian life, at times in things like ordinary morality, common honesty and decency quite apart from certain other sins of the flesh.

Now it is not difficult to see how these things arise. Any profound movement in the spirit of man in a sense always exposes such a man to unusual attacks from the devil, who is always anxious to come in and to bring the work into disrepute. And thus it comes to pass that you get these two extremes generally being advocated at the same time. People say, 'It does not matter, I have been baptized with the Holy Spirit; look at the powers that I have got, look at what I am doing' – and so the life becomes neglected and this has often led to real disaster. And remember I am still talking about honest, good, spiritually-minded people, who are anxious to get the best, as they put it, that God has got to give them and who really were originally concerned with the glory of God and with that alone.

In the light of all this, then, what is the relationship between the baptism with the Holy Spirit and sanctification? My first answer is that there is no direct connection. I mean that the primary purpose and object of the baptism with the Holy Spirit is not sanctification, but it is, as I stated earlier, something that is concerned with power – power in witness and in testimony.

This of course is stated quite plainly and explicitly, as we have seen, by our blessed Lord himself, when he says, 'But ye shall receive power, after that the Holy Ghost is come upon you: and ye shall be witnesses unto me both in Jerusalem, and in all Judaea, and in Samaria, and unto the uttermost part of the earth' (Acts 1:8). There is our Lord's own statement with respect to this – 'tarry ye in Jerusalem until ye be endued with power from on high.'

We have seen this so clearly in the transformation of Peter in Acts 2 and in the story of Paul in Acts 9, and the subsequent history of the Christian church demonstrates this same point abundantly. Baptism with the Holy Spirit is primarily and essentially a baptism with power. It gives us great certainty and assurance, and there is a kind of 'must' about it and an ability and the power to do it in the way that we have indicated. I am therefore arguing here that there is no direct connection between the baptism with the Holy Spirit and sanctification.

A second argument is that surely the case of the church at Corinth ought to be enough in and of itself to settle this question. Here were people boasting about their gifts and manifesting them – the church itself was excited about the gifts. But the apostle shows the spiritual state and condition of that church and it was in many ways deplorable. He tells us in the fifth chapter that there was a sin being condoned in the church at Corinth which even the Gentiles would not condone.

This is the extraordinary thing, that you can get these two things at one and the same time; a low state of spirituality, and indeed, of morals, Have you ever noticed that the apostle even has to say a thing like this over their love feasts followed by the communion service. Not only was their selfishness being displayed, but it is quite clear that some were drinking too much before they went to the love feast and were not quite sober. That was actually true of the church at Corinth. Now the state of spirituality, or of sanctification, if you like, was low, and yet there was this mighty evidence in terms of gifts, and so on.

All I am concerned to show is that there is obviously

therefore no direct connection between these two things, and, of course, the apostle settled it once and for ever for us in the famous thirteenth chapter of the first epistle to the Corinthians. 'Though I speak with the tongues of men and of angels, and have not charity, I am become as sounding brass, or a tinkling cymbal. And though I have the gift of prophecy, and understand all mysteries, and all knowledge; and though I have all faith, so that I could remove mountains, and have not charity, I am nothing. And though I bestow all my goods to feed the poor, and though I give my body to be burned, and have not charity, it profiteth me nothing.'

There it is! That is demonstration and proof; the whole epistle does the same, but there it is concentrated into that tremendous statement that there is obviously no direct and immediate connection between these two things. And all this, of course, is so important, because it is the failure of people to grasp this that leads to the tragedies to which I have already been referring. People have assumed that because they have got these gifts and are having experiences then all must be well. It is not always; these things must be applied, and if we do not apply them there will be trouble.

The third argument which demonstrates that there is no direct or immediate connection is that the work of the Spirit in sanctification is always presented in the New Testament in terms of exhortation. Now take that statement again in Ephesians 5:18 – 'Be not drunk with wine, wherein is excess (or riot); but go on being filled with the Spirit. 'Now that is an exhortation. The apostle does not urge them there to seek an experience which would put them right, he is commanding them, and telling them what to do: it is an appeal to them to go on yielding themselves to the Spirit that is in them.

He states it negatively also. He tells them not to 'grieve the Spirit'. 'Grieve not the Holy Spirit of God, whereby ye are sealed unto the day of redemption. 'Now this again is a command. It is possible for us to 'grieve' the Spirit.

Elsewhere, in 1 Thessalonians 5, he says, 'Quench not the Spirit'. Now these are all of them exhortations; they are all addressing us, telling *us* what to do and what not to do. That is the characteristic way in which the New Testament always presents the doctrine of sanctification.

Take another illustration in Philippians 2 – this great statement in verses 12-13 – 'Wherefore, my beloved' – take note – 'as you have always obeyed, not as in my presence only, but now much more in my absence, work out your own salvation with fear and trembling. For it is God which worketh in you both to will and to do of his good pleasure.' There is a typical statement of it. We have to do the working out because God has already made it possible for us to do so. It is God that works in us but we have got to work it out; it does not happen to us. Whereas the whole point about the baptism of the Spirit, as we have seen, is that it is something that happens to us. You cannot do anything about being baptized with the Spirit except to ask for it. You cannot do anything to produce it.

I referred to that elsewhere when I pointed out the terrible danger of trying to produce it or to induce it or to help it to come by relaxing yourself and breathing in deeply etc. All that belongs to the realm of psychology. You can do nothing about the baptism of the Spirit. It is 'given', his operation, his action. It is altogether of God. It happens to us. But here in the realm of sanctification it is always exhortation, always an appeal to us to apply what we have already learned.

What the apostle writes in Ephesians 4:17 is so typical of the New Testament teaching concerning sanctification: 'This I say therefore, and testify in the Lord, that ye henceforth walk not as other Gentiles walk, in the vanity of their mind....' He is appealing to them; he says, 'Look here, you have been born again.' He later exhorts them, 'Be ye therefore followers of God, as dear children.' 'Remember who you are,' he is saying. 'Walk in love, as Christ also hath loved us, and hath given himself for us.' Later on he writes, 'Ye were sometimes darkness, but now are ye light in the Lord: walk as children of light.... Have no fellowship with the unfruitful works of darkness.' This is sanctification and it is all an argument and an appeal. He reminds us of who we are, and what we are, and what has happened to us, and says 'Now, in the light of this, apply it, realize who you are; do not live as you used to live, show that you are different, show that you are "dear children of God."'

It is all appeal, exhortation, argument, and that is the typical method of the New Testament in teaching us sanctification. Sanctification is ultimately the work of the Spirit. No man can sanctify himself unless he has the Spirit of God in him. But the moment a man is regenerated the Spirit is in him and the work of sanctification has already started.

But, by definition, the baptism with the Holy Spirit is something that happens to such a man. It can only happen to the Christian. But a man may be a Christian, a good one, too, 'growing in grace and in the knowledge of the Lord', a man may be progressing in sanctification and still not know the baptism with the Holy Spirit. This is something that is given; a tremendous experience. It is something that can be isolated, whereas sanctification is a continuing and a continuous process. So, for these reasons I am arguing that it is wrong to identify them, and that indeed we must teach and say that there is no direct connection between them.

However, having said that, I come to my second point which is that while it is clear that there is no direct connection, it is equally clear that there is a very definite indirect connection between them. What I mean is that the very experience of the baptism with the Holy Spirit must affect and have an influence upon our sanctification. How? Well, it is something like this, is it not? When a man is baptized with the Holy Spirit what really happens to him is what Paul talks about in Romans 5:5: 'The love of God is shed abroad in his heart' – that is the term of the apostle and the translation is quite a good one – it is poured out in great profusion, his heart is flooded with a realization of the love of God. When men and women have such an experience of the love of God to them, of God telling them that 'he has loved them with an everlasting love', that they are 'his dear children', that he has got his eye upon them and has had it before the foundation of the world, and that he loves them and is concerned to bring them to himself and the glory everlasting in absolute perfection and glory, when God does this, it is quite inevitable that at that moment they abhor sin with the whole being, sin is to them at that moment unthinkable. They know nothing except the love of God to them and their love welling up back to God in return. That is the experience of being baptized with the Holy Spirit, one which is essentially experimental. That is where those people who say that it happens to everybody at regeneration seem to me not only to be denying the New Testament but to be definitely quenching the Spirit. Regeneration is unconscious, non-experimental; but the baptism with the Holy Spirit is essentially experimental.

Look at the second chapter of Acts – fancy saying that that is non-experimental! But that is what some have taught. Because they have been afraid of the excesses of Pentecostalism they have driven themselves to that impossible, indeed ludicrous position of saying that the baptism with the Holy Spirit is non-experimental. As we have seen, it was not only experimental, it was so experimental that the whole of Jerusalem knew that it had happened to the people; they knew it themselves and everybody else knew it. Indeed it is characterized essentially by this tremendous experimental or experiential happening. It is great and most amazing. It is the most wonderful and glorious experience a man can ever have in this life. The only thing beyond the experience of the baptism with the Spirit is heaven itself. In that experience, then, a man feels that he can never sin again – how can he sin against such love? So it is not at all surprising that people have tended to identify it with sanctification.

But we must be careful here. Though that is what one feels at that point, it does not mean that sin has been entirely eradicated. That is what one feels at the time, but it is not so. Because if it were so, I again argue that all these great exhortations in the New Testament epistles would have been entirely unnecessary, you would never have had all these arguments, appeals and reasoning; all the apostle would have had to say was, 'Well now then, seek this and you will be delivered from all problems, you will be entirely sanctified.' But he does not say that, as I have shown you.

Let me give you some further arguments to substantiate what I am saying. Look at the apostle, for instance, writing in Romans 6:11. He says, 'Likewise reckon ye also yourselves to be dead indeed unto sin, but alive unto God through Jesus Christ our Lord.' Then immediately comes an appeal: 'Let not sin therefore reign in your mortal body that ye should obey it in the lusts thereof.' Do not allow it, he says. It is in your control. 'Neither yield ye your members as instruments of unrighteousness unto sin: but yield yourselves unto God, as those that are alive from the dead, and your members as instruments of righteousness unto God' (Romans 6:11-13). That would never have been said if this other teaching were the truth and were correct. Clearly it is not. Sanctification is always presented in terms of exhortation.

And so you get it again in Romans 8:12 'Therefore, brethren, we are debtors, not to the flesh, to live after the flesh. For if ye live after the flesh, ye shall die: but if ye through the Spirit do mortify the deeds of the body, ye shall live.' Now if sin is taken right out of us by the baptism of the Spirit, the apostle would never exhort us to 'mortify the deeds of the body'. But he does. He reasons, he gives us arguments to present to ourselves. But the exhortation is this: 'If ye through the Spirit' – the Spirit will enable you and help you, but you have got to do it – 'do mortify the deeds of the body, ye shall live.' We must not say that the baptism of the Spirit inevitably guarantees sanctification. But I still say that there is this indirect connection between them. What, then, is it? Well, I would put it like this. The baptism with the Holy Spirit is the greatest possible encouragement to sanctification.

Let me use an illustration, which I have used elsewhere, from Ephesians 1:13, in connection with the sealing of the Spirit. I cannot think of a better way of illustrating the relationship between the baptism with the Spirit and sanctification. Look at it like this: think of spring, when people have been digging their gardens and sowing the seed. The gardener has done his work, he has dug it up, broken up the earth, put the seed in, levelled it off. Now there is life in that seed but it may be that it is a bad spring – cold, no sunshine, no rain. Weeks pass and the poor gardener goes to inspect his garden and he sees nothing and he begins to wonder whether the seed that he has sown really was good seed. Something is wrong, nothing is happening, and he feels a bit discouraged.

But at long last he just begins to see this seed sprouting and appearing just above the surface, just a kind of green haze and no more. Then it remains like that for days. Nothing seems to be happening and again he is almost filled with despair; and on it goes like that for some time. But suddenly a day comes with glorious sunshine, and then a shower of rain and you can almost see the whole thing springing up.

Now that is the relationship, it seems to me, between the baptism with the Spirit and sanctification. You see, there was life there all along; the man couldn't see it but there was life in that seed and it is bound to come up. But it is very slow you can scarcely see it, it is imperceptible almost, and on it goes at that pace. But when the sun comes and the rain, then the whole thing is stimulated and it springs up, you can almost see it growing with your naked eyes.

The moment a man is born again, the seed of divine life is in him. 'We are made,' says Peter, 'partakers of the divine nature.' John says, 'The seed remaineth in him.' However poor the Christian may be, the seed is there. The Christian cannot go on living a life of sin; he does not 'abide in sin'. Why? Well, the seed abides in him. The life is there but it is like that garden, you are almost doubtful as to whether there is anything there at all.

In other words, the moment a man is born again and this divine seed or principle enters into him, the life has started and there is this imperceptible growth. But let a man like that be baptized with the Holy Spirit, let the rain and the sunshine of the Spirit come upon him, let the love of God be shed abroad in his heart, and you will see him springing up into life and vigour and activity; his sanctification, everything about him, is stimulated in a most amazing and astonishing manner. But, it is an indirect connection, not direct and not the same thing. There is an inevitable and intimate relationship and yet the two things must be thought of separately; otherwise there will be nothing but confusion. And the confusion has often taken place in the long history of the Christian church.

Then there is just one other step in this matter, another tremendously important one, that is emphasized everywhere in the New Testament. Because these various operations are the operations of the same Holy Spirit there is always this connection between them. Because the baptism with the Spirit is the greatest stimulus and incentive to sanctification, we always have a very good test, therefore, which we must always apply to anything and everything that claims to be the work and the operation of the Holy Spirit, and it is, of course, the test of the other works of the Holy Spirit. In other words, if you see something very dramatic and spectacular claiming to be of the Spirit, you are entitled to look in that person for the fruit of the Spirit: for 'love, joy, peace, longsuffering, goodness, gentleness, meekness, faith and temperance'. It is because at times certain sections of the church have failed to do this, that they have made shipwreck, as I have been indicating.

There is a consistency about the work of the Spirit. There may be times when you may get the very thing described in 1 Corinthians. We must be clear about this. You must not say that the members of the church at Corinth were not Christians. Many people would say so. They look at this one side only, that of sanctification, and say, 'But surely a man who is guilty of that terrible sin mentioned in 1 Corinthians 5 a man who has his father's wife – a thing that is not even mentioned amongst the Gentiles – that man,' they say, 'cannot be a Christian, the thing is impossible. I don't care what he knows, what experience he has had, what gifts he may possess, I say he is not a Christian.'

Well you have no right to say that, and you are judging without knowledge. The apostle Paul talks about that man as a brother. A brother! In 1 Corinthians Paul exposes some of these grievous sins, these awful faults, and scandals into which the members of the church at Corinth had fallen, and yet – and this is the wonder and the glory of it, thank God for it – this is how he addresses them: 'Paul, called to be an apostle of Jesus Christ through the will of God, and Sosthenes our brother, Unto the church of God which is at Corinth, to them that are sanctified (set apart) in Christ Jesus, called to be saints' – 'called saints.'

They are saints! You do not have to be perfect to be a saint. (The Roman Catholics have abused this word 'saint' by calling only certain Christians saints. Every Christian is a saint – every one). We are all 'called saints'. So I say we must be careful at this point. Here is the apostle, though he shows these grievous sins into which these people had fallen, still saying that they are saints. But at the same time he does not excuse them; he reprimands them. He says, it is no use talking about your wonderful gifts if you are thus denying the very Spirit in your daily life. Be consistent, he says, there is a wholeness about the Christian life.

So there is always this connection between the baptism with the Holy Spirit and sanctification, so that we must always examine and check everything that claims to be of the Holy Spirit by the test of sanctification; and if we do not find obvious evidences of sanctification in those who are claiming great experiences or great gifts, we must warn them solemnly in the name of God, show the danger to them, remind them that gifts can be given by the devil, and that evil spirits can counterfeit in a terrifying manner some of the choicest manifestations of the gift of the Holy Spirit himself.

Chapter 17

The Sealing of the Spirit

We come now to another term which is used with respect to the Holy Spirit, and that is the 'sealing' of the Spirit. Here is a term that you find in particular in 2 Corinthians 1:22. In verse 20 the apostle says, 'All the promises of God in him are yea, and in him Amen, unto the glory of God by us. Now he which stablisheth us with you in Christ, and hath anointed us' – there is another of the terms – 'is God; Who hath also sealed us, and given us the earnest of the Spirit in our hearts.'

Another use of the word is in Ephesians 1:13: Now the apostle here is referring to the Gentiles. He has said in verse 11, 'In whom also "we" have obtained an inheritance' – that is a reference to the Jews. They were the first, as he says in verse 12 – 'who first trusted in Christ'. Now here he says, 'In whom ye also' – the Gentiles – 'trusted, after that ye heard the word of truth, the gospel of your salvation: in whom also after that ye believed, ye were sealed with that holy Spirit of promise, which is the earnest of our inheritance until the redemption of the purchased possession, unto the praise of his glory.'

It occurs again in Ephesians 4:30, 'And grieve not the holy Spirit of God, whereby' – by whom – 'ye are sealed unto the day of redemption.'

Now those are the main uses of this term. There are others which are not quite as explicit, but that is sufficient for our purpose here. And what we are told is that these believers have been 'sealed' by 'the holy Spirit of promise'. The Holy Spirit is often referred to in the New Testament as 'the promise of the Father'. There is a great promise running through the Old Testament of a day which is to come when the Spirit will be poured out upon all flesh. It is in the prophecy of Joel, you remember; and you find it in Ezekiel 36, and in many other places in most beautiful and pictorial language, where it is quite often compared to the 'dew' or a 'shower of rain'. Now, therefore, the Holy Spirit in this way is referred to as 'the Holy Spirit of promise' and what the apostle teaches is that we are sealed unto the day of redemption by the giving and the receiving of this Holy Spirit so long promised.

Some questions immediately arise. What is the relationship of this to the baptism with the Spirit? What exactly does 'sealing' mean? The best way, it seems to me, is to take those questions in the reverse order: by discovering what exactly the 'sealing' is we shall see what its relationship is to the baptism with the Holy Spirit.

What, then, is this 'sealing with the Spirit'? What does the apostle mean when he reminds the Corinthians and the Ephesians of it like that? (And what he says to them, of course, can be true of all other Christians – they can be 'sealed' with this Holy Spirit of promise.)

The tendency, again, on the part of some is to identify this also with sanctification. There is a teaching, which has been one of the prevailing and one of the most popular of the teachings in evangelical circles ever since about 1873, that all these terms really are just different ways of describing sanctification. So when we are told, therefore, that we have been sealed by the Spirit, it is just another way of saying that we all are undergoing this process of sanctification, and that all the promises of God are sealed to us by producing the 'fruits' of sanctification in us; and that therefore the sealing of the Spirit means that we are manifesting love, joy, peace, longsuffering, gentleness, goodness, meekness, faith and temperance – the fruit of the Spirit. On this view there is nothing special or separate or unique about the sealing with the Spirit.

Now I indicated earlier on the question of sanctification that there are people who take that same view with regard to the baptism. And then there were the others who identified the baptism with sanctification. So again it is necessary that we should clear this matter, and I want to suggest that this identification of the sealing with the Spirit with sanctification is again nothing but confusion. It becomes important and serious because I believe that eventually it leads to a quenching of the Spirit. Men and women come to the conclusion that all that is meant here is that because we are born again and have got the seed of life in us which is growing, our sanctification is proceeding; and that because this is the work of the Holy Spirit, that is what is meant by saying that we are sealed, and therefore they look for nothing further.

Now it seems to me that the danger all along the line with this question is that of reducing the New Testament terminology to the level of our own experiences. It is the danger of interpreting the New Testament teaching not in terms of the life of the early church, but the life of the church as it has become, unfortunately, during the centuries. To put it another way, it is the danger of interpreting New Testament teaching in terms of the life of the church when she is at her lowest, instead of when she is at her highest, in periods of revival and quickening and awakening and the manifestation of God's glorious power. Nothing to me is more serious than this. If it is all a matter of sanctification there is nothing further for us to live for. We just go on as we are, yielding ourselves to the work of the Spirit and you never expect anything from outside, never any 'shower' or 'outpouring' of the Spirit, and that, of course, is, alas, the prevailing attitude with so many at the present time.

All this is wrong, because it is to do violence to the actual words used by the apostle in the statement in Ephesians 1:13. Let us study this for a moment. 'In whom ye also trusted, after that ye heard the word of truth, the gospel of your salvation.' Now I am taking it from the Authorized Version and it goes on like this 'in whom also after that ye believed, ye were sealed with that Holy Spirit of promise, which is the earnest of our inheritance until the redemption of the purchased possession.' 'Ah yes,' say these friends who want to identify it with sanctification, 'I see exactly how you fall into error, you have been misled by the Authorized translation.' It is always interesting to me to see how these friends seem to think that some special translation is always going to solve the problem.

Of course, we are well aware of the fact that the Authorized translation here is not literally accurate. Now I emphasize that. I am not saying it is not accurate, I am saying it is not 'literally' accurate. They should not have actually said: 'after that ye believed'. The better translation is 'believing', or 'having believed'. You can take it in both ways. 'In whom also believing, ye were sealed with that Holy Spirit of promise'; or again, 'Who having believed….' Now both those translations are correct and the authorities are divided between the two.

But this does not make any difference at all to the meaning. What the apostle is saying is this: you also having heard the message of the truth of the gospel, you have believed it, you have received it, and believing (or having believed) ye were sealed with that Holy Spirit of promise. So that it leaves the meaning exactly the same. It is presumed and taken for granted that they have believed, they were already believers when they were sealed.

Now I want to quote the comment of Charles Hodge at

this point because it seems to me that it cannot be improved upon. Charles Hodge referring to this Authorized translation says, 'This is more than a translation; it is an exposition of the original,' and he is undoubtedly right. What he means is this: though, perhaps, they should not have actually said 'after that ye believed' they really were expounding the original Greek. These men were great Greek scholars and they translated it like this. They knew all about the exact meaning, but they were anxious to help the readers. So in order to help them, they 'expound' rather than translate at this point. 'Whatever is meant by "sealing"', says Charles Hodge, 'it is something which follows faith.' Now that is the important point.

Or take Charles Simeon with regard to this same statement. Referring to the sealing of the Spirit he says, 'This was vouchsafed to many of the saints at Ephesus' – notice he does not say all of them. And then he continues, 'There shall always be some in the Church who possess and enjoy it.... This higher state of sanctification and assurance is reserved for those who "after having believed" have maintained a close walk with God.'

In other words these two authorities, differing so much from one another in many respects – Charles Hodge the great American commentator and theologian; Charles Simeon, Cambridge, evangelist, pastor, teacher – are both agreed about this, that this is something that assumes faith, and it is something given to those who possess faith. And Simeon is particularly insistent upon this point, that it is not true of all Christians. Now take that other view which says that this is sanctification and, of course, you have to say it is true of every Christian, that every Christian has automatically been sealed unto the day of redemption by his very regeneration. As they say that the baptism with the Spirit is true of all, that it is the same as regeneration and nothing separate and different, so they say about this. But here it seems to me the very words, plus what we are told by these authorities, make it impossible for us to accept that exposition.

In other words, what you have here in Ephesians 1:13 is exactly the same order as you have in Acts. Look at it; look at the apostles themselves. Here are these men who had been with our Lord and who believed in him, whom he contrasts with the world and of whom he has said, 'Now are ye clean through the word which I have spoken unto you', the same men upon whom he had 'breathed' the Holy Spirit in the upper room after his resurrection, whom he had told to remain until they received power – these men who were already believers, and regenerate – but it was only on the day of Pentecost that they were baptized with the Spirit. That is the order.

And you remember the case of the believers down in Samaria. Philip had preached, they had believed the message and he had baptized them, but still they had not been baptized with the Holy Spirit. It is this same order. Then Peter and John came down and prayed and laid their hands upon them, and the Holy Spirit descended upon them. It is always this order. 'Having believed', 'believing' – then.... It is precisely a repetition of that.

And in the same way, in Acts 19, the apostle Paul having again preached to these people and having then 'baptized them in the name of the Lord Jesus Christ', still had to lay his hands upon them before they received the baptism with the Holy Spirit. That is the sequence. And I suggest you have exactly the same order here in what the apostle says to these Ephesians about 'sealing'.

What, then, is this 'sealing with the Spirit?' 'In whom believing, ye were sealed with that Holy Spirit of promise.' Here again is an interesting point. There are those who say, 'Ah, yes, a seal. 'Sealing always means ownership. When a man owns something he puts his seal on it to say, 'This is my property'. Quite right—people do that. It is one of the meanings of the term 'sealing'. Others say, 'No, it is more a question of security', and that again is quite right. You tie up a parcel, you are particularly anxious that this should go safely, so you register it and you cannot register a thing without sealing it. So the idea, they say, is security. And again, of course, we know that sealing is used in that sense. But it is a very dangerous thing just to turn up your dictionary and see the meaning of a word, and then apply the first one you come to and say, 'Ah, it must be this.' No, there are many different meanings to sealing, and there is another meaning which I want to commend to you as being the most appropriate meaning at this point.

Another purpose of sealing is to authenticate, or to confirm as genuine and true. Now you do that in signing a document, do you not? You put a seal on it, and the object of that sealing is to authenticate this document, to confirm that it is genuine and true. And I want to suggest that that is the main meaning here. It is not the only one, the other two I think are involved; but I believe the main object of the sealing is that the thing has been authenticated. You believed, says Paul, we believe, you believe, and then you were authenticated by the Holy Spirit of promise, who is also the earnest of our inheritance until the redemption of the purchased possession.

Why do I say that this is the meaning that we should select rather than the others, or at any rate give it the greatest prominence? Well, I believe the first argument should be that the very context suggests it. The apostle here is reminding these Ephesians of what they are as Christians. That is the whole object of this letter. So he starts off with the great eternal purpose of God, and he shows what God's great purpose is. It is, he says, really this, that 'he hath chosen us in him before the foundation of the world, that we should be holy and without blame before him in love: Having predestinated us unto the adoption of children by Jesus Christ unto himself' – that is what he really is proposing for us. And so he 'hath blessed us with all spiritual blessings in heavenly places in Christ Jesus.' This is the great eternal plan and purpose of God, as he puts it in verse 10, 'That in the dispensation of the fulness of times he might gather together in one all things in Christ, both which are in heaven, and which are in earth; even in him. 'God redeeming the cosmos, making a people for himself. And he has done this, he says, out of these Jews and out of these Gentiles.

What he wants these Ephesians to know is that this is true of them. He is writing to encourage them, which is why he goes on to pray, 'I cease not to give thanks for you, making mention of you in my prayers; that the God of our Lord Jesus Christ, the Father of glory, may give unto you the spirit of wisdom and revelation in the knowledge of him: The eyes of your understanding being enlightened; that ye may know what is the hope of his calling'. That is the context, you see, and even here, in this immediate context, he says that the Spirit is the seal and the earnest: sealed with that holy Spirit of promise, which 'is the earnest of our inheritance until the redemption of the purchased possession.'

Paul means that Christ, by his work on earth, his life, death and resurrection, has purchased for us a great inheritance, a great estate. But as we are here on earth and life is difficult and we are weak and failing, the question is, how can we know that all this is true, that this inheritance belongs to us? He has done the work but we have not yet possessed it. It is there and we are going to receive it, 'until the redemption of the purchased possession'.

Now, he says, the security that you are given while you are here is the Holy Spirit. The Holy Spirit is the seal, the earnest: he is both. You have got the title-deeds, you have got your document and the stamp is on it, and the stamp is this promised Holy Spirit. So the stamp has been put upon us; we have been 'sealed' by the Spirit. Not only as God's 'possession' – that comes in – of course, I have accepted it; but I do not forget this. Not only the question of security, that is also involved. But the greatest thing of all is that we might have this authentication and confirmation that this is true of us.

There is my first argument for this, and I would argue that that is the way in which it is used also in Acts. As I have reminded you, the apostles, Peter and John, had to go down to Samaria, in a sense to confirm the work that had been done by Philip. Philip had preached, the people had believed, Philip had baptized them. Yes, but still that is not the highest form of authentication, so the apostles go down, and they pray for them and lay their hands upon them and the Spirit comes upon them. There is the authentication, to them in particular, but also to others who were looking on.

But the most striking case of all in many ways is Acts 10:44-48, the story of what happened in the household of Cornelius, which we have already considered more than once.

You see, what happened was this: Peter says in effect 'I was confronted by an unanswerable argument.' He was a Jew and he was in trouble. He had been given the vision in order to persuade him that the Gentiles should be admitted into the church. It took a vision to persuade him. He had all the prejudices of a Jew – 'How can a Gentile be a Christian?' That was the question, and here he is preaching. And what Peter is saying in effect is this: When I saw God putting his seal on these people, who was I to say that they could not be received or that they should not be baptized? God, he said, put the seal upon them and therefore I was speechless.

But, you remember, Peter was called to account for this and he had to go up to Jerusalem to explain his action in baptizing these Gentiles and receiving them into the Christian church. In Acts 11 Peter gives his account of what happened. He says, 'And as I began to speak, the Holy Ghost fell on them, as on us at the beginning. Then remembered I the word of the Lord, how that he said, John indeed baptized with water: but ye shall be baptized with the Holy Ghost. Forasmuch then as God gave them the like gift as he did unto us, who believed on the Lord Jesus Christ; what was I, that I could withstand God? Then when they heard these things, they held their peace, and glorified God, saying, Then hath God also to the Gentiles granted repentance unto life' (verses 15-17).

You see the argument. God had given the evidence, by putting his seal upon them. So I am arguing that what you have got here in Ephesians 1:13 is in conformity with what you find there described in Acts.

I have still a stronger piece of evidence, one which should determine us in our decision as to what exactly is meant by the sealing with the Spirit. It is what we are told about our blessed Lord himself in John 6:25-27. This is about the Jews who were arguing with him: 'When they found him on the other side of the sea, they said unto him, Rabbi, when comest thou hither? Jesus answered them and said, Verily, verily, I say unto you, Ye seek me, not because ye saw the miracles, but because ye did eat of the loaves, and were filled. Labour not for the meat which perisheth, but for that meat which endureth unto everlasting life, which the Son of man shall give unto you: for him hath God the Father sealed. 'Exactly the same term! Here our Lord is saying about himself that he has been 'sealed' by God the Father.

Now this was said to these Jews who did not believe in him. Then in verse 28 we read, 'Then said they unto him, What shall we do, that we might work the works of God?' Then later they asked him, 'What sign shewest thou then, that we may see, and believe thee? what dost thou work?' They wanted a sign, they wanted some seal, some proof that he was the Son of God as he claimed to be. He is saying, 'I am the bread of life', 'I am the water of life', 'I am the light...' and so on, but they wanted some proof. And he says, you have had the proof, God the Father hath already 'sealed' me.

What does this refer to? Well, there is only one answer to this question. It cannot be sanctification here, can it? You do not talk about the sanctification of the Son of God. Of course you do not. He was born the Son of God, he was born filled with the Spirit of God, he is God the Son. But he has been sealed he says. What is he referring to? There is only one answer to this – he is referring to what happened to him at his baptism. It was there that God authenticated him. He insisted, you remember, that John the Baptist should baptize him, and as they stood in the Jordan the Holy Spirit descended upon him in the form of a dove, and, as we see in John 1:33, it remained on him. 'And a voice came from heaven, saying, This is my beloved Son, in whom I am well pleased.'

Now that is the sealing, the authentication. Jesus of Nazareth, the carpenter suddenly steps forward, begins to teach, and everybody says, 'Who is this ?' Then God answers the question. God 'seals' him, and authenticates him. He says: 'This is my son; the Spirit is sent upon him.'

It is after that he begins to do his work. So, having come back from the temptation in the wilderness, he goes to his home town of Nazareth, enters the synagogue on the Sabbath, is handed the scroll, and begins to read out of Isaiah. 'The Spirit of the Lord is upon me, because he hath anointed me to preach the gospel.'

He has been sealed, set apart. God says, here is my messenger, my Messiah, 'God giveth not the Spirit by measure unto him,' says John at the end of John 3.

Bishop Westcott's comment on this is, I think a particularly clear one. He says that sealing means 'solemnly set apart for the fulfilment of a charge and authenticated by intelligible signs'. That is what happened there to our Lord; to Cornelius and his household; to the Samaritans and to these people in Ephesus. This is what the apostle is saying about them.

This then is clearly something that is concerned not with sanctification but with power to witness and to testify, something visible, intelligible, tangible; something has happened that men can understand. And so when you read about our Lord's ministry you find that people were amazed. They said: We cannot dispute the power, but after all, this is Jesus of Nazareth, how do you explain these things?' And he keeps on saying to them: Cannot you see the explanation? What I am doing, what I have been enabled to do is the proof of who I am and what I myself am training for. Up until the age of thirty our Lord apparently lived a life like everybody else, but suddenly as he set out upon his work of witness and testimony he receives this 'sealing of the Spirit'.

In other words, I am suggesting to you that the sealing of the Spirit and the baptism with the Spirit are the same thing. These terms are synonymous but they are used, one here and one there, according to the immediate context. When it is purely a question of witness and testimony you get the term 'baptism' used; but when it is put more in terms of our inheritance and the certainty that is given to us that we are the heirs of God, then the term 'sealing' is used, and the term 'earnest' elaborates the meaning a little further. The earnest and the sealing generally are found together for that reason.

We have defined baptism in these terms – that the baptism with the Spirit is the highest form of assurance of salvation that anybody can ever receive, and that with this assurance comes the power. If we are uncertain, doubtful and hesitant, our witness is going to be affected. If we are uncertain about the word of God, as to what is true and what is not true, or if I am uncertain about my relationship to him and the truth of these things in my case, I shall, as we have seen, be an advocate, not a witness. But when a man is baptized with the Spirit or sealed with the Spirit, he knows; the Spirit is the certainty.

That leads not only to certainty in the individual, it leads to power. It must do. It is when we are certain, that we speak with authority and power. We do not merely 'suggest' something. Our statements are not contingent, they are not qualified, we 'declare' – that is the great word of the New Testament. 'Whom therefore ye ignorantly worship,' says Paul to the Athenians, 'him declare I unto you.' He knew! That is the great characteristic of the Christian church in every period of revival and of reformation.

In order to make this yet clearer I want to go a step further and suggest that what the apostle Paul says in Romans 8:16 is again the same thing. 'The Spirit itself beareth witness with our spirit, that we are the children of God.' But go back; let me give you the context, from verse 14: 'For as many as are led by the Spirit of God, they are the sons of God. For ye have not received the spirit of bondage again to fear; but ye have received the Spirit of adoption, whereby we cry, Abba, Father. The Spirit himself beareth witness with our spirit, that we are the children of God: And if children, then heirs; heirs of God, and joint-heirs with Christ; if so be that we suffer with him, that we may be also glorified together. For I reckon that the sufferings of this present time are not worthy to be compared with the glory which shall be revealed in us.'

You note the context? How interesting these things are. The apostle there is saying exactly the same thing as in Ephesians 1:13, but he varies his terminology. Here, in writing to the Romans, he is concerned about Christians who are passing through a very difficult time. 'I reckon that the sufferings of this present time are not worthy to be compared with the glory which shall be revealed in us.' How do I know that? Here I am having a hard and a difficult time as a Christian in this world, I am told about these glorious things – how do I know that these belong to me?

The apostle answers the question. He says: You believed the truth; the Spirit is working in you, and in you yourselves there is a Spirit of adoption, a cry in your heart to God saying, 'Abba, Father'. You may not have it often but you know what it is. As when a little child runs to his father or mother in trouble, you have known what it is to run to God and say, 'O Father! Abba, Father!' 'The Spirit of adoption'!

That is a great help to you, says the apostle. You are no longer in a spirit of heaviness and of bondage, or under the law, trying to make yourselves Christian, thinking sometimes that you are Christians, then falling into sin and saying: 'But am I a Christian at all?' and becoming uncertain about the whole of your justification. That is the spirit of bondage, that leads to fear, so that you do not know whether you are a Christian or not. But you are not that, says the apostle, you have not received that 'again'. You once were like that, but no longer. No, you 'have received the Spirit of adoption, whereby you cry, Abba, Father'.

All right; but the devil comes to you at that point and says, 'Yes I know, but the human spirit is a very uncertain and a very unreliable thing, perhaps it is just good animal spirits. You know how variable you are. You wake up two mornings in succession and you may find yourself entirely different; you are in a good mood one day and a bad mood the next. You cannot control these things. You may feel like this today, and say "Abba, Father", but what will you be like tomorrow? Are you going to rely upon your own feelings?'

The devil as 'the accuser of the brethren' comes and says things like that to us, and it is very difficult to answer him because he is subtle and clever, and he manipulates his arguments. He brings in modern psychology and so on and you begin to doubt the whole thing.

Well now, wait a minute, says Paul. I have not finished, I have got something stronger. Over and above your spirit which cries 'Abba, Father' there is this other thing – 'The Spirit himself also beareth witness with our spirit'. Now this is not something in me, but is something outside me. This is the Spirit himself bearing witness with my spirit. In other words, if you like, as a stamp or a seal upon my spirit. Here is my title-deed with the stamp upon it; the stamp is the Spirit. 'He beareth witness with my spirit that I am a child of God.'

Now my dear friends this, you see, is not sanctification. Sanctification is included in what we are told in verse 15 – 'My spirit'. We have all known this I trust, every one of us. Not only those moments in prayer when you just say, 'Father!' and you rest in his love and in his arms as his child. But you know also about experiences in which when you read the Scriptures they speak to you. They do not speak to everybody but they do to the Christian. They have been indicted by the Holy Spirit and he is in you. You know what it is to find the Spirit bringing the word out and speaking to you, and that gives you great assurance, you have got it in your spirit. You know that you are a child of God. You may remember a day when you felt the Scriptures were boring and you did not understand and they meant nothing to you. But now they do! Well, that is your spirit, in a sense, crying 'Abba, Father'. Or you may have known it in a service when you have felt things which have given you assurance that you are a child of God.

Do you know the story about William Wilberforce and his close friend, William Pitt the Younger, one of the great Prime Ministers of this country? Wilberforce was a very fine Christian man and he was deeply concerned about his friend William Pitt, who was a nominal Christian, but no more. Wilberforce was always trying to speak to him about these things. He was particularly anxious that Pitt should go with him to listen to a famous evangelical preacher, called Richard Cecil. So Wilberforce worked on Pitt for weeks and months. At last Pitt promised that the next Sunday morning he would go with him to listen to this preacher, so Wilberforce was praying, full of anticipation, and they went to the service and sat together. Richard Cecil preached and expounded the glories of the kingdom of God and the relationship of the child of God to the Father, and Wilberforce was in ecstasy, rejoicing, revelling in this glorious truth, and he was wondering what was happening to Pitt.

Now Pitt was, I suppose, an abler man than William Wilberforce – he was the Prime Minister. At the end of the service they walked out and Wilberforce wondered what this had all meant to Pitt. He did not have long to wait. Just as they got outside the vestibule, Pitt turned to Wilberforce – who had been so ravished by the exposition of the truth of God – and said, 'I didn't understand a word of what that man was talking about, what was it?'

Now that is how we get assurance, is it not? If these things move you and ravish your heart it is because you are a child of God. You have a nature that can receive 'the sincere milk of the word' and it gives you assurance. So you get it in prayer, in reading the Scriptures, in services, and in various other ways.

But what the apostle is saying is this: All that is wonderful, but there is something still more wonderful, and it is 'the Spirit himself bearing witness with our spirit' – the seal, the baptism, 'the love of God shed abroad in the heart'. This is something unanswerable. You are looking on and listening. You are not deducing it from yourself or from the signs of sanctification in you. That is another way in which you can have assurance. This is external, as it were, objective, 'given' – this 'happens' to you.

There is only one thing beyond that, as I have said and that is to be in heaven itself, in the glory. This is the nearest we ever get in this world to heaven – when 'the Spirit himself beareth witness with our spirit, that we are the children of God: And if children, then heirs; heirs of God, and joint-heirs with Christ.'

My dear friends, I am telling you that these things are the same: 'baptism with the Spirit', 'sealing with the Spirit', 'the earnest of the Spirit', the assurance of the

Spirit with our spirits that we are the children of God.

Let me quote Charles Simeon again: 'To many,' he says, 'alas, the sealing of the Spirit is mere foolishness. 'Unfortunately there are many such people in the church today; they regard all this as 'foolishness'. But Simeon continues, 'Those who account it so speak evil of things that they understand not. Let us seek to experience it ourselves, instead of censuring those who do.' And I repeat and commend those words to you.

Let Whitefield have the final word. This is an entry in his Diary: 'Was filled with the Holy Ghost.' (This is long after his conversion.) 'Oh, that all who deny the promise of the Father might thus receive it themselves! Oh that all were partakers of my joy!'

Have you been sealed with the Spirit? Has the Spirit testified with your spirit that you are a child of God? I do not mean that you deduce it from your sanctification or from your reading of the Scripture or prayer or services or any of these others.... I am asking, has he himself authenticated, attested, sealed it to you; let you know beyond any doubt or uncertainty that you are a child of God, and a joint-heir with Christ? Thank God for the very multiplicity of the terms, for they all together, in showing us this same great truth from different aspects, help to enhance its glory and its wonder.

'Oh that all who deny the promise of the Father might thus receive it themselves! Oh that all were partakers of my joy!' Can you say that? That is possible to you. Seek it. Seek it until you find it and have it and are able to say, 'Oh that the whole world knew the joy that I now know, as the Spirit fills my life and bears witness with my spirit that I am a child of God.'

Chapter 18

Something Worth Striving For

We have seen that it was only after the apostles had been baptized with the Holy Spirit that they really came to understand the meaning of what had happened to their Lord and Master. If you read the pages of the four gospels, you will find the disciples slowly coming to a belief in the deity of our Lord but still stumbling, especially when he referred to his forthcoming death. They were unable to take that and to receive it, and we have the pictures of them even after his resurrection still disconsolate, and still failing to understand. Our Lord has to rebuke them and to reprimand them, and he then goes on to expound to them in the Scriptures the truth concerning himself. He points out how the Scriptures had prophesied that the Christ must needs have suffered and that 'Jesus is the Christ'. That was the essence of his teaching as you will find it, for instance, in Luke 24. Then he instructs them and promises them that in a few days' time they shall be baptized with the Holy Spirit. And they were, on the day of Pentecost, and what you find immediately is that the apostle Peter, acting as the spokesman and the preacher, is able to expound the meaning of the death of Jesus Christ in a way that he was never able to do before.

In other words, our Lord had promised that when the Spirit came in his fullness he would give understanding, he would lead into all truth, he would enable them to grasp things that they could not grasp at the time.

Now that is a principle which is as true today as it was then. We have looked together at the testimony of many men who have lived in the past, the saints of God, and we have noticed that there is one element that is common to all and it is this: in this experience they all testify they have come to an understanding of the truth concerning the Lord and into a knowledge of him which they have never had before.

Very well then, it is therefore essential, if we are to grasp the meaning of the events leading up to the cross and the crucifixion itself, that we should be anointed with the Holy Spirit, because it is only as our eyes are truly enlightened that we shall understand. You all know how many have misinterpreted the meaning of these things, and still do; alas, even in the name of Christianity, our Lord's death is depicted as the death of a pacifist, it is depicted as a great tragedy, and they wish it had not happened. My dear friends, if it had not happened, you and I would not be here now; no one would have any hope of heaven at all. But we cannot understand these things with the natural mind. 'The natural man receiveth not the things of the Spirit of God: for they are foolishness unto him: neither can he know them, because they are spiritually discerned' (1 Corinthians 2: 14). The greatest need of the church from every standpoint is a great visitation of the Holy Spirit, and it is only as she receives this she will be enabled to understand again, to grasp and to preach to others, the saving message of the gospel of the Son of God. So we shall go on with our study: nothing is more vital.

Now it seems to me that there is one other thing we must do. There are a number of difficulties that people have always had and still get with regard to certain texts.

The difficulty is that these texts seem to say on the surface that every Christian has received this baptism with the Holy

Spirit and it is wrong, therefore, to urge Christian people to seek this blessing, since because you are a Christian you of necessity must have received it. Or sometimes they put the difficulty in this way – that if the promise is made that this is something that is going to happen to all believers, well then, either all believers have received it, or else they are in difficulties as to why those who ask for it have not received it.

Let us look at one or two of these verses, because I do find that people who are concerned about this matter – and they are the ones I am anxious to help – are in a genuine difficulty about this. A verse which they often quote is Luke 11: 13: 'if ye then, being evil, know how to give good gifts unto your children: how much more shall your heavenly Father give the Holy Spirit to them that ask him?' Now that is one of these verses that perplexes people. 'Either,' they say, 'we have all received the Holy Spirit in this way as Christians or else we are left in difficulties. There we seem to be told that we have only to ask for this gift and we shall receive it.'

Then the argument continues like this: people say, 'Well, I have asked him and I have not had any experience such as you have been describing. Therefore there is only one conclusion to come to, either that you are wrong in saying this is something special and unique and it *is* the possession of all Christians whether they know it or not, or else the answer seems to be that somehow or other God is not fulfilling his promise.'

How do we deal with this? Here, I think, is a most important principle which governs not only this particular text, but also many similar statements. You notice that our Lord is referring only to children, the children who ask. Here is something interesting in and of itself. He seems to be taking it for granted that those who are going to ask the Father for the Holy Spirit are those who know that they are children and who address him as their heavenly Father. This suggests that here, once more, we are being told that it is only those who are children who ask for this. It is not something that happens automatically therefore at regeneration, but it is the regenerate, the 'children', who make this request; nobody else will do so.

Our Lord has made it plain that 'the world' cannot receive the Spirit. He makes that perfectly clear in John 14:16-17 where he says, 'I will pray the Father, and he shall give you another Comforter, that he may abide with you for ever; Even the Spirit of truth; whom the world cannot receive, because it seeth him not, neither knoweth him: but ye know him; for he dwelleth with you, and shall be in you.'

There we have the same kind of distinction. You, he says, know; the world does not. I am arguing therefore that those who make this request are already 'children', already Christian, and they, as children and as Christians, go to their heavenly Father. That is their way of approaching him, not as God in the distance, but as their heavenly Father and they make their request to him in that way and in those terms. Now that is one important principle.

But still more important I think is this – what exactly is meant by asking? The impression people seem to have is that you have only to ask and God immediately gives. That is how they interpret these words: 'How much more shall your heavenly Father give the Holy Spirit to them that ask him?' So they assume that anybody who has asked God for this gift of the Holy Spirit should receive it at once. But now here arises this most important question as to what is meant by asking, and it is here that we tend to go astray. You notice that our Lord suggests a kind of gradation in this question of asking. 'And I say unto you,' he says in Luke 11:9, 'Ask, and it shall be given you; seek, and ye shall find; knock, and it shall be opened unto you.' Then he says, 'For every one that asketh receiveth; and he that seeketh findeth; and to him that knocketh it shall be opened.'

Now many no doubt have had this perplexity with regard

to the whole question of answers to prayer. There are statements in the Scripture which seem to suggest that you only have to ask and you will receive. So people say, 'But I have asked, and I have not received', and they do not understand this. I am suggesting that the answer is that there is a greater content to this word 'asking' than we tend to think, and our Lord suggests that, in varying the expression, 'Ask; seek; knock.'

True asking, I am suggesting, is the knocking. In other words, asking does not mean a casual request. You suddenly feel like it and you make your request, then you forget all about it by the next morning. That is neither true asking, nor true seeking. In true asking there is a kind of urgency, there is a refusal to be content with anything less than the answer. That is where this knocking comes in. You do not merely shout from a distance, you go on and you approach nearer and nearer, and at last you are, as it were, hammering at the door.

This is clearly the teaching of the Scripture itself. Our danger, all of us, is to reduce the great blessings of the Christian faith to some almost automatic process. I have often compared it to the slot machines into which you put your coin and draw out your chocolate or drink – there it is. That is simply not true in the Christian life. It is not true at all. There is this element of real seeking, 'hunger and thirst'. 'Blessed are they that do hunger and thirst after righteousness.' That does not mean that in a service you wish you were living a better life and you would like to be better, or when you are at a funeral you feel the same thing, and then forget all about it and go back and live the same old life. No, hungering and thirsting after righteousness! 'Asking; seeking; knocking!'

And as that is the teaching of the Scripture, you will find this abundantly confirmed in the testimonies and the experiences of people who testify to having received this great blessing. Many of them have had to strive sometimes for years before they have had this wonderful experience, and they say, furthermore, that looking back they can see that their difficulty was that their seeking was fitful – they would do it in spasms and then forget all about it. Then they would come back to it, and then forget about it again. But then they reached a point at which they became desperate, and like Jacob of old they, as it were, said, 'I will not let thee go except thou bless me.' Now that is the thing, typified once and for ever in that great story of Jacob. And it has been repeated so often in the lives and the testimonies of people.

The trouble with us is we are all half-hearted about this. Our Lord is speaking here about importunity; hence the illustration, which he gave in order to deal with that point, of a man suddenly finding friends landing on him and he has no food to give them. So he goes to a friend of his and says, 'A friend of mine in his journey is come to me, and I have nothing to set before him. And he from within shall answer and say, Trouble me not: the door is now shut, and my children are with me in bed; I cannot arise and give thee. I say unto you, Though he will not rise and give him, because he is his friend, yet because of his importunity he will rise and give him as many as he needeth' (Luke 11:6-8).

This man is not going to take a refusal though the man in the house has said, 'I cannot get up, I am in bed and my children are in bed with me.' That is exactly what it means; they were in bed with him, and he says, 'I cannot disturb everybody.' But the man outside goes on bothering and asking and shouting and says, 'Get up, give me these loaves. I must have something to give my friend who has suddenly arrived.' The man in the bed at last says, 'Well, we cannot sleep. There is only one way of getting rid of this man; I had better get up and give him the loaf' – and he does so 'because of his importunity'.

Now that is the point our Lord is making and enforcing. So

that if we just almost casually, as it were, ask God for this blessing and then nothing happens, we must not blame God. We have not fulfilled the conditions, and have not really asked. Do not forget – 'Ask; seek; knock.' Importunity! 'I will not let thee go!' This whole element is of vital importance in this matter. It is in the teaching of the Scripture, it is confirmed by the testimonies and experiences of the saints.

The whole human analogy is surely of importance here. A human parent does not always give the child its request immediately. There are times and occasions when it is not wise and not right to do so for the child's sake. There are advantages in withholding and in refusing under certain given conditions. That is familiar in ordinary human life. God is our Father and he does not give us the blessing we want immediately, always. Thank God he doesn't. We would never grow up if he did, and this is a part of our whole process of sanctification. By withholding the blessing God searches us, examines us, makes us examine ourselves, and realize the terms and the conditions, and he deepens the whole of our spiritual life.

This again is something that the generation to which we belong is tending to forget. We are a people who always desire some short cuts, some easy method, some kind of 'package' blessing. And that is one of the great differences between the Christian literature of this present century and of the Christian church up to about the middle of the last century. People would seek a blessing for years before they received it. But there was a purpose in it all; God was dealing with them and leading them along a given path. You will never know the heights of the Christian life without effort. You have to strive for these things – there is a seeking, knocking, and an importunity. And it is because so many have missed that element that they get into confusion at this point.

Now let us take a second, very similar, yet slightly different difficulty which people find. It is in Acts 2:37-39. The apostle Peter is preaching on the day of Pentecost: 'Now when they heard this, they were pricked in their heart, and said unto Peter and to the rest of the apostles, Men and brethren, what shall we do? Then Peter said unto them, Repent, and be baptized every one of you in the name of Jesus Christ for the remission of sins, and ye shall receive the gift of the Holy Ghost. For the promise is unto you, and to your children, and to all that are afar off, even as many as the Lord our God shall call.'

'Now,' they say, 'this is quite simple. Peter says to them, "Repent, and be baptized in the name of the Lord Jesus Christ, and ye shall receive the gift of the Holy Ghost." And not only you but "to your children, and to all that are afar off, even as many as the Lord our God shall call."'

'There is,' they continue, 'only one way in which that can be interpreted and that is, that it is saying quite clearly and plainly that if you do repent and believe you will receive the gift of the Holy Spirit and it is promised to all. How then do you say that a man can be a Christian without it? How do you say that every Christian has not received this, whereas that statement seems to promise it universally to all who repent and are baptized in the name of the Lord Jesus Christ?'

Here again we are faced, of course, with a great principle with regard to biblical teaching. 'The promise!' they say. '"The promise is unto you, and to your children." Very well, a promise is a promise and therefore it must happen to all.'

Many people have been in trouble about this. I imagine that if I had kept a record, I would find that I had had to answer people's questions concerning this matter more frequently than any other single question. They say, 'The promise is plain, "Ask, and ye shall receive." I have asked, but I have not received.' They do not understand this. They tend to think that sometimes God does not keep his promise.

They do not realize that all the promises of God are always conditional – invariably.

Let me put it to you like this. The promise does not mean that it will be given automatically to everybody. No, the promise is a general one accompanied by conditions. Take some of these great statements which are made to us in the Scriptures. The apostle Peter, for example, in 2 Peter 1:1 says 'Simon Peter, a servant and an apostle of Jesus Christ, to them that have obtained like precious faith with us through the righteousness of God and our Saviour Jesus Christ: Grace and peace be multiplied unto you through the knowledge of God, and of Jesus our Lord.' Now notice this! 'According as his divine power hath given' – 'hath given!' – 'unto us all things that pertain to life and godliness, through the knowledge of him that hath called us to glory and virtue: whereby are given unto us exceeding great and precious promises: that by these ye might be partakers of the divine nature. . . .' But the question that immediately arises is this: are we all, every one of us, ready at this moment to testify that we have received these exceeding great and precious promises in all their fullness?

Now on this other argument we all should be able to do so, but the apostle Peter in that very chapter goes on to base an argument on this. He says in effect: that is what is promised and offered you, but you people do not realize this, you know, you have not approached this truth in the right way. He then says, 'Beside this, giving all diligence, add to your faith virtue; and to virtue knowledge; and to knowledge temperance; and to temperance patience; and to patience godliness; and to godliness brotherly kindness; and to brotherly kindness charity. For if these things be in you, and abound, they make you that ye shall neither be barren nor unfruitful in the knowledge of our Lord Jesus Christ.'

You can be a Christian and aware, theoretically, of all these exceeding great and precious promises, but be barren and unfruitful. Why? Well, because you have not given this diligence, you have not 'added', 'furnished out', your faith with virtue etc. Peter goes on, 'But he that lacketh these things is blind, and cannot see afar off, and hath forgotten that he was purged from his old sins. Wherefore the rather, brethren, give diligence to make your calling and election sure: for if ye do these things, ye shall never fall: for so an entrance shall be ministered unto you abundantly into the everlasting kingdom of our Lord and Saviour Jesus Christ.'

That is a perfect illustration of this great principle. We must get rid of this automatic notion and stop saying, 'The promise is – therefore I must have or else there is something wrong. No. All Peter is saying is this: if you repent and believe on the Lord Jesus Christ you are a candidate for these promises; these are the promises that will then confront you. You are then in a position to receive the gift that we the apostles have already received.

Peter is speaking to people who have only just believed the message – under conviction. They cry out, 'Men and brethren, what shall we do?' And he says: all right, you see what has happened to us – this is what you must do, then these things are open to you. He does not say they are going to happen automatically because they do not and they have not done throughout history.

Now there we have one illustration of it and, of course, I could give you many others. The apostles have to keep on making this point. Paul writes to the Ephesians – here are saved Christian people, and yet he prays for them that 'the eyes of your understanding may be enlightened; that ye may know what is the hope of his calling, and what the riches of the glory of his inheritance in the saints, And what is the exceeding greatness of his power to usward who believe' (1:18-19). It is all available, but do we know it? – That is the question. So we must understand the nature of these promises.

Now let me give what is, perhaps, one of the most crucial examples. I remember having to deal with a person in great distress of soul about Matthew 18:19, which reads, 'Again I say unto you, that if two of you shall agree on earth as touching anything that they shall ask, it shall be done for them of my Father which is in heaven' – and the problem was that two of them had agreed but they had not received that for which they had asked. Here, you see, is exactly the same problem. It is no use saying, 'There is that verse, what could be plainer? But it does not happen.'

Well, there must be something wrong then in your thinking – and there is of course. That verse must never be interpreted as meaning that if two Christian people agree about anything at all and ask God for it they are bound to receive it. Thank God that is not true! Disaster would often have come and have happened to such people if their request had been granted. No; these things are put in this way to encourage us and to show what is possible, but we must not assume that we have, as it were, a lever that we can pull and God is bound to respond; that is not Christian teaching. Such thinking belongs to the realm of mechanics and you do not find mechanics in the New Testament.

Now these things must be regarded in the way that I have explained. They are indicative to us of possibilities that are open to us in Christ; but we never receive them automatically. No, the whole relationship is involved, the fatherhood of God, our own good, our own ignorance and darkness and many other things. And therefore we must never interpret Acts 2:38-39 as teaching that automatically everybody who repents and believes, is baptized with the Holy Spirit. It is not true to the teaching of the New Testament, and it is not true in experience.

That, then, brings me to the third and last difficulty which I am anxious to deal with, and which is to be found in 1 Corinthians 12:13 – 'For by one Spirit are we all baptized into one body, whether we be Jews or Gentiles, whether we be bond or free; and have been all made to drink with one Spirit.' Now the emphasis is here placed upon the 'all' by those who believe that all Christians are baptized by the Holy Spirit. This, they say, is true of all, therefore the baptism of the Spirit must be true of all.

That is the familiar argument and it is being used a great deal at the present time, as it has always been used by those who do not believe in the baptism with the Holy Spirit as a separate experience. They maintain that this one verse is enough in and of itself. It says that all have been baptized with the Spirit. But that raises the real question – does the verse say that? I want to try to demonstrate, further, that the verse not only does not say that, but that this verse does not deal at all with the doctrine of the baptism with the Holy Spirit.

'Ah,' says someone, 'I can see what you are going to do; you are going to read that Authorized Version again which says "For by one Spirit are we all baptized into one body." But the original Greek does not say that. It says, "For in one Spirit are we all baptized into one body." So that verse does not say that the Spirit has baptized us, as you suggest, it is rather saying that we have been baptized "in" the Spirit into the body of Christ.' And such people claim that this can be established because the apostle used the Greek word *en* which people maintain, always means 'in' and not 'by'.

Now this is a most interesting matter. Practically all the translations that we have, apart from the Revised Version and the New English Bible*, translate this as the Authorized Version does, saying, 'For by one Spirit'. The Revised Standard Version says that, Dr Moffat says that, the American Williams says that, Arthur S. Way in his famous translation of Paul's Epistles and J. N. Darby puts it in the margin. The Amplified New Testament translates it like this: 'For by (means of the personal agency of) the Spirit'. 'By'!

Now here is the interesting thing – why is it that virtually

*The Jerusalem Bible, which also translates *en* as 'in', was not published when Dr Lloyd-Jones gave this address.

all these translations knowing all about the fact that the word *en* is the word used, deliberately translate this by the word 'by'? There is only one answer – it is that this word is used in Greek in a causal sense. Turn up the great lexicons – Arndt and Gingrish, which is the latest and one of the best, gives a section showing that it is used in this causal sense. And the older lexicons likewise say exactly the same thing.

Let me give you an example or two of this same word *en* used in this instrumental sense. Take this, for instance, from Matthew 26:52: 'Then said Jesus unto him, Put up again thy sword into his place: for all they that take the sword shall perish with the sword' – and there is the little word *en* and it means of course 'perish *by* the sword'. You could not possibly translate that '...perish *in* the sword'.

Or take Matthew 7:6 where you find exactly the same word used and it can only have one possible meaning. 'Give not that which is holy unto the dogs, neither cast ye your pearls before swine, lest they trample them under their feet...' – which is really, 'trample them *by* their feet'. They cannot 'trample them *in* their feet', but it is the word *en* that is used.

It is the same in Luke 1:51 and then there is a famous instance of it in Romans 5:9 where the apostle says this: 'Much more then, being now justified by his blood', but it is *en*. They should say, 'Much more then, being now justified in his blood.' But nobody would dream of saying that 'we are justified in his blood. 'So this word is used and represented as 'by' quite as definitely and quite as much as by the word 'in'. Purely, therefore, on grounds of grammar there is no objection whatsoever to the Authorized translation.

But let me quote a statement in a book called *The Untranslatable Riches from the New Testament Greek*, written by a famous Greek scholar from America, Dr Wuest. He deals with this very verse. Now I have to disagree with Wuest in his final interpretation, but I am quoting him here only as an authority on the grammar, as a linguist. He says:

> Baptize means "to place into" or to "introduce into".... The word Spirit is in the instrumental case in the Greek. Personal agency is expressd occasionally by the instrumental case. At such times the verb is always in the passive or middle voice. The Greek construction here follows this role of Greek grammar. The personal agent in this case who does the baptizing is the Holy Spirit. He places or introduces the believing sinner into the body of which the Lord Jesus is the living Head. We could translate therefore "by means of the personal agency of one Spirit we all were placed in one body".
>
> It is not the baptism with the Spirit, or of the Spirit, in the sense that the Holy Spirit is the element that is applied to us; it is the baptism by the Spirit. This baptism does not bring the Spirit to us in the sense that God places the Spirit upon us or in us; rather this baptism brings the believer into vital union with Jesus Christ. This means that the baptism by the Spirit is not for power, for in this baptism there is nothing applied or given to the believer.

Then he goes back and compares and contrasts this statement with the statement that you have in Luke 3:16 where John the Baptist said to the company: 'But one mightier than I cometh, the latchet of whose shoes I am not worthy to unloose; he shall baptize you with the Holy Ghost and with fire.' And it is the same little word *en* there. Dr Wuest takes that statement and John 1:31, with which we are dealing, and Acts 1:5, and Acts 11:16 and so on and states:

> This kind of a verb is not found in the passages quoted from Matthew to Acts, but is found in 1 Corinthians 12: 13. Therefore our rendering "baptized by means of the Spirit" is correct for the Corinthian passage but not correct for those others commented upon. The phrase "with the Spirit" therefore defines what baptism is referred to, and the words "by means of the Spirit" speak of the fact that the Holy Spirit is the Divine Agent who himself baptizes, the purpose of which baptism is to place the

> believing sinner into vital union with Jesus Christ and thus make him a member of the body of which Christ is the living Head.

That to me is most important because there you have one of the greatest authorities on these matters in this present century, and I could have quoted even more. His whole argument comes to this – that here in 1 Corinthians 12:13 there is something quite different from all the other mentionings of baptism with the Holy Spirit. This is not referring to the baptism *with* the Spirit, and he gives his grammatical reasons for saying that.

But there are other reasons, quite apart from grammar, which make this perfectly plain and clear. In every reference to baptism with the Spirit, the Baptizer is the Lord Jesus Christ, and what he does when he baptizes with the Spirit is what we have seen. It is a baptism to give power, to create witnesses, to enable us to testify. 'Tarry,' he says, 'at Jerusalem until ye shall have received power.' The whole object, as we have seen so abundantly, of the baptism *with* the Spirit, is to give us such an assurance and to fill us with such power that we become living witnesses and testifiers to the truth as it is in Christ Jesus; we become *his* witnesses. That is the purpose of the baptism with the Spirit and it is a baptism that is done by the Lord Jesus Christ.

But here the apostle is dealing with something entirely different. His whole object in this passage in 1 Corinthians is to deal with the confusion that had arisen in the church at Corinth, because they were dividing up in various ways, including over the question of the various gifts that they had received. In this chapter the apostle says: This is a monstrous thing to do. It is the same Spirit who has given all these gifts to you. 'All these worketh that one and the selfsame Spirit, dividing to every man severally as he will.' It is the Spirit, he says, who is acting in all these, and who decides which to give to one man and which to another; but do not quarrel about them, do not be jealous and envious, do not despise one another, because you have all received the gifts, whatever they are, from the one and the selfsame Spirit. He is the Agent who has given you them all.

Then he goes on. Listen, he says, I have got an illustration. 'As the body is one, and hath many members, and all the members of that one body, being many, are one body: so also is Christ.' He says it is because by one Spirit we have all been baptized into one body of Christ, whether we are Jews, or Gentiles; and we have all been made to drink into the one and only Spirit. He is continuing with the activity of the Spirit and that is why, undoubtedly, these Authorized translators and all the others, apart from the Revised Version, have deliberately translated this with 'by' – '... by the Spirit'.

It is a continuation of his account of the action and the activity of the Holy Spirit, and what he is talking about here is not power, it is not witness, he is here reminding them that every Christian is one who is born again. That is true of all Christians. You cannot be a Christian without being born again, and the rebirth is the activity of the Holy Spirit; it is the Holy Spirit acting in regeneration.

But the Holy Spirit at the moment of regeneration also takes each person who is regenerated and puts him into the body of Christ – places and introduces him into it. That is the force and the meaning of the word. And what he is saying here, therefore, is this: Now the Spirit who has given you these different gifts, the same Spirit also has taken every one of you and has put you into the body of Christ, so that you must never think of yourselves as separate units. He is reinforcing his main and general argument. It is no part of his concern here to deal with the doctrine of the baptism with the Holy Spirit. The illustration is simply to show that all Christians, whether they were Jews or Gentiles, whatsoever they were, are now 'one in Christ Jesus', they are all different members of this one body of which he is the Head. And that, he says, is the action and the work of the Holy Spirit.

Now you see the contrast; it is the Lord himself who baptizes us 'with' the Spirit, but it is nowhere taught in the Scripture that the Lord engrafts us into his own body. No, that is the work of the Spirit. His work is to regenerate us, to engraft us into Christ, to place us in him, to 'baptize' us if you like into the body. All along, this is the activity of the Spirit. It is the Spirit who applies salvation to us right the way through, and that is true of every Christian.

You cannot be a Christian without being regenerate. You cannot be a Christian without being a member of the body of Christ. Every Christian is baptized into the body of Christ, as the apostle tells us in verse 13: 'By one Spirit we are all baptized into one body, whether we be Jews or Gentiles, whether we be bond or free; and have been all made to drink into one Spirit.' Of course we have. We partake of this one Spirit. The Spirit is in every Christian. 'If any man have not the Spirit of Christ, he is none of his.'

That is what this statement is saying. But it has no reference whatsoever to the doctrine of the baptism with the Spirit or the blessing which comes to those who have been baptized with the Spirit. So this verse, which some people seem to think is crucial, not only does not contradict what we have been saying, but tends to prove it, and that to the very hilt, because we have seen so clearly and in so many different places that there are people described in Acts who have believed and have been baptized but still the apostles had to lay their hands upon them before they received the gift of the Holy Spirit. They were already regenerate, as the apostles themselves were before the day of Pentecost, but they had not been baptized with the Holy Spirit.

'No,' says John the Baptist, 'I indeed baptize you with water; he shall baptize you with the Holy Ghost, and with fire.' This statement is in series with all the others. It does not contradict it, it does not deal with the question of the baptism of the Spirit at all.

We have, therefore, dealt with these main difficulties which seem to confront certain people as they look at this great doctrine of the baptism with the Holy Spirit. But in conclusion, let me ask you a question: do you know him? Do you know his love to you? Do you know anything of his power within you? Do you understand the meaning of his death and of his agony? Have you passed from the condition of the disciples before Pentecost to their condition afterwards? These are the things that finally matter. These are the ways in which we test whether we have or have not been baptized with the Holy Spirit.

Chapter 19

Receive the Spirit

There are some further difficulties that I would like to deal with, but let me first say again I am doing this for one reason only. To me the most urgent question of the hour, is the need of this power for witness, the need of this power in our lives. The early church turned the world upside-down as the result of this baptism, and without it we shall avail nothing. So it is important for the church as a whole and for the individual Christian.

The next question therefore that people often put is this. 'All right,' they say, 'I will accept what you have said to the effect that every Christian is not automatically and of necessity baptized with the Holy Spirit, but do not the New Testament Scriptures suggest that at any rate all the early Christians, all the members of the early infant Christian church, were baptized with the Holy Spirit?' They then adduce certain texts which seem to teach that, or which always seem to assume that. Here are the three main ones:

First, Romans 5:5, where Paul says, 'And hope maketh not ashamed; because the love of God is shed abroad in our hearts by the Holy Ghost which is given unto us.' It should be read, 'the Holy Ghost has been shed abroad in our hearts', or 'the love of God has been shed abroad in our hearts by the Holy Ghost which is given unto us.' Paul seems to be saying there that this is true of every single member of the church in Rome.

Second, the apostle writes in Ephesians 1:13 'In whom ye also trusted' – he means by 'ye' the Gentiles. He has been saying what has happened to the Jews, now he says, 'In whom ye also trusted, after that ye heard the word of truth, the gospel of your salvation: in whom also after that ye believed, ye were sealed with that holy Spirit of promise.' 'Is he not saying there,' it is asked, 'that this was true of every single member of the church at Ephesus and the other churches to which this letter was sent?'

And then, finally, take 1 Peter 1:8. Peter writing 'to the strangers scattered abroad throughout Pontus, Galatia, Cappadocia, Asia, and Bithynia' says: 'Whom having not seen, ye love; in whom, though now ye see him not, yet believing, ye rejoice with joy unspeakable and full of glory.' Now as I have often pointed out, he was not writing that to apostles, but to people whom he did not even know, 'strangers scattered abroad', Christian people in different countries in different parts of the world. What he says about them is that they are rejoicing in this Lord whom they have never seen with their naked eyes 'with a joy unspeakable and full of glory'. He seems to be saying that about all of them.

What do we make of all this. It is, I admit, a difficult question and I suggest that the answer is that the apostles, in writing these letters, obviously have to assume a kind of norm, a standard, a pattern. They always write in terms of the church as she should be. And therefore these descriptions which they give of the early Christians are descriptions of the church as she is meant to be in the purpose of God. There is no question at all about that. We find depicted in the New Testament the ideal Christian church. But that, of course, is where these epistles are of such value to us. We should always be examining ourselves in the light of this and testing ourselves and asking certain questions – are we like that?

Take, for instance, what I have just quoted, 1 Peter 1:8. Do you and I rejoice in the Lord Jesus Christ with a joy that is unspeakable and full of glory? Do we? – That is the question.

There is the norm and pattern for the Christian church. That is one answer then – that the apostles are writing with that supposition, with that assumption; here is the description of the true church.

But, secondly – and I think perhaps this second point is even more helpful, at least I find it so myself. Our danger – as I have pointed out many times during our discussion of this subject – is always to estimate things in terms of what we know, what we are familiar with in ourselves. That is a fatal thing to do, because if you start regarding the church as she is now as the norm, then you have to reduce these great New Testament statements to this level and you thereby evacuate them of their glory. But that is quite wrong.

We must constantly remind ourselves of the great story of Acts Chapter 2. We must recapture this picture of the New Testament church receiving wonderfully and gloriously great outpouring of the Holy Spirit on the day of Pentecost. You remember the circumstances, the ecstasy and the excitement, the thrill and the power. Another example of it is found in what happened in the case of Cornelius and his household. Are you familiar with something like that? Have you ever seen anything like that happen? That is what we call revival. The New Testament church was blessed in this way with this tremendous outpouring of the Spirit; and therefore it seems to me that it is more than likely that most members of the early church received the baptism of the Holy Spirit.

That becomes most helpful in approaching this matter when one reads the history of subsequent revivals in the long history of the church. You will find churches in an ordinary state and condition such as, alas, you and I have known in this present century. Oh yes, the people are Christians and they read their Bibles and they pray and they attend the services and God is pleased to grant a measure of blessing upon the preaching of the word. People are converted and added to the church and they are built up in the truth.

All right! But there is no more than that. Many of them – perhaps most – cannot say that they rejoice in him 'with a joy unspeakable and full of glory'. They cannot say that honestly. They are aware of a deadness within themselves, of having to force themselves and to press themselves. They know nothing about abandon. They are unlike the early church 'praising God with gladness and singleness of heart', daily eating their meat from house to house. They know little about the thrill that you feel in Acts and in the remainder of the New Testament.

That is how the churches have been, so frequently. Then suddenly something happens. It may happen to one man, or to a group of people. The Holy Spirit comes down upon them and they are utterly transformed and changed. It may then spread throughout a whole district or throughout a whole country or perhaps many countries at the same time. That is the great story of the history of revivals. And what you find at such a time is that large numbers of people get this experience; some of them begin to doubt whether they had even been saved before. They say, 'In the light of this were we Christians before or not?' They were Christians, but they had not received this baptism with or of the Spirit. But now they have received that baptism, and it happens to a large number at the present time. And if you were to describe the church at the time of revival, you would find that you would be saying something very similar to what you read in the New Testament itself. And you might think at such a time that every single member of the church has been baptized with the Holy Spirit. The point is that most of them have, but not all.

If that is true of the subsequent revivals of history how much more so is it true of what happened at the beginning? There God was initiating the church and there was this overwhelming outpouring. So that I do not find any real difficulty about this at all. It seems to me that the vast majority of the early Christians had received the baptism with the Holy Spirit. So when the apostles come to write their letters to them they can assume that, they can act on that assumption and supposition – and so the difficulty is resolved.

But it is very dangerous to argue from that and to say, 'Very well, then, is it not equally true now?' I say 'No', because I apply the tests. When a man is baptized with the Holy Spirit, and when a number of people are, there is no difficulty about knowing it. You do not have to assume it or persuade yourself that it is true, it manifests itself as we saw earlier with those people in the household of Cornelius. And unless there is evidence of this kind of life and of experience it is not only dangerous, it is sinful, to assume that it is true of all, always because we are reducing these great New Testament statements to our level. No, we are not in a state of revival. Let us face that. That is the first thing we have to realize. There is no hope for the church until she realizes that. The Christian church of today does not conform to the New Testament pattern; and that is the whole cause of the trouble.

We start, then, with that first point. We cannot say that all the early Christians had been baptized with the Holy Spirit but we can say that clearly the majority of them had been and that the norm in the New Testament church was men and women manifesting in their daily lives the fact that they had been baptized with the Holy Spirit.

One is often asked another question: Should we seek this baptism with the Holy Spirit? And of course the answer must be obvious in the light of what I have just been outlining. That is why I have put these things in this particular order. It is our business to desire to attain always to the New Testament norm; we have no right to do anything else. We do not judge the Christian life by what we are, but by what the

New Testament says; and we judge ourselves in the same way. And there I have put before you the picture of the norm, the standard, and pattern of the Christian church and of the individual Christian.

I sometimes think that it would do us all great good if we faced that statement in 1 Peter 1:8 every morning of our lives. There it is. Remember, these people had never seen the Lord Jesus Christ with their naked eyes. They were in exactly our position in that respect. They were not Palestinian Jews. They were people who lived in these various other countries; they had never seen him. So Peter says, in effect: Whom having not seen ye love; in whom, though now ye see him not, yet believing, ye rejoice with a joy that baffles description, beyond description and full of glory. Philip Doddridge, in his note on that, says that this phrase 'full of glory' means that you rejoice in him with a touch of the rejoicing that the saints in glory rejoice in him who are seeing him now face to face.

You must not reduce that statement. That is how these people were; that is what you and I should be. Therefore I argue that seeing that and recognizing it, I should say to myself that I must become like that. I must not be content with anything less than that. If I allow myself to be content with anything less than that I am sinful. I am deliberately sinning. Surely this needs no demonstration. As you read about it here in the New Testament you see it. You then read the subsequent history of the church and see the church in times of revival. As you do so, you find the same experience in most ordinary people that the world has never heard of. And then you can read it in the lives of the great men, the men of whom everybody in the church has heard.

It does not make any difference, great and small, you will find that they have come to this New Testament position; they have lived this kind of life, they have 'rejoiced with a joy unspeakable and full of glory' in the Lord Jesus Christ. And I say that the inevitable deduction to draw is this – 'I must be like that. I want this.' So you must seek it. You must not try to argue it away or to try to explain it away by saying that times have changed, and so on. No, the teaching of the New Testament, as we have seen many times over, is that 'the promise is to you and to your children, and to as many as are afar off.' There is nothing in the New Testament which says that all this was limited only to the early church. History proves that it was not so limited. The history of revivals demonstrates that. What is there about today which makes it exceptional? There is nothing. God is the same, the power of the Spirit is the same, our needs are the same. Put all these things together: 'Should I seek it?' Of course you should!

But then somebody argues, 'We are not told to seek it in the New Testament.' Well, the answer to that again is a twofold one. We are! I have dealt with Luke 11:13, which deals with this very thing. 'Ask, and ye shall receive; seek, and ye shall find; knock, and it shall be opened unto you.' 'If ye then, being evil, know how to give good gifts unto your children: how much more shall your heavenly Father give the Holy Spirit to them that ask him?' And, further, there is this argument which I have just been deploying, that in view of the condition of the New Testament church obviously there was no need for instruction for them to seek it because they had already received it.

So the emphasis in the New Testament is upon the control of the manifestations of the gift already received. In a time of revival you do not have to exhort people to seek this blessing, they all do seek it automatically when they see what happens. At such a time you have to deal with the problems which arise as the result of it. So it seems to be quite clear that everything urges us in the same direction; that this is something we should all seek, and seek with the whole of our being.

But that brings us to the next problem which seems in many ways to be yet more difficult. People ask this question:

'How is this blessing received, how does it happen?' It is indeed a most important question. And what makes it so very important is the danger of the counterfeit. If there were no danger of counterfeit, the problem would be so much easier, but we call the Holy Spirit the 'holy' Spirit in order to show what he is by contrast with certain other spirits, evil spirits, headed up by the devil, who, as the apostle reminds the Corinthians, is able 'to transform himself into an angel of light' in order to deceive God's people. Various agencies – psychological agencies and evil spirits – can counterfeit so much of what is promised us by the Holy Spirit, so that it is doubly important that we should be extremely careful in our consideration as to how this great and glorious blessing is to be received.

Now let us look at it like this: start with the New Testament again. Is it not clear that in the New Testament times the commonest way for the Spirit to 'fall upon them' is what happened in the case of Peter preaching in the household of Cornelius? That is typical. But start with the apostles themselves and the company with them in the upper room. 'When the day of Pentecost was fully come, they were all with one accord in one place. Suddenly there came a sound from heaven as of a rushing mighty wind, and it filled all the house where they were sitting. And there appeared unto them cloven tongues like as of fire, and it sat upon each of them. And they were all filled with the Holy Ghost.'

Then in the case of the household of Cornelius, we read, 'And while Peter yet spake these words the Holy Ghost fell on all of them which heard the word.'

Then if you want a bit of negative evidence, in Acts 8 there is the case of the people at Samaria to whom Philip the Evangelist had preached. Later Peter and John came down from Jerusalem and verses 15-16 say: 'Who when they were come down, prayed for them, that they might receive the Holy Ghost: (For as yet he was fallen upon none of them:

only they were baptized in the name of the Lord Jesus.)' Now there again, is clearly the norm, and pattern in the New Testament itself, that the Spirit 'fell' upon them. And certainly as you read subsequent history, as I will show you, it is the same, but let us keep ourselves for the moment to the New Testament.

It is equally clear from the New Testament teaching that the apostles had the ability and the gift of being able to transmit this blessing to others by laying their hands upon them. This is again clear in the case of those Samaritans in Acts 8: 16, 'Then laid they their hands on them, and they received the Holy Ghost.' And the apostle Paul did exactly the same thing with the disciples whom he found in Ephesus. In Acts 19:5 we read: 'When they heard this, they were baptized in the name of the Lord Jesus.' Then verse 6: 'And when Paul had laid his hands upon them, the Holy Ghost came on them.' It happened clearly as the result of his laying of his hands upon them.

Then there is the interesting case of the conversion of the apostle Paul himself. I put this before you simply in order that I may demonstrate that I am not concerned to argue a case, but to give the evidence. It would be very convenient in many ways for me if I could say that only the apostles had this ability, but I am confronted by this fact. The apostle Paul on the road to Damascus, was struck blind having seen the risen Lord. Here he is, a converted man, and someone called Ananias is sent to him. Ananias did not want to go, but we read: 'The Lord said unto him, Go thy way: for he is a chosen vessel unto me, to bear my name before the Gentiles, and kings, and the children of Israel: For I will shew him how great things he must suffer for my name's sake.'

So Ananias went and entered into the house; and putting his hands on Paul said, 'Brother Saul, the Lord, even Jesus, that appeared unto thee in the way as thou camest, hath sent me, that thou mightest receive thy sight, and be filled with the Holy Ghost.' And he was. But that took place through the hands of Ananias who was not an apostle, and who, as far as we can tell, was not even a leader in the early church. Nevertheless that did happen.

Now what do we say with regard to all this? It is a very important point and the only conclusion we can come to is this—that this is a gift that is given to some; it was clearly given to the apostles, and clearly given to Ananias in that special instance of the apostle Paul. We must therefore not say that it is impossible now. We are not entitled to do so. But I think we are entitled to say that taking the New Testament evidence as it is, we do see it in the case of the apostles and in the case of this man sent on a special journey with a very special commission.

I would suggest that it is very dangerous to argue from this that it is possible to all who have themselves been baptized with the Holy Spirit. I say that all the more for this reason – that, looking at what we know can happen in terms of psychology and in the power of suggestion, we realize that there is a very great danger here. I would certainly not hesitate to say this: that no man should venture to lay his hands upon another unless he has received a definite and a special commission to do so. He must not do it automatically. We must not say that everybody can do this. Unless a man receives a very definite commission and has examined himself honestly in the light of the word, he should certainly not do so.

Now there we have the New Testament evidence, but turn to the subsequent history of the church, which is also important. What happens in the case of the great revivals in the history of the church to which I have referred? Or in the case of the many individuals of whom we can read? I have mentioned people like Thomas Aquinas, Pascal and certain Puritans. We have considered Jonathan Edwards, John Wesley and George Whitefield, Charles Finney and D. L.

Moody. We can also mention R. A. Torrey, Howell Harris, Daniel Rowlands and other men who have been used in a mighty manner. How did it happen in these cases?

It is most interesting. I do not know of a single instance among such men where they received the blessing as the result of the laying on of the hands of someone else; not a single one. What is interesting is that in the long history of revivals in the Christian church in general, or in individuals – for a revival is nothing but a large number of people being baptized with the Holy Spirit at the same time – what has happened has been that the Holy Spirit has 'fallen' or has come upon them. There is great variation in the history. It is most interesting to notice this. Sometimes this has happened to people without their expecting it at all, without their even seeking it.

That is important because it demonstrates the Lordship of the Spirit. You will also find that it happened to some people without their knowing what had happened. Take a man like Finney. He was converted one day, the next day this happened to him. He knew nothing about it, he just found it happening to him. He had not prayed, he had not sought it. It happened to him. That is true of many others.

But then you find others who had been seeking this for months and sometimes for years, and had almost given up in despair, when suddenly God graciously caused the Spirit to fall upon them. There is almost endless variation. And it is important we should realize this. And as this is true in the case of individuals, so too it applies to the larger groupings in the Christian church. You will find sometimes that people in a church, having become dissatisfied, having examined themselves, having realized the lack and the need, or having seen the problem of the church and the problem of the unconverted masses going to hell outside the church, these people have met together and have prayed, and prayed, and agonized, and have done so for a considerable time. God then answers them.

But there have been other times when the church has not been aware of all this. This was more or less the position two hundred years ago in the evangelical awakening both in this country and in America. The Church as a whole had been doing nothing. But God suddenly began to deal with certain people individually – one here, one there, unknown to one another. And through dealing with one man he has roused the church and showered the blessing in a more general manner upon them.

But the point I am making is that in this long history of the Christian church, both in individuals and in larger groupings, this has happened, not as the result of the laying on of hands, but as the result of the Spirit coming or falling upon them. There is an individual in his room, perhaps reading his Bible and the Spirit comes upon him suddenly; or another may be on his knees praying to God, sometimes praying for this particular blessing, or perhaps for something more general, and suddenly the Spirit falls upon him and he becomes aware of this tremendous thing taking place in him and upon him. And it is the same with churches.

There is a wonderful description of this in the biography of Andrew Murray of South Africa. He was presiding at a prayer-meeting in one of his churches when suddenly he heard a noise, a kind of rumbling, something analogous to that which happened on the day of Pentecost at Jerusalem as described in Acts 2 – and there suddenly the Spirit fell upon them and a revival broke out, which led to many conversions among church members and outsiders. Now that has been the testimony and the history of the church throughout the centuries until this present century. I am simply putting facts of history before you. This whole idea of giving the gift by the laying on of hands has been restored by the Pentecostal movement in this present century, but until then you do not find it. You find rather what seems to have been the norm in the New Testament itself – namely, that the Spirit has 'fallen upon' people in the various ways I have tried to describe to you.

This is something, then, which we must bear in mind. That seems to have been the way and the method of the Spirit throughout the centuries. I am not saying that a man cannot have the gift of being able to give the gift to others. I am not excluding it, but I am saying that we must be careful. If the Lord has acted throughout the centuries in the manner we have been considering, why should it suddenly become common that people can lay hands on others and give the gift of the Spirit; especially when you bear in mind the psychological danger and the power of suggestion and hysteria and various other possibilities? There, it seems to me, is the evidence.

But now we come to the particular term 'receive'. What is the meaning of this word? We have found in dealing with this subject, that 'receive' is the term that is constantly used. Take the apostle Paul, for instance, in Romans 8:15: 'For ye have not received the spirit of bondage again to fear; but ye have received the Spirit of adoption, whereby we cry, Abba, Father.' Or the question put by Paul to those people at Ephesus: 'Did you receive the Holy Ghost when you believed?'

There is a great deal of confusion, it seems to me, with regard to this particular word. I am not going to enter into it in detail – I have done so elsewhere in dealing with Romans 8:14-16. Let me try to summarize the position by putting it thus. The danger with regard to this word 'receive' is to put too much emphasis upon our activity in receiving, as if it entirely depends upon us. You will find that many teach that you can receive this blessing whenever you like; 'there it is for you'. The trouble is, they say, that you have not received it, you have not taken it, but you can have it whenever you like. Now that is because of their false emphasis.

Another way in which it is put is in terms of the phrase

which is commonly used: 'Take it by faith.' They quote: 'The promise is to you and to your children, and to as many as are afar off.' Then they say: 'Take it, take it by faith. Don't worry about your feelings, don't worry whether you feel anything or not. Do you believe that promise? If you do, take it and thank God for it. You can take it by faith whenever you like, just as you are. It is by faith, and therefore you can take it.' That is how this word 'receive' is frequently interpreted.

They produce certain Scriptures to try to support their contention and the ones adduced most commonly are Galatians 3:2: 'This only would I learn of you, Received ye the Spirit by the works of the law, or by the hearing of faith?' and 3:5: 'He therefore that ministereth to you the Spirit, and worketh miracles among you, doeth he it by the works of the law, or by the hearing of faith?' Again, Galatians 3:14 is quoted: 'That the blessing of Abraham might come on the Gentiles through Jesus Christ; that we might receive the promise of the Spirit through faith.' And they link that up with the great statement of our Lord as recorded in John 7:39 where John says: (But this spake he of the Spirit, that they which believe on him should receive.')

This is to me a most important matter because I am convinced it is a misinterpretation of the meaning of the word 'receive'. It is not active; but passive. I was able to demonstrate that from the grammar of Romans 8:14. It must be taken in a passive not an active sense. This is seen clearly in descriptions in the New Testament of people being baptized with the Holy Spirit. Take the apostles on the morning of the day of Pentecost; there they are, praying in the upper room, and while they were praying they received the baptism of the Holy Spirit did they not? Yes, but do you put your emphasis upon their taking? Of course you do not. They received in this way because it was sent upon them. They were passive. The activity comes from the Lord who sent down the Holy Spirit upon them. That is what is meant by receiving.

And it is the same with all the others. You must not say that they 'took it by faith'. They did not, it happened to them. The New Testament makes it clear, and the subsequent history of the church supports it, that this is something that happens to people. They do not decide to take the baptism of the Spirit by faith. No! You cannot do that actually. I know many people who try to do it, and who have tried many times. They have heard this teaching, so they have 'taken it by faith'. They say 'I must have had it, I do believe, I thank God for it.' But they do not feel any different and they are no different. They do not show the evidence of baptism with the Spirit, and nobody else can see that they have been baptized with the Spirit. The fact is they have not been baptized with the Spirit. So it is very important that we should not misunderstand this.

Let me use an illustration which may help. I have used it before in connection with this word 'receive'. Let us imagine that I decided to send you a gift, so I sent you a parcel last week and I have been expecting to hear from you that the parcel has arrived safely. But I have not heard from you. So I write you a letter and I ask, 'Did you receive a parcel from me last week?' Now what do I mean by that word 'receive'? Am I saying, 'Did you go to the door when the door-bell rang and by a great effort of the will take that parcel out of the hands of the postman?' Of course not. No, what I am really asking is this, 'Did the postman deliver my parcel to you last week?' You were passive. I am the sender and the postman is my agent. You just receive it. You must not put the activity into your receiving. Yet that is the word that we use. 'Receive.' It is passive, the activity is entirely on the part of the giver, and here it is the Lord Jesus Christ himself.

Now of course this becomes yet more serious when this teaching about the activity of the receiver or 'taking it by faith' is pressed in a mechanical manner. I know of nothing that is more unlike the New Testament than this – when people are taught, 'You can have this whenever you like. Do you want it? Very well, stay for an after-meeting.' Then in the after-meeting you are put to sit in chairs, you relax and you are told, 'Now you can breathe in, in the Spirit, breathe in deeply, breathe in rhythmically; breathe in, and as you are breathing in, you are breathing in the baptism of the Spirit into yourself.'

One simply has to ask a question: is there anything in any sense whatsoever suggestive of that in the New Testament? Is there anything suggestive of that in the subsequent history of the church in revival? And the answer is, 'Nothing whatsoever.' That is pure psychology. I do not hestitate to say that, and there is nothing more dangerous. You and I can do nothing about receiving this gift, nothing at all. It is the prerogative of the Lord and it is in his sovereign will. You can keep all the conditions – and many I know have tried to do this – and you can breathe deeply, and you can 'take it by faith' – you can do everything that you are told to do and you will get nothing.

I must not say that in these circumstances the Lord will not give you the blessing. He may give it to you even in spite of your wrong teaching. But this does not mean that the teaching is right. No. He gives it to you in spite of the teaching. When I say you will get nothing, I mean that men and women have done all this and have received nothing. It is a gift! It is the gift of the ascended Lord and he gives it when he chooses and to whom he chooses, and you and I must not emphasize our activity in receiving it.

Go back to the New Testament and see how it always happened. Read the subsequent history of the church and see how it has continued to happen. When this happens it is unmistakable, and a man knows that it has happened. That is why Paul was able to put the question: 'Did you receive the Holy Spirit when you believed?' And in Galatians 3, as I have already expounded, the apostle is simply saying the same thing. He is contrasting law and faith. He says everything in the Christian life comes to us as the result of faith not our work or activity. It is through faith you have everything, even the gift of the Holy Spirit. It is the faith relationship that makes all these things possible, but that does not mean that it happens to all. That is all the apostle is concerned to say. He is not teaching that you can 'take it by faith' whenever you like. All he is saying is that it is always in the realm of faith and never in the realm of law.

There are still a few problems and questions and difficulties left that we must deal with, but God forbid that anybody should finish this with only the details or the particulars in his or her mind. The great question I would like to leave with you is this – did you receive the Holy Ghost when you believed? Have you received him up to date? Have you been baptized with the Holy Spirit? That is the question. We all of us either have or have not, and we know exactly which it is. Has the love of God been shed abroad in your heart? Does the Spirit 'bear witness with your spirit that you are a child of God?' I am not talking about deducing evidence, but the Spirit himself directly, immediately letting you know that you are a child of God. Those are some of the evidences, and there are others.

He died for you, his body was broken, his blood was shed. Do you rejoice in him with a joy unspeakable and full of glory?

Chapter 20

Seeking the Baptism with the Spirit

In our study of the baptism of the Holy Spirit, we have reached the point at which we are considering the sovereignty of the Lord and the Giver. This is a baptism by the Lord Jesus Christ. 'Upon whom thou shalt see the Spirit descending, and remaining on him, the same is he which baptizeth with the Holy Ghost' (John 1:33). This is his prerogative, something that he does, a baptism performed by the Lord Jesus Christ. It is not an activity of the Spirit himself primarily, but of the Lord pouring forth, shedding abroad upon us, causing to descend upon us his blessed Holy Spirit in this particular manner.

We must start, then, with this great realization that it is his gift. We must not talk about 'claiming' or about 'taking'. He gives, we receive. And, as I think I have indicated, it is very interesting to notice this thing historically. Sometimes the Spirit descends in this way upon an individual or a company without their doing anything at all – unexpectedly, surprisingly and they are amazed and astonished. That has often happened. But it is not always like that and it is to this other aspect that I am now particularly anxious to direct attention – this aspect of 'seeking'.

In chapter 10 we dealt with the statements in Luke 11:9, 13, 'Ask, and ye shall receive; seek, and ye shall find; knock, and it shall be opened unto you....' If ye, being evil, know how to give good gifts unto your children: how much more shall your heavenly Father give the Holy Spirit to them that ask him?' How, then, do we do this?

This is entirely practical but nevertheless I suggest most important. If we stop at a mere theoretical consideration of this great doctrine, this great truth, it will avail us nothing. The whole object of dealing with the doctrine is to create within us a desire for this great blessing which characterized the early church as we have seen, and which has always characterized the church in days of revival, true quickening and awakening, when the church, vibrant with power, is acting truly as the body of Christ in this sinful world. So, what do we do?

Firstly, we must realize the possibility. I must start with that because, of course, if you do not believe the doctrine concerning this, well, you seek nothing – and that is the position of large numbers at the present time. They say the church was baptized with the Holy Spirit once and for ever on the day of Pentecost at Jerusalem and everybody who believes at regeneration is baptized into the church.

There is utter confusion there. They no longer talk about the Spirit 'descending', they now identify the baptism of the Spirit with the teaching of 1 Corinthians 12: 13, which we have looked at, where we read that 'by one Spirit are we all baptized into the one body'. That happens at regeneration; that is being put into the body of Christ. By identifying these things, of course, they seek nothing further, and this has been popular and prevailing teaching, which says that it is all there, and all you have to do now is just to yield yourself to it. You have already had everything you ever can have, all that remains now is for you to go on surrendering yourself to this and allowing it to play a greater part in you.

That is the confusion of regarding Ephesians 5:18 as dealing with baptism with the Spirit. But it does not of course, as we have seen. That is concerned with sanctification. So I start with this proposition – you have to realize that there is something possible to you which hitherto you have not known. I am addressing those who cannot claim to have been baptized with the Holy Spirit. You start by facing this evidence. You ask yourself certain questions; I have already put them to you.

Let me hurriedly remind you of some of them again. 1 Peter 1:8, 'Whom having not seen, ye love; in whom though now ye see him not, yet believing, ye rejoice with a joy unspeakable and full of glory.' If that is true of you, well, all right – God bless you. But I am talking to people who cannot say that and who feel that that is not true of them. What do you do? Well, you say to yourself, 'That ought to be true of me.' Peter assumes that, with these unknown Christians to whom he is writing. He says, I know this is true of you, you strangers who are scattered abroad in these various countries.

Well, you and I, we read that in our New Testament, we look at the New Testament church, we see this amazing life that was in it – this power, this joy, this abandon, this thrill, and we ask ourselves, 'Are we like that?' We then read the history of the church and we see that it is not one of a dead level of life, nor of achievement, but a graph that goes up and down. We see that there have been periods in the church like this present era when the church has been weak and lethargic and ineffective. And then we read of those other periods, Reformation and Revival, when the church again seems to go back into Acts, and life and power come, and people are transported, as it were, into another realm and are amazed at themselves and wonder whether they have ever been Christians at all until this happened to them.

Now we examine ourselves in the light of all that and if we feel that we know very little about it, well then we start by saying, 'I should not be like this, I must not remain like this. I see that there is this other possibility and I want that, I want to be like that. I see the need of this and I see the urgency of this need.'

Now that is obviously the first step. There are many who do not take it, who speak actively against it. There are people today – I do not understand how they can possibly do so, but there are many people – who are very satisfied with the present state of affairs. They seem to think that everything is going well in this country and in others. How anyone reading the New Testament and looking at the church as she is today can do that passes my comprehension. No! This is the first step: the realization of the need, of the possibility and the urgency of the need, not so much in terms of ourselves as of the whole situation of the church in the world as she is at this present time. There is this paramount need of authority, of power, of a holy boldness, of apostolic witness, if you like. It is the greatest need of all. And nothing can give us this but the baptism with the Spirit. That has been the history of the church throughout the centuries.

But then, secondly, the next important step, is to watch our motive, and this is particularly important perhaps at the present time. The moment you deal with these matters and give an account of them, there are always people who become interested because they are always interested in some new or some fresh experience. They are the people who go round the world, as it were, always looking for experiences and if they hear of anything, they are there. It is a certain mentality and a very dangerous one. These people have often tried the various cults and have gone the round of them, and are interested, as I say, in experience as such, per se.

Now I do trust, in the light of the doctrine concerning all this, as we have considered it in the Scriptures, that we are all free from that particular danger and tendency. Thank God for every experience in the Christian life but the importance of the experience is not the thing itself, it is what it means, what it represents. We are not merely to seek experiences. No, let us remember that.

Or, and in the same way, let me say we must not be concerned only about power. Now here again is another temptation particularly, perhaps, to preachers – the desire for power. You read in the New Testament about a man like Peter, frightened, timorous, cowardly before Pentecost; afterwards filled with boldness, preaching a sermon and there are three thousand converts. 'Ah,' you say, 'that is what I want, this power.' And many men have coveted it. You read about people like Whitefield, the Wesleys and the rest, and the great preachers of the Reformation era and you say, 'Ah, this is what I want, this power.'

Well, we do need power but, again, if you isolate it and are merely concerned that you should have power, you put yourself into a very dangerous position. The danger is, as we have already indicated, the counterfeit. The enemy is always ready to bring in his counterfeit, something that simulates what is given by the Spirit. So that if you concentrate on any aspect save the central one, you are exposing yourself to danger.

The same thing exactly applies, as I have said elsewhere, to the gifts. People want to speak in tongues, to have the gift of healing or this or that. Now their whole interest is in these phenomena and in these gifts and they are always talking about them; this is the thing they read books about – they want to be able to do this or that. This is a part of the same danger.

Let us be clear in our doctrine. The Spirit does give experiences. I have tried to show that there is no experience possible to the Christian in this world higher than this experience of the baptism with the Spirit. There is only one thing beyond this and that is the glory itself. As Peter puts it there in 1 Peter 1:8, 'rejoice with a joy unspeakable and full of glory.' It is a touch of the glory everlasting and there is nothing that brings a man nearer to that than this, the baptism with the Spirit. This is the universal testimony of all men who have ever had this experience. He gives experiences, he gives power, he has gifts that he can give. But the point I am making is that we should not seek primarily what he gives.

What should we be seeking? We should always be seeking the Lord Jesus Christ himself, to know him, and know his love and to be witnesses for him and to minister to his glory. That is what you find, of course, in the New Testament itself. The apostle Paul says that the height of his ambition is 'that I might know him'. Not that he might have experiences but that he 'might know him, and the power of his resurrection, and the fellowship of his sufferings' etc.

This I think is something that should be obvious to us. Our Lord said of the Holy Spirit that he would not glorify himself but that he would glorify him. The Spirit is sent to glorify the Lord Jesus Christ, and those who are familiar with Acts will know that this is what happens there. All along when the Spirit has come upon these men they preach about the Lord Jesus Christ, and that is therefore what we should be seeking. We should seek to know him and his love. You see, we are told of the Spirit, 'The love of God is shed abroad in our hearts by the Holy Spirit given to us.'

Now take that great term again, 'shed abroad'. Do not put your little limit to it and say, 'Oh yes, I love God.' Paul says that the love of God is 'shed abroad' in great profusion, overwhelmingly, in our hearts. Now that is what we should seek. We believe in God, in the Lord Jesus Christ, in the doctrines of salvation. All right! But the question that confronts us at this particular point is not that of believing but love! A belief that does not lead to love is a very doubtful belief, it may be nothing but intellectual assent. The emphasis of the Bible is always upon love. The relationship of man to God is to be one of love. 'What is the first and the chiefest commandment?' Not that 'thou shalt *believe* in the Lord thy God', but that 'thou shalt *love* the Lord thy God, with all thy heart, and all thy soul, and all thy mind, and all thy strength.' Is this true of us?

There is nothing that will enable a man to do that but the baptism with the Holy Spirit. You can believe, and in a sense have a measure of love; but the thing put before us is not just a measure of love it is an abounding love. Paul says in Romans 8:15, 'Ye have not received the spirit of bondage again to fear; but ye have received the Spirit of adoption, whereby we cry, Abba, Father.' That word 'cry' has a depth of meaning in it – it is an elemental cry going up from the depth of the being.

Here, then, is the question – to what extent do we know this love of God to us and how do we love God? We are meant to love him with the whole of our being and there is nothing that can make us do so but the love of God shed abroad in our hearts. 'We love him, because he first loved us.' You can believe in his love to us, but you only feel it in its fullness when you are baptized with the Spirit, and that in turn forces your love to rise up within you to him.

This is New Testament Christianity! New Testament Christianity is not just a formal, polite, correct, and orthodox kind of faith and belief. No! What characterizes it is this element of love and passion, this pneumatic element, this life, this vigour, this abandon, this exuberance – and, as I say, it has ever characterized the life of the church in all periods of revival and of reawakening. That is what we must seek – not experiences, not power, not gifts. If he chooses to give them to us, thank God for them and exercise them to his glory, but the only safe way of receiving gifts is that you love him and that you know him.

In other words, you put 1 Corinthians 13 in the centre. Concentrate on love and then all these things will fall into their right respective positions. So we must be careful about this question of motive. The history of the church, here again, holds up a great warning sign to us. Many a true servant of God has been led astray by the devil at this point. He has been side-tracked and has concentrated on gifts and eventually he loses his power and everything else. The motive is all-important.

Then I come to the third matter, the question of obedience. Now there is a statement in Acts 5:32 which directs our attention to this, however you may interpret it. Peter is speaking with the other apostles and he is addressing the authorities. In verses 29-31 he says: 'We ought to obey God rather than men. The God of our fathers raised up Jesus, whom ye slew and hanged on a tree. Him hath God exalted with his right hand to be a Prince and a Saviour, for to give repentance to Israel, and forgiveness of sins.' Verse 32 continues, 'And we are witnesses of these things; and so is also the Holy Ghost, whom God hath given to them that obey him.' I do not stay with 'so is the Holy Ghost'. The Holy Ghost is a witness, apart from us. 'We are witnesses ... so also is the Holy Ghost.' That is his work in his demonstrable, visible effects and influence and power. But the interesting thing here is 'whom God hath given to them that obey him.'

You may well interpret that word 'obey' as having reference to obeying him in the sense of believing the gospel. I am sure that that is included. But it may well go further, as many suggest, and be added in order to emphasize that God gives the Holy Spirit only to them that obey him. Whatever the interpretation of that text may be, the point, I think, is a valid one. Read again chapters 14-16 of John's gospel and you will find that the emphasis is that love shows itself in terms of obedience. This is the gift of the Lord and he gives it to those who love him, and they show that they love him by their obedience to him.

Let me put it like this. Is not this something that is of necessity true? Take it in the realm of human relationships. We always try to please those whom we love. That is, in a sense, an obedience, and if you want anything from them, you show that by doing everything you can to please them. Whenever a man desires anything truly, he will show it with the whole of his being. If you merely want gifts from God and are only interested in gifts, you will ask him for them and then you will probably forget all about it, and then ask him again. But if you really want to know him and want to know his love, and want to love him, then you concentrate upon your relationship to him and that will lead to your obedience; you will want to do everything you can to please him and to be near him.

Let me quote Charles Simeon on this, as he puts it perfectly. He says, 'This higher state of sanctification and assurance is reserved for those who after having believed have maintained a close walk with God.' And he is undoubtedly right. That is certainly true to the whole history of the Christian church.

Now I am putting this in terms of obedience. You believe the truth, you are a Christian, you are a born again person. Very well. 'But', you say, 'as I read the New Testament and the subsequent history of the church in periods of revival, and look at God's great servants, I just feel I am living on a different level. I know I ought to be there on that higher level and I want to be there. I want to know God, to love him with the whole of my being, and to know his love.' If that is your consuming passion you will show it, you will do everything you can to please him, and you please him by keeping his commandments. 'He it is that 1oveth me that keepeth my commandments.' Love is not just a sentiment. Love is not just something that you feel now and again in a service or as you are reading a book. No! Love is a great controlling passion and it always expresses itself in terms of obedience. And so the Scriptures themselves give us advice and exhortation with regard to this matter. To look at it negatively you must avoid 'grieving the Spirit' because when you grieve the Spirit you grieve the giver of the Spirit also.

How do you grieve the Spirit? You do so by disobeying. The Spirit is within us. You cannot be a Christian without having the Spirit in you. 'If any man have not the Spirit of Christ, he is none of his.' That is not the baptism of the Spirit; that is regeneration. So the Spirit is in you and the Spirit works and he reprimands you, upbraids you, makes you feel unhappy and uncomfortable and that you have done something wrong. Now if you deliberately ignore that and go on doing that same thing, that is grieving the Spirit.

The moment a man is born again the Spirit begins to work in him. He works in him to produce his sanctification. And he will stimulate him and cause him to feel certain impulses; he may direct you to read the Scriptures, but you say, 'No, no, not now, I want to finish that novel or I want to talk to somebody or read a newspaper.' That is grieving the Spirit. You must obey him, and if you deliberately ignore his promptings you are grieving him.

We all know about this. You know the things that make you feel uncomfortable and ill at ease. You know the sense of condemnation that is within you; but you try to rationalize it, to explain it away, or say, 'I am going to....' Now all that is grieving the Spirit, and as long as we do that we shall not be baptized with the Spirit. We must do everything we can in the way of obedience. Negatively, you must neither grieve nor quench the Spirit.

What is the difference between these two? It is along the lines I am indicating. 'Grieving' has special reference to this matter of obedience in details in our daily life and living. 'Quenching' is something different, in this sense, that it is more applicable to what Christians do when they are gathered together and the Spirit moves upon a meeting or upon an individual in a meeting. It can happen when you are by yourself, as well as in the gathering of the saints. But this has often happened: in a meeting, when the Spirit is dealing with us in general, rather than in details, you begin to be afraid as to what is going to happen and to say, 'If I do this what will take place?' That is quenching the Spirit. It is resisting his general movement upon your spirit. You feel his gracious influence, and then you hesitate and are uncertain or you are frightened. That is quenching the Spirit. Remember the context in which the apostle Paul puts this in 1 Thessalonians 5:19-21, 'Quench not the Spirit. Despise not prophesyings. Prove all things; hold fast to that which is good.' Now the Spirit came upon people in this matter of prophecy and if they did not respond or if others discouraged them from responding, then that is quenching the Spirit.

But we turn now to the positive side of obedience: it is that you put yourself, as you are, and all your affairs and concerns and interests into God's hands. If you believe that you are his child, well then you say, 'I am not my own, I have been bought with a price.' 'I am his, I am at his disposal whatever happens, whatever it costs, I do not mind.' That is utter obedience; that is really abandoning ourselves to God and to God's gracious purposes. We must be very careful concerning this whole matter of obedience. There are people who never mention it; they think that all you have to do is go to a meeting and 'take it by faith' and you have got it. That is not how it comes. God deals with us in this matter, and obedience is very central. You show the depth of your desire by the extent of your obedience.

But I come now to the next matter which is that of prayer. Note the order in which I place these things. I put prayer as the fourth principle. You do not start with prayer but you come up to it. In other words you realize this: Though I do everything I can, I have no claim upon him, I cannot demand anything. I do not 'claim' anything from God. This is a gift. I show my desire for it, my longing for it, by my obedience, such as it is. But that is never going to purchase it. I can never say 'I have paid the price, give it me'.

That has often been taught; but it is all wrong. You do not

in any sense deal with God in that way. Having done all, you say, 'I am an unprofitable servant; I am dependent solely upon the grace, the free grace of God and his mercy and his love and his compassion. I do not obey him in order that I may get something; I obey him because I love him and I want to know him.' But having done all I can I am still a suppliant; I ask him for it; and that is prayer. I have quoted elsewhere this great word of Thomas Goodwin at this point. Thomas Goodwin in his Exposition of Ephesians 1 uses the expression: 'Sue Him for it.' It is a way of describing persistent, urgent, and importunate prayer. Let me quote further from Charles Simeon of Cambridge, who puts it thus:

> To many, alas, the sealing of the Spirit is mere foolishness but those who account it so speak evil of things that they do not understand. Let us seek to experience it ourselves instead of censuring those who do.

What wise words! They are badly needed today. There are people who are censuring those who seek this blessed highest form of assurance that is given by the baptism with the Spirit or the sealing of the Spirit, whichever you prefer to call it. He says:

> God is willing to bestow this blessing on all who seek it. If we possess it not we should inquire what there is in us which has occasioned God to withhold it from us. We should beg of God to take away from us the hardness of heart which incapacitates us for it, and we should live more on the promises that by them it may be imparted to our souls.

That is it! I really have nothing to add to that.

If you read the biography of Simeon you will find that well after his conversion and regeneration he received this great blessing of the sealing or the baptism of the Spirit. It was the profoundest experience of his life and led to his ultimate ministry. This is what he says: 'God is willing to bestow this blessing on all who seek it.' And the only people who seek it are believers, regenerate people. If you do not have it, well he says, 'Inquire what it is in us which has occasioned God to withhold it from us.' That is the way to look at it. God has withheld it from us for some reason or another and that is why you cannot take it whenever you like. When you begin to seek this blessing God will show you certain things. He will let you know what it is in you that makes him withhold it from you.

How do you pray for this blessing? You plead the promises. 'The promise is unto you and to your children, and to all that are afar off, even as many as the Lord our God shall call' (Acts 2:39). Tell God that. The Fathers used to use this great term – 'Pleading the promises.' You never hear it now. Why? Because people do not really pray any longer, they send little telegrams to God. They think that that is the height of spirituality. They know nothing about 'wrestling' with God and 'pleading the promises'.

You go to God and you say: 'What was that promise you made in the Old Testament which is referred to in the New Testament as the 'promise of the Fathers?' Why is he called 'the Holy Spirit of promise'? You have promised to give this to your people, you have promised that when your Son came into the world and made atonement for sins and ascended, you would give him this gift to give his people. You have promised it, so cannot I receive this?' You plead with him, you beg of him, you supplicate at his throne.

This is the way that has ever been taught by men who not only interpret the Scriptures truly but who themselves know this experience and do not censure those who are seeking for it, but rather are anxious to encourage them. You see the way to pray for this blessing is to use the language of Jacob of old, 'I will not let thee go'. I want to know thee, I want to love thee, I want to know thy love shed abroad in my heart. I know this is possible and I have not got it. 'I will not let thee go.' You go on and on and on.

I could illustrate this at great length from the lives of those who have gone before us and whom God has signally blessed in this matter and used to his glory. You will find in almost all these cases that they had to seek this for some time. The actual time varies. It is he who fixes the time; we cannot lay down any time. Read the story of Whitefield and you see the agony through which he passed before this happened to him. Then again, John Wesley's straggle went on for months, perhaps even longer.

Look at the story of Dwight L. Moody. Here was a converted man; not only so he had started his mission work in Chicago and thought he was very successful. Two ladies went to him at the end of a service and said: 'Mr Moody, we are praying for you.' He rather resented this; he was a successful preacher! He said, 'What are you praying for?'

They said, 'We are praying that you may have greater power.' He really resented this. He thought he was a preacher with power and that all was well.

But he could not forget their words. He began to realize what they meant, to have an insight into this whole doctrine, and to pray himself for this. He went on for at least six months, pleading, in the way that Simeon describes, that God would hear him in this matter. And we have seen how walking down Wall Street in New York City one afternoon God suddenly answered and the Spirit fell upon him. That is the story – six months at least of praying and of pleading of yearning, longing – 'I will not let thee go!' And at last...!

R. A. Torrey describes and teaches exactly the same thing. This is what is so extraordinary to me that so many people in this and other countries, who revere the memory of Moody and Torrey and their great campaigns, completely depart from them and deny their teaching at this most vital point. The same is found in A. J. Gordon and in A. T. Pierson – it is the story of all these men. I could give you a very long list of witnesses in this great matter.

All these men had to pray, had to plead. They did not 'take it by faith,' or 'demand' it, or 'claim' it. Certainly not! They did all they could and yet they felt, 'No we do not know, we have not felt this love; we want to know him.' And then God in his own time answered them. The Lord baptized them with the Holy Spirit. In the words of a well-known hymn, we must pray:

> 'O Love Divine, how sweet Thou art!
> When shall I find my willing heart
> All taken up by Thee?
> I thirst, I faint, I die to prove
> The greatness of redeeming love,
> The love of Christ to me.'

Have you ever really offered up that prayer? That is it!

> God only knows the love of God;
> O that it now were shed abroad
> In this poor stony heart!

Had you ever realized that you had a heart of stone and not of flesh? 'Stony heart!'

> For love I sigh, for love I pine:
> This only portion, Lord, be mine,
> Be mine this better part!

Or take another prayer, that of William Williams of two hundred years ago who knew something about this experience. Here is a translation of his hymn:

> Speak I pray Thee, gentle Jesus,
> O how passing sweet Thy words,

Breathing o'er my troubled spirit
Peace which never earth affords.
All the world's distracting voices,
Its enticing tones of ill,
At Thine accents mild, melodious,
All is stilled.

And on he goes:

Tell me Thou art mine, O Saviour,
Grant me an assurance clear;
Banish all my dark misgivings,
Still my doubting, calm my fear:
O my soul within me longeth
Now to hear Thy voice divine,
So shall grief be gone for ever
And despair no more be mine.

And finally a verse quoted by Spurgeon in a sermon. He does not give the author but here it is:

If in my Father's love
I share the filial part,
Send down Thy Spirit like a dove
To rest upon my heart.

That is the way to pray. Plead with him like that, let him know the despair of your heart. And as certainly as you do so he will grant you your heart's desire. He will speak to you, manifest himself to you, shed his love abroad in your heart. And you will begin to love him and to rejoice in him with a joy which is unspeakable and full of glory. Oh that the Christian church today were filled with such people! Let us make certain that we become such people and then the revival for which we are longing will have already started.

Chapter 21

When Discouragement Comes

We have seen that baptism with the Spirit is for today, but that those seeking it must always watch their motive. We should not be concerned merely about experiences, nor even power. Our desire must be to know him, and his love to us, and to become such that he can use us in the extension of his kingdom, and to make known his glory. Obedience is vital – and so is prayer.

At this point, someone may ask: does this mean that we should not start praying until we have rendered perfect obedience? Well obviously not. These are distinctions only in the mind. You do all these things together at the same time. You will never be perfectly obedient. In that case one would never pray at all. No, this is what I regard as the intellectual order, the way in which these things should present themselves to our minds. I mean that it is idle for people just to pray for a blessing if they are not concerned about doing everything they can in the way of obedience to please him. I have been making a general statement which applies to the whole of the Christian life. It is no use in this life just asking for things and feeling that your own obedience and responsibility do not enter in at all.

Now that is the point at which we have arrived, but we must go on from there. So now, having seen that there is this great blessing, that of baptism of the Spirit, with the results and the consequences that we have noted so frequently in terms of the New Testament description and what we find in the lives of others, we now desire this and we are praying and pleading for it. What is the next principle?

Here is a very important point and I cannot put it in a better way than to say that in this situation nothing is more important than for us to be prepared for surprises. We must always remember that the Holy Spirit is the Spirit not only of power and of might, but also of truth, of holiness and of purity (you remember that he has often represented himself as a dove) and because we always fail to remember that, we must be prepared for surprises. All this is of extreme importance in this matter of praying for the baptism with the Holy Spirit.

Then take with that the state of our own hearts. We are all the children of sin, 'born in sin and shapen in iniquity', and when we are born again we are not made perfect. There is much that is wrong and evil and which belongs to the old nature still remaining in us – not the 'old man' but the old nature.

It is vital that we should bear these two things in mind for this reason, that when we pray for the baptism with the Holy Spirit, we have to realize that what we are asking is that the Holy Spirit should come upon us and fill us till our hearts shall overflow and that he shall dwell within us in a powerful manner and bring to us in that way God the Father and God the Son.

That is what we are really asking for and the moment, therefore, you realize the truth concerning the character, nature, and being of the Holy Spirit and the state of our hearts, you realize at once that you must be prepared for surprises. That is the case for my argument: that because the Holy Spirit is who and what he is, he must have a dwelling place that is suitable and that is meet for him. And so it comes to pass that the saints have often testified to this – that when they have begun to realize the possibility of this blessing and have started praying for it all kinds of things have happened to them, things which they had never imagined. They have begun to be conscious of sin within themselves in a way that they had never realized before. They feel they are much worse than they were before they began to pray. They are conscious of pollution within, in a manner that was beyond even their imagination.

Not only that, but they find that they are tempted, and tried in a more acute and virulent manner than they had ever known; things seem to go against them, evil is ever present with them, and they find themselves in the midst of a most painful, terrible conflict such as they had never experienced in the whole of their lives. Indeed they are pressed at times to such an extent that they even begin to doubt their salvation and to wonder whether they are Christians at all.

Now this is something they had never known before and it seem to be the direct outcome of their praying for and desiring this baptism with the Holy Spirit. And there are many who, because of this, have given up in a sense of hopelessness and despair, beginning to feel that there is something wrong, and that the main result of all this endeavour has been to confuse them, and make them unhappy, to make them feel that they are further away from God than they have ever been in the whole of their lives, so that they are utterly confused by it all. I suggest that there should be no confusion about this but rather that it is something which we should have anticipated.

Again I am not saying that this is an invariable rule. I have tried to point out as we have gone along that there is no standard pattern in these matters. Indeed, I have tried to show that anybody who presents you with one is not only being false to the New Testament teaching but also to the whole history of individuals in the church and of the church in general throughout the centuries. Anybody who comes to you with a formula or a cut and dried method is already on the side of the psychologists and the cults. But in the spiritual realm there is almost endless variation. There are some people who pray for this gift and receive it immediately. There are others who have spent months and even years of agonizing and of trial and of trouble. He is Lord, as I have reminded you, and he has his ways of dealing with us. But here is something that has often been testified to by many of God's people. The immediate result of beginning to pray for this blessing has been a kind of aggravation of their troubles, their trials, their problems and their difficulties; and above everything else, this vision of themselves has been something which has been startling and terrifying.

Now it has occurred to me that it might be of some help at this point if I quote some statements made by a great master in these matters of the soul, an American called George Bowen who spent many years as a missionary in India in the last century. He puts it very clearly. He says:

> You, entertaining a certain conception of the Spirit, ask for the Spirit and suppose that His influences will all correspond with a conception that you have formed. You expect Him, for instance, to be to you a spirit of consolation, and compass you about with the ambrosial airs of paradise. You understand that He is to lift you into a supermundane ethereal sphere where poetic visions of the islands of the blessed shall come flashing upon you upon the right hand and upon the left.
>
> But the Spirit is Truth and He must come in His true character or not at all. You have solicited His ministrations and they are not withheld. But how surprised you are when He takes you by the hand and you prepare for a rapturous ascent into the Empyrean to find that He has taken you by the hand for the purpose of conducting you down into some deep, dark dungeon-like chambers of imagery. In vain you shudder and draw back. You only discover thereby what an iron grasp He has.

He bids you look upon those hideous images and observe how they body forth the great features of your past life.

One abominable statue is named selfishness and its lofty pedestal is completely carved with inscriptions of dates. You look at these dates – your Guide constrains you to – and you are appalled to find that what you regarded as the most beautiful and most consecrated hours of your past life are there; even there. There is a repulsive image called covetousness, and you say boldly, Sure I am that no date of mine is there inscribed. Alas, there are many, and some that you thought golden connecting you with heaven – anger, wrath, malice, see how the odious monsters seem to wink at you from their seats as at a well-known comrade; how the picture of your past life is made ugly on their pedestals. You have looked unbelief in the face, and frowning tell him that you know him not. Whatever your faults you have never been an unbeliever. The Spirit constrains you to observe that unbelief claims, and justly claims, the whole of your past life.

A profound humiliation and a piercing sorrow possess your heart. At least you say, standing opposite the image of falsehood, I am no liar, I hate all falsehood with a perfect hatred. The Spirit of God points you to the fatal evidence. You examine the dates and you see that some of them refer even to your seasons of prayer. At length, altogether humbled, dispirited and conscience-stricken you acknowledge that here in these damp subterranean galleries, and in the midst of these abominable images is your true home. You remember with shame the ideas with which you have greeted the Spirit, and you fall at His feet confessing all your folly. There does He raise you and lead you into the open air beneath the blessed canopy of heaven, and you find a chariot in which you may unforbidden take your place beside the Spirit and visit the places of joy that are above the earth.

That is an excellent and perfect summary of the experiences that some of the greatest saints of God, including George Bowen himself, had to pass through before they had this wonderful experience. In other words, we are so ignorant of ourselves. We say, 'Yes, I am a born again Christian, all I need is this further blessing', and ask for it without realizing the subtle evil that is still here. Even our prayers and our best and noblest desires are selfish. Now the Spirit, being the Spirit of truth and of holiness, has to open our eyes to these things. We have to be humbled before we are exalted. We have to see the real state in which we are before we can expect such an exalted experience.

But consider a well-known hymn by John Newton, in which he puts in verse precisely the same thing. Again, he is writing of his experience:

> I asked the Lord that I might grow
> In faith, and love, and every grace,
> Might more of His salvation know,
> And seek more earnestly His face.
>
> Twas He who taught me thus to pray,
> And He, I trust, has answered prayer:
> But it has been in such a way
> As almost drove me to despair.
>
> I hoped that in some favoured hour
> At once He'd answer my request;
> And, by His love's constraining power,
> Subdue my sins, and give me rest.

That is what we all feel is it not? We hear something like this, 'Ah,' we say, 'we want that.' And we pray, and that is how we anticipate it is going to come.

> Instead of this, He made me feel
> The hidden evils of my heart,
> And let the angry powers of hell
> Assault my soul in every part.

Yea, more, with His own hand He seemed
Intent to aggravate my woe,
Crossed all the fair designs I schemed,
Blasted my gourds, and laid me low.

'Lord, why is this' I trembling cried,
'Wilt Thou pursue Thy worm to death?'
''Tis in this way' the Lord replied,
'I answer prayer for grace and faith.
These inward trials I employ,
From self and pride to set thee free,
And break thy schemes of earthly joy,
That thou may'st seek thy all in Me.'

There is no question about this my dear friends. It is possible for us to go through this world, Christian people, saved, sins forgiven, and yet living on such a low level that we know nothing about the great conflicts that are described in the Scriptures and in the lives of the saints. Take the great apostle Paul: 'We wrestle not,' he says, 'against flesh and blood, but against principalities and powers, against the rulers of the darkness of this world, against spiritual wickedness in high places.'

There are many Christian people who simply do not know what that means, and have never experienced it. They know nothing about the depths of evil within them. They took a decision at a meeting, and they have gone on like that ever since; and cannot understand what all this is about. 'What more is needed?' they ask. That is based on nothing but sheer ignorance of themselves. They are certainly Christians, but they are infants and they may go to their graves as 'babes in Christ'. Saved? Yes! But as the apostle puts it, 'saved; yet as by fire' only.

But on the other hand, the moment you begin to realize the possibilities of grace and what is possible to you in Christ Jesus by this great baptism of the Spirit – the moment you enter that realm, the devil is obviously going to be disturbed. He is going to exert all his efforts to stand between you and that. He does not want anybody to get near to the Lord Jesus Christ. He wants us to remain as children. He will keep us there, ignorant, not desiring anything more. But the moment you have these longings and desires for something bigger and deeper, then the devil will attack you, as these two men have shown us. I could quote many others. Read the lives of men who have lived before us and who have had this great blessing, and you will find that they, most of them, have had to go through this terrible conflict. So I am not promising you something easy and quick and glib. No! I am trying to show that such teaching is entirely foreign to the New Testament. You do not simply ask, and receive immediately.

Did you notice again – we have referred to this before but I want to re-emphasize it – that our Lord spoke that parable about the man going to his neighbour to borrow the loaves in this very context; and did you notice that what he was stressing was the principle of importunity, which obviously suggests difficulty and strife and struggle.

I would put it, then, like this in general – that the moment we begin to seek this baptism in every way I have described, we must be prepared for surprises, but we must realize that we are in God's hands. There is nothing better, therefore, that I can do at this point than to give the advice based upon the experience of D. L. Moody. He often said that during those months while he was praying for this baptism, as he walked down a street, or whatever he was doing, he would pray, 'O God, prepare my heart and baptize me with the Holy Ghost power.' But note the order. It is dangerous to have power unless the heart is right; and we have no right to expect that the Spirit will give us the power unless he can trust us with it. So you get, 'prepare my heart' before the request to 'baptize me with the Holy Spirit power'. This is a very vital principle.

But let me go on to another obvious principle: let him lead

you on. This again is vital. If you are putting yourself in the hand of God, let him lead you; and it is he who decides where he leads you. As George Bowen puts it, he does not lead you straight up into the heavens, into the Empyrean as you think: he will probably lead you into some dungeon. Whatever it may be, let him lead you. Go on! Do not be foolish, and because you are disappointed, turn back and say, 'This is unpleasant, and uncomfortable.' Wherever he leads you, follow him. Go on! It is obviously ridiculous to ask God at one and the same time to bless you and then to resist what he is doing to you. God knows what he is doing, and God has his method and his plan – and here it is. He will lead you into all sorts of places, He may give you strange experiences. But looking back you will see that every one of them was a part of the purpose.

This is to me one of the most amazing things in the Christian life. We all have our ideas, and they are all short and glib and easy: short cuts always. We are all given to that by nature. It is the result of sin within us. But looking back across our lives we see very plainly and very clearly that God had to do certain things with us. God has often had to knock us down before he lifts us up. We always think we can start from where we are; we generally cannot; we have to be taken down, we have to be humbled and humiliated, and God will deal with us in almost incredible ways.

This is, of course, the great romance of the Christian life; things that appear to be quite accidental at the time can have the most momentous consequences. It has all been a part of God's plan and purpose with respect to us.

In other words, the moment you enter into this realm and realize that you are in the hands of God and put yourself into them, you must be prepared for anything. But go on – do not bring in your reason, do not reject things because you do not understand them. Realize that God's ways are not our ways, and that his thoughts are not our thoughts, and that if you genuinely and honestly do seek this blessing to his glory, he will bring you to it; but he will do so in his way and not in yours. And therefore, I say, let him lead you on, do not resist, and do not put down your conditions.

It is a great and a wonderful thing to be in the hands of God but it can be frightening and alarming until one begins to know something about this realm. I say trust God, put yourself in his hands. Say, if you like, with Newman – 'I do not ask to see the distant scene; one step enough for me'; and take every step as it is indicated to you.

That leads me, of course, to the next principle, which is: keep on! Keep on! How this needs to be emphasized. I am sure that I am speaking to the experience of most people when I emphasize the all-importance of this particular principle. Look back across your lives and is not this what you find?

And you will find it in the lives of God's saints throughout the centuries – our greatest danger is to be spasmodic. It works like this, does it not? We seek this in fits and starts and then we are surprised, looking back, that nothing has happened to us. You may perhaps be reading a book, or the life of some great saint, and see how, having lived a humdrum Christian life, sometimes up, sometimes down, failing, succeeding, all on a low level, this saint was suddenly lifted to a higher level, and continued to live on it. And immediately you feel, 'Well, I would like to be like that, to have that.' And so you begin to pray and to seek this. But nothing happens, and after a few days you begin to forget all about it. Or it may be the result of listening to a sermon, or it may be some experience you have had; it may be an illness, an accident, or someone's death.

All these things have the effect of stirring you up and making you feel you would like to know this, and so you begin to pray, and pray really with earnestness. But you do not keep on with it, and after a while you almost forget all about it and you go back to where you were before. And you may live like that for months or years. Then again something happens and again you start – but you do not keep on, you forget. And so you go on for years, seeking spasmodically but never really receiving.

Now this I think is a most important point for us all to observe, and there are many passages in the Scripture that bring it out very powerfully. There is the one which we have already considered, in Luke 11. Importunity! Our Lord makes the same point again in Luke 18 about the woman who went and bothered the judge and would not take no for an answer. And at last the judge answered her. He said, 'I cannot get peace from this woman, I must grant her her request. She is pummelling me and bothering me, she is a nuisance to me.' Our Lord actually uses a parable like that to encourage us to pray to God. Importunity!

This is the principle expressed in that gradation of 'ask, and seek, and knock'. A half-hearted, spasmodic desire is never likely to be granted. And again, you will find in all the literature on this great matter that there is always this element almost of desperation that comes in before God really hears this prayer and grants our request. You notice it came out in the case of John Newton and of George Bowen. They were brought to the point at which they really were almost complaining and wondering what was happening, and were almost at the point of despair and of giving in. Then suddenly, at that point, God granted their request and blessed them in such a manner that they could scarcely contain it. It is the principle, of course, that we find in the old story of Jacob and his wrestling that night – 'I will not let thee go!' These are the people whom God blesses.

How far this is removed, how remote all this is, from the teaching which says glibly, 'Take it by faith,' or 'The moment you ask you receive.'

It is not true. It is not true in the Bible, nor in the

subsequent history of God's saints and people. No! God brings us to the point at which we feel we cannot live without this. He creates such a hunger and thirst for it, such a desire for it, that you do not just pray now and again; you say, 'Life is hardly worth living if I do not get this. I must! "I will not let thee go."' That is the prayer.

If you read again the great story of revivals and how they have come – and this is an exact parallel – you will find that it has generally been like that. Revival does not come the moment people begin to pray for it. Neither does this personal blessing. A revival is as we have seen, this baptism of the Holy Spirit happening to a large number at the same time. There are people who have prayed for revival for years but nothing has happened. But they go on, and rightly so. Read the history of all the great revivals and you will find that God has always dealt with people in some such way as this: that they have been brought to the point at which they realize that without revival everything is lost.

But we tend to be confused about this. We come to points when we feel that nothing will do but a revival, but then we get tired of praying for it and say, 'We must start doing something', and begin organizing an evangelistic campaign or some other activity and we stop praying for revival. We carry out our plans but nothing much comes of it; and then we are exhausted and we do not know what to do. Then we are cast down again; then we pray again. But it is all so spasmodic. Is not that the trouble?

It is exactly the same with the individual. Without an element of importunity and persistence, or urgency and almost a holy violence with God, we have little right to expect that God will hear our prayer and answer it. Indeed, as we have seen, in holding back the answer God is preparing us. He wants us to come to this place in which we realize we are indeed helpless and hopeless, and so become desperate and cry out unto him.

You recall the event which happened to John Wesley on May 24th 1738 in Aldersgate Street in London on that famous occasion? It had happened a few days before to his brother Charles Wesley. If you read the lives of those two men just at that time you will find that both of them had reached a point in which they were so hopeless that they were physically ill. They were utterly cast down; the thing seemed further away than it had ever been. It was just then, when they were physically as well as spiritually prostrated, that God was pleased to hear their cries and the prayers of their friends and to send his mighty blessing upon them.

I therefore urge you to keep on and to measure your real desire for this in terms of urgency. You can think of many illustrations from the natural realm to prove what I am saying: 'Faint heart never won fair lady.' Of course not! And faint heart has never won this blessing of the baptism with the Holy Spirit. If you really want something, you are persistent and you cannot be put off. You keep on and on and on until you almost make a nuisance of yourself. I say, with reverence, we must become like that in the presence of God if we really understand this and truly desire it. Keep on! Be persistent! Be importunate! 'I will not let thee go!'

I must of necessity add immediately that you must at the same time be patient. Now that sounds as if it is a contradiction; and yet it is not, because if we become impatient, then our spirit has gone wrong again. The fact that a man is urgent and importunate does not mean that he is impatient. If you are impatient it means that you are impatient with God, and you must never be that.

The combination of these two things works like this: your urgency is born of your consciousness of need and of the greatness of the blessing. But you are not impatient, because you have now come to see that you are entirely unworthy of this blessing, you are unfit for it. The moment you become impatient what you are really saying to God is that you deserve this, and that he should give it to you, and that he should not be keeping you waiting in this way. That is impatience and it is always wrong. That proves again, that you are not fit, and that you need to be prepared much further.

This is important because it is impatience that always leads people to give up. 'It is no use,' they say, 'I have striven for many years.' They really have a sense of grudge against God. They say to him, 'I have done everything you have said but I have not had the blessing.' The end, that is unspoken, is, 'Why is God treating me like this?' The answer is, because you are like that, because of your very impatience, because of your restlessness of spirit. So we must neither be impatient nor discouraged. The prayer at this point is,

> Thy way, not mine, O Lord,
> However hard it be.

Or as another hymn puts it:

> Nearer, my God, to Thee
> Nearer to Thee!
> E'en though it be a cross
> That raiseth me.

That is the prayer – one of utter submission, a desire to know God and his love, to be filled with his love, to be his servant, to live to his glory. You must say, 'It is your way, not mine. I don't know, I have lost confidence in myself and my understanding. I am leaving myself in your hands.' Urgent, importunate, but not impatient and not discouraged.

So I come to the encouragements – and thank God for them. There are great encouragements to us. There are those wonderful invitations in the Scripture. Take John 7:37 – 'If any man thirst, let him come unto me, and drink.' Now the word 'thirst' is a strong one. It does not just mean that you are conscious of a certain amount of thirst and you would be rather glad if there was something there to slake your thirst, but as there is not you do nothing about it. No!

'If any man thirst, let him come unto me, and drink.' This is a description of a man who feels he cannot go on; thirst means a deep desire. Our Lord says the same to the woman of Samaria, 'If thou hadst known who it is that speaketh unto thee, thou wouldest have asked of him, and he would have given thee the living water.' He explains what he means when he goes on to say – 'Whosoever drinketh of this water' – this water that is here by our side 'shall thirst again. But whosoever drinketh of the water that I shall give him shall never thirst; but the water that I shall give him shall be in him a well of water springing up into everlasting life' (John 4: 13-14).

These are the great encouragements. So let us read the Scriptures and concentrate on the offer. Look at the reasons for Christ's coming, his life, death and resurrection, and what he has made possible for us. Look at this and listen to the gracious invitations.

Another great encouragement, as we have seen, is to read the lives of others who have gone before us. I must add a note to that. There is a right way and a wrong way of reading Christian biography, and I have often felt that we need instruction concerning this. (I am speaking partly out of my own experience.) The value of reading these lives and these biographies in the history of the church is that they remind us of the possibility, they show us what can happen. And, thank God, what they show is that it does not depend upon us, it depends upon God's power to give. It makes us realize that this blessing is not only for certain outstanding saints, it is for all God's people – the invitation is 'to you, and to your children, and to as many as are afar off, and to all that the Lord our God shall call.' This is a great encouragement. You see men and women like yourselves and you see that this blessing came to them, and so it encourages you.

But there is a wrong way of reading such stories and records and it is that you just concentrate only on their experience and think of that alone. The result is that you just want their experiences or their power. You do not learn the whole lesson that they teach you. You do not see that they were more concerned about holiness and about God and his love and the knowledge of him than they were about the experience. You can misappropriate these histories; you can become a gatherer, a collector of experiences. That is always bad. And still worse is the danger of living on their experiences and never having the experience yourself. Do you know something about this? It is a very, very real danger.

Look at it like this. You may be in a dry, arid spiritual condition, and you read a biography somebody gives you. And as you read it your heart is warmed and moved and you feel altogether better and different. It leads you to a season of prayer for this blessing and great diligence in your Christian life. But that only lasts for a while. Then you read another such book and the same thing happens again. You can spend your life like that. You have been given a temporary satisfaction by reading the experiences of others, and you tend to live on that.

This is a very common condition. It is not confined to the reading of books; it can happen equally well in meetings where people give experiences. I sometimes think it is one of the greatest dangers in connection with missionary meetings. People sit back and they hear these wonderful experiences of conversions that happen, and it gives them a nice comfortable feeling, but it leaves them exactly where they were. They are living on the experiences of others and they have never had the real deep experience themselves. If someone who has had some remarkable experience is announced to speak in a meeting concerning this, it will be packed, crowded. Many will get a thrill out of it, as they say. But the question is, have they ever partaken of the experience itself? So while I am commending and really advocating urgently the reading of everything that stimulates this desire, we must use this in the right way. These things are meant to be stimulants; we are not meant to live on them. You do not live on stimulants. If you do you will soon be in a very bad state. It is like people who live on pep pills. There is far too much of that, it seems to me, in the religious world today.

The value of these histories is that they should lead you to seek the thing itself. And so, next to the invitations of the word and the encouragements in the word itself, I would put the reading of the history of the church throughout the centuries. I say with this proviso, that you use it in the right way and do not abuse it. You must say at the end of the reading, 'Very well, that happened to that man, that happened to that woman; has it happened to me? Why has it not happened to me? It must happen to me! Because it happened to them it can happen to me, I therefore will seek it.' Thus it will urge you to greater prayer.

If your reading or your attendance at meetings does not lead you to that, you are abusing them, you are using them as drugs, and are trying to live on stimulants instead of on true food.

But, for me to finish this particular section, let me say just a word about what used to be called 'Tarrying meetings'. This comes in our logical sequence. Having grasped that this is not something which you can take whenever you like, but that it is something for which one has to pray and perhaps for a long time, the whole notion of tarrying comes in. This is based partly on what we read in Acts 1 where our Lord said to those disciples, 'Tarry ye in Jerusalem until....'

Now here again is a statement that can be misinterpreted completely, and I think it has been misinterpreted very frequently in the past and still is. There are those who say, 'Ah yes, but that has got nothing to do with us, that is a purely dispensational statement. All it meant there was that the

Holy Spirit was not to come until the day of Pentecost, in order that the Old Testament types might be fulfilled. They in particular had to tarry but nobody else has to.'

That has been the popular exposition of those who do not regard the baptism with the Holy Spirit as a separate experience, and in that way they think that they can get rid of it. But surely they are proving too much. I am prepared to grant that the dispensational element did come in, but I suggest that that typical teaching, the teaching through the types, is designed to apply to all times and is designed to emphasize the point that regenerate Christian people do have to wait for this haptism, this power to witness. It need not be ten days but there is a distinction, there is a difference between regeneration and baptism with the Spirit. Those who are already regenerate have not received this baptism automatically, and there is an interval. It may be a moment; it may be an hour; it may be a day as in the case of Finney; it may be six months as in the case of Moody; it may be years as in the case of George Bowen and many others whom I could mention to you.

The actual length of time is irrelevant and unimportant. But what is important is that we realize that we must wait until we have it and know that we have it. And it is quite certain that if those apostles were not capable of acting as witnesses to him without this baptism the same is equally true of us. Their belief in him was now strong and certain. He had instructed them himself; they had faith in him. Yes, but they cannot be powerful witnesses 'Until....' Neither can we. We need full assurance; the testimony of the Spirit with our spirits that we are the children of God.

But there is another side to this subject. It was the custom in certain religious circles during the early part of the last century and the end of the eighteenth century to hold what they called 'tarrying meetings'. These were meetings in which Christians were advised to meet together and to pray to God that he would baptize them with the Spirit, and that they should wait there until he had done so. This was very popular in America at that time and was introduced into this country in a measure by a man called Lorenzo Durand. It was particularly practised by the early Primitive Methodists.

What does one say about holding 'tarrying meetings'? I must confess that I find this a difficult subject. We certainly cannot prohibit such things, and yet again there is surely the need of a great and a grave note of warning. Any body of people (or any individual), which takes up this attitude of saying that they are going to go on praying until God does this to them, are really dictating to God. They are missing the entire point made by John Newton and George Bowen. We have no right to put a time limit upon God. Not only so, but you are again opening the door to the psychological and to the spurious. If you continue in this manner, perhaps with inadequate food, and the atmosphere gets tense and excited, you are simply exposing yourself to psychological and even evil spirit influences; and oftentimes such meetings did lead more or less to spiritual disaster. Therefore I say again: wait! Tarry! – But be careful not to do it under time limits, and don't put conditions upon God, saying, 'I will not leave this meeting until....' By doing so you are not only exposing yourself to these other influences, but in any case you are violating the great principle and doctrine of the sovereignty of the Lord Jesus Christ.

It is he who gives this gift. He knows when to give it, when we are fit to receive it. All we can do is to long for it, yearn for it, cry out for it, keep on doing so and to be importunate. But above all we must leave ourselves unreservedly, and the great issue itself, entirely in his blessed and loving hands, as John Newton reminds us in his hymn. If you are in this position of seeking, do not despair, or be discouraged, it is he who has created the desire within you, and he is a loving God who does not mock you. If you have the desire, let him lead you on. Be patient. Be urgent and patient at the same time. Once he leads you along this line he will lead you to the blessing itself and all the glory that is attached to it.

May God give us grace to understand and to implement these spiritual principles. The possibilities are there for any genuine child of God who longs to know the love of God in its fullness! Go on pleading. Go on asking.

> O love divine, how sweet thou art!
> When shall I find my willing heart
> All taken up by Thee?

Go on offering that prayer, and in his own gracious good day he will grant you your heart's desire, and you will begin to know that 'joy unspeakable and full of glory'.

Chapter 22

Blessed Are They That Mourn

As we reach this point in our consideration of this vital and all important doctrine of the baptism with the Holy Spirit, let us remind ourselves that this is not a theoretical matter. There is nothing more practical than this. I have given, I think, abundant evidence to prove that it is men who have been baptized with the Holy Spirit whom God has used most signally in the long history of the church. It is certainly the great characteristic in the lives of the saints who have known most what it is to enjoy God. You remember the definition of the Shorter Catechism: 'What is the chief end of man?' And the answer is, 'The chief end of man is to glorify God, and to enjoy Him for ever'; and the men and women who have known most of that blessed enjoyment are those who have testified to this baptism with the Spirit, something which has come to them and happened to them subsequent to their original conversion.

There is therefore nothing that is more urgent than this. This is undoubtedly the greatest need in the church today. The greatest need of the church as a whole, the greatest need of individuals within the church.

We must measure ourselves in terms of the pictures and the portrayals that we have in the New Testament of the Christian. Not by what we see today, nor by contrasting ourselves with others who are obviously below us or unworthy. It is not enough for us as Christian people to make sure that we are orthodox and to bemoan the statements that are made in the name of Christ that are denials of the Scriptural teaching. That is all right, that is very simple. But what you and I have to do particularly is to examine ourselves in the light of this picture. Are we – let us ask it again – are we rejoicing in the Lord Jesus Christ with a joy which is unspeakable and full of glory? That is what we are meant to be.

Let us remember, too, that there is nothing the devil is more anxious to prevent than that a Christian person should be baptized with the Holy Spirit. A formal Christian does not worry the devil. The formal Christian does not do much harm to the kingdom of the devil. But once a Christian is filled with the Spirit he becomes a menace to the devil.

I want now to continue our consideration by putting this question to you: how is this blessing given, or, how does the baptism of the Holy Spirit come to men? Now I do not mean by that something which we have already considered, namely the question of laying on of hands or these mechanical methods of rhythmic breathing, which suggest auto-suggestion and psychology. I mean rather the circumstances in which this blessing has generally come to people in the past. It is very helpful, very instructive, and very encouraging to consider that.

You will find that it has generally happened in one of the following ways: one is while the Christian is actually praying. The Christian may be praying alone, or he may be in a prayer-meeting. Perhaps that is the most frequent manner of all in which the blessing comes. A very interesting point I must emphasize here is that it is not always when the Christian is praying for this particular blessing. That is where that incident in Acts 4:23-31 is such an interesting and important one. The Christians were not praying for another outpouring of the Spirit; they were simply putting their case as it was into the hands of God and praying that they might be enabled to continue with their witness and their testimony. And as they were praying for that, God sent the blessing down upon them. And it has often happened like that. But it does happen often that while someone is actually praying for this blessing, it is suddenly given. That is something that we would expect – while engaged in prayer, either individually or collectively.

Then another very common way is that while one is reading the Scripture, this blessing suddenly comes. This is again something one would expect. The Holy Spirit is the author of the Scripture. It is he who inspired and guided and filled the men who have written these Scriptures. So there is this association inevitably between the word and the coming of the Spirit. And what often happens is that the Christian is reading a portion of Scripture which he may have read many, many times before. He may have read it hundreds of times and always enjoyed it, and had a blessing as he read it, but suddenly this portion of Scripture seems to stand out, is lifted out, and applied directly and immediately to him with great power.

What happens is not so much that the man is again convinced of what he already knew and believed concerning the way of salvation or some other truth of the gospel; but suddenly a scripture is taken out and speaks in a very direct manner. It is as if an audible voice said – 'This is for you!' The scripture suddenly is given and applied directly to the soul. And the recipient knows this and is filled with the sense of rejoicing and of praise – as we have seen so many times in the Scriptures themselves and in the testimony of others throughout the centuries.

So if you are praying for this blessing and seeking it – asking, and seeking, and knocking – never be surprised but that at some favoured moment while you are reading your Scriptures he suddenly comes. This is the place to find him, because this is his. So keep with the Scriptures, read the

Scriptures. Read them in general, read in particular about every aspect of salvation. You never know when, you never know where. There are no strict rules about this; you cannot stereotype this blessing. The Spirit is free, he is like the wind, he 'bloweth where He listeth', and this is very true in this particular matter.

Then sometimes it happens while the word is being preached in a service. This is what makes a service in the house of God so wonderful, so marvellous, and – I use the word deliberately – so romantic. We have a right to expect that he should come when his people are gathered together to praise God and to worship him. Christian people, you neglect the services of the house of God at your peril and to your great loss. To me the most wonderful thing as I walk up into a pulpit is that I never know what is going to happen. How often I am wrong in my anticipations, in both ways; wrong in that something that I had expected does not happen, but, thank God, much more frequently wrong in that my poor expectations have suddenly been falsified and God has suddenly been pleased to look upon us and bless us.

How often that has happened in the past while God's people are met together and the word is being expounded and unfolded. That is the way in which it comes. And again let me make this clear; the exposition need not be about the Holy Spirit, or about the baptism of the Holy Spirit. Many friends need to be reminded of this at the present time. There is a danger that some people only speak and preach about the Holy Spirit, because they feel that if you do not you will never receive this baptism.

But if you read Acts, you must be struck at once that that is not what happened. The early preachers preached about the Lord Jesus Christ. It is as they were preaching about him that the Spirit was sent. This is, of course, what you would expect. Our Lord said: 'He will not glorify himself, he will glorify me.' So if you really desire this blessing, concentrate on the

Lord Jesus Christ; and it is so often, as men of God have been expounding the Scriptures and have been unfolding the truth about the Lord in the glory of his great salvation, that the Spirit has come and has set his seal upon the message by baptizing men and women as they were listening to it.

That has happened so frequently; but, you see, the ways in which he comes are almost endless. Another way is that sometimes when the Christian is in a state of meditation and thinking about these things, about the spiritual life, about the whole state of the church, mourning about its condition, and generally exercising himself in these matters – not reading the Scriptures, not praying at the moment but simply meditating – the blessing comes. As you read the biographies you will find that happening constantly and constantly being emphasized.

But we today are so busy, weare so active, we have no time to think or to meditate; and that is why we often miss the blessing. Meditation! Suddenly as they were meditating a Scripture was brought to the mind. They had not been thinking about it, nor seeking it, but suddenly a Scripture is brought to them, put before the mind, implanted in it almost, and is suddenly applied to them. And when they least expected it, they were thus filled with a spirit of rejoicing and of praise and of thanksgiving.

But – and I want to emphasize this last one also – sometimes this blessing is given quite apart from the Scripture altogether. I mean by that a direct and an immediate impression is made on our spirits by the Holy Spirit. I am concerned to emphasize this because some of the leading Puritans have emphasized that the Spirit never comes in this way of blessing, or baptism, or of sealing or of giving the earnest, apart from the word. Now I suggest that at that point they are going beyond the Scriptures; that there is no scripture that says that, and that furthermore, they are denying what has so often happened in the experiences of the saints throughout the centuries.

Now I understand why they said this. They did so for the reason that the man who tries to hold the balance of Scripture always has to fight on two fronts.

Many of the leading Puritans had to do that. They had to fight the Romanists and the dull formalists in Anglicanism; but on the other hand there were a number of wild enthusiastic sects in their day. Those who are familiar with the history of the seventeenth century will know the story of the Quakers and others; a kind of left wing Puritanism. Some of these enthusiasts went so far as to say that they did not need the Scriptures at all, that because of the 'inner light' and the inner witness of the Spirit and the direct dealings of the Spirit of God they did not need the word. Now the main Puritans in their desire to control that excess which they could see was going to do harm to the truth over against the formalists, went so far as to say that you must never trust anything unless it comes directly with the word.

But that, it seems to me, goes beyond Scripture, and is wrong, not only for the reasons I have given but for this further reason. The early Christians did not have the Scriptures as we have them; some had their Old Testament Scriptures but they had not got the New Testament Scriptures.

How, then, did the blessing come to them? There is a danger that we may go too far and set a limit upon the freedom of the Spirit and his sovereignty in his determination of the way in which he grants this particular blessing. So I am asserting that this blessing may come to the believer apart from the word altogether, directly and immediately. Let me, in order to support this, quote some words that were uttered by Charles Haddon Spurgeon on April 28th, 1861 on this very matter, in a sermon that he preached on the subject of full assurance. He had been dealing with preaching, as I have been trying to do. He had also been dealing with reading the word. But then he says,

> God has a way of speaking without the Word, and without the ministers to our hearts. His Spirit can drop like the rain and distil like the dew as the small rain upon the tender herb. We know not how it is but sometimes there is a deep, sweet calm. Our conscience says, I have been washed in the blood of Christ, and the Spirit of God saith, Aye, 'tis true! 'tis true! In such times we are so happy – so happy – that we want to tell our joys, so blessed that if we could but borrow angels' wings and fly away we would scarce know the change when we were passed through the Pearly Gates, for we have had heaven below and there has been but little difference between that and heaven above.
>
> Oh! I wish that my whole congregation without exception consisted of men and women who had heard the Spirit say, "I am thy salvation." What happy hymns! What happy prayers! You might go home to some poor single room, you might go to a scantily furnished house, and to a table that has barely bread upon it, but happy man – happy man – better would be your dinner of herbs than a stalled ox without confidence in Christ; better your rich poverty than the poverty of the rich who have no faith in Jesus; better all the griefs you have to endure when sanctified by assurance than all the joy the worldling has when unblessed by faith and unhallowed by love to God. I can say now, Grant me the visits of Thy face and I desire no more.

That is it! That is how Mr Spurgeon put it. 'Without the word,' 'without the preacher,' but the Spirit like the dew dropping and falling. Suddenly he distils this and he speaks. The conscience says, I know that I am washed in the blood of the Lamb, and the Spirit replies in an unmistakable manner saying, 'Tis true! Tis true!' That is it. It can happen, then, immediately and directly without the use of the Word.

There, my friends, are some of the ways in which this happens. We have already dealt with the discouragements. I am saying this now to encourage you.

Sometimes a light surprises
The Christian while he sings;
It is the Lord who rises
With healing in His wings.

That is the glory of this blessed life into which we have been brought – that you never know what is going to happen. There are surprises and you never know when they may come – after rain, after storm.

Let us now go on to consider the question: when is he given? When are we most likely to receive this blessing? When have we a right to expect it? Well, in addition to what I have just been saying, there are a number of points which to me are most encouraging and are always most comforting. Once more I would emphasize the element of variableness, and that is where I do bemoan the teaching that has mechanized all this. You cannot teach in that way if you really believe the Scriptures, and if you know the long history of the church in general and in the particular lives of God's people. Oh the variety of the ways! Oh the variableness in his dealings! There is nothing fixed, set, stereotyped. That is again always the characteristic of the cults. 'Do this and there it is!' That is not the freedom of the Spirit, and that is why I must issue that warning once more.

But there are certain chosen ways along which he comes. Here is one of them. If you have truly mourned because of sin, because of your sinfulness, do not be surprised if the blessing is at hand. I mean that you *really* mourn because of your sinfulness. How much mourning is there today? It is not surprising that we have heard so little in this century about the baptism with the Spirit; it is not surprising that people should even oppose the teaching of this truth. They know nothing about mourning for sin. We live in days of 'easy salvation', 'easy conversion' and 'decision'! But when you read the old biographies you find men mourning because of their sin. John Bunyan was eighteen months in an agony of soul; and he is but one of many, many witnesses in this respect. It seems to be a rule that when a person has been led by the Spirit into this terrible mourning and grief because of sin it is generally the prelude to the baptism of the Spirit.

Now the apostle Paul in a sense puts that to us in Romans 8:15, 'For we have not received the spirit of bondage again to fear; but we have received the Spirit of adoption, whereby we cry, Abba, Father.' Now there is such a state as 'a spirit of bondage to fear'; and that is the work of the Holy Spirit. The Holy Spirit can cast a man down, as you see in the case of the apostle Paul in Romans 7. He is beside himself, he does not know what to do. He says, 'In me (that is to say, in my flesh) dwelleth no good thing.' 'The law is holy: but I am carnal, sold under sin.' He is in an agony and he is grieving, he is in bondage under 'a spirit of heaviness', and he can simply cry out, 'Who shall deliver me from the body of this death?'

A man who has ever known this terrible spirit of bondage is one who is more likely than anyone else to have the baptism of the Spirit. The people who have never known a spirit of heaviness and of bondage are scarcely ever able to testify to the baptism of the Spirit, indeed they are not interested because they think they have got everything. That is because of the superficiality of their whole position. But the deeper you go in conviction and repentance and agony of soul, the more likely you are to be lifted up to the heights. I could give you many, many illustrations of this. I have reminded you of how Whitefield and the Wesleys went through such an agony of repentance and conviction that it almost ruined their health. Then came the great and the blessed moment.

A person who is led to some special act of self-denial in promoting God's glory is also on the way to this blessing. The Spirit leads us, as we have seen, and should he ever lead you to some act of special self-denial for the sake of God and his glory and his church and his cause, you can be confident that he is taking you along that road because He has something in store for you. It is not that you are purchasing it by your act of self-denial, but in your act of self-denial you have shown your obedience. You remember that Abraham, when he was ready to offer his Isaac, received a great word with respect to the Covenant.

There is another route by which the blessing may come and for which we thank God. Those who have often had some special season of conflict with temptation and the devil have often found that that has been the prelude to the receiving of this great blessing. This is satanic attack. The devil does not stop merely at tempting people; that is, as it were, his regular business. But there are times when he deals with the Christian as he did with our Lord himself in the wilderness, and makes a special onslaught upon us. He attacks with great force and hounds the soul and pursues it! It often happens that when a soul has passed through such a period of conflict and temptation with Satan, then round the corner there awaits this great and mighty and delivering blessing.

I am simply saying these things for your comfort. If you feel that you are in the position that things seem to be worse than they have ever been with you, and that you are having to fight for your very faith, I say 'hold on'. Hold on, and it may be that just at the least expected moment the Lord will pour forth his Spirit upon you to comfort you and to reward you and to gladden your heart.

Another fact – and it follows from the last one and is most interesting in the history of the church – is that the blessing often comes in connection with some great trial. I do not mean temptation, or a satanic attack; I am thinking of trials in a more material and external sense. This has often been associated with illness or with an accident or with disease of some kind. Those who have ever read the biography of the great Dr Thomas Chalmers in Scotland will know that it was after a long illness, when he was on his back for ten months or so that he was blessed in this way and his whole ministry was completely transformed.

But it has often happened in connection with circumstances – wars and trials of that kind. You will often find that a country is visited with revival before it has to face some great trial. There was a revival in Korea before they had their main troubles back in 1906 and again after the last world war. There was a remarkable revival in the Congo (Zaire) some years before it passed through agonizing political trial and upheavals and sufferings.

God does this special thing for his people before the time of crisis and difficulty comes, in order to give them this consolation, in order to enable them to endure. I believe that the incident in Acts 4:23-31 can be put into that particular category. God is gracious and he prepares his people for a testing. It also happens sometimes that when God has some special task for a Christian to perform he gives him this blessing. Why? Because he knows the man is inadequate in and of himself. Our Lord says to the apostle, 'Tarry in Jerusalem', as if to say: I have taught you how, I have instructed you; you have the knowledge; but you cannot do this, you cannot be witnesses unto me until you have been baptized with the Holy Spirit. So wait until.... Then.... That is what you find throughout the running centuries. God, when he wants to use a man, prepares him, leads him through a process of preparation and then gives him this authority, this power, this assurance, this certainty. Then the man goes to perform the task to which God has called him and to which he has set him.

This does not only apply to preachers; it is a task that falls to the lot of many of God's people who are not in the ministry as such, or in whole time Christian work. But whenever God has a special work for somebody to do he equips them, and gives them this enduement of power. You would expect that.

My final point under this section is that sometimes his blessing is only given to God's people on their deathbed. You will find that the fathers – and I mean by that everybody until about eighty or ninety years ago – were very interested in the way in which people died, and rightly so. John Wesley used to boast about his people, saying, 'Our people die well.' What a testimony that is to the truth of God and of Christ! So it has often happened that people have only received this sealing, this blessing, this baptism just before they have entered into the glory.

There was a notable man and preacher in America last century of the name of Edward Payson. He was a godly man who had sought this blessing throughout his life but he only received it on his deathbed. His acount of it is most remarkable; and he is but one of many. It is as if God was anxious to put his seal upon the faithful witness of this soul, to give this longing soul a foretaste of the heaven which he was about to enter. The ways in which the blessing comes are almost endless. We must be careful lest we restrict them or lest we try to systematize them over much, or, still worse, lest we mechanize them.

Let us turn, then, to another section: how can it be known exactly when this has happened? I have already partly answered that question earlier when I gave some of the main results of the baptism with the Spirit. But let me emphasize one aspect now. Again, we must be very careful that we do not standardize this but there are a number of tests which we can apply. Let me quote a short word from a Puritan called Thomas Houghton, writing in 1664. This man preached a great number of sermons on Romans 8, which were published in a huge volume. He puts it like this: 'Whenever it comes in the reality and fullness of it and so long as it remains upon the soul it silences all objections, scatters all temptations, removes all scruples and doubts whatsoever to the contrary, and sets the heart at perfect rest. It is secret and inexpressible, certain and infallible.'

Has your heart ever been set at perfect rest? Have you known this luminosity, this clarity when all scruples, doubts, hesitations and objections are scattered, and your heart is at perfect rest? 'Secret', he says 'and inexpressible, certain and infallible.'

But let me quote Edward Payson, to whom I referred above. This blessing came to him when he was on his death-bed. He did not live very long afterwards, but this is how it happened. Somebody asked him, 'Do you feel reconciled?' People used to put such questions to one another in those days. When you visited a sick or a dying person then, you did not do your best to conceal the facts from them, and talk about the weather or politics or everything else; you talked about the soul.

What has gone wrong with us Christian people? What has gone wrong with us evangelical people? Somebody, then, asked Edward Payson, 'Do you feel reconciled?'

'Oh,' he said, 'that is too cold. I rejoice, I triumph; and this happiness will endure as long as God himself, for it consists in admiring and adoring him.' That is it! That is the test. He added, 'I can find no words to express my happiness. I seem to be swimming in a river of pleasure which is carrying me on to the great Fountain.'

This is something inexpressible, something given, and you can only describe it in terms of superlatives. Here again the thing that strikes us above everything else is the variety and the variableness. There is nothing so fatal in this matter as having everything cut and dried and documented. There is infinite variety because it is the liberty of the Spirit. But I would say in general that this experience is not permanent; it tends to pass.

It is sometimes the case that people have had the experience once only and never again; but the memory of it has remained with them all their lives, as long as they lived, as the most wonderful and the most glorious thing they had ever known. I happen to have known a man who was a perfect illustration of this. He was a minister, and I first got to know him some twenty-three years after this great experience came to him. It was the time of the Welsh Revival of 1904/5 and he was a ministerial student in a theological college with a number of other students. The lecturer that morning was the Principal of the College and he was giving a course of lectures on the doctrine of the atonement. He was not lecturing on the Holy Spirit, or the gift of tongues or other gifts.

The students had entered the lecture room one morning, as they had done every other morning, but something strange and unusual then happened. My friend said that he remembered the lecture starting somewhere about ten o'clock, but that the next thing he remembered was that just before one o'clock in the afternoon he found himself on his knees in one of the corners of the room. He looked round and found that the other students were all on their knees and were all praying. He remembered the joy that was in his own heart, and the expression on the faces of his fellow students. Their faces were shining with some strange glory. Nobody knew exactly what had happened.

The Spirit had suddenly come down upon them, had fallen upon them, and my friend had been transported, taken out of himself, in a sense had lost his consciousness and been taken out of time and filled with a great spirit of freedom and rejoicing and praise, in his praying in particular. This had lasted for several months. Then it had gone! I met this man twenty-three years later. His ministry had been a barren one; all he could do was tell us about this experience, and when he did so he became transformed for the time being. His great longing and desire was that he might know this again, but he never did!

The memory of that experience had carried this man through the period of barrenness and of trial. But, you see, this is an experience that can be lost. If you grieve the Holy Spirit you will lose it. There is no question about this. It has happened to many a man. Many men have been blessed like this and filled with the Spirit; they have then fallen into sin, and have lost the joy and peace. The agony of soul comes back to them and they are in great trouble. They still know that they are Christians, although at times they are tempted even to doubt that because they have lost this blessing.

But I must hasten to say this: you can lose it but, thank God, you can receive it again. There is no limit; you can be blessed again. It may be repeated many times. The people of whom we read in Acts 4 were the same people of whom we read in Acts 2 – the apostles and the others who were now part of the company. They were filled on the day of Pentecost, but they were filled again on this other occasion. The same people! This can happen many, many times.

It is so wrong to say that it is 'once and for ever'. No! It can be repeated. If you read the Journals of Whitefield, you will find that this happened to him many times. He always lived on a high level but there were moments when he was transported into the heavens. He did not remain there, he came back again. Then he would be taken up again.

This is true of many others. If you know anything about the Methodist Revival in Wales in the eighteenth century you will know that after the tremendous movement and excitement from 1735 to 1750, even under the ministry of the great Daniel Rowland from 1751 to 1762 there was a period of aridity. He was still a great preacher, he still preached with great authority and power, but there was no freedom, no abandon. But again at the end of 1762, the blessing returned, with a spirit of rejoicing and of praise which continued with occasional intermissions until Rowland's death in 1791. And, perhaps most remarkable of all, the very news of the death of Daniel Rowland led to another outpouring of the Spirit and a time of revival.

Do not take it for granted that if you have lost this blessing you have lost it for ever. No. The blessing can be repeated if you truly seek it. Do not feel that you have sinned against the Holy Spirit, or that it is 'once and for ever'. Seek it, for it can be repeated many times.

Let me substantiate this assertion with some quotations. A man called Joseph Smith of Charleston in the United States preached a sermon on George Whitefield, whom he knew well; and amongst other things he said this:

> He (Whitefield) renounced all pretensions to the extraordinary powers and signs of apostleship; gifts of healing, speaking with tongues, the faith of miracles.

Joseph Smith regarded such things as being peculiar to the age of the apostles only. We disagree with him concerning that. He was simply saying what he regarded as a fact. He then continues:

> Whitefield also allowed that these feelings of the Spirit were not in every person, or at all times, and in the same degree. And that though a full assurance were attainable, and what every one should labour to attain, yet [it was] not of absolute necessity to the being of a Christian.

That is what Whitefield taught regularly in his ministry in this country and in America. In other words, you can be a Christian without this blessing, but you should seek it and labour to attain it.

Let us also consider Philip Doddridge, the man who wrote some of our great hymns, such as: 'O God of Bethel, by whose hand Thy people still are fed'. He puts this truth thus:

> And I judge it the more necessary to expatiate upon that thought because the devil sometimes takes an advantage to bring all into doubt and to raise a storm in the soul merely on

account of the cessation of these extraordinary experiences.

He was a wise pastor; he knew that when people who had had a great experience seemed to lose it, the devil took advantage and created a great storm in the soul, trying to make them doubt even whether they were Christians at all. Doddridge goes on to say:

> These things were never intended as our daily food but only as the rich dainties with which our heavenly Father thinks fit now and then to delight the souls of his children and to make, as it were, a feast for them.

This is not food, says Doddridge, but some special feast, a kind of birthday party that God in his infinite grace gives to his children now and again. So if it goes, do not feel that you are not a Christian; do not let the devil get an advantage over you. This is not food; but dainties prepared by the heavenly Father in his love for us.

Let me end this chapter with a quotation from J. C. Philpot who with William Tiptaft was one of the founders of a branch of the Strict Baptists. This is how he puts it:

> Those who enjoy it (he is referring to this experience) have it only at favourite moments and peculiar seasons. If once enjoyed, they cannot lose the recollection of it, but they may, and do, lose the enjoyment, and through temptation and desertion sink into those dark and miserable spots where nearly all seems lost and gone.

Such is the testimony of these men of God in different ages and circumstances and in different places and times. They all agree that it may be lost, but that it can be obtained again. There is universal testimony to the fact that once a man has known this he is never the same again. Whatever may happen to him, whatever trials may beset him, whatever desertions he may know, the recollection of this is as an anchor of the soul, something never to be forgotten.

Well there it is; those are some of the ways in which this blessing comes, the time at which you are entitled to expect it, its character, its nature, and this variable element in connection with it. It all comes to this: it is within the lordship of the Lord Jesus Christ himself. You cannot hold it; it is given, it is taken. We can but go on to seek his face, to rejoice before him, to seek his glory and to ask him to seal all the promises to us, to grant us this blessed baptism, especially at an evil time like this, to fill us with such power and authority and assurance that our word shall indeed go out as the word of God, and many shall be humbled at hearing it and brought to seek salvation, and then to have this blessed assurance that Jesus is among us.

Chapter 23

The Church and Pentecost

We have been dealing with the way in which we should seek the baptism with the Holy Spirit, and how we are to expect that the blessing is likely to come to us. But now I want to look at another problem which has often presented itself to many Christian people, and indeed should present itself to all who really know their Scriptures. This problem is one which raises the whole question of the timing, or the time relationship, if you like, of this baptism of the Holy Spirit to various other incidents in connection with our blessed Lord's life and work. I mean in particular the relationship of this to the Resurrection and to the Ascension.

These matters are of considerable importance, as I hope to show you, and the great question is that of order, or time. Now let me put it like this. It is a part of my whole exposition to show that a teaching has come in during the last seventy or eighty years which is at variance with what had been previously the customary general teaching in the church, especially amongst evangelical people, concerning this matter.

Now, let me remind you, the common popular teaching during this present century has been something like this. It regards what happened on the day of Pentecost as the constitution of the Christian church. The teaching has been that the Christian church 'began' on the day of Pentecost, that there was no church as such before that but that the whole object and purpose of the baptism with the Holy Spirit was to form the church as a body and as an organism and enable it to function.

And then, taking that view of what happened on the day of Pentecost, they have gone on to say, as I have shown, that what happens to us ever since then is that at the moment of regeneration we are all baptized with the Holy Spirit, for the baptism with the Holy Spirit simply means that we are baptized into the body of Christ which is the church.

That has been the prevalent teaching this century, that the baptism with the Holy Spirit is contemporaneous with regeneration and non-experimental. We must think, according to that, of the baptism with the Holy Spirit as being the constitution of the church, the formation of the church as a body and as an organism, which then by this power proceeds to function.

This obviously is a very important matter. We have been dealing with it from a different angle before, and have tried to show that that is a complete misunderstanding of the baptism with the Holy Spirit. But now I want to show it in particular in the light of John 20. Let me first of all give you two typical characteristic statements of this modern teaching. Here is one:

> In the upper room was a company of witnesses all together as a bodily association yet separated from the Lord and from each other. By the mighty fire baptism of the Holy Spirit the separated units were fused into one unity, every individual member was joined to Christ and so shared the common life, thus becoming an organism through which Christ was able to carry on his work.

Here is another:

> The Holy Spirit came at Pentecost to dwell in believers individually – and yet that individual indwelling by the Spirit naturally resulted in a corporate work uniting them all in one body which is the Church of Christ. Since that day whenever a sinner believes in the Lord Jesus Christ he shares in that baptism and becomes a member of that one Body of which Christ is the Head.

Now those are two typical statements of this particular teaching and attitude towards both the baptism with the Holy Spirit and what happened on the day of Pentecost. Their point is that since that is the case you do not seek this baptism; there is nothing further that you can have. You have really had everything at the moment you believed, when you were regenerate, and all you have to do now is to go on yielding yourself to this, and you should not seek anything that comes upon you. You see it excludes, as I have been showing, the whole doctrine concerning revivals; and that is why we have heard so little about revivals of religion in this present century. We have heard a great deal about campaigns, but very little about revival, and that is where this great departure has taken place from what had been the rule amongst evangelical people in the Christian church ever since the Protestant Reformation. So this is indeed a very crucial matter.

But I want to take it from this standpoint. If this modern teaching which I am putting before you is correct, then the question arises as to what did happen on that occasion on the evening of the day of the Resurrection when our Lord appeared in the midst of his disciples. We can read the account in John 20:19-23:

> Then the same day at evening, being the first day of the week, when the doors were shut where the disciples were assembled for fear of the Jews, came Jesus and stood in the midst, and saith unto them, Peace be unto you. And when he had so said, he

> shewed unto them his hands and his side. Then were the disciples glad, when they saw the Lord. Then said Jesus to them again, Peace be unto you: as my Father hath sent me, even so send I you. And when (now here is the crucial statement) and when he had said this, he breathed on them, and saith unto them, Receive ye the Holy Ghost: Whose soever sins ye remit, they are remitted unto them; and whose soever sins ye retain, they are retained.

Obviously the question to ask people who take the modern view of the baptism with the Holy Spirit is – what was it that happened there? They are of course, of necessity in difficulties immediately, and the explanation that they put forward is that this which happened in the upper room, when our Lord breathed upon them saying, 'Receive ye the Holy Ghost', was just a kind of prophecy. Let me quote again one of the two authorities. He says: 'This was a prophetic breathing, symbolic and suggestive. They did not receive the Holy Spirit then. Did he not tell them in the course of those days that they were to wait until they received the Spirit?'

Their explanation, in other words, is that our Lord was only saying in effect: 'Now in some such manner as this you are going to receive the Holy Spirit. So that nothing really happened here. It was a kind of picture, a dramatic enactment, in order to encourage them and to assure them that this was going to happen to them. So the question that arises is whether that is the true exposition and explanation of this statement in John 20.

How, then, do we understand this passage? Well, you have to take it in connection with what we are told in Acts 2 – before us is this whole matter of the relationship between the two passages. The first comment, therefore, that I would make upon this modern outlook and teaching is that in connection with Acts 2 there is not a single word said in the Scripture about the constitution of the church or about the formation of a body or of an organism – not a single word.

This is, therefore, something that is imported into the Scripture. Read again for yourselves the first two chapters of Acts and I just defy you to find any suggestion, any statement which says in any way that what was happening there was the formation or the constitution of the Christian church as a body and as an organism.

However, that is merely a preliminary remark. Let's come back to John 20. Here again, if you just read the account, I think you have got to agree with me when I say that there is nothing in the text whatsoever that suggests that this was a prophetic enactment. Take the words as they are and this is what you find: 'Jesus said to them again, Peace be unto you: as my Father hath sent me, even so send I you. And when he had said, this, he breathed on them and he saith unto them, Receive ye the Holy Ghost.'

Surely if our Lord was merely telling them that this was going to happen to them, he would have done what he is reported as having done in Acts 1 where he tells them, 'Tarry ye in Jerusalem until....' There he is telling them that something is going to happen and he puts it quite plainly and quite clearly. But there is no suggestion at all of that in John 20. He says, 'Receive ye the Holy Ghost.'

Let me be still more specific. If you consult the learned authorities on the whole question of Greek grammar and the meaning of the words, you will find that they are unanimous in saying that in the Greek the word 'receive' in verse 22, is the aorist imperative. And the authorities are also unanimous in saying that the Greek aorist imperative never has a future meaning.

This is a purely technical point, but a very important one. So many of our friends, who hold to the other teaching that we are criticizing, do so in terms of the Greek and the original. So let us meet them on their own ground. Here – and again I defy you to find a single exception – the authorities are all agreed in saying that the Greek aorist imperative never has a future meaning – and I would emphasize the word 'never'. So you see, the very word that is used is a word that wants us to see that what we are told happened then, *did* happen then; that when our Lord said to them 'Receive ye the Holy Ghost' they did receive the Holy Ghost. The very word that he used, I repeat, makes it impossible that he was here uttering a prophetic utterance and preparing them for something that was going to happen. That ought to be enough in and of itself to get rid once and for ever of this false view of Pentecost.

But there is still more. When we are told that our Lord 'breathed' on them and said, 'Receive ye the Holy Ghost', this same word 'breathed', here in the Greek, is the word that was used in the Septuagint translation of the Old Testament in two most important instances. The first is Genesis 2:7 which reads: 'And the Lord God formed man of the dust of the ground, and breathed into his nostrils the breath of life; and man became a living soul.' The other striking example of this is to be found in the book of the prophet Ezekiel in a very well known passage in chapter 37:5-9 – the vision of the 'valley of dead bones'.

> Thus saith the Lord God unto these bones; Behold I will cause breath to enter into you, and ye shall live: And I will lay sinews upon you, and will bring up flesh upon you, and cover you with skin, and put breath in you, and ye shall live; and ye shall know that I am the Lord. So I prophesied as I was commanded: and as I prophesied there was a noise, and behold a shaking, and the bones came together, bone to his bone. And when I beheld, lo, the sinews and the flesh came up upon them, and skin covered them above: but there was no breath in them. Then said he unto me, Prophesy unto the wind, prophesy, son of man, and say to the wind, Thus saith the Lord; Come from the four winds, O breath, and breathe upon these slain, that they may live.

The Septuagint translation of the Hebrew word breathe

used there, is exactly the same word as is used here in our passage, and surely this is a most significant fact.

Matthew Henry, the great commentator, says on John 20:22, 'As the breath of the Almighty gave life to man and began the old world, so the breath of the mighty Saviour gave life to His ministers and began the new world.' In other words, Matthew Henry sees this extraordinary parallel in the original creation of man. God forms man's body out of the earth – well, there is the body but it has not got life in it. Now he breathes into it, and that as it were constitutes man as man. The body is now fully constituted and has life in it; an exact parallel, as Matthew Henry points out, with what happened here in this upper room when our Lord came to these disciples and breathed on them and said, 'Receive ye the Holy Ghost'.

The statement in Ezekiel 37:9 in particular obviously carries the same connotation and is teaching the same general idea. The bones have come together and the flesh and so on; there was a body but now the life is put in. Here it really is vivified, as it were, and constituted.

Now if you just allow the Scriptures to speak to you, I think you are bound to come to that conclusion. If our Lord was doing something prophetic he would have said so. But he was not. He was doing something there and then. He was obviously constituting the church and commissioning her and it is at that very point that the church really comes into being as such.

I know that there are those who would argue that the church was already in existence even before this, and there is certainly a great deal more to be said for their point of view than there is for this other view which says that the church was only constituted on the day of Pentecost. For instance, you remember the statement and the teaching in Matthew 18 where our Lord says in verses 15-17:

> If thy brother shall trespass against thee, go and tell him his fault between thee and him alone: if he shall hear thee, thou hast gained thy brother. But if he will not hear thee, then take with thee one or two more, that in the mouth of two or three witnesses every word may be established. And if he shall neglect to hear them, tell it unto the church: but if he neglect to hear the church, let him be unto thee as an heathen man and a publican.

There are those who argue that our Lord was speaking and giving instructions there and then, and that the church was already in being. I think that is doubtful, but whether it is or not there is more to be said for that view than there is for the other. But what is abundantly clear in John 20 is surely that the church was constituted as a body and as an organism there and then. Our blessed Lord, having finished his work and having presented himself and his blood in heaven, is now the head of the church, and he comes here to these chosen disciples and apostles and makes it clear to them that they are already the body. He breathes this Spirit of life into the body, in this extraordinary parallel with what happened in man's creation at the very beginning.

There is still further proof of the correctness of this exposition. Notice what follows. 'And when he had said this, he breathed on them, and saith unto them, Receive ye the Holy Ghost: Whose soever sins ye remit, they are remitted unto them; and whose soever sins ye retain, they are retained.' This is of course of extreme importance. Our Lord here now is giving the commission to the church that has been constituted and formed into a body and into an organism. He is sending them out now to do the work and gives them the authority. He has given them the life, the body is as it were constituted, and here he immediately gives them this commission.

Have you not often been struck by the way in which that particular commission and command come at that particular point? I confess that for years I was troubled by this – I could not understand why it came here. The whole thing has been confusing, I think, to believers during this present century because of this other teaching. But if you take the passage as it is, surely there is no difficulty at all. Here is the church. She is constituted, she is the body of which he is the head. The head is speaking to the body giving it the commission, telling it what it has to do and that it will do it in his name and with his authority and power. Here, of course, we have the other side, as it were, of what you can read in our Lord's High Priestly prayer as it is recorded in John 17:18-19. Our Lord says to his Father, 'As thou hast sent me into the world, even so have I also sent them into the world. And for their sakes I sanctify myself' etc. There is the other side. He is praying to his Father and saying: You have sent me, I am sending them, I have in a sense already given them the commission. But he prays on their behalf.

Then having completed the work on the cross and in the resurrection and in the presentation of his blood, he comes back to them and says: Now, it has happened, everything is finished, you are my body. Go; this is what you have to do and this is the authority and the power that I am giving to you.

In many ways there is a parallel again with all this at the end of Matthew 28 where our Lord came to them and said, 'All power is given unto me in heaven and in earth. Go ye therefore, and teach all nations, baptizing them in the name of the Father, and of the Son, and of the Holy Ghost: teaching them to observe all things whatsoever I have commanded you: and, lo, I am with you alway, even unto the end of the world.' That is before the day of Pentecost, of course, and I am suggesting that all these passages work together to show us that the church is already in being.

Let us take another step. One of the quotations I gave earlier read something like this: In the upper room was a company of units all together as a bodily association yet separated from the Lord and from each other. The writer has to say that, obviously, in order to make it consistent with his theory that the church was only constituted and only became a body and an organism as the result of the baptism with the Holy Spirit on the day of Pentecost, so he describes them as 'a company of units'.

'But,' he continues, 'by the mighty fire baptism of the Holy Ghost, the separated units were fused into one unity, every individual member was joined to Christ and so all shared the common life, thus becoming an organism through which Christ was able to carry on his work.'

Now I have already pointed out that nothing of that is said at all in chapters 1 and 2 of Acts. It is all imported. There is not a word there about these disparate units all being fused together into one body; indeed there is most striking evidence to the contrary. If you look at Acts 1:13 (this is, remember, immediately after the ascension, ten days before Pentecost) you find that having seen him ascending into heaven on mount Olivet, they went back to Jerusalem, 'And when they were come in, they went up into an upper room' – and then we are given the names of the people who were there. 'These all continued' – take note – 'with one accord in prayer and supplication, with the women, and Mary the mother of Jesus, and with his brethren.'

Luke goes out of his way to say that they were 'with one accord', which means, 'of one mind' primarily, but also 'of one Spirit'. You remember the other description – disjointed units. They were together in a sense but they were a gathering and a collection of units, 'separated from the Lord' – how anybody can say that passes my comprehension – 'and separated from one another'. Then the baptism of the Holy Spirit comes and at once they are all 'fused together'. But you see they were already that – 'one accord'.

Then you come to the first verse of chapter 2: 'When the day of Pentecost was fully come, they were all with one accord in one place.' I know you do not find the words 'one accord' in the Revised Version, and in more recent versions. Why? They say that in the oldest manuscripts the 'one accord' is not there. That is something that cannot be decided. It is in some manuscripts but not in others. I am not going to attach any weight to this. All I am showing you is, that in the light of the statement in Acts 1:14, surely the instinct of the Authorized translators was right when they put it in here and accepted the manuscripts which have it in Acts 2:1.

But even leaving it out, what you find is: 'When the day of Pentecost was fully come, they were all in one place' – as they had been, we are told, in Acts 1:14. They continued like that, that is how they went on; one mind, one spirit, already fused into one. A different people because of what had already happened to them, as described in John 20 when he had 'breathed' the Spirit. It was there they became one; it is there that this great thing happened. And so they were waiting now with one mind and with one spirit.

What makes this still more interesting is this: if you go on to Acts 2:46 – this is now, of course, after the falling of the Holy Spirit upon them – you read this: 'And they continuing daily with one accord in the temple, and breaking bread from house to house, did eat their meat with gladness and singleness of heart.' Here is the interesting thing; the very word translated here 'with one accord' is the same word exactly as was used in 1: 14.

Now those who hold this other view say: 'Ah, here you are you see, Acts 2:46, "They continuing daily with one accord" – all fused together into this great unity.' It was there, my friends, ten days before Pentecost, and it continued during the ten days before this great event that took place on that day of Pentecost. The thing had happened in the upper room, and it had happened on the very night of the resurrection of our blessed Lord and Saviour. It was then the church was constituted as such.

Someone, then, may ask me, 'What do you say happened on the day of Pentecost?' Well surely that is the question I have already been answering throughout our consideration of this matter. What happened is what our Lord had promised should happen. He never promised that the church was going to be constituted on the day of Pentecost, but he did say this. (Acts 1:7-8): 'He said unto them, It is not for you to know the times or the seasons, which the Father hath put in his own power. But ye shall receive power, after that the Holy Ghost is come upon you: and ye shall be witnesses unto me.'

In other words, as I have been trying to show, the baptism with the Holy Spirit is one of power. It was never designed to constitute the church. Its object and purpose was to give power to the church that is already constituted. It is as if our Lord was saying to them: All right, you are already my body but you must have this power in addition; so stay where you are in Jerusalem until you have received it.

There is not a single suggestion anywhere that the church was formed as an organism on the day of Pentecost at Jerusalem. All we are told is that this was the day when they received the power; they were already in existence but lacking the power. And I think you will realize the significance of all this for the present time. This is just exactly a repetition of the same thing which our Lord said to these people at the end of Luke's gospel where he expounds the Scriptures to them and then ends by saying: 'Repentance and remission of sins should be preached in his name among all nations beginning at Jerusalem. And ye are witnesses of these things. And, behold, I send the promise of my Father upon you: but tarry ye in the city of Jerusalem, until ye be endued with power from on high.'

Our Lord did not say: Stay where you are in Jerusalem, until ye are fused into one body, and are no longer separate units; wait until you are brought together and are given one mind and one spirit, constituted as the body, and then....' All he keeps on saying – and Acts 1 and 2 are exactly the same – is that the one great function of the baptism with the Holy Spirit is something that applies only to power; power to witness. This is the great assurance, this 'love of God shed abroad in the heart'; this amazing certainty that leads to such confidence and boldness in witnessing and in preaching.

I trust that this may come to you as the only satisfactory and adequate explanation of what happened in that upper room as it is recorded in John 20:22-23. But if you want a final proof, I would adduce this. What was the feast of Pentecost which brought all those people up to Jerusalem on that famous occasion? It is generally taught that this marks the beginning of the church. But actually the feast of Pentecost was not to celebrate any beginning, it was to celebrate an end, the end of the harvest. The celebration of the harvest began at the beginning and that was fifty days before, when they waved the sheaf.

In other words, surely, it is fairly clear what all this represents. I know there is a teaching which has come in during this present century which would have us believe that the main function of the feast of Pentecost was to commemorate the giving of the Law. But I think if you take the trouble to read that up you will find that it is on most shaky foundations. It cannot be established. It is a later idea that came in. It is a part of the teaching of the Pharisees probably and the Judaisers and others. But quite apart from that it does not fit the picture at all.

Pentecost is a feast of joy and of rejoicing. The harvest is finished, and so people give themselves to this feast of joy and of enjoyment and of praising God. That is the very thing that we see happening to these people on the day of Pentecost at Jerusalem. The Spirit fell upon them and they were all filled with the Spirit, and they began to praise God and to tell forth the wonderful works of God. This great harvest, as it were, that had been completed by the perfect work of Christ. Here, the enjoyment of it all comes, the certainty and the enthusiasm and the boldness that led to the subsequent witness; and if we take it like that, it all fits in so happily and so perfectly.

I want just to say a word about another difficulty that has often presented itself to people. You remember what we are told in John 7:37,39, where our Lord lifted up his voice on that last great day of the feast and gave out that glorious invitation: 'If any man thirst, let him come unto me, and drink. He that believeth on me, as the scripture hath said, out of his belly shall flow rivers of living water.' Then John explains, '(This spake he of the Spirit, which they that believe on him should receive: for the Holy Ghost was not yet given; because that Jesus was not yet glorified.)'

People use these verses in this way: 'It is quite impossible,' they say, 'that the church should have been constituted before the day of Pentecost; it could not possibly have been constituted in John 20 on the very night of the resurrection, because Jesus was not yet glorified.' Here again, surely, is a grievous misunderstanding. You must not confine the glorification of our Lord to the ascension.

If you take the passages in which this word glorified comes, you will see clearly that he was glorified by the voice that spake to him just before the end. It is recorded in John 12 that the voice spake from the glory when our Lord prayed: 'What shall I say? Father, save me from this hour: but for this cause came I unto this hour. Father, glorify thy name.' And the reply came, 'I have both glorified it, and I will glorify it again.'

But not only that, he was glorified in his resurrection, and before that even in his death. The death is one of the most glorious things of all; it is one of the greatest manifestations of his glory. But certainly the resurrection is quite unique in this respect – the raising from the dead! There he is 'declared to be the Son of God with power, according to the spirit of holiness.'

So we must not confine this idea of our Lord's being glorified simply to the time of his ascension. Indeed it seems to me quite clear from John 20 that the glorification had already taken place. Have you noticed the difference between verses 17 and 27? Look at verse 17: here is Mary clinging to our Lord: 'Jesus saith unto her, Touch me not' – which means, 'Do not go on clinging to me.' Why? – Well, 'I am not yet ascended to my Father: but go to my brethren, and say unto them, I ascend to my Father and your Father; and to my God, and your God.' Go and tell them that, said our Lord to Mary.

Then he came and appeared to them, and in the incident with Thomas we read: 'Then saith he to Thomas, Reach hither thy finger, and behold my hands; and reach hither thy hand, and thrust it into my side: and be not faithless, but believing.' He tells Thomas to do the exact opposite of what he said to Mary. Why? I suggest to you that the answer is that he had already ascended to the Father. He was about to do so when he spoke to Mary. If this was something in the future he would have given the disciples themselves the message, because he appeared to them but a few hours later. He said, 'Go and tell them that I am ascending,' but he was with them in a few hours and did not mention about going to ascend. The fact is he had already been.

What had he been doing? He had been presenting his own blood in the heavenly tabernacle. Read Hebrews 9 and you will see exactly what I mean. In the old days they presented the blood of bulls and of goats in an earthly tabernacle; he had taken his own blood and presented it in the heavenly tabernacle. That was when he did it, immediately after his resurrection. And then having done that which was the final completion of the work, he came back, as I have shown, and said to these apostles: 'You are now my body, I am now henceforth the head of the church, which is my body, and you are members of it. You are one, you have become this organism and I give you this commission.'

That, of course, is what proves all this to be true. If you go back to the Old Testament types, which are but foreshadowings of all this, you will find that when the beast was killed and the blood was collected, it was not kept for some forty days before it was presented in the tabernacle or in the temple. No – it happened at the same time and was one action. It is quite wrong to think that our Lord only presented his blood in the glory and was then glorified after the ascension. No. That happened immediately after the resurrection, and these different statements I suggest to you prove that beyond any doubt or peradventure whatsoever.

So I end with this particular point. There are people who are confused and troubled by this whole question of the tarrying at Jerusalem. You are familiar with the teaching. We have been told that it is quite wrong to tell people to wait. You must not tell people to 'tarry' for the Holy Spirit or to 'pray' for the baptism with the Spirit. 'Of course,' they say, 'that is all wrong. That had to happen in the case of the disciples, because the Holy Spirit could not have come before the day of Pentecost; because if he had come before the day of Pentecost, it would not have fitted in with all that we read in the prophecies of the Old Testament. They had to wait in order that the Old Testament prophecies might be fulfilled.'

But is not that rather an extraordinary thing to say? Which of these Testaments controls the other? Their argument is based on the view that the Old Testament controls the New and that things cannot happen because of what the prophecy has said. So *they* had to wait ten days; but nobody else does. You can get the Holy Spirit, as it were, whenever you like.

But this is where the confusion comes in. The important question to ask is this – why was there that interval in the Old Testament? The answer is that it was there because it was prophetic of what was going to happen. It is the New Testament that controls the Old, not the Old the New. In the Old Testament God has his plan from eternity; in the Old

Testament he gives a foreshadowing of it in these pictures, of what he has already determined and decided is going to happen. So you get these intervals simply because this is God's chosen way and method. I suggest to you that the deduction from that is quite inevitable – that you can be a Christian, you can be a member of the body of Christ, you can be a part of this organism, without having received this baptism of power, without knowing this highest form of assurance, without having this overwhelming experience of the love of God shed abroad in your heart so that you rejoice with a joy unspeakable and full of glory.

I am not advocating Tarrying Meetings but I do advocate that we should realize our need of this power, assurance and certainty, this love of God shed abroad in the heart, this thing that makes us like these disciples and apostles, not only on the day of Pentecost but as described in Acts 4 and as described repeatedly, this experience that people have had in times of revival and of reawakening, which, I have shown you so abundantly from the subsequent history of the church, has always happened to the men whom God has used most signally. This is what gives the power to witness, the authority, and absolute certainty and assurance, which is, ultimately, the absolute necessity of true witnessing and acting as representatives of our blessed Lord and Saviour.

Above all, I commend to you a very careful study again of that tremendous statement in John 20:22-23. Can you dismiss that as prophetic? Can you say dogmatically, as the teacher I have quoted said, that they did not receive the Holy Spirit on that occasion? Work it out in terms of the Greek, the language, the context, the parallel passages, and everything that I have tried to put before you, and I think you will find that there is only one satisfactory conclusion to which you can come.

May God give us all grace in this matter. It is not a matter for controversy, nor for proving who is right and who is wrong. The issue before us is the state of the Christian church, her weakness, her lethargy, with a world on fire, a world going to hell. We are the body of Christ but what do we need? The power! The pentecostal power! Shall we not with one accord, mind and spirit, during these coming days, wait upon him and pray that again he may open the windows of heaven and shower down upon us the Holy Spirit in mighty reviving power?

Chapter 24

The Way to Revival

Every Whit Sunday, Christians are reminded that the day of Pentecost is a historical fact – just as much as Christ's birth, his miracles, his death on the cross and literal physical resurrection, and his ascension. This needs to be emphasized more than ever today – our gospel and our salvation is not a mere teaching or a philosophy, but primarily a series of acts, with meaning and purpose. We should never lose sight of the historicity of what we are considering here.

So what we read in Acts 2 is something that literally happened in the way that is described. Luke was primarily an historian and his concern was to give to Theophilus, to whom he had already written his gospel, a further account of the continuing action and activity of the Lord Jesus Christ; and so he is dealing here with something that belongs solidly and purely to the realm of history.

What happened in Acts 2, as the records make so plain and clear, was that the early church was baptized with the Holy Spirit. Remember the promises with respect to that in the Old Testament, and remember how it was the great theme of John 1:26,33, and in a sense of the preaching of John the Baptist: I am not the Christ. I baptize with water. There is another. You do not know him, there was a time when I did not know him, but the one who sent me to baptize – in other words, God – called me and gave me my commission. He said to me, 'The one on whom you shall see the Holy Ghost descending, and remaining on him, he is the one who shall baptize with the Holy Ghost.'

Our Lord himself repeats the same thing and tells the disciples to stay in Jerusalem; not to go out to start upon their work to which he has already commissioned them, but to wait until they shall be baptized with the Holy Spirit. Now here in Acts 2 we read of that thing which had thus been prophesied so much, literally and actually taking place.

What is the relevance of all this to us? What are we doing exactly when we celebrate Whit Sunday? Is this merely a commemoration of something that once happened? Are we just looking back at a great fact in history? Is it just that? Or is there more than that to it? Has it a greater and a deeper significance for us?

The answer to that question is determined entirely by our attitude to the doctrine concerning the baptism with the Holy Spirit. This is, as we have seen the most urgent, vital and crucial matter for the Christian church at the present time. Unfortunately, it has become a point of division with respect to the whole doctrine of the Holy Spirit and his work.

People who are evangelical in their outlook are agreed with one another about practically everything in connection with the doctrine of the person and the work of the Holy Spirit apart from this one matter. They are agreed about his activity in creation, about his position in the blessed Holy Trinity, and about his operations upon certain men, giving them gifts to perform certain tasks, as you see it described in the Old Testament – in the prophets, and in certain men working in the temple, like Bezaleel, and so on. They are agreed about all that.

They are also agreed about his activity in connection with the Lord Jesus Christ himself, how the Holy Spirit came upon him and enabled him to preach and to do his work while he was here in this world. They agree about his activity in our Lord's death and resurrection, about the work of the Holy Spirit in convicting people of sin, and about his operation in the great and mighty act of regeneration. They are agreed more or less in general also about his activity in sanctification. There is a slight difference there. But the point I am establishing is that in almost the entire range of the details of the great doctrine of the Spirit and his work, there is agreement, but when you come to this matter of the baptism with the Holy Spirit there is a divergence and a disagreement. So, then, what is the significance of what happened on the day of Pentecost to us?

There are in the main two views with regard to this. (We need not be bothered about minor deviations here and there, or minor differences.) The first, as we have seen, is the view that teaches that what really happened on the day of Pentecost at Jerusalem was that the Christian church was born. It follows, therefore, that they say, with regard to this event, that it was of necessity a once and for all event, never to be repeated, and all we can do is to look back to this unique happening.

There is a good deal of confusion in what they say, but I am trying to give you what I would regard as the commonest view. They would say further that since then, and especially since what happened in the household of Cornelius, recorded in Acts 10, when a man is regenerated he is at the same time baptized by the Spirit into the body of Christ and becomes a part of this one body that was formed on the day of Pentecost.

I emphasize that it is since what happened in the household of Cornelius for this reason: of course, they are in difficulties over the people in Samaria, the account of which is given in Acts 8, and have problems in the case of the apostle Paul. But, they say, in the case of the household of Cornelius, while Peter was yet speaking the Spirit fell – obviously regeneration and the baptism with the Spirit happened at one and the same time. They have to gloss over the incident of the Ephesians recorded in Acts 19: 1-7. In general they say, 'This, now, has become the norm. Obviously the case of the disciples was a unique one and a special one, but now ever since, the baptism with the Holy Spirit is an event which is synchronous with and practically identical with regeneration.'

The regenerate person is thus one who has received the baptism, has received the Holy Spirit, and has received all that it is possible for a Christian to receive. Therefore, they say, all he has to do is go on living and walking in the Spirit. He must not expect or long for anything further.

Now, they say, it is possible, of course – and alas – for the Christian who thus has been baptized and filled with the Spirit to fall away from that. He may fall into sin, become slack, backslide, and, as he does so, he will lose this blessing. He grieves and quenches the Spirit; he may offend the Spirit in this way. The Spirit does not leave him, and is still there in him, but as he has grieved the Spirit he is not now experiencing the Spirit's gracious influences. What is he to do? Well, they say all that is necessary is for him to realize this, to repent of it, to surrender himself once more, and to go on living a life of obedience to the Spirit that is in him. If he does this, what he has lost will be restored unto him and he will be able to go on his way rejoicing and happy.

This is what has been the prevailing and the most popular and common evangelical teaching with regard to the meaning of the baptism with the Holy Spirit. Now there is a most important and interesting corollary to this teaching and it is the one I want to emphasize again here. Such a teaching rarely, if ever at all, speaks about revival. It is not interested in revival and, of course, obviously cannot be. There is no room left for revival in that teaching. I have made it a practice now for many years, whenever I see a book on the doctrine of the Holy Spirit which I have never seen before, to look first at the synopsis or the table of contents at the beginning, and the index at the end. I look for 'Revival' and I do not find it.

I commend that to you as an interesting exercise. Look at the books on the person and the work of the Holy Spirit that have been published during this century and look for a section, a chapter or even a part of a chapter, on the subject of revival and you will not find it. And of course they are perfectly consistent. It has been excluded, there is no possibility, there is no room left for it, it cannot happen.

The result is that the activity of the church, the way in which she has conducted herself and her outlook during this present century has been this: when things are not going too well, the church does not exhort people to pray for revival, but decides to have an evangelistic campaign; she organizes one and then, of course, asks God to bless that. That is her solution. This has become the kind of pattern. People are converted in meetings, campaigns, evangelistic efforts, and it is believed that if they believe and respond, they are born again and are baptized with the Spirit, and all they need now is a further teaching which will tell them to go on yielding, surrendering, giving obedience, allowing the Spirit who has come into them in his fullness, to possess them wholly. And that is the sum of evangelical teaching: conversion, regeneration, then this further teaching with regard to sanctification.

You notice that the whole time the emphasis is placed upon what we do, it is all in our hands. There is nothing further to be expected; it is all a matter now of our surrendering and our obedience. And so the whole of the effort is put on that; pressure is brought on the will both in the first decision and in the subsequent surrender.

But there is another view and the other, of course, is the old evangelical view. I call it that because I am speaking strictly historically. The view I have been dealing with is still not fully a hundred years old, but prior to that and even continuing since, there is this other view, the one that has obtained in the church throughout the centuries. Let me put it like this to you. What happened at Pentecost, according to this second teaching, is that the church was baptized with the Holy Spirit, as our Lord had promised and as the others had prophesied – it was a baptism of power for the church was already formed. We have dealt with this earlier, but I just want to remind you of the sequence so that you may have it clearly in your mind. These men were regenerate. Our Lord said to them, 'Now are ye clean through the word that I have spoken unto you' and he prayed to his Father: 'I pray for these: I pray not for the world....' These and many other statements in the gospels confirm that they were all regenerate. And, you remember, the church was formed in the Upper Room, when our Lord breathed his Holy Spirit upon the disciples, and gave them the authority to remit sins, and so on. Then, on the day of Pentecost, what happened was that the Lord sent upon the church this power to witness that he had promised: 'You shall receive power.'

Before that we see them waiting in accordance with his command, waiting constantly and instantly in prayer; and then suddenly, on this day of Pentecost, this tremendous thing happened. There they were, met together in this one place, and 'Suddenly there came a sound from heaven as of a rushing mighty wind, and it filled all the house where they were sitting.'

This was a baptism with power and with fire! And you notice what is emphasized: not some secret operation of the Spirit in the depths of the personality, but the Spirit 'falling' upon the gathered church, 'descending' upon her, being 'poured out' upon her. Those are the terms that are used, and that is exactly what happened. The very sound of the rushing mighty wind emphasizes this objectivity, this given-ness. It is not a secret work such as happens in regeneration. No, it is a power coming upon the church, something happening to the assembled company, and she finds herself filled with power and authority, with certainty and with a sense of glory.

It is the action of the risen Lord. God had told John the Baptist: It is the one upon whom you will see the Holy Spirit descending and remaining – that is the one who is going to do this.

He is the One who did it. He said he would, and he did.

I must then ask the question that I asked under the first section – was this therefore something once and for all? The answer is that it was once and for all in one sense only, in that it was the first time it ever happened; but it is not once and for all in any other sense, as I am now going to try to prove to you. When something happens for the first time – well, you cannot go on repeating the first time, but you can repeat what happened on that first time. I first entered the pulpit of Westminster Chapel on the last Sunday morning of the year 1935. I cannot repeat that particular occasion, but I have repeated the action many hundreds of times since.

We can demonstrate the truth about Pentecost like this. What we are told about those people there on the day was that 'they were all filled with the Holy Ghost'. That is the term that is used. 'There appeared unto them cloven tongues like as of fire, and it sat upon each of them. And they were all filled with the Holy Ghost, and began to speak with other tongues' – and all the rest that followed.

But if you go to Acts 4 you will find the incident where Peter and John were arrested as the result of their performing of the miracle on the man who sat at the Beautiful gate of the temple. They were put on trial but the authorities decided that they would let them off this time, and straitly charged them 'not to speak at all nor teach in the name of Jesus... So when they had further threatened them, they let them go, finding nothing how they might punish them, because of the people.'

Then, you remember, Peter and John went back to the

company, to the church, and reported what had happened to them. And when the church heard this, 'they lifted up their voice to God with one accord', and they began to pray. What they prayed for of course was that God might behold the threatenings of their enemies. 'And now, Lord, behold their threatenings and grant unto thy servants, that with all boldness they may speak thy word, By stretching forth thy hand to heal; and that signs and wonders may be done by the name of the holy child Jesus.' Then, notice this: 'And when they had prayed, the place was shaken where they were assembled together; and they were all filled with the Holy Ghost, and they spake the word of God with boldness.'

Exactly the same thing as had happened on the day of Pentecost! The same people!

Notice the objectivity again: 'the place was shaken.' It is something happening outside them. They are not here just yielding themselves. They had no need to, they had not been disobedient, but very obedient. They had borne a wonderful witness before these authorities and powers; they had said to them without any hesitation, 'Whether it be right in the sight of God to hearken unto you more than unto God, judge ye. For we cannot but speak of the things we have seen and heard.' They had witnessed with boldness and yet they see here that they need something further and they pray and God answers; the place is shaken and the Spirit descends upon them.

The shaking of the building corresponds to the sound of the 'mighty rushing wind' and they are all filled with the Spirit. And the same result follows, 'they spake the word of God with boldness', and later, 'with great power gave the apostles witness of the resurrection of the Lord Jesus: and great grace was upon them all.'

I ask you to read again for yourselves the account of what happened in Samaria (chapter 8); read, too, what happened in the household of Cornelius (chapter 10). We have already considered this story in detail. We are not told that some secret action took place in their souls leading to regeneration. That did happen, of course, but in addition the Holy Spirit 'fell' and you remember how Peter and those that came with him recognized that exactly the same thing had happened to these Gentiles as had happened to the apostles and others on the day of Pentecost.

There is the evidence as we have it in Acts, but look at the history of the church – and this is where the whole matter becomes to me so vital. The graph of church history is something like this. She starts up there on the day of Pentecost, but after a while she seems to have lost much of her power and becomes more or less ineffective; then she rises again in power, and so it goes on. How do you explain this? Well, this is what has happened: the church has become worldly, she has forgotten her true nature and condition. She has absorbed a lot of Greek philosophy and Roman law – a man like Constantine decides to bring the Empire into the church for political reasons because it is going to help him and pay him in certain respects – and the church becomes an institution.

Then what happens? Certain men, you will find, become concerned and disturbed and unhappy, and they say, 'What we need is another baptism with the Holy Spirit, we must seek the face of God.' They do everything they can; they repent and render obedience; they try to go on walking in the life of faith, a life of surrender to the Spirit and they do so genuinely. But nothing happens. And they go on and on like that and are almost at the point of despair, when suddenly something happens, often when they least expect it. When they are on the verge of utter despair, suddenly upon an assembled company the Holy Spirit falls again.

It is simply wonderful to read the accounts of these events. Sometimes the writers have described actually hearing a sound, as if there were another rushing mighty wind. Not always. But what does happen invariably is that they are aware of a Presence and of a power, something has come upon them and has happened to them and they are lifted up out of themselves and out of time, they scarcely know where they are, and phenomena take place. I am not talking about speaking with tongues, but about joy and abandon, sometimes so great that people even faint and become unconscious, and great power and liberty, great authority follows in preaching – and that is what is called a revival.

Now this is what has been happening in the church throughout the running centuries, and the thing that I am emphasizing is that it is always the action of God. It is not man. Man has done everything. He has been surrendering, but nothing happens. He may organize nights of prayer, every night – still nothing happens. Then suddenly something does happen, and nobody understands and nobody can explain it. There is only one explanation, it is God again, the One who sent the Holy Spirit on the early church, the One who sent it on that building and shook the walls. It is the God who did it then who is repeating it and has gone on repeating it throughout the centuries.

My dear friends, if you read the history of the church you can come to only one conclusion: this has been God's way of keeping the church alive. The Christian church would have been dead and finished centuries ago and many times over were it not for revivals. This is the true meaning of the word 'Revival'. It is God pouring out his Spirit on an assembled church or company, or many churches or countries even, at a time. What he did at the beginning he has done again. When the life has gone he has sent it again; when the power has vanished he sends it again. That has been the history of the Christian church from the first century until today.

Let me remind you of some of the examples of this. There was something like it in the second century. The church had been absorbing Greek philosophy and she was so anxious to show that there was nothing strange about her doctrine, that the apologists who held sway then were governed by that idea. The result was the church had become lifeless and lost her power. Certain people were aware of this and they began to seek the face of God, and God answered. I am referring to what is called Montanism. I know there were excesses, and that they went wrong at certain points, but at any rate the church was alive again and there was power in her. One of the greatest intellects and brains of the whole history of the church – Tertullian – entered into this movement when he saw that this was New Testament experience as over and against the formal dead church.

There was another example of it in North Africa in the third century – the Donatist Movement, which rebelled against the formality that had come in when Constantine and the Roman Empire came into Christianity. It was denounced of course. The church always denounces every revival. The Montanists and the Donatists were both condemned by the church as the Methodists were condemned two hundred years ago, and as people who are filled with the Spirit are almost invariably condemned by a dead formal church.

Then you get it in the Middle Ages here and there amongst various people – God visits and blesses them. There were revivals in the South of France in the Middle Ages, revivals in connection with the Waldensian Church in Northern Italy, revivals amongst the Brethren of the Common Life in Germany and parts of Holland; all this prior to the Reformation. Then the great Reformation itself undoubtedly was a revival. A man like Hugh Latimer who used to preach at St Paul's Cross was a man who was clearly filled with the Spirit and preached in an apostolic manner; and there were others.

Then in the seventeenth century there were remarkable movements: local revivals in Northern Ireland and in parts of Scotland. I have already reminded you of that tremendous thing that happened at Kirk-'o-Shotts when John Livingstone was preaching, and just preached that one sermon which led to the conversion of so many. The Spirit came down upon them: a repetition of Pentecost.

Everybody knows, of course, about the eighteenth century in the United States and in this country – the revival that broke out in Northampton under the ministry of Jonathan Edwards, that soaring genius. Read the account of it which he wrote. Then you will know what a revival is. It is the Spirit coming down, not man controlling and just deciding to yield and to give obedience; no! People have done that and still nothing happens. Then God does something. God sends down his Spirit and visits them. *That* is revival.

Of course, the same happened in this country under the ministry of Whitefield and the Wesleys, and in Wales under Daniel Rowlands and Howell Harris. In each case keep your eye on the objectivity, how suddenly it happened – when nobody was expecting it. Daniel Rowlands, for instance, had been in trouble for months. He had believed the truth at last. He had been in the ministry without believing it but then he saw it and was trying to preach justification by faith and still he did not feel it. But there he was one Sunday morning in a Communion Service in his little church, actually reading the liturgy in connection with the communion service, when he came to the words about 'Christ's precious blood'. As he was reading these words the Holy Spirit fell upon him and upon the church. He wept, he broke down, and a revival broke out.

Look at the last century, the nineteenth century. Have you ever read of the great revival in the United States which began in 1857 and went on to 1859; of the little prayer-meeting that a man began in Falcon Street in New York City and how they went on praying for months and nothing happened? They did all the surrendering they were capable of – still nothing happened. But then it did happen – God! It is always God. It is always 'pouring forth', it is always 'shedding abroad', it is always 'falling upon'! Then there was one of the greatest revivals in the whole history of the Christian church. It was not confined – it began in Ulster in 1858, in Wales in 1859, and went right through the country. Amazing! Astonishing!

You can read these accounts for yourselves. You will not find them in books written on the Holy Spirit in the twentieth century, but you read the books of the nineteenth century and the eighteenth, and you will find they are there. Buy a book like that of Sprague on the history of revivals.

Then in 1904/5 the same thing happened again in Wales; in 1906 in Korea; still more recently, in the 1950s, in the Congo. Several revivals have happened in the Island of Lewis, not only the one connected with the Rev Duncan Campbell but before that. This has been the story of the Christian church throughout the centuries. And all this I am suggesting to you is a repetition of Pentecost. The church waiting: God sending down his Spirit upon the church.

Now you see the importance of this doctrine of the baptism with the Holy Spirit. It is this truth and this alone that holds out any hope for us today. Here is the lesson for us. What has the church to do? Well, of course, she should go on yielding and obeying, she should do all that. But, oh, if we had to stop at that I would despair; I would be without hope. I know of men, individual ministers, who have been teaching this for twenty years and more trying to persuade their people to do it. They have obeyed, they have sacrificed, they have surrendered, they have had special prayer meetings every morning at seven o'clock; it has been going on for years but nothing has happened so far. And, you see, if it all depends upon us what hope is there?

But the message of the day of Pentecost is that what God has done, God can still do. This is something that God has gone on repeating throughout the running centuries and what the church needs to do is to realize her weakness, her impotence, that the power is always of God and not of man.

There is nothing so fatal as the reliance upon man's ability to deal with the situation of the church.

The first step is to realize that man, having done everything, has in a sense done nothing. He can produce a number of converts, thank God for that, and that goes on regularly in evangelical churches every Sunday. But the need today is much too great for that. The need today is for an authentication of God, of the supernatural, of the spiritual, of the eternal, and this can only be answered by God graciously hearing our cry and shedding forth again his Spirit upon us and filling us as he kept filling the early church. Here are men filled on the day of Pentecost, again a day or two later the building is shaken and filled again. And God has gone on filling the church in revival. That is the greatest need, and our only hope.

But you have to believe in the possibility of that! If your doctrine of the Holy Spirit does not leave any room for revival, then you cannot expect this kind of thing. If you say the baptism with the Spirit was once and for all on Pentecost and all who are regenerated are just made partakers of that, there is no room left for this objective coming, this repetition, this falling of the Holy Spirit in power and authority upon a church.

But, thank God, there *is* room left! The teaching of the Scripture, plus the long history of the Christian church shows this so clearly. You and I are called upon not only to believe this but to pray to God without ceasing for it; to ask him to open the windows of heaven and to send down the Spirit, to pour him upon us, that he may fall upon us in mighty power.

Here is, to me, the great encouragement. I have told you how in Fulton Street in New York just one man began to pray at first, and then two or three joined him, and then more and more came until they had to move to a bigger building. They went on praying for months and God answered. The story in

Northern Ireland was this – there was a very simple labourer, called James McQuilkin. He began to pray alone. Then persuaded a friend of his to join him, just two of them. They prayed in a little school-room for months. But then others began to pray and on and on they went, and at last God heard and answered; and so it has always been.

There has always been this preliminary period when just one man, or two men, or a group of men, realizing the truth of this doctrine, have turned to God and have started pleading and praying urgently and without ceasing, and then suddenly, in a prayer-meeting perhaps, or in a preaching service, or anywhere, God suddenly sends down the Spirit; he comes again. Sometimes he almost comes again as a mighty rushing wind, as we saw in the story of Andrew Murray of South Africa.

There is not always the noise, but there is always the sense of glory, the sense of awe, of the majesty of God; a sense of power, an assurance of salvation. It always leads to great joy, and always gives boldness in witness, whether from a pulpit or in private, a convicting and a converting power. What happens always is that the believers are revived. Revival can only happen to a man who has got life. It means revivifying. The church has lost her power, and is given the power again. He gave the power at the beginning, he goes on repeating this. That is revival and God, I say again, has kept his church alive and going by this succession of revivals throughout the centuries.

To me, as I mentioned at the very beginning, there is nothing that is more urgently important than this. Do you believe in revival, my friend? Are you praying for revival? What are you trusting? Are you trusting the organizing power of the church? Or are you trusting in the power of God to pour out his Spirit upon us again, to revive us, to baptize us anew and afresh with his most blessed Holy Spirit? The church needs another Pentecost. Every revival is a repetition of Pentecost, and it is the greatest need of the Christian church at this present hour. Oh may God open the eyes of our understanding on this vital matter, that we may look to him and wait upon him until in his infinite mercy and compassion he once more sends down from on high the power of the Holy Spirit upon us.

Scripture Index

Acts

The Martyn Lloyd-Jones Recordings Trust

Over 1600 tape cassettes of Dr Martyn Lloyd-Jones' sermons are available from The Martyn Lloyd-Jones Recordings Trust, and a catalogue can be obtained from their office at 25 High Street, Ashford, Kent TN24 8TH. Special albums are available on *The Baptism and Gifts of the Holy Spirit*, *Revival*, and other great biblical themes.